THE **TRAVELLER**

NOTES
FROM AN IMPERFECT JOURNEY
AROUND THE WORLD

by
Daniel Baylis

with guidance from
Monique James

The Traveller: Notes from an Imperfect Journey Around the World

Sparks Publishing books may be purchased for educational, business or sales promotional use. For further information contact *info@sparkspublishing.ca*.

Please encourage burgeoning writers by paying for what they write. Purchase only authorized electronic editions, and do not participate in or encourage piracy of copyrighted material. Your support is vital.

Editing by Monique James, *www.moniquejames.ca*.
Proofreading by Jennifer McFee, *jmcfee@outlook.com*.
Cover design by Michel Vrana, *www.michelvrana.com*.

Interior typesetting in Futura and Arno Pro
by Emrys Miller of Rocketday Arts, *www.rocketday.com*.

FIRST EDITION
ISBN 978-0-9920882-0-0

Printed in Canada, eh!

100% post-consumer recycled paper, Processed Chlorine Free.

*"Believe in a love that is being stored up for you like an inheritance,
and have faith that in this love there is a strength and a blessing so large
that you can travel as far as you wish without having to step outside it."*

— RAINER MARIA RILKE

This project is dedicated to my four teachers

Mom,
Dad,
Cathy
& Lisa.

I have been to the far corners of the world.
Yet I have not been to a single place
where I could not feel your love.

Thank you.

PROLOGUE

*W*hat compels a person
to embark on a year-long journey around the world?

I suppose there are several reasons. Some people want to gargle wines from the most distinguished vineyards across the globe. Others are interested in getting fresh blisters from hiking the world's tallest mountains. More romantic types set out on a quest for love (or maybe just lovemaking) in exotic locations. And then there are those who are simply running from the law.

For me, however, it was plain old curiosity.

I will elaborate.

But first, let me go back and tell you a bit about me. We are, after all, going to be spending some time together. And, heck, I want you to know who I am — or at least how this trip came to be.

I was born in the northern city of Prince George and grew up in a typical Canadian family. On Sunday nights, we ate roast beef for dinner, usually accompanied by a dish of microwaved creamed corn. On weekends, my father took pride in maintaining a green lawn, while my mother tended to carrots in the garden. My only sibling, an older sister, consistently made the honour roll while collecting MVP awards at soccer and volleyball tournaments. I was a less notable child. I enjoyed mud puddles and took piano lessons (but I progressed little further than an unremarkable version of "Für Elise"). As a family, we would take

1

the truck and camper to a nearby lake, where we'd paddle our red canoe and play card games while listening to country music. If we deviated from the other households on our freshly constructed suburban block, our "rebelliousness" came from the fact that the fifth member of our clan — a German Shepherd named Kinda — was a lesbian. That's about as weird as it got.

Throughout my childhood, both of my parents worked as teachers. My mother taught at an elementary school and my father at a secondary school (instructing math and physical education). Their salaries provided the family with enough means to own a home, to drive an imported car (Subaru!) and to even vacation in Disneyland. If you ever need snapshots of middle-class Canada from the 1980s, look no further than my family's photo albums.

After graduating high school, I did what was largely expected of me: I went to university. There I toyed with new lifestyle choices such as vegetarianism and novel concepts such as alcohol. Unfortunately, my grades were below par due to my inability to understand what on earth was occurring in my Economics 101 course, paired with a general lack of passion for my program (recreation and leisure studies). Consequently, I did what confused kids do: I dropped out. I didn't know what in the blazes to do with that term everyone seemed so focused on — "career."

For nearly a decade, I drifted and tinkered. I tried my hand at a variety of activities that were eye-opening but didn't necessarily lay a foundation for a clear future. I improved my music skills at a community college, worked as a barista at a café and spent a string of summers planting trees in the mountains of British Columbia. Eventually, I moved across the country to Montreal. It was there where I successfully failed at a couple of romantic relationships, learned to speak a bit of French (albeit with a really bad English accent) and made a few great friends along the way. Midway through my twenties, with a deeper sense of resolve to explore that notion of "career," I returned to school to finish a university degree. I wanted to make something of myself. ○

THE SEEDS OF this journey — and subsequently this book — were planted on a rainy April afternoon. I was at a café with a latte in hand and all the intentions in the world to study diligently. With only a few final exams remaining, I was mere days away from actually graduating. To the detriment of my grades, however, my attention refused to focus on the class notes strewn in front of me. Instead, I was lost in daydreams about the future.

At that point, I could only see a few months in advance. I had confirmed a summer job as a community service tour director for a group of teenagers. But what would happen after that? I had no idea. September would bring a new abyss: no more classes to attend yet no professional life to gracefully transition into. Unlike training in nursing or engineering, the degree I was about to acquire in Human Relations did not equate to a job or even a specific profession. The unknowns of the situation were both exciting and daunting.

Between sips of coffee, I flipped my notebook to a blank page. And then I asked myself a small question (one that all those university credits still hadn't managed to solve): *What do you want to do with your life?*

That afternoon, I gave myself the go-ahead to think big and not sensor myself — to keep my feet on the ground but also to shoot for the stars. A bunch of ideas came out of that brainstorm, some more realistic and achievable than others:

- *Travel the world*
- *Improve my French language skills*
- *Record an album*
- *Run a marathon*
- *Get a motorbike*
- *Open my own café*
- *Write a book*

I knew it would be helpful to choose one thing and start working toward it. So I selected the first thing that had come to mind, the top item on the list: *I was going to travel the world.* ☼

So there I was, a twentysomething kid with a dream to see the world — how precious! Despite my lofty desires, however, I knew I wasn't actually ready to ride a donkey across Chile or meditate on a Nepalese mountain. For starters, I didn't have any money. Sure, it wouldn't necessarily take exorbitant amounts of cash to explore foreign countries. But at that stage, my financial worth was a two-figure savings account and a rusty 10-speed bicycle.

Even if I had been blessed with a trust fund, I had a more pressing reason to defer an adventure. If I took off to travel immediately after school, I'd only be prolonging the "career" question that remained unresolved: *How will I contribute to this world?* Travel, I feared, wasn't going to give me the sense of greater social involvement that I craved.

I was done with being a drifter.

I was sick of being a student.

I wanted to contribute.

Fortunately, my expectations of what it meant to "contribute" were low. I was relatively confident that the cure for cancer was *not* residing inside my cranium. My goal was just to get a job. Basically anything beyond slinging coffee would suffice. I was certain that I could be, at minimum, a non-inept administrative assistant or even a mildly entertaining flight attendant. I wanted to support myself. To stand on my own two feet. To become more than an overgrown zygote feeding from the umbilical cord of society. So I got to work getting work.

After a few months of botched interviews and too much time spent alone in my underwear, I finally landed a job and began my professional career in a cubicle at McGill University. For days on end, I gazed into Excel sheets, talked about my weekends around the water cooler and became a master at alphabetizing stuff.

A half-year later, I caught a bigger break. Based on my previous experience writing for my university's student newspaper and maintaining a personal blog (yeah, before it was even cool!), I landed a job as a content producer with the Montreal tourism bureau. For the next two years, I threw myself into my role by writing articles, taking photos and creating videos about a city that I loved.

Were my contributions to society great? Well, if you value cutting-edge online tourism articles — such as "Montreal Museums Matched to your Personality Type!" — then, yes, my contributions were great. Perhaps more importantly, I got a sense of my capabilities: I could meet deadlines, I could pitch ideas (and get them approved), and I could entertain people. Ultimately, the bigger breakthrough had nothing to do with contributing. Instead, I learned that I had the ability to step up to a challenge and accomplish something. With that in mind, I could now wrap my head around a bigger goal. ○

As the months hurried past, thoughts of travel marinated in my mind. In my everyday life, I began to exhibit the symptoms of a person dreaming of international adventures. I spent working hours covertly opening tabs of various travel websites. On the weekends, I browsed through outdoor adventure stores for the sole objective of ogling backpacks. Maps of the world became an increasing source of arousal. The more I entertained the notions of travel, the more I began to ponder my own game plan. If I were to set off into the world, what type of trip would I take?

First and foremost, a big journey was something I would need to do *alone*. I saw it as my own self-determined rite of passage. Besides, being alone meant that I could call all the shots.

Furthermore, unless a thunderstorm of cash came showering down upon me, any type of long-term adventure would have to be done on the cheap. There'd be no fine dining at exclusive restaurants. Fancy elephant safaris were out of the question. There was no point in dreaming of swanky spas. On the other hand, I had no interest in tormenting myself either. I wasn't going to starve on a fixed "one-meal-per-day" budget or fool myself into thinking that hitchhiking from Berlin to Beijing would make an attractive cost-saving option. I envisioned low-cost flights and inexpensive ways of engaging with people. Yup, practicality would be my ticket.

Perhaps the most pragmatic option for adventure-seekers on a tight budget is to find international work opportunities. If I opted for this approach, I could set up a job teaching English in South Korea. Or I could nab an internship with an NGO doing development work in Ghana. My main concern with these types of undertakings, however, was that I'd be locked into a single experience, at a single location. Is that what I wanted? I wasn't certain. If I were to embark on a trip of a lifetime, I might feel more compelled to cover ground.

Whatever my approach would be, my central objective was to travel in the most basic sense of the endeavour: to see different landscapes, meet new people, taste exotic foods and, in turn, to see how all these things would impact me. I sought adventures that had elements of connection, of insight, of education. Essentially, I was curious, not simply to just see new places but to experience them.

What I really wanted, I realized, was *involvement*. ○

TWO AND A half years after that fateful April afternoon spent dreaming in a café, my 30th birthday was approaching. Up until that moment, the journey that stewed in my head was primarily a lofty pipe dream, something that I lusted for — but ultimately as real as Santa Claus riding a unicorn across Neverland.

It was one morning in early autumn when an interaction at the office catalyzed a life-changing decision. I was sitting at my desk writing a blog post about the cobblestone streets of Montreal's historic district when the campaign manager approached me and began to discuss next year's marketing plan. Things were scaling up. They had a new and prestigious role with my name on it.

"We've got big plans for you, Daniel!"

I was flattered, of course — what favourable sentiments! I had gone from a lowly non-contributing social leech to having an agency incorporate *me* into their strategy. Wowsers. Who wouldn't appreciate such fawning? However, after the manager continued on his way and the initial ego swelling subsided, I realized another aspect of the announcement. And I was slightly alarmed. Somebody else had plans *for my life*.

That night I went home and had a long, hard soul-searching session about what these big plans really entailed — and, more importantly, what they meant *for me*. On the verge of entering a new decade, was I at the steering wheel of my own life? Was I putting down the foundation for a future that I'd feel proud of? What about my list of dreams?

The evening's existential crisis made a couple of things clear: 1) the call of travel was not getting any quieter, and 2) I had never been better equipped to respond. To make world travel feasible, countless variables needed to align. My personal health had to be robust. My family's health had to be steady. I needed to be without larger financial obligations, such as mortgages or Mafia debt. As far as I could see, my ducks were all in a row. Left without any big excuses, I faced an unavoidable question.

If I didn't do a trip now, then when would I?

Before going to bed that night, I wrote a sincere email to my boss. If the agency was incorporating me into their strategies (which, again, was terribly complimentary), I thought it was necessary to intervene sooner than later. I expressed my gratitude for the opportunities granted. And then I revealed that I wasn't planning on renewing my contract.

I needed to start planning something else. ○

AFTER SENDING THE email, I felt like puking.

What the hell had I just done?

As the days went by, little by little, the shock of my career suicide became less pronounced. I even grew giddy. I wasn't going to be a travel writer anymore. I was going to be an actual traveller. As such, it was time to stop dreaming and start scheming. What would be *my* strategy for the upcoming year? Where would I go? How would I get elbow-deep into cultures that were different than my own?

I wasn't so starry-eyed to believe that I could see the *entire* world. I determined that if I were to allocate one month each to 12 different nations over the course of the year, I might achieve a happy medium between community participation while still seeing a significant amount of the globe. I'd purposefully choose distinct microcosms — with varying geography, cultures and backgrounds — to provide a diverse sampling of the world. This is where it got interesting. If I were to visit two countries (on average) on each of the six inhabited continents, I would need exactly 12 months. The math involved in planning the project seemed rather serendipitous.

I had heard about certain online networks that matched independent projects — farms, guest houses, vineyards, schools and more — with people looking to help. This made sense to me. It was the practical way I had envisioned travelling. I'd exchange labour for room and board. This way, I could engage with local communities, and maybe I'd even pick up some new skills.

The trip began to take form. I would leave in January. I'd go into the world, visit 12 countries and do what people did before money even existed: engage in reciprocal relationships. ☺

THAT DECEMBER, I signed over my cherished rent-controlled apartment to one of my best pals. My most important items — photos, books, tax receipts, a suitcase of plaid shirts, a stovetop espresso maker and my Leonard Cohen vinyl records — were neatly tucked into a storage space the size of an airplane lavatory. The rest I gave away. One by one, I hugged my Montreal friends with a mixture of guilt and glee.

I went west for Christmas. In British Columbia, I kissed my family and packed a final backpack. Then, on the first day of January, I eagerly stepped forward into the world and into a journey born from curiosity.

Not looking to give or receive charity. Simply seeking to participate. ☺

JANUARY

"Ladies & gentlemen," the chief steward announced, "please stow your tables and return your seats to their upright position. We've begun our descent to the Louis Armstrong Airport. Thank you for flying with us — and have a great year."

My stomach turned a bit. What had I signed myself up for?

Curled up in seat 35F, I was staring out the window into the night sky, contemplating my situation. Stretched below were flickering lights of freeways and oil refineries. Surrounding me was an arena of stars. I had never felt so little.

My tongue was dry against the roof of my mouth. The other passengers on the flight were acting as if everything was completely normal. But everything did not feel normal. It was as if I had approached an unknown forest and then convinced myself that it would be a fun idea to enter, explore and see if I might come out the other side. And now that I had taken a few steps forward, the setting seemed a hell of a lot darker and more isolated than I had initially imagined.

It was the first day of January, and I was only a few hours into what was supposed to be a year-long personal odyssey around the world. I had quit a cushy job, renounced my rent-controlled

9

apartment and bid my friends and family farewell, downplaying the significance of the drastic lifestyle change. But already, I found myself second-guessing my decision to cut all ties and pursue a highly romanticized travel dream.

Thus far, my approach to managing the emotions that surfaced as my departure grew nearer had been to reiterate a series of self-affirmations:

- *This trip is no big deal.*

- *I'll be back in a year.*

- *People are always doing this sort of stuff.*

- *I'm going to meet wonderfully fascinating people.*

- *Whatever happens is simply "meant to be."*

- *Suck it up, buttercup.*

But at that moment, as I soared a couple thousand metres above the earth, it finally sunk in that everything familiar was officially surrendered.

My heart raced.

My breath quickened.

My eyes grew damp.

My mind raced with self-doubt.

Why do you have such grand fantasies of doing something "special" with your life? Everything was just fine and dandy. Leaving everything was a big mistake, bucko. Don't you think you're being a tad self-indulgent? You have a family back in Canada that could really use your support and presence. Do you think you're actually going to be happier? You're going to return exhausted and confused and overloaded with debt.

My head was spinning with uncertainty. Would this year be worth it? Would the returns justify what I'd given up? ○

THE PLANE TOUCHED down unceremoniously. I located my backpack on the luggage carousel and stepped out of the airport. I had expected Louisiana to be semi-tropical, but the night air was crisp. I hailed a taxi and threw my bag in the trunk.

"How much to get to the Lower Ninth Ward?" I asked as I sat on the cracked leather seat. I felt proud to be negotiating a price before departing, as some of my better-travelled friends had advised me to do. I was determined to be a good traveller.

"Why do you want go to the Lower Ninth Ward, brother?"

"I'm going there to volunteer."

The driver's eyes scanned me through the rearview mirror, reading my face.

"Well ... we can let the meter run," he responded slowly, "or I'll give you a flat rate of 40 bucks."

Considering that I would not have any income for a year, $40 seemed awfully steep. But metered rates were always a gamble with variables such as traffic accidents and unforeseen road construction.

"Let's go with the flat rate," I conceded.

The taxi pulled away from the airport and into the night. I peered out the window, attempting to soak in as much as I could: the concrete freeway, the glowing billboards, the haunting immensity of the Louisiana Superdome (where thousands of people sought refuge after Hurricane Katrina). Late-night Saturday traffic was minimal, with no road delays to slow us down.

We were heading to a volunteer house that served as the headquarters of Common Ground Relief, an organization where I had arranged to help for the month of January. I had an address but no map, and the driver did not have a GPS system. He was guiding us on instinct; I was proceeding on trust.

We passed over the ominous-looking Claiborne Bridge and crept gradually through the Lower Ninth Ward, slowing to read road signs and trying to determine where exactly Deslonde Street was located. The taxi rolled past buildings boarded shut, vacated properties with the skeletal remains of houses, and entire strip malls that had no apparent signs of functioning business. After

20 minutes, two things were evident: firstly, we were lost, and secondly, I was pleased that I had chosen the flat rate.

A rescue phone call would need to be made. I dug out a phone number that I had been given and convinced the driver to lend me his mobile phone. Luckily, someone at the volunteer house picked up the line, and it was rapidly determined that we had missed a turnoff immediately after crossing the bridge. And so we retraced our steps along the same empty streets — the taxi ride becoming an informal tour but without any historical commentary or appropriate photo ops.

Shortly before midnight, the taxi finally turned onto Deslonde Street and came to a stop at an unassuming two-storey blue house with a small porch decorated in climbing vines. Painted onto a piece of plywood hanging from the porch, the Common Ground Relief logo — a fist holding a hammer — confirmed that I was in the right place.

"Good luck, brother," said the driver. He didn't bother waiting to see if I got into the house.

Under the weight of my backpack, I wobbled up the front steps and knocked tentatively. The door crept open, revealing a sleepy-eyed young woman in sweatpants and a paint-streaked T-shirt. She introduced herself as Denise, the volunteer coordinator, and invited me into a bright orange living room with unfinished plywood floors. In the corner sat a Charlie Brown-style Christmas tree decorated with paper snowflakes. Apart from the drone of cars on Claiborne Bridge, all was quiet.

"Everyone's pretty chilled out tonight," Denise whispered, watching my eyes wander around the room. "We all went pretty hard last night for New Year's celebrations. All of the other volunteers are in bed."

"Darn. I'm always late for the party," I joked, wanting to make a friendly first impression.

Denise smiled and proceeded to give me a quick tour of the main floor of the volunteer house, which included a lemon-coloured kitchen, a simple bathroom complete with a basket of sunscreen and condoms, a couple of administrative offices and the living room, which also doubled as an eating area. Overall, it was stark, but the bright colours helped make it feel lively.

"I'll show you to where you'll be sleeping," Denise said, leading us out the front door. "It's a room called The Shaft."

"Great. I'm definitely ready for bed myself." I wondered why we were going out the front door and how a room gets a name like The Shaft.

I followed her down the stairs and along the outside of the house to a separate entrance to the basement. She pushed a door open into a dorm room, flipping on the fluorescent overhead lights and stirring a couple of bodies from their New Year's Eve recovery comas. Denise directed me to a vacant bunk and bade me goodnight. I quickly turned off the lights, trying to minimize my intrusion and hoping to escape being branded as the obnoxious new guy who turns on all the lights in the middle of the night.

Using the glow of my iPod, I rooted through my backpack to extract a clean shirt, my sleeping bag and a toiletries bag. I located my toothbrush and toothpaste and then made my way into the adjacent hallway, only to see a series of closed doors. Which one was the bathroom? Since I didn't want to risk intruding on any other volunteers, I returned to The Shaft, slipped on my fresh shirt and crawled into a cramped lower bunk, mossy teeth and all.

I lay in the dark and took a deep breath. I was doing it. I was living out my dream of travelling for a year. In the ghetto of New Orleans. In a dark, foul-smelling dorm room. ◌

TO LAUNCH THEIR adventures, some world travellers might have immediately bought a ticket to a far-flung exotic destination. But not me.

Don't get me wrong, distant lands were definitely on my travel agenda, but I also reasoned that you don't necessarily have to go overseas to find transformative experiences. With this in mind, North America became an important stop on my list of destinations. My home continent, despite being terribly un-exotic in the eyes of friends and family, would make a great starting point. The culture shock would be less jarring, and the jet lag negligible.

To make things interesting, I decided to select a place that I had never visited before. I examined a map of North America. The energetic appeal of New York City immediately grabbed my attention. I could spend a month starring in a Broadway show, no? However, I had already been to the Big Apple, so that option was ruled out. Northern California called with its progressive culture and world-class wine, but I was afraid that it wouldn't provide enough of a departure from the type of social circles I gravitated to at home. The Canadian province of Newfoundland had its quaint charms, but was perhaps a little too sleepy to be a rousing first destination. And Texas was ... well ... Texas. I wasn't sure I was ready for that level of culture shock.

When my eyes fell on New Orleans, all other options evaporated.

New Orleans had been a longtime fascination. After taking a college course in jazz history, I added the city to my list of urban dream destinations — places that I wanted not only to see but to really experience. With a unique culinary heritage, racial intricacy and history of dramatic natural disasters, the city beckoned like a smooth Louis Armstrong trumpet solo. And since I had the Cajun flair of a moose, there would be just enough cultural difference to make the month intriguing.

Plus New Orleans had the word "new" in it, and this was a small but significant quirk. This would be the first month of my big journey. It was a new chapter in my life, where I would have new experiences, meet new people and face new challenges. Sure, it was a minor semantic coincidence, but I couldn't resist the parallel. ☼

DAYLIGHT ARRIVED, REVEALING slats of wood a mere foot from my nose. The cramped bottom bunk was so compact that I could smell my morning breath rebounding off the top bunk.

I turned my head and took a better look at this dormitory mysteriously called The Shaft. The room featured three wooden bunk beds, along with a couple of shelves spilling with wrinkled clothes, torn books, empty liquor bottles and well-worn boots. The walls were the colour of mint chocolate chip ice cream, but instead of speckles of chocolatey deliciousness, they were dotted with nail holes and splotches of dirt. A two-foot Buddha statue, wearing colourful Mardi Gras beads around his neck, sat serenely under the window.

Suddenly the bed swayed as someone rolled over on the upper bunk. I sensed a set of eyes peering over the edge, but I pretended to still be asleep. I wasn't quite ready to make conversation. ○

I HAD ASSUMED that one of the benefits of arriving on a Saturday night would be that I'd get to spend Sunday adjusting to my new surroundings. But that's not exactly how it worked out.

On my first real day in New Orleans, I found myself in an off-centred state, not really knowing what to do with myself. I longed to be assigned a task, a small responsibility that would provide me with structure and help me navigate this foreign situation less awkwardly. It's the same thing if I go to a party where I don't know anyone. I appreciate it when the host gives me something to do, like circling the room and offering up the bread bowl filled with spinach dip. Such tasks prevent me from getting drunk by myself in a corner.

That first morning, I eventually rose, dressed, found a bathroom and wandered around the premises. The house was quiet, and people were few and far between. I overheard a couple of other volunteers casually talking about going to see Second Line, the weekly big brass parade. But they concluded that their immediate concerns involved sipping tea on the porch, doing laundry and tackling other Sunday chores. It was also clear that sleep and rehydration were still high on their to-do lists after all the New Year's Eve debauchery. So after a lacklustre breakfast of toast and jam, a quick flip through *The Times-Picayune*, and a total failure to successfully engage with the other volunteers — *Where was a bowl of spinach dip when I needed one?* — I decided to take matters into my own hands. I set off on my own to see a bit of New Orleans.

I walked and then I walked some more from the Lower Ninth Ward, over the canal on the St. Claude Avenue Bridge and through the Bywater district. I spent more than an hour ambling the quiet streets, noting the litter and boarded-up homes, before eventually coming across a massive two-storey concrete levee, evidence of the city's vulnerability to greater natural forces. I decided to follow it, happy to have a clear and stable point of reference.

The levee led me to the famous French Quarter. Resting on a park bench in Jackson Square, I sat in the sunshine and watched a high school brass band performing swing standards. Across the square stood stately French colonial buildings and an imposing church with a pointy steeple. The smell of horse manure and deep-fried *beignets* (southern doughnuts) drifted past. When the performance ended, I wandered through the covered French Market, gazing across piles of cheap leather purses, Cajun spices, shot glasses adorned with saxophones, and voodoo dolls of various sizes. A foam trucker's hat with the words "Big Easy" embroidered across the front appealed to my tourist sensibilities, so I purchased it. Back in the open air, I meandered along Bourbon Street, where a man walked past flailing his arms and praising Jesus for his abilities to heal.

It was then that I realized what I had really wanted to find that afternoon: something tangible from my first day, some affirmative evidence that I had made the right decision to renounce my comfortable lifestyle for a year of drifting. But between the tackiness of Bourbon Street, the lineups for doughnuts and the tired expressions on most people's faces, I couldn't help but feel like the French Quarter was a cheap caricature of the New Orleans that I had envisioned. The sentiment surrounding this important first day was a quiet anticlimax summarized in one syllable: Meh. And a larger question arose that frightened me: *After dreaming of this trip for so long, had I set myself up for disappointment?*

An intense craving for caffeine led me to an unexceptional café on a side street lined with cast iron balconies. With a steamy cup of coffee in hand, I crouched on the sidewalk against a stone wall and observed a four-piece band. The performers had enough musical chops to rival any jazz band I would have paid to see at home. But what was more entertaining was how they interacted with the pedestrians who passed by, playing a bit more boisterously whenever a generous individual dropped a bill in their open guitar case. The bass player looked at me and tipped his hat. I smiled and nodded back. It was kind of him to acknowledge me. ☼

WHEN IT CAME time to choose a place to help out in New Orleans, I knew I wanted to join an organization that dealt with the consequences of Hurricane Katrina. I had heard that rebuilding efforts were *still* ongoing, years after catastrophe had struck, and I wanted to understand more about this significant event in recent American history. There were, however, a couple of hitches. Such as the reality that most organizations charged volunteers an arm and a leg to become involved. And perhaps more importantly, the fact that I possessed absolutely no building skills. What organization would even want me?

With less than a month remaining before my big departure from Canada, I had yet to secure a host for that important first month, and I began to accept that I might have to pay for my first work-exchange experience. The thought of paying to volunteer was contrary to my travel strategy of finance-free trading; I was seeking opportunities to exchange a few hours of work per day for food and accommodation. I was willing to bend my travel guidelines, however, for the sake of compelling and educational experiences. At the last minute, I finally found a good compromise.

Common Ground Relief was suggested to me by an acquaintance in Montreal who, after discovering I would be heading to New Orleans, messaged me with an unsolicited recommendation that would shape my first month. He had spent many months with the organization and mentioned that it had offered him "rewarding work and community." As I researched more, I discovered that Common Ground Relief had been formed to respond to the devastation created by the catastrophic flooding brought on by Hurricane Katrina. With thousands of residents suddenly lacking food, water and shelter, the organization's initial mandate was to provide basic survival necessities to anyone who needed support. Once the emergency response was over, the work transferred to basic clean-up efforts. Volunteers might have found themselves wielding a crowbar as they gutted thousands of homes or staffing a health clinic and women's shelter. Today, projects revolve around repairing and rebuilding homes (painting, flooring, drywall, insulation and more), as well as offering free advice at a legal clinic, testing residential soil quality and providing education about gardening.

Common Ground Relief sounded like a place where I could give a little and learn a lot. They required $10 per day to cover food, but I reasoned that working for a reputable host was worth the money — *especially* for the first month. So I completed the application and waited with fingers crossed that they might accept an unskilled guy like me.

In the days that followed, I received an email of approval and got in touch with Thom, the director of operations. He outlined what I should expect — to get splattered in paint and sleep in a dorm room — while warning of overly strict American customs officers who had unsympathetically denied entry to Canadian would-be volunteers in the past. He also cautioned me about the chilly winter temperatures that New Orleans could experience (to which I chuckled and thought to myself: *I'm a Canadian. We practically invented cold temperatures*). Thom quelled my fears about having no discernable skills to offer and assured me that if I could use a wheelbarrow, my presence would be appreciated and put to good use. ◌

"DANIEL, YOUR RESUMÉ said that you have experience planting trees, right?" Denise called over to me. I was standing in the kitchen, packing a brown bag lunch with a peanut butter sandwich and a waxy apple. It was Monday morning, my first day on the job.

"Uh, yeah." I responded. "I used to plant trees in the summertime, in the wild mountains of British Columbia." I added the "wild" part rather gratuitously, hoping she might perceive me as strong and capable.

"Great. I need you to lead a crew. You'll take them to plant trees."

"Wow ... um ... sure." My emotions — a nervous form of excitement — were predictable to a certain extent. But I never expected to be thrust into a leadership role. This would be my first big surprise of the day.

"Great. You'll be working with Mary Ann — you know, the girl from New Jersey," said Denise before ducking out of the kitchen.

Once I finished packing my lunch, I headed out to the front porch where I found my co-captain standing in a grubby pair of jeans and a bandana. About to begin her final semester as a nursing student specializing in burn care, Mary Ann had also recently arrived to Common Ground Relief herself for a two-week volunteer stint. We had met the night before when she was assigned a bunk in The Shaft. I had told her about my plans for the year, and she had shared stories about the time she hitchhiked across South America and subsequently got a staph infection so bad that sores popped up all over her body. Her left leg got so swollen and painful that she couldn't walk. What struck me more than her grandiose tales was her nonchalant way of relating each experience.

With our hands in our pockets, we stood strategizing. Or at least pretending to strategize.

"So, you know what we're doing?" Mary Ann asked, peering over her wire-rimmed glasses.

"Not really."

"Cool. Me neither. But I've got the new Black Keys album.

So whatever we do, we got good music." Mary Ann nodded her head to an imaginary beat.

Minutes later, Denise hopped up the porch stairs with a clipboard in hand and began to brief us. We were to be released into the Lower Ninth Ward with a beat-up truck, a couple of shovels and a collection of four-foot-tall magnolia, maple and cypress saplings. We also had a list of residents who had expressed interest in free trees. Our crew would be a group of insurance-industry professionals from the Deep South who had been flown to New Orleans to watch an important football game — a "rewards trip" for strong corporate performance. While in town, they were also scheduled to do some community service.

"That sounds doable, right?" Denise asked. Mary Ann and I both gave her the thumbs-up. But before she rushed off to brief a house-painting crew, Denise emphasized one important detail. "Please let the corporate folks do the digging." She smiled and looked me directly in the eye to make sure I understood. I did.

The next thing we knew, a massive bus turned onto Deslonde Street and approached with a cloud of dust and engine noise. It pulled to a stop in front of the two-storey blue house. One by one, the businessmen and businesswomen waddled off the coach in matching corporate-branded T-shirts — a swarm of pasty skin and southern accents.

Muting my skepticism, I forced a welcoming grin. Internally, however, I couldn't help but wonder about the efficacy and ethics of a corporate group dropping into a fractured neighbourhood for a few hours of tokenistic volunteerism. Who was really benefiting from this? Then again, the insurance company had probably made a hefty donation to make it worth the logistical feat of accommodating 40 volunteers for only one day.

Once my crew was assembled, we set off into the neighbourhood to knock on doors. We asked residents where they wanted their new trees and began digging holes. That's when I had my second big surprise of the day: planting trees in the Lower Ninth Ward was not just a landscaping effort, it also bordered on archaeology. Each time we opened up the earth, we found debris and treasures that the post-hurricane flooding had brought in from around the Mississippi basin. Buried in the ground were shards of broken bottles, chunks of dishware, gnarled utensils, toy marbles and, perhaps most hauntingly, dirt-smeared Barbie dolls.

At our third house, we uncovered a large piece of plastic that might have been a piece of car bumper. That's when one of the corporate crew members — a woman with high hair and breasts that barely fit under her T-shirt — approached me.

"So, Dane-yul," she drawled, "why are we planting them types of trees?"

"Well, from what I know," I responded, "cypress trees have an ability to soak up a lot of water, to act like sponges. Which is important in an area prone to flooding."

I might have sounded smart, but I really wasn't — I had asked the exact same question to the wetlands coordinator at Common Ground Relief earlier that morning.

As much as I enjoyed that split second when I nailed my job as crew boss, I soon regretted positioning myself as a knowledgeable go-to person. Suddenly, the rest of the gang started to pipe up with a deluge of questions: *Is it really safe to build houses here again? How does Common Ground Relief get its funding? What measures have been made to ensure that another disaster will be avoided? Who owns all the abandoned homes?* I answered the inquiries as best I could, sharing the nuggets of information I had acquired over my meagre 36 hours in the city. But more often than not, I simply had to own up to my own ignorance on the subject.

As we headed to our fourth house, I began to feel remorseful about how quickly I had dismissed my crew at the outset. I had braced myself to deal with a group that was steeped in over-privileged ignorance or, at best, simply wrought with middle-class apathy. But their questions were relevant and spoke to an awareness that was anything but indifferent.

In fact, if I could gauge anything from our short time together, I'd say they were good-intentioned folks who genuinely wanted to help out while gaining a better understanding of the events and issues related to Hurricane Katrina. They had come to the Lower Ninth Ward, if only for a morning, to help and to learn.

So were their intentions any less valid than my own? ○

THE NEXT DAY I was assigned to lead another tree-planting team. But instead of directing a group of insurance folks, Mary Ann and I were in charge of a cohort of college freshmen and freshwomen from the University of Virginia on a goodwill mission during their winter holidays. Again, we set off into the neighbourhood. Given their eager attitudes and youthful physiques, this crew of six could plant a four-foot sapling in a matter of minutes. This meant we had plenty of leftover time to hang back and listen to residents share their tales from the neighbourhood. These were the folks who came back after Hurricane Katrina, the people who were either brave enough to return to ground zero or had no other options.

The residents we met spoke of loved ones lost as a result of the storm, as well as from other causes, such as old age or disease. They seemed nostalgic for days gone by, days when their families were still together. Few locals actually used the words "Hurricane Katrina." Instead they referred to it as "The Storm." Immense squalls hit the Gulf Coast every year, but whenever someone mentioned The Storm, we knew exactly what they meant.

Late in the afternoon on that second day, an old man with a purple ball cap and a limp approached as we dug holes for cypress trees at a retirement community.

"The insurance companies have not honoured the protection policies of hundreds of homeowners in the Lower Ninth Ward," said the old man, who had introduced himself as Mr. Jackson.

We paused from digging and gathered in a circle around him, a wide-eyed audience.

"Those corporate bastards refused to pay out in fear of bankruptcy. They were worried about their own bottom dollars. But we are people. They don't see that."

Several of the students averted their eyes. I wondered what

yesterday's corporate folks would have thought if they had heard what Mr. Jackson had to say.

"We made agreements with them, and they didn't follow through. We were abandoned."

After his speech, Mr. Jackson took the time to offer each of the crew members an encouraging pat on the back. He might have been angry with the insurance companies, but he was welcoming with us. And to be honest, I couldn't help but think that he must be the life of the party at the retirement home.

We continued forth, planting more trees and chatting with more residents. Each tree was a small gesture, but the smiles and appreciation we received led us to believe we had done something greater. In a neighbourhood where abandonment from corporations and governments had become part of daily life, the simple symbolism of planting a cypress tree was laced with the potential for regeneration and hope. And I felt honoured to participate in the gesture. ◌

IT WASN'T JUST the smell of beer farts and paint fumes in The Shaft that posed a threat to my slumber cycles. It was also the soundscape that arises when living in close proximity to energetic young people who value good times over bath times. During the night in that basement dorm room, it was not unusual to be confronted with a variety of auditory stimuli: a drunken volunteer returning from a blues concert, the murmurs of two volunteers cavorting on a lower bunk or, the worst offence of them all, chronic snoring.

You might think that because I was an aspiring world traveller, I would be an adventurous and extroverted character — you know, the type of person who embraces communal living as some sort of ideal model for collectivism. Sure, I dig socialism. And I certainly appreciate my fellow humans. But my preferred way to appreciate my fellow humans is after I've had an uninterrupted eight hours of sleep in a spacious bed in a soundproof room. The fact of the matter is that I've always had hermit tendencies. If given the option between a boisterous party with energetic music and tequila shots or a quiet night at home with a book and duvet, I've always been apt to choose the latter. In fact, after many years of living solo in my own apartment, I can be quite territorial over personal space. Thus, the shared accommodations at Common Ground Relief were a direct affront to my curmudgeonly boundaries. There was rarely an instance when I might sit and read the newspaper alone, and even though I did get a moment of respite in the shower, the act of pulling someone else's hairball out of the drain made me weep quietly.

The saving grace, however, was that everyone was kind of awesome. The Shaft, it turned out, was an acronym for "Short-term Housing And Fun Times." The room was one part functional bunkhouse and one part ever-evolving scrappy art installation: six unmade beds, a ladder hanging from the ceiling, incense ashes scattered across the dresser, a map of New Orleans taped loosely to the wall. The cast of volunteers staying in the dormitory fluctuated, and over the course of the month, I shared the space with a string of eccentric dorm-mates. For example, there was a wise-beyond-his-years 18-year-old from Seattle named Lukas, a Parisian bundle of awkward English and absolute joviality known as Boris, and Mary Ann, the unflappable New Jersey nursing student.

In the evenings, after the working day was finished, my fellow volunteers and I would often pile onto the organization's rickety old bicycles and take mini-adventures around the city. We enjoyed free mouth-watering curry at the local Hare Krishna centre. We danced to the Treme Brass Band's vintage big band songs in the heart of the famous neighbourhood with the same name. In a dingy local drinking hole called Kajun's Pub, we watched the New Orleans Saints in a tense playoff game, celebrating touchdowns with fluorescent Jell-O shots. Most adventures were concluded with a late-night bicycle parade of woozy volunteers returning to the Lower Ninth Ward.

As for my interrupted sleep, I soon developed a special technique that helped me get through the night. While the standard way to use a pillow is to place it under the head, I discovered that it was more effective when used *on top* of the head. Positioned just so, it acted as a surprisingly good defence against smells, sound and light. The trick was to apply just the right amount of pressure, to crush it forcefully enough over my skull to block out Boris's snoring or the odour of damp socks, but just delicately enough so as to not suffocate myself. When The Shaft was particularly noisy, I used earplugs as backup. Still, the pillow would remain in place to filter the smells and to mitigate any instances of a foolish person flipping on the fluorescent overhead light.

In a way, the combination of working during the day and sleeping in The Shaft at night felt like a radical version of summer camp, but instead of tug-of-war and Kool-Aid, we had power tools and whisky. Just never at the same time. ○

ONE AFTERNOON DURING my first week as a crew boss, all the trees that needed to be planted had been planted. Consequently, I was released early from my volunteer duties for an afternoon of leisure. Curious to explore more of the Lower Ninth Ward, I left the volunteer house and started walking north, away from the Claiborne Bridge and into uncharted territory. Along the avenue was a series of newly constructed houses — angular buildings with elevated foundations and solar panels, built to withstand storms and architectural boringness alike. (These were the hip eco-friendly homes of Brad Pitt's rebuilding organization, Make It Right.)

Eventually I reached the end of Deslonde Street, which was cut off by an immense brush-covered levee. The wall was impossible to see over or climb, so without any specific destination in mind, I decided to hang a right and kept strolling through what seemed to be a "less rebuilt" corner of the neighbourhood. The levee was on my left, boarded-up houses on my right. A few blocks further along, I came to a signpost marked "Bienvenue" and a set of stairs leading up the side of the levee to a visitor's platform. I was immediately curious because the platform provided a vantage point over something I had never actually seen before: a bayou.

Like folks who are not from the southern U.S.A., my impressions of a "bayou" had been informed by steamy Louisiana-based movies and Hank Williams songs. I had certain expectations of what a bayou might be, and they generally involved either a dark form of voodoo drama or, conversely, a knee-slappin' swampy good time. I imagined gloomy trees dripping with vines, lily pads the size of sombreros, and a menagerie of toads, dragonflies and alligators — and maybe even some slow-moving mist to really set the mood. Yet as I stood atop the platform and looked across "Bayou Bienvenue," I couldn't help but feel slightly underwhelmed, that perhaps something was missing from the scene.

Bayou Bienvenue looked like an oversized mud puddle. The brown expanse of water stretched for a couple of kilometres, the distant shore lined with overgrown bushes. The most notable landmarks were a series of scattered weather-washed vertical stumps in random spots throughout the bayou. The slough was anything but mystical. It looked like a place where trees went to die. A sort of cypress abyss.

During my stint as a tree-planting crew boss, and through subsequent interactions with the Wetlands Coordinator at Common Ground Relief, I had learned more about the environmental complexities of the New Orleans region. One of the most important take-aways of my month thus far was a new respect for wetlands. The spongy attributes of swamps, marshes and bogs act as a form of protection against natural disasters, with the potential to absorb water and to maintain the ecological balance essential to the region. In fact, Common Ground Relief had started a tree nursery to ensure the restoration of native ecosystems throughout the Gulf Coast region and to repair the damage done by the saltwater intrusion, a consequence of human-built canals. And by the looks of the broken-down bayou, the organization had its work cut out for it.

Having seen enough, I stepped down off the platform to continue on my stroll through the Lower Ninth Ward. As I walked, I sang to myself quietly: *Dress in style and go hog-wild, me-oh my-oh. Son of a gun, we'll have big fun on the bayou.*

But I tagged an extra few words on the end: *That is, if it still exists.* ☼

AFTER MY INITIAL late-night arrival to The Shaft, I later relocated to a much-coveted upper bunk bed. One evening, I was sitting on that top bunk plucking gobs of sticky white mess from my hair (after a day spent painting ceilings) when a new volunteer sauntered into the dorm. She was taller than average and wore a knee-length dress cut from red fabric with a jalapeño pepper print. Her ragged shoulder bag was adorned with a series of buttons that attested to various personal beliefs and identities: "Not gay as in happy, but queer as in fuck you" and "Food Not Bombs" and "P is for Polyamory!" From first appearance, she was the kind of character you might expect to see in an art film. Except this was real life.

"Hiya. I'm Edda," she said self-assuredly in an Australian accent, dropping her backpack onto one of the lower bunks. The rest of us in the room took turns introducing ourselves politely and then returned quietly to what we were doing.

"Do you mind if I turn on some bounce?" Edda interjected, an open question to the room.

"What does it mean to turn on some bounce?" I asked.

"You know, New Orleans 'bounce' music?" She read the look of confusion on my face and continued. "It's like a luscious version of hip hop from New Orleans," she explained, "but where you lean over and thrust your ass in the air."

Edda put her hands on the dresser beside the Buddha statue and proceeded to demonstrate. After a couple seconds of booty thrusting, she fell over laughing.

It was a fine introduction to an individual who would subsequently affect the course of my year-long journey. ☼

THE MORNINGS FELL into a reliable groove, which suited my affinity for predictability just fine. The average daybreak ritual was to wake up early, head upstairs to the kitchen to pack my lunch and enjoy a moment of personal space — a short meditation before the other sleepy-eyed volunteers stumbled into the kitchen. Then I would escape to the porch with a steamy cup of Earl Grey, a bowl of instant porridge and the local daily newspaper tucked under my arm. For the sake of planning my trip, it was important to keep up-to-date with world events — I would need to avoid war zones or areas of political instability.

But, more imperatively, I needed to check my daily horoscope. If the Sagittarius blurb was favourable, I soaked up every word and shared my fortune with the morning zombies as they trudged up the stairs. If the prognosis warned of impending doom, I would toss the paper aside and mumble something along the lines of "Astrology is bullshit!"

Eventually, the other volunteers would join me on the porch and wait patiently for Denise to assign our duties for the day. And each morning while waiting, I wondered if that would be the fateful day when my complete lack of handyman skills would be exposed. It's not that I was uninterested in the trades or renovations or building work. It's just that I had never really had the opportunity to explore my handyman potential. (No, correction: I never had the *right* opportunity to develop these skills.)

You see, in high school I was a bit of a runt. The guys who signed up for woodworking, auto mechanics and other trades-based endeavours were the same guys who ritualistically slammed me against the hallway lockers. Thus, for my own personal protection, I avoided those classes with the same brand of avoidance that prepubescent boys use to circumvent the gymnasium shower room (which is a comparison I employ with experience).

Outside of school, the role of family handyman was played by my under-qualified father, who earned the position primarily because he has hands and is a man. Dad is famous for saving the house from a dead pine tree that risked falling through the roof and into the bathroom. With his chainsaw, he managed to fell the tree but subsequently snapped a set of power lines and left the neighbourhood without electricity for a couple of hours. Luckily, only a squirrel was killed during this episode. His general approach was to get projects done quickly so that we could focus on more interesting activities: cross-country skiing excursions, canoeing in the local lakes and stealing road signs. Besides, I was often too busy accentuating my nerddom with piano lessons or Toastmasters Club or gymnastics training — which incidentally proved helpful to dodge shoulder checks in the high school hallways — to really learn how to be a handyman from my dad. And in light of the aforementioned events, that was perhaps for the best. Any way you slice it, I had arrived at the age of 30 with a handyman skill set comparable to that of a trombone. A sad trombone.

And so it happened that late one evening during my first week, Denise approached me with a look of conspiracy and inquired deeper into my handyman history.

"Hey, Daniel," she tilted her head and grinned, "have you ever laid tile before?"

Her optimism was adorable.

"No," I admitted. "But I have laid some other things … " I paused and raised an eyebrow for comical effect. She refrained from rolling her eyes and continued.

"Would you be into helping John and Myke with a tiling project? There's a lot of work to be done, and they could use an extra set of hands."

"Such as bringing them coffee?"

Denise just shook her head, smiling.

"No," she continued. "You are going to learn how to tile. It's easy."

The next morning, after a cup of tea and a frightfully discouraging horoscope, I stood beside one of the company trucks in a faded flannel shirt and well-worn blue jeans. Around my hips was a crusty leather tool belt, which had been left in The Shaft by a previous volunteer. I posed with a tentative sense of pride, knowing that I had achieved, at the very minimum, the esthetic of a handyman.

Eventually, Myke and John came strolling down the steps of the volunteer house and toward the truck. They said nothing about my staged outfit — which I interpreted as a good sign — and soon we were off to the construction site: a new house that had relatively few remaining jobs before the homeowners could move in.

I followed my two comrades up the front steps and into the unfinished kitchen, where we began planning our work.

"Well, it's usually best to start laying the tile from the first visual entry point of the room," said Myke.

"True," replied John. "Let's just make sure we don't end up with some really awkward strips of tile around the cupboard toe kick."

"Good point," added Myke. "We also have to be careful because sometimes the backer board can be a bit blistery in places. Any thoughts, Daniel?"

Both guys looked at me. I froze. "Uh ... nope." I tilted my head and rubbed my chin, as if to give the impression that I was deep in thought. "I ... uh ... I think it's going to look mighty fine."

"Great! Let's get to work," concluded John. I followed the guys outside.

Myke began to mix mortar, telling me about the delicate balance of powder and water as he proceeded. Maybe he could smell my inexperience, since he carefully explained the steps as he moved along. What a relief to be with someone who seemed to have no expectations of my knowledge or ability! That said, I still wondered if one of them would crack a passing joke about my ineptitude or apply a quick shoulder check in response to my obvious bookishness. But as the hours progressed, Myke proved to be a patient and accommodating teacher. If he had any issues with my rookie status, he did a remarkable job of concealing them. And John didn't even complain when I put in my earphones and began to sing along to Ray LaMontagne.

Throughout the course of the day, I learned how to cut tile, carefully apply mortar with a trowel and correctly space each tile with these delightful foamy devices named "tile spacers." It turned out that Denise was right — basic tiling wasn't all that hard. In fact, it was sort of fun. I was having a great time and felt like I was the one who was gaining. In a neighbourhood recovering from a catastrophic natural disaster, was that even allowed?

That evening, during our Friday night spaghetti dinner, I boasted to the other volunteers about my wizard-like abilities in tiling. The others nodded graciously, none of them stating the obvious: *Yeah, but a toddler could lay tile.* For me, the experience was a minor victory. Later on, after beer, darts and more tipsy bike riding, I crawled into my bunk bed and drifted to sleep, dreaming of the house that I would construct when I returned to Canada — oh, what beautiful floors it would have! ☼

EVEN THOUGH SHE arrived to the volunteer organization after I did, Edda had already spent some time in New Orleans and was familiar with the various festivities happening around the city. Her personal belief system — equal parts Catholicism and mystic witchery — meshed well with the voodoo vibe of The Big Easy. And since I love an oddball, they meshed well with me too.

Hailing from Lismore, a small town in New South Wales, she had funded her international travels by offering services ranging from doula work to nude modelling to festival planning. Each of these experiences provided her with a unique point of view, complemented by her university studies in Community Trauma. It was not surprising that she was consistently the first volunteer to initiate conversation with citizens of the Lower Ninth Ward. She usually approached them with a guiding question: "How can we best facilitate healing?" The answers involved lengthy yet insightful sentiments about rebuilding the neighbourhood. And Edda would simply listen.

When the working day was through, most of us volunteers crashed, exhausted from painting or demolition work, but Edda often went out alone to one of the many parties happening around town.

"Edda," I asked one evening as she prepared herself for a bondage workshop, "aren't you tired?"

Standing in front of a cracked mirror in The Shaft, Edda paused from applying her cherry-coloured lipstick. She looked up toward my bunk bed through the reflection.

"Yeah," she replied. "But we only live once, right?"

And then she stood up, put a spiked collar around her neck, blew me a kiss and headed out into the night. ☻

CAMPFIRES ARE THE original entertainment system. They have always appealed to me more than television or movies (or, dare I say, books). Not only is the mixture of heat, colour and crackle intoxicating, but the stories that emerge around a firepit are somehow more poignant, more gripping than in any other setting. On the quieter evenings at the volunteer house, a popular activity was to round up scrap pieces of wood, light a fire in the backyard and huddle around with a guitar and a flask of whisky.

However, when Edda decided to host a "Full Moon Ceremony" around the campfire, I greeted the idea with reluctance. My 21st-century social conditioning has blessed and cursed me with a great deal of cynicism. Any activities involving "moon" and "ceremony" leave me with notions of long-haired, flower-clad pagans dancing around a fire chanting appropriated Eastern mantras. Which is all fine and dandy, but miles away from anything that I've ever been able to relate to spiritually. My mystical moments are achieved when walking in solitude through nature or popping a zit in a really difficult place to reach on my back. And the general theme is that I do these things alone.

At first, I hummed and hawed over whether I'd attend. Because Edda had become a friend, I felt a certain obligation to go. But then again, Edda had also invited me to a kinky party, which I bashfully declined. In the case of the Full Moon Ceremony the kicker was my own inner dialogue, which stated matter-of-factly: *Daniel, if you don't try this, it could be evidence that your spirit is suffering from a great degree of boringness. This is why you are travelling. Buck up and get out there.* And so I pulled myself off the bunk bed, traded my suspicions for a warm sweater and headed out to the backyard to explore a potentially meaningful moment with my fellow volunteers.

A handful of folks had already gathered and were sitting casually around the wheelbarrow-turned-firepit. I sank into a squeaky wooden chair and placed my palms over the fire. The evening was surprisingly cold. Even though Thom had warned me about the potential for icy temperatures, I hadn't truly believed it until now.

Edda was wearing her long chili pepper dress and had a blanket over her shoulders. She walked from person to person with a bundle of smoldering sage. One by one, she invited us to stand and then wafted smoke over each of our bodies as part of a smudging ritual. The custom, I was told, served as a cleansing agent to the spirit. I could not recall the last time I had interacted with another person in an intentionally spiritual fashion. The fact that someone had decided to take the time to help me do my divine housework was considerate.

"We gather at the full moon as people have done since ancient times, on the brightest night of the month when the moon has come to the end of its cycle," said Edda.

To my right, I noticed a small altar constructed of photos, candles, incense, fruit, flowers and trinkets.

"The moon has a major impact on the tides, women's fertility cycles, human behaviour, the growth of plants — everything upon which it casts its light, really." Edda's tone was neither syrupy nor unnecessarily precious. "It's helpful to pay attention to the moon's power so we can better harness its energies and consciously work with the shifts that this celestial body effects."

I scanned the other participants. Denise watched attentively, with her head tilted to one side. Mary Ann pushed her glasses up her nose, occasionally nodding. Myke was cleaning mortar out from under his fingernails. Boris stared into the fire.

"By honouring the moon, we honour the passing of time, we focus on the sacredness in our lives and we celebrate being a human being on this earth."

With the calming glow of the fire, the lingering smell of sage and the soft intonation of Edda's voice, the space felt safe, even sacred. I couldn't help but appreciate the purpose of the moment, the deliberate celebration of "being a human being on this earth." This was definitely not something I did in my day-to-day life.

"I invite you each to take a piece of paper," Edda said, moving the service forward. "On this paper, write down an intention that you wish to explore, a goal that you'd like to send out to the universe or an emotion that you'd like to purge."

Again, I looked around the fire and saw contemplative expressions from my fellow full-moon ceremony devotees. I pondered my own wishes and intents. They came simply: good health for my loved ones and strength to continue my journey. After we had scribbled down our thoughts, Edda invited us to individually share our sentiments aloud or to simply throw our notes into the fire. When my turn came, I read my items without explanation and then threw the paper into the flames, watching it momentarily light up the silent faces around me. Then, as a personal contribution, I passed a bottle of Johnnie Walker around the fire. One by one, we cheers'ed the moon and then took ceremonious swigs.

"Now we'll each select a Goddess Guidance card," Edda announced, producing a deck of cards that contained 44 goddesses from various spiritual practices around the world. "I encourage you to focus your energy and then select a card that speaks to you." Soon the cards were in my hands. Unsure of what it meant to "focus my energy," I simply imagined that I was Gandalf and placed a hand magically over the deck, hoping for the best. I drew Maat.

"Maat is the Egyptian goddess of integrity, fairness and justice," I read from the card. "She brings order to chaos and advocates for honesty and truthfulness in social interactions."

"What does that mean for you, Daniel?" Edda asked.

"It means I need to stop lying," I stated and then paused for a dramatic effect. "Guys, my real name is Chuck."

Edda shook her head and smiled.

"I'll bet it's a simple reminder to be a good guy," I followed up more truthfully and then passed the deck to Boris, who accepted the deck neither with eagerness nor reluctance.

As the other volunteers drew their cards, I continued to ponder the possibilities of Maat's messages. I was hesitant to attribute too much meaning to it all, yet curious to see how a mere suggestion might challenge my thinking. Ultimately, I decided that the card was a subtle encouragement to be respectful over the forthcoming months as I made my way across the planet.

After we had all drawn our cards, Edda closed the ceremony with a final blessing, and as a group we sent another round of whisky salutations to the moon. Then some folks headed off to bed, but I stayed behind, hypnotized by the twinkling embers of the bonfire. ☼

DESPITE THE FULL moon ceremonies and tipsy bike rides, it was impossible for me to forget where I was — in a neighbourhood that had a hefty share of adversity. Yes, many reconstruction efforts had taken place, but the Lower Ninth Ward still had numerous apocalyptic nooks and crannies: hollowed homes, piles of debris and lots overgrown with tall grasses. Many roads were in disarray, with potholes that could swallow small cars. For every house that had been rebuilt, there seemed to be two abandoned ones, and the strip malls along the main avenues of North Claiborne and Saint Claude were like frontier ghost towns. Years after the destruction of Hurricane Katrina, the Lower Ninth Ward had still not been restored to the community it once was.

Prior to the storm, the neighbourhood boasted the highest percentage of African American home ownership of any corner of the United States. People were invested in the area. After the storm, however, thousands of folks opted to relocate to different corners of New Orleans, if they chose to return to the city at all. And subsequently, in the Lower Ninth Word and throughout the city, a sort of "Cajun diaspora" has occurred.

A stronger levee has since been constructed around the perimeter of the Lower Ninth Ward. And, as it stands, the region has been deemed a safe and reasonable place to rebuild homes and reconstruct community. But after an event of such magnitude, trauma had intruded (and refuses to leave) the neighbourhood's psyche. The community still struggles with a number of challenges — inadequate housing, unemployment, crime and an aging population — and, from what I sensed, continues to grapple with a bigger question: *Who are we now?*

A number of community organizations, including Common Ground Relief, are committed to the redevelopment of the Lower Ninth Ward. Some of these projects are strictly community-driven initiatives to restore the neighbourhood to the way it once was. Other organizations have contemporary and externally led mandates that aim at shifting the architectural legacy of the area, such as constructing futuristic-looking houses that are more sustainable and built high on stilts. The collective future of the community is, understandably, a contentious issue with residents and stakeholders. You might say that the immediate forecast for the Lower Ninth Ward is still somewhat stormy. ○

ON ONE OF my last days in New Orleans, Edda took me to visit Smitty, an 80-year-old man who often helped out at Common Ground Relief as a residential advisor. Smitty was one of the great elders of the Lower Ninth Ward; he had grown up in the neighbourhood and knew it better than anyone. Among the volunteers, he was something of a legend. Smitty's house was located on a street that had been more successful in recovery efforts. The houses surrounding him had new weather-resistant siding. There were even flowers in some of the yards.

We arrived in the early afternoon, locked our bikes to the chain-link fence, wandered up a set of creaky steps and knocked on the door.

"Welcome, welcome," he said as he waved us in. "Just let me finish up here."

The elderly black man was settled in front of an old desktop computer, working on his soon-to-be-released memoirs. We took our shoes off and stepped onto the plush grey carpets of his living room. The walls had been recently painted and still remained bare. The only décor was the books, which were sprawled out on knee-high shelves that lined the room. It looked more like a library than a living room.

After finishing with the computer, Smitty darted into the kitchen and quickly returned with a pot of green tea. We settled onto a simple grey couch (the only place we could sit other than the floor) and blew the steam off our teacups. Smitty pulled off his glasses. He told us about growing up in the Lower Ninth Ward and how he had left to work for a couple decades in Hollywood. The steadily increasing cost of living in California eventually drove him back to New Orleans, where he could afford to live out his days in a home that he actually owned. He had returned before The Storm and had been one of the last people to leave the neighbourhood during the flooding, mainly because he had nowhere else to go. His house — the one we were sitting in — had been largely destroyed by the surge waters, and then gutted and rebuilt by Common Ground Relief.

With the subject of the Lower Ninth Ward on the table, Edda posed her classic question.

"Smitty," she began with her honest sense of curiosity, "how can we best facilitate healing in the Lower Ninth Ward?"

A look of frustration fell over Smitty. He shook his head and exhaled forcefully.

"Forget about healing!" he exclaimed, much to our surprise. "Every organization rolls in here and wants to make a difference. They do great work and we're very much appreciative. But they're not going to do a damn thing to change the future of this neighbourhood unless the people of the neighbourhood want to change themselves."

Smitty took a second to collect his thoughts and then unfolded his wrinkled hands.

"What we need is to expand our minds," he continued,

illustrating his point by extending his fingers out from around his head. "The only way we are going to reach a better place is if we educate ourselves. The path to the future is made possible by education."

And that's all he had to say about healing. ⟡

JANUARY PASSED QUICKLY. The first leg of the journey would be nostalgically recalled as a meaningful debut to my adventure. Common Ground Relief set the standard to which I would subsequently compare all other months. It provided the setting for a series of winning travel variables: the opportunity to learn new skills, experience a culturally textured location, engage with locals, hang out with a memorable confluence of volunteers and, most importantly, contribute to a project that was doing some great work.

The month provided some important lessons that would inform the rest of my journey and beyond. Possibly the most significant nugget was that it is permissible to have both good times and educational experiences in a struggling setting. Residents of New Orleans will attest to the importance of the first Mardi Gras celebrations after the storm. The annual festivities helped bring a sense of normalcy and enjoyment to a city facing an unknown future. Of course humour and festivity are not appropriate for every situation, but the intention to rebuild or renovate emotional spaces is as important as the physical spaces. A smile works differently but as effectively as a trowel. Not only is joyfulness legitimate, but I'd say it is vital to the recovery process.

The celebratory tone of New Orleans and of the people at Common Ground Relief also enabled me to move past some of my hesitations about leaving home. And, at the risk of sounding sentimental, I began to see that this voyage, in its own way, could be a year-long full moon ceremony — a simple celebration of being a human on this earth.

Eventually, the moment of my departure from the volunteer house arrived. I slipped a bottle of whisky under Denise's pillow for the gang to discover later, as there would be more moons to salute. I administered boisterous hugs to my fellow volunteers. I took a final inhalation of The Shaft's unique aromatic blend.

A horn beeped impatiently, informing me that the car was waiting. Thom had offered to drive me to the airport, and Edda insisted on coming along for the ride. I tossed my backpack in the trunk, and we were soon zooming along the New Orleans freeway, passing the same billboards and urban concrete sprawl as when I had arrived late that night on the first day of the month. Perhaps it was the daylight or perhaps something in me had shifted, but the Louisiana Superdome, an iconic image of Hurricane Katrina, seemed less immense.

The car pulled into the departures level. Thom hopped out and gave me a no-nonsense hug, the kind of quick adios you'd expect from someone who runs a non-profit organization with a high turnover rate. I turned to Edda. She took my cheeks in her hands. "Be safe and brave on your journey," she whispered into my ear. And then she wrapped her arms around me, squeezing the air from my lungs. A small salty storm formed on my cheeks.

I stood watching as the car pulled away. But Edda didn't look back. Instead, she stuck a hand out the window. It wasn't waving goodbye. It was waving me forward. ☺

FEBRUARY

The Jungle, Costa Rica

Perched on a bar stool, I stared into a glass of Merlot. It was like looking into the eyes of a lover who I would not see for a long time.

"I'm going to miss you," I whispered, caressing the stem of the glass and inadvertently attracting the attention of the barman. He raised an eyebrow and inquired if everything was all right.

I was fine. Just a little concerned about the next four weeks of the journey. It wasn't going to be easy.

Outside the window of the nondescript bar at the Denver airport, flakes of snow twirled in the dark evening air. I was on a convoluted route to Costa Rica, where I'd be spending the next month. The cheapest tickets tend to offer up the most creative trajectories. In this instance, I squeezed a dirt-cheap ticket out of a discount flight website that had me jetting north to Denver, waiting a few hours, and then hopping a red-eye flight south to the capital city of San José. The land of *pura vida* was calling, and my volunteer project would be in an alcohol-free setting. The glass of Merlot sitting before me was my last taste of booze.

I'm not a heavy drinker, but I do enjoy a daily glass of wine or whisky, generally in a social context or to catalyze creative juices for a writing assignment. That evening, however, the only thing I needed to write was my signature on the bar tab. My sips were slow and intentional and relished.

"I'll be seeing you soon," I said before taking the final swig.

Then I tipped my trucker's hat to the bartender, threw my backpack over my shoulder, sauntered to my gate and boarded a flight bound for San José. ○

"I'M SORRY FOR the delay, folks," the captain announced loudly on the airplane intercom, jerking me awake. "We have to do another loop around the area to buy a bit of time. Apparently there are children playing on the runway. And we'd prefer them not to be there."

Yawning, I rubbed my eyes with the palms of my hands, stretched out my stiff neck and then turned my attention out the window. In contrast to the snowy darkness of Denver, the scenery below was heavenly: rolling hills of luscious green abruptly stopping at the expansive, shimmering Pacific Ocean. Even from a thousand metres in the air, it looked like a tropical utopia. A tingle of excitement rushed down my spine.

After the 10-minute bonus loop, the airplane touched down onto the San José tarmac safely, without plowing over any unsuspecting children. Following the other passengers as they plodded off the plane, I ducked out the low doorway and was immediately engulfed with sweet, humid air. I chuckled to myself, knowing it was at least -15° C back home.

In a matter of minutes, I cleared customs and immediately went to work trying to locate an Australian fellow who would be heading to the same volunteer destination as me. The arrival area was a sea of tourists struggling to manage their suitcases while fending off opportunistic taxi drivers. In the middle of the chaos stood a beacon of calm: a tall, blond-bearded, smiley chap sporting an elegant fedora, complete with a feather sticking out its side.

"Daniel?" he inquired loudly, above the noise of honking.

"Yup. That's me."

"I'm Matt," he said. "Let's get outta here, mate."

Matt had already found our pre-arranged taxi driver who would drive us from the San José airport to the local bus terminal. Soon we were buzzing toward the city centre. Multinational corporate billboards and American fast-food restaurants lined the highway, defying my impression that Costa Rica was an untouched tropical paradise.

Apart from charging us a higher fare than we had anticipated, the taxi driver delivered us to the bus terminal without incident. Matt and I sat in the sterile station waiting for the garbled intercom voice to announce the next bus to San Isidro de El General, a large transportation hub in the south of Costa Rica. The wait gave us an opportunity to get to know each other better. Matt mentioned that he had grown up on a vineyard, so I figured he had Merlot in his blood — we'd obviously get along smashingly.

The bus to San Isidro de El General was a sleek air-conditioned machine. As it curled out of San José, I discovered the Costa Rica that I had envisioned: humble concrete homes with corrugated iron roofs, small fields with bony cows, scruffy dogs that could benefit from an extra meal. The route took us over a mountain pass and included many hairpin turns. If I had been in a smaller vehicle, I might have been sick.

In San Isidro de El General, another pre-arranged taxi driver was waiting. After tossing our bags in the bed of his 4×4 truck, Matt folded himself into the confines of the backseat. He graciously offered me the front and the chance to chat with the driver, a small weathered man who seemed charmed — at least initially — by my beginner-level Spanish.

"Soy Daniel."

He smiled and nodded.

"Soy de Canadá."

He asked me if I liked Costa Rica.

"Sí, me gusta Costa Rica."

And then I think he asked me what I did for a living. Although, for all I know, he might have asked politely if I had a walnut where my brain should be.

"*Soy escritor.*"

He opened his mouth as if to say something but ended up just nodding his head. And then he started whistling a tune. Any further attempts at communication were pointless. I had exhausted my entire repertoire of conversational Spanish.

Eventually we turned off the highway and onto a gravel road cutting through a valley. The Costa Rican jungle grew denser, with thick foliage permanently blocking direct sunlight from the forest floor. It was so thick that I couldn't tell how tall the trees were. At one point we approached a dark line across the dirt track, and as we drove over it, I realized that it was the unfortunate route of army ants. After an hour, the "road" deteriorated into a rocky mess, and I figured that we had to be approaching our final destination. At a walking pace, the truck crawled down an embankment so steep that I feared the rear bumper would tip over our heads. But the driver managed to keep the truck's wheels on the ground, and eventually we broke out of the forest at the top of a hill.

To describe the vista as stunning would be a disservice. The valley was a horseshoe of rolling emerald peaks, the dirt track was the colour of adobe bricks and the sky a joyful indigo. Halfway down the hill on a small outcrop, I spotted a modest hut, evidence that humans did indeed inhabit the wilderness. This would be my home for the coming weeks: a humble farmstead in the heart of the jungle. ○

THERE ARE MANY approaches to adventure. For instance, one method is to grab a feather, throw it into the wind and bravely follow wherever it might go. Free-spirited and spontaneous, this strategy inevitably leads to hidden surprises and unexpected encounters. However, for the sake of my budget (and to preserve my sanity), I decided against randomly drifting across the planet in loose pants and with wooden beads dangling from my neck — no, the romantic "follow the feather" approach was not for me. Instead, at the risk of sounding like a human missile, I chose to carefully plot and maintain an intentional trajectory.

Since I had chosen the U.S.A. as my first destination, it made sense to continue south to other corners of the Americas before taking a long-haul flight across an ocean. With mind-boggling biodiversity, ferocious seismic activity and a unique pre-Columbian history, Central America promised to be fertile ground for discovery. After researching volunteer opportunities and flights, it became apparent that Costa Rica was a practical destination: airfare was reasonable and there was a plethora of work-exchange projects to choose from.

Since the first leg of my journey was in an urban space, I decided that the month of February should be spent in a rural setting. Looking for a host organization, I scoured an online network of organic farms that accepted volunteers. One listing — a raw vegan farm — intrigued me.

The online profile stated that the farm was a tropical sanctuary for residents and guests to heal and explore sustainability. It was located within a lush rainforest setting, complete with stunning waterfalls and freshwater pools. Furthermore, the white-sand beaches of the Pacific Ocean were just a quick drive away. To a guy raised among pine trees, snowdrifts and buck-toothed beavers, this description of the farm was nothing short of landscape erotica. Plus, there was also a rare experience to be had — the opportunity to learn a bit about sustainable farming while potentially improving my health through a raw vegan diet. One can never get too many vegetables, right? Furthermore, I figured that a raw vegan farm could not possibly exist without a cast of intriguing personalities.

The Farmer in charge of the project was an American expat who, judging by our brief phone conversation, seemed like a spacey yet easygoing hippie. The only catch was that he requested a $10 daily contribution to offset the costs of what he mentioned were "higher-than-average quality of healthy meals and natural lifestyle education." Once again, I revisited my game plan. Did I want to bend my personal travel guidelines of money-free work

45

exchange? I really did *not* want to pay to volunteer, but then again I had a trifecta of reasons to go: the geographic splendour (i.e. sexy waterfalls!), the opportunity for a "niche" food education and the potential to meet unusual people.

So I bit the bullet and sent a deposit to reserve my place on the farm. For the month of February, I was going vegan. Raw vegan. ◌

THE FARMER MUST have heard the truck because he was waiting at the end of the track on a grassy vehicle turnaround. He was short and lean and had a head full of unruly white hair. With an awkward smile, he shook our hands, welcomed us to the farm and directed us along a manicured grassy path that led to the *rancho*, the modest A-frame structure we had seen upon entering the valley. The building was simple in its construction, featuring a palm-frond roof and bamboo screens that allowed air to circulate. The space was minimally furnished with a large wooden table and kitchen counter. There was also a modest sink, a stack of dishes and a shelf filled with fresh fruit and vegetables. The rancho, I would learn, functioned as the kitchen, dining room, office space and The Farmer's sleeping quarters. It was the heart of the farm.

The sliding doors at the far end of the hut opened onto a veranda that featured a hammock and mesmerizing views of the valley. I stood there and stretched my arms over my head, absorbing my surroundings. This would do just fine.

"Would you like a glass of hibiscus tea?" The Farmer inquired from inside.

"Uh, sure," I said as I pivoted toward the kitchen. "I don't think I've ever had hibiscus tea."

"It's delicious," he assured me. "Most people don't realize that you don't need a kettle to make tea. Nope, just a bit of sunshine and time."

The Farmer handed Matt and me each a glass of liquid that was the same colour as cherry Kool-Aid. I raised the flowery infusion to my lips and was pleasantly surprised by its light, earthy flavour. Perhaps a daily glass of hibiscus tea would provide the same psychological effects as a glass of Bordeaux. Perhaps I wouldn't even miss wine or whisky or espresso or Earl Grey tea.

"So where's everyone else?" I inquired, curious about the other residents and volunteers.

"Oh, it's just us for the moment," The Farmer responded casually. "There will be more volunteers coming next week."

This caught me by surprise. Based on our previous communications — and the project website — I was under the impression that this was a permaculture *community*, a term that commonly implied more than one permanent resident. I thought about asking him why there were no other people living on-site, but I didn't want to come across as impolite or critical. First impressions are terribly important.

Before I could pose any other questions about daily life on the farm, a zippy insect resembling a hyperactive bumblebee caught my attention. Darting from flower to flower, it had far more focus than your average meandering bee.

"That's the smallest species of hummingbird in the world," The Farmer explained, seeing the intrigue on my face.

After draining my glass of flower-power tea, I rummaged through my backpack to look for the cache of food I had bought for The Farmer. Before I left New Orleans, he had forwarded me a shopping list of non-perishable items that were difficult to find in Costa Rica and promised to reimburse any purchases I made on his behalf. I pulled out bags of organic sunflower, pumpkin and flax seeds with the eagerness of a kindergartner during show and tell, happy to have arrived with a contribution. The Farmer was impressed with how much food I had managed to stow in my backpack. When I presented him with the receipts, however, he winced.

"Yeah, that's not what I pay my seed-and-nut dealer," he said, furrowing his brow. "This is way too much."

"Uh ... sorry?" I responded tentatively.

In the rush of preparing for the next leg of my journey, I had done my shopping at the closest health food store I could locate (which wasn't exactly the easiest task, considering that I was staying in the Lower Ninth Ward). I thought for sure this gesture of goodwill would help me start the month on a good note. But I suddenly felt like I had done something wrong. I wasn't really sure what to say.

"Okay ... well, why don't you calculate the difference of what you would have paid and tack it on to my fees?" I suggested.

"Yeah," he replied. "I'll do that." The numbers were crunched, and an additional $22 was tacked onto my $280 bill.

I'm aware that people everywhere have their idiosyncrasies — heck, I even welcome unconventional thinking — but The Farmer's penny-pinching shocked me. That said, I *really* did not want a couple bags of seeds to sprout a conflict, especially considering that it was my first day. So unenthusiastically, I handed over a stack of American bills.

With the finances settled, The Farmer led Matt and I out of the rancho and down a hill to our accommodations — a series of tent platforms, each with enough space around it to afford a sense of privacy. I selected the first option: a ragged green tent on a grassy knoll sheltered by a giant tarpaulin. While Matt and The Farmer continued further down the path to the next site, I unloaded my backpack and then collapsed onto the thin mattress. Between the planes, buses and 4×4 taxis, it had been more than 24 hours since I left New Orleans.

I breathed in deeply, inhaling that particular smell of sun-baked tent: a mix of outdoors and nylon that is partly organic, partly artificial. The accommodations were basic yet comfortable enough for me. I'd even go so far as to say I was pleased to have a small space all to myself. A little fort to call my own.

A light drizzle began to fall on the tarpaulin, and a cool breeze snuck through the mouth of the tent. Soon my eyes grew heavy, and I surrendered to the gentle emancipation of a much-needed siesta. ۞

BEFORE ARRIVING IN Costa Rica, I did a bit of research on what it meant to eat a "raw" diet — and, more importantly, why people might select this regime. From my reading (and subsequent experience on the farm), I came to understand that choosing rawism can be based on one of many personal motives — or a combination thereof.

One of the main arguments for a raw diet is that foods lose their "life force" when heated (as beneficial enzymes are destroyed above certain temperatures). Another belief is that the digestive system is forced to work harder to process cooked foods; therefore, more effort is required to extract nutrition and energy from a traditional cooked diet. Proponents of these theories attest to increased levels of energy when eating raw. Others claim that going raw has helped alleviate problematic skin conditions, high blood pressure, allergies, menstrual complications and other health concerns. For folks with a history of obesity or Type 2 diabetes, the raw diet has been said to promote weight loss and help stabilize insulin levels. Spiritually driven individuals describe a stronger sense of unity with the universe, thanks to the powers of raw food. There are even people who claim that a raw food diet slows the aging process.

Going into the experience, I thought that the raw vegan lifestyle sounded excessively austere. But, heck, I was willing to try it out for a month — besides, what's a fella got to lose? (I mean, other than a few pounds?) I approached my time on the farm with curiosity about a diet that had the potential to cleanse my system of impurities and recharge my body with new-found vitality. Plus, if the raw vegan folks were correct about obtaining a clearer spiritual connection, then perhaps I could summon the great divine to help guide me toward work-exchange arrangements that didn't involve me having to pay to volunteer. Or at least provide me with tipoffs on winning lottery numbers.

Still, the diet wasn't going to be easy for a cheddar-loving wino such as myself. Raw veganism would mean cutting out many of my favourite provisions — meat, milk, yogurt, cheese, sugar, alcohol, coffee, tea, soda, junk food, processed food, not to mention any form of baked or cooked food such as potatoes, rice, pasta or bread. With so many items being off-limits, the next rational question on most people's minds is "Well, what in tarnation is left to eat?" Ultimately, my diet would consist of four basic categories: fruits, vegetables, nuts and seeds. ☼

ON MY SECOND day in Costa Rica, I awoke shortly before dawn, discovering the harmonious relationship between the sun and the animal world. The sun acted as choirmaster to a chorus of birds and insects, starting with staccato peeps and squeaks, slowly rising with more elaborate calls, and climaxing to a deafening cicada song. It was nature's alarm clock saying "Up and at 'em, Vegan Boy."

My feet found their way into my paint-stained hiking boots, and I headed up the hill to the rancho. Halfway up the path, I paused and scanned the surrounding valley. The rays from the sun slowly snuck over the eastern ridge and began to warm my face. Turning west toward the opening of the basin, I felt affirmed in my decision to come to the farm — it was, to put it simply, a beautiful place to be.

I found Matt standing outside the kitchen doors, watering a raised bed of two-inch sprouts and baby vegetables.

"Mornin' mate," he said, smiling in his chipper way. "How'd ya sleep?"

"Oh, not too bad," I replied. "But I think I have some sort of robust nocturnal creature living under my tent platform."

"Sounds deadly."

"If he stays noisy and I get hungry, I figure I'll just eat him."

Matt smiled again and nodded. I wasn't sure if we were allowed to crack jokes about eating animals. But inappropriate jokes can be a lot of fun. And I like fun.

In the kitchen The Farmer was busy preparing a selection of fruit and vegetables for our breakfast smoothies. We exchanged some morning pleasantries, and then I was put to work peeling ginger. I started immediately, doing my best to remove the skin off the irregularly shaped root while casually describing the sound I had heard coming from beneath the tent platform during the night.

"It sort of sounds like it could be something the size of a prairie dog, which would make sense because it lives in the ground, but I'm pretty sure there are no prairie dogs in —"

"Hold up," The Farmer said, stopping me mid-sentence. "You're wasting too much ginger."

I looked down at the small pile of ginger skin, confused.

"Yeah, don't use a vegetable peeler. Use a knife and scrape off the skin." He grabbed a chunk of ginger root and proceeded to demonstrate the most effective way to remove the peel. A flurry of grey ginger skin fell onto the cutting board, exposing a smooth golden nugget.

"That's how it's done." He returned to washing kale. I continued prepping the ginger, using his knife-scraping method. But in silence this time.

Once the fruit and vegetables were prepped and peeled, they were tossed into a Vitamix — a normal blender on steroids. The ingredients included pineapple, mango, kale, celery, coconut and some soaked *Salvia hispanica* (commonly known as chia, the stuff that we use to sprout hair on beloved terracotta pet figurines). The electricity for the blender came from a turbine near the creek, and there was more than enough power to send the Vitamix into its full roaring glory. A green soupy texture was achieved, and breakfast was officially ready.

Matt came in from the garden, and we gathered around the table. In front of us sat wooden bowls filled with avocado-coloured muck topped with shredded coconut, berries and raw almonds.

"Well, bon appétit, guys!" I stated with a false smile on my face.

A bit of fake cheerfulness is always better than crying in one's green, boggy breakfast. I tried not to think about golden runny egg yolks or warm buttery croissants or the intoxicating odour of a steamy cup of café au lait.

Surprisingly, the green smoothie was more agreeable to the

tongue than it was to the eyes. In fact, with the sweetness of the fruit and the zing of the ginger, it was likeable and healthy. I scraped the bowl clean with my spoon, unsure of when my next meal would be — or if it would be any more satisfying. But before even thinking about the next meal, which was many hours away, we had morning chores to tackle. And, as luck would have it, I was assigned to the tremendously glamorous task of emptying the compostable toilet. ○

WHEN I DECIDED to travel using a method of trade-based currency, I knew there was a good chance that I'd have to face grimy and arduous tasks. I figured that grit would come with the territory. And I was right. It took less than five weeks for me to be assigned to the crappy job — pun most definitely intended — of dealing with human fecal material. It would be one of many sobering instances that were charmingly emblematic of low-budget travel.

In our modern lives, most of us city dwellers never have to think about the by-products of consumption, which fall into two general categories: poop and garbage. We do our business, flush the toilet, and our little turd logs magically disappear. The same goes for trash. We put it on the curb and someone else deals with it. These systems that we have established relieve the individual of the bothersome consequences of consumerism, both in the digestive and material senses. And I, for one, appreciate the easiness of it all.

Because the farm was off the grid, it employed a "humanure" composting system that processed organic human waste. (For the record, I did not invent the word "humanure" — some folks, it turns out, are really into composting their own feces.) The toilet system sort of looked like an outhouse but required a bit more intervention and produced surprisingly less odour. Here's how it works:

1 *When nature calls, position your bottom over a bucket framed with a well-balanced plastic toilet seat for improved comfort and aim.*

2   *After pinching a loaf, instead of flushing, simply sprinkle sawdust over your human by-product.*

3   *Every day or two, empty the "buckoilet" (I did actually invent that word) into a large manure compost pit.*

4   *Wait a few months, harvest your nutrient-rich soil and share it with all your favourite people.*

5   *So on that first morning in Costa Rica, it was my job to empty the buckoilet, bringing a whole literal dimension to the pop-psychology adage "You gotta deal with your own shit."*

After the breakfast smoothies were swallowed and the dishes were washed, I sauntered to the rudimentary restroom to begin cleaning. With a pitchfork in hand, I grabbed the weighty buckoilet and turned my attention to the wooden compost bin. The bathtub-sized container was covered with corrugated iron roofing and, to my surprise, lacked the pungent odour that one might anticipate. I propped up the lid and got to work digging a hole. Once I had created a decent crater, I hoisted up the buckoilet and tipped in the contents, which fell like chunky kitty litter dropping onto a flowerbed. Then I covered the dookie-sawdust brew with a heaping pile of dirt. Soon the wonders of nature would commence, transforming the poop into soil. And perhaps someday, down in the vegetable garden, a rutabaga would lounge in what once was my bowel movement.

Unfortunately, that was not the end of my latrine duties. Someone had been less than accurate while defecating, and the wall of the pail was smeared with a familiar avocado colour — apparently on the farm, what went in and what came out of the digestive system were not entirely unlike. Using water and a fortuitously long-handled brush, I scrubbed the buckoilet to a state of renewed splendour and returned it to the little hut where the vegan poo babies were birthed. I tossed a handful of sawdust into the bottom of the bucket, replaced the toilet seat, arranged the sanitary paper into a welcoming pleated fold (life is all about the small touches) and then I moseyed off to discover what splendid task might come next. ○

I FOUND THE Farmer and Matt in the greenhouse repotting young jackfruit and avocado trees. They indicated that I should grab a hand spade and help scoop topsoil into large plastic bags, where the seedlings would be relocated and subsequently have more space for their developing roots. After a few minutes of silently shovelling dirt, and feeling less concerned about a perfect first impression, I asked about the coming weeks.

"So who's arriving next?"

"I'm glad you asked." The Farmer paused from removing mulch from an adjacent wooden compost bin and leaned against his pitchfork. "This morning I got an email from a young woman in Munich who wants to live here permanently."

"Oh, is that right?"

"Yeah, she's sick of all the corruption in the West. But I just want to make sure the hot tub is finished by the time she arrives."

"Hot tub?"

"Yeah, I'm building a tub from rocks that I hauled up from the creek and moulding them with ecological cement that I've had shipped from Arkansas."

"Wow, sounds high-tech."

"Yeah, but it's worth it." The Farmer nodded his head. "Women love hot tubs."

I tried to picture an anti-capitalist raw vegan German with a penchant for hot tubs. Over dinner she'd wax poetically about the injustices of factory farming, and then later she'd slip into a bikini (which wouldn't be able to adequately conceal her untamed bush of pubic hair) and enjoy a relaxing soak in the ol' heated love tank. *Es ist wunderbar*, she'd say.

But even if this person didn't *actually* care for hot tubs and even if she wasn't the quarterback for Team Merriment, I was sure that she would still be an interesting person. Like I had forecasted, she would be one of those uncommon characters drawn to a raw vegan farm. And meeting uncommon characters was what I signed up for, wasn't it? ☺

As THE SUN crept higher on that first day of work, my level of hunger increased from "noticeable" to "urgent," and I became very curious to find out what we would be having for lunch. In my non-travelling life, lunch might involve rustling up a grilled havarti cheese sandwich accompanied by garlic pickles and potato salad. Or if I were on a lunch break from work, I'd order a smoked chicken panini with roasted-tomato chutney and a bowl of minestrone soup. But I knew that none of these things would be found on a raw vegan menu. Thus, I was sort of surprised when The Farmer said we were having pizza.

Before our arrival the previous day, The Farmer had crafted a batch of tortilla-size dehydrated rosemary and flaxseed crackers, which would act as the pizza crust. Back in the kitchen he began concocting a white "cheese" sauce using macadamia nuts, garlic, a splash of olive oil and an exotic fruit called *noni* (or cheese fruit or morinda or dog dumpling, depending on who you ask). My job was to prepare the toppings, and I made a point of peeling the vegetables with utmost precision to prevent another "ginger incident." When all the ingredients were ready, we spread the vegan cheese blend across the dehydrated crackers and then layered on sprouts, avocado, tomato and other veggies. By the time I had finished assembling my meal, the mini personal pizza looked colourful and downright appetizing.

The cracker was chewy and it folded under the weight of the toppings, sort of like wrapping the produce department in a flaxy pita. And although it wasn't as satisfying as, say, a roasted-veggie, gooey-goat-cheese, crispy-thin-crust pizza, it wasn't too shabby, all things considered.

After we finished our pizza party, The Farmer suggested some afternoon yoga. A free weekly class was hosted by his neighbour, who lived in a bungalow on the other side of the valley. I expressed immediate interest. My travel-weary muscles were pleading to be stretched, the price was right and it meant sidestepping unknown tasks that, for all I knew, might be worse than cleaning human feces out of a bucket. I quickly bounded down to my tent and changed into some loose yoga-appropriate clothing. We were soon piled into a red 4×4 truck en route to yogic nirvana.

However, upon arrival at the neighbouring estate, we were greeted with a handwritten sign taped to the gate: *No Yoga Today*.

"That's too bad," said The Farmer. He paused and then asked in a tentative tone, "You guys want to check out a waterfall instead?"

Matt and I looked at each other and responded in sync. "Yes!"

The truck continued further along the bumpy track and eventually pulled to a stop under the shade of an enormous walking tree — a variety of tree that is able to move by growing new roots and then pulling itself toward more idyllic conditions. We unloaded from the vehicle and started hiking down a red dirt trail. As we wandered I was baffled by a seeming impossibility: the air felt wet, yet there wasn't a cloud in the sky. After seeing Matt and I looking upward for the source of the moisture, The Farmer informed us that the delicate tempest falling on our faces was actually cicada urine. We were caught in a sort of non-consensual creepy-crawler golden shower, which only confirmed that the theme of the day was destined to be excrement.

We marched forth, hiking approximately a kilometre along a crumbling trail that sharply etched itself down the steep wall of a ravine. Before I could see the waterfall, a roaring echo alerted us that it was near, as did the mist, which provided a much-appreciated rinse from the cicada pee. We rounded a bend to see a river dropping more than 50 metres through the U-shaped gorge into various tiered pools, which spilled into a final swimming hole. Small yellow leaves tumbled like tickertape from the tree canopy, creating the same effect as confetti at a surprise party.

I have a firm belief that when given the chance to swim in a tropical waterfall, one should not decline. Plunging into a body of water, though, hadn't been on our original afternoon itinerary. I was sporting an ensemble fit for yoga; my swimming trunks were back at the farmstead, neatly folded in my backpack.

What to do?

I scanned the situation. At least a dozen other folks were enjoying the waterfall, all wearing swimsuits. I didn't want to assault their eyes with the blinding glare of my albino buttocks.

Therefore, no skinny-dipping.

I turned to Matt. "You going in?"

"You bet I am," he said as he dropped his backpack, slipped off his shirt and crept forward — *in the swim trunks he had worn for yoga class.*

A practical option, I decided, would be to wear my undergarments into the watering hole. Yet, as obvious a solution as this might seem, it was not actually an easy decision to make. After a busy few days, including the long-haul journey from New Orleans to Costa Rica, my clean-clothes options were dwindling. That morning, I had been forced to put on my "last resort" pair of ginch — and they were not the kind of thing you want for romping around a waterhole. The briefs I had selected were more in the style of a flashy Chippendale dancer than of a practical hiking enthusiast.

While on the road, there are crucial moments when a traveller must navigate a major dilemma: *Am I willing to look like a fool in exchange for an experience I simply cannot have at home?* Or in this case, it was more like: *Am I prepared to show these people my red bikini-style manbriefs, which I am incidentally wearing inside out, in exchange for access to this waterfall?*

We've all been there before.

Ultimately, I did what any reasonable man would do. I slowly removed my yoga shorts, exposing the loud undies, and crept discreetly into the pool. I hoped that my fellow waterfall waders would not see me as a skinny degenerate who intentionally wore a banana hammock in public places. Perhaps they'd just think I was a Speedo-sporting athlete. Or a European.

Anyone unfortunate enough to have caught a glimpse of my scarlet nut-sarong was probably left wondering why the manbriefs were inside out. Truth be told, I've actually been wearing many of my pairs of underwear inside out for years, as they are more comfortable with the seams on the exterior. It's quite rational. Oh yes, and for those wondering why a husky and masculine character such as myself owned crimson bikini briefs — well, I purposefully left home with a diverse artillery of seven undergarments, which included relaxed boxers, fitted boxers and briefs. Like most menfolk, I most often opt for a multi-pack when purchasing underwear, and it just so happened that one of the pairs in the selection was red. And the red pair ended up in my backpack. Which was actually beneficial because over the course of the year, I came to learn that skimpy underwear is ideal for travel: it's comfortable in the heat and occupies the least amount of space in a backpack.

So that's that.

We stayed at the swimming hole for a good hour. Despite my initial bashfulness, I quickly lost all concern about my fashion dilemma. I was swimming in one of the planet's most picturesque locations, and I couldn't let a little pair of red undies blush my experience. ○

THE FIRST COUPLE of days on the farm turned into a week, yet I can't say that the time flew by. The physical setting was consistently impressive, but my interactions with The Farmer were awkward and often involved coarse criticism. Furthermore, the diet, despite being visually appealing, often left me feeling hungry. Each morning began with a variation of the green smoothie, usually served with chunks of fresh fruit, such as mango, papaya or pineapple. For protein we'd sprinkle a few nuts or seeds on the top. I was not unhappy with my morning swamp juice, but a steamy morning cup of coffee or tea (and the subsequent caffeine nudge) was most notably missed.

Lunch varied but was typically the most complex and filling meal of the day. We had lasagna made with a chunky uncooked tomato sauce and a "ricotta" substitute mixture of palm hearts and cashew, all layered between noodles of thinly sliced zucchini. There was soup made with pumpkin seed and cactus, "stir-fry" with an avocado-macadamia sauce, and "sushi" featuring blended coconut and cauliflower instead of rice. The Farmer deserved credit for his inventiveness in the kitchen, and he seemed to be more buoyant and positive when food was involved.

Dinner, on the other hand, tended to be meagre. Often we'd simply eat the leftovers of what we had prepared earlier that day. On a good day, The Farmer might whip up some chocolate pudding made from unroasted cacao beans and avocado. The most lacklustre evening meal, however, consisted of nothing more than a large slice of watermelon. (That night I stole some almonds from the food box but still went to bed with a growling stomach.)

The working tasks varied from day to day. In the morning, Matt and I might build nurture nests around the fruit trees. Then after lunch and a period of rest, we would landscape around the half-finished hot tub or provide assistance in the woodworking shop. One afternoon we lifted heavy rocks for a couple of hours, restoring a riverbed near the turbine that generated electricity for the homestead. Projects were generally start-and-stop, and The Farmer was usually around to ensure that everything went exactly to his liking. Although the tasks I did in New Orleans were equally as mundane, they were made enjoyable thanks to enthusiastic colleagues and encouraging guidance. But in raw vegan "paradise," even Matt's cheerfulness could not counteract the dreary atmosphere. In general, I felt micromanaged (do you know how patronizing it is to be subjected to a personal tutorial on how to correctly use a salad spinner?) and that my presence was unappreciated, which was disappointing. I had hoped that as a volunteer, my contributions would be valued, if not valuable.

Sure, the vistas were beautiful and I was learning to make raw vegan dishes. Yet there was still one big discrepancy on the farm: not only did I fail to meet an alternative-minded community, I failed to meet *anyone* (apart from The Farmer and Matt). Throughout the weeks, I was told that other volunteers had confirmed their arrival. The Farmer even continued to share messages from the people around the world who expressed interest in coming to live permanently in the community. But I learned to take these announcements with a grain of salt. Because during all the weeks I was on that farm, no one else ever arrived. ۞

MY SAVING GRACE was the daily siesta. Each day after lunch we were granted a couple of "non-working" hours. Matt tended to retire to his tent to nap or strum his guitar, but I preferred to hike down to a set of small natural pools located at the far edge of the multi-hectare farm. My route took me along a spiny ridge, which provided optimum views across the valley before descending deep down into the jungle. The rainforest was decorated with a thousand shades of green: leaves bigger than my face, lengthy vines that reached skyward, tight fern spirals and carpet-like moss near the streams. I regularly saw howler monkeys, toucans, vultures, wild turkeys, frogs, lizards, spiders and army ants. One afternoon, a four-foot-long emerald-coloured snake with a golden underbelly and an inquisitive tongue blocked my path. I stood in awe of the stunning predator — and obviously gave him priority of passage.

The snakes, however, were not the most fearsome creatures of the jungle. That title belonged to the supposedly aggressive Costa Rican wild boar. The Farmer warned that the boars would attack if they felt threatened, and if they attacked, you'd best have your last will and testament in order. Thus, during my solo excursions, much of my attention was given to searching for climbable trees. Despite having a healthy appreciation for irony, the idea of being mauled to death by angry pigs while staying at a raw vegan farm was a bit too rich for me.

Upon arrival at bottom of the ravine, I walked along the shallow creek and carefully scouted for one of many freshwater pools. Knowing that the nearest person was at least a kilometre away, I stripped off all articles of clothing and the forest basins became my own personal baths. I sat on a boulder located directly under cascading water for a natural shoulder massage. After the hydro-rubdown, I sprawled naked on a sun-baked volcanic rock, allowing my body to air-dry while I gazed at the jungle canopy above. This was nature's spa.

Thankfully I never came across any boars. In fact, apart from the goggling eyes of a monkey or the curious head tilt of a toucan, I always had the personal baths to myself. That month, it was the time alone, the peacefulness and the natural beauty that kept me sane. ☼

"DID YOU KNOW that 100 per cent of chickens have cancer?" The Farmer blurted as I stood at the kitchen counter peeling a mango. "Well, it's true. And to think I used to put that into my body. Disgusting."

He searched my face for a response. I raised my eyebrows in acknowledgement, while digging for the strength to force a smile.

More than a week had passed since the start of my adventure on the raw vegan farm. That morning I had emerged from the tent and, with the same gusto as one would rush for a colonoscopy, I commenced my daily trudge up the hill to the rancho. As soon as I stepped into the kitchen, I sensed agitation. The Farmer was worked up over a health debate he had heard on a satellite radio program. The topic was rawism, and the dietary paradigm had been critiqued and called into question.

"Wow. Cancerous chickens. That's really ... something." I wanted to inform him that, as far as I knew, most living creatures had cancerous cells at any given point in time. I decided to skip the biology lesson for fear of instigating an argument.

"It's true what they say," he continued. "If you're not raw, you're cooked!"

I took a deep breath. "I recall that the compost toilet was getting pretty full yesterday. I think I'll go tilt it over my head and pack some more shit into my ears. Because, really, one can never have too much." I wanted to say this. But I didn't. I bit my tongue and went to water the garden.

Later that evening, The Farmer had gone into town to buy vegetables for the coming week. I found Matt on the rancho balcony, removing the skins from cacao beans. Since we were rarely alone together, I seized the opportunity to weigh in with him about the unique situation we were in.

"Dude, how are you not going bonkers here? I feel like there's a full serving of crazy being snuck into each green smoothie."

Matt chuckled. "You gotta keep it cruisy, mate," he said. "I figure we're in paradise. Why not just enjoy it, right?"

"Yeah, but that's easier said than done," I retorted. "How do you keep your cool with The Farmer? Don't you ever want to explode and tell him that he's lost his mind?"

Matt paused. "I just figure he's just doing his best to live a really strict set of values."

"No kidding. It's like the frickin' raw vegan Taliban around here."

"But I am thinking of heading out a bit earlier," Matt confided. "I'd like to get to the Caribbean coast to relax and do more reading." Beneath the chillaxin' Aussie exterior, I sensed that he was also dealing with a bit of dissatisfaction. Recognizing this made me feel less alone in my frustration.

"Well, if you're taking off early, so am I. There's no way I can be alone with The Farmer," I added. "That would be a raw vegan recipe for disaster."

Again, Matt smiled but didn't respond. I picked up a handful of cacao beans to peel, popping the occasional one into my mouth, and left all concluding sentiments to the sinking sun. ☼

THE NEXT DAY, Matt informed The Farmer that he would be leaving a week earlier than anticipated. The announcement was greeted with a head scratch and a harsh exhalation. "Well, it's free world," said The Farmer after a moment. Matt downplayed his early departure by emphasizing that he was eager to work hard during his remaining days, and all tension seemed to quickly dissipate.

Meanwhile, I took a couple of extra days to ponder my approach. For some reason I was nervous — yet what was there to be afraid of? Hurting The Farmer's feelings? Burning bridges? Backing out of a commitment? I'm a guy who usually feels capable of navigating conflict and disagreements. (Not to boast, but I have a university degree in Human Relations with an emphasis on interpersonal dynamics and conflict resolution.) However, this man had displayed traces of lunacy *and* he had control over all the farm resources: the food, the only vehicle and the only mobile phone. I didn't fear for my physical safety, but I did worry that The Farmer might overreact and that consequently the situation would get much more complicated. I *really* did not want to end up hiking five kilometres to the nearest road with all my gear in the 35°C jungle heat. And on an empty stomach.

With only a week left before my new departure date, I finally worked up the nerve to broach the subject. The Farmer, who appeared to be in a relatively good mood, was clacking away on his laptop computer when I approached.

"Just wanted to let you know that I'll be heading out the same time as Matt."

Realizing what I had said, The Farmer closed his computer and stood up.

"No, no, no. This won't do." He started pacing across the rancho. "We had an agreement that you would spend the month of February here. I declined other volunteers because you made this agreement."

"Yes. I understand. That's fair," I stated. "I'm not going to ask for any money back. You can keep my full deposit."

"You guys all do this. I can't rely on anyone ... everybody leaves early."

He hesitated for a moment at the veranda and looked into the night. I had no idea what was going to happen next. Was he going to scream? Or worse, cry?

Finally, The Farmer turned, looked in my direction and pointed his index finger at me.

"Well, if you want to leave, I can't stop you. But you've got your own karma to consider."

At that point, there were a few specific things I wanted to say — or better yet, to yell. *"KARMA? Are you kidding me? I've given you $300 to volunteer on your farm, offering you 30-plus hours per week of labour! And you have the audacity to suggest that I should be concerned about my karma?"* Did he think I lived in trembling fear of the Karma Police? I'm fairly certain that if the great divine wanted to communicate, the only thing to be said would be this:

"Daniel, you don't have to torture yourself. Extract the learning that you can and then go sit on a beach. And, dude, have a hot cup of freshly roasted Costa Rican coffee while you're at it!"

I waited to see if there were any other rousing statements to be tossed in my direction. The Farmer stayed quiet and simply returned to the table, opened his computer and resumed his work. Figuring that there was nothing else to be said, I exited and walked down the hill. The refreshingly cool night air was filled with frog croaks and cicada buzz, and a familiar amphitheatre of stars provided just enough light to navigate the footpath with relative certainty.

Back in my tent, I crawled directly into my sleeping bag, but I couldn't fall asleep. A post-conflict knot had metastasized in my stomach. It was partially due to the unfortunate argument with The Farmer and partially due to a deeper realization of sorts. The charming semantic "newness" that came with New Orleans was definitely gone. If there were a honeymoon phase of this journey, it was officially over. For the first time since I left Canada, I truly understood that this trip around the world was not going to be all magic and wonderment. ○

THE MORNING AFTER I announced to The Farmer that I would be leaving early, he acted as if nothing significant had happened. During breakfast prep he didn't say much. There were no impromptu lessons on how to peel fruit. He didn't offer any mantras for the merits of raw veganism. We were sitting around the picnic table eating our breakfast when he did finally speak.

"I'm looking forward to the day that I'm petting a jaguar," he said, nodding his head in deep thought.

I had just shovelled a spoonful of the chunky breakfast mush into my face, and the arbitrary announcement caused me to choke on a piece of papaya.

"Uh ... what?"

"Yes, as we return to an era of peace and awareness through the conscious global awakening, we'll have a new relationship with the animal kingdom. We're going to be able to interact with animals without fear," he stated matter-of-factly. "I've seen some small jaguars around here. I think it's happening already."

"Wow," I replied, nodding my head cautiously. "Let me know how that works out for you."

I excused myself from the table to clean the breakfast prep dishes. At certain moments throughout the previous weeks, I had been flabbergasted and frustrated by The Farmer, but as I scrubbed squished avocado off a bamboo cutting board, I felt a new emotion. This time it was sadness. The Farmer was relatively alone in his belief system — how did he feel about a world that was different than him? His response was to isolate himself in the back hills of the Costa Rican jungle. Sure, he was committed to his ideals. To a certain extent, I even respected him for that commitment. If anything, we were both dreamers. Yet I had never met anyone so forlorn with his dream.

It must have been a mighty lonely place to be. ○

THE THREE OF us were laying slate stones inside the new hot tub when Matt paused and asked about transportation off the farm. The Farmer grumbled something about buses and then instructed me to mix more mortar. I sensed that he didn't want to talk about our departure, so I decided to change the subject.

"We'll have to pack up and get ready for lunch if we're going to make the afternoon yoga," I stated in my most encouraging tone. We had attended a class the previous week and the experience had been among the more enjoyable aspects of life in rural Costa Rica.

"Well, since you guys are leaving early, I'm afraid we'll have to skip yoga today," The Farmer said coolly. "We've got a lot of work to do." He didn't look up. Instead, he splattered more mortar against the walls of his fantasy tub.

Ugh. This was *not* about getting work done. This was a little game of tit-for-tat: you're leaving early, so I'll take away your yoga class. I looked over at Matt. He shrugged his shoulders and then returned to his task of rinsing stones while humming softly.

Figuring that nothing more could be said, I continued working with my lips pinched together. However, the knowledge that The Farmer was intentionally punishing us made the situation gradually intolerable. Finally, I stood up, exited the hot tub and walked up to the rancho to sit down and cool off. After a self-imposed 10-minute time out, I heard Matt calling for my help. He had moved onto the next chore, which involved scrubbing the inside of the water tower, and needed an extra set of hands. As we stood there drenched in water and green algae slime, The Farmer approached us.

"The practice of yoga is very important, so I'll drive you guys to the studio so you can take the class. But I'll be working on my laptop."

Matt expressed his gratitude immediately, which was just the type of generous response that made him an overall classy guy. Conversely, I kept my mouth shut, feeling far from indebted. My internal dialogue raced: *Here's an idea. Don't be a punitive dickhead in the first place! How about that?* According to my personal approach to social etiquette, I don't feel it necessary to express gratitude to someone for *not* engaging in spiteful behaviour. It would be like someone punching me in the face repetitively and then, when they finally stopped, saying, "Wow, it feels really great not being punched in the face at this moment. Thanks a lot for not punching me in the face."

Humility has never been my strong point.

After a quick lunch, we loaded into the truck and bounced down the same bumpy track to the yoga class. I sat in the bed of the pickup, still frustrated and tense. Why were my interactions with The Farmer continually challenging? What was *my* role in the dynamic? Before I could come to any major conclusions, we arrived to the studio. I jumped out and walked to the open-air platform. As I took a deep breath and looked over the lush tropical valley, the tension drained from my body into the wooden planks beneath my bare feet. An opportunity to stretch and clear my mind would do me good.

It was our second class with Julie, an American yoga teacher who stood about three mangoes tall. At the start of each practice, she passed two decks of cards around to the students. Every card had a virtue or a sentiment that served to germinate reflection. The previous week, my Angel Card read *"TRUTH,"* while my Buddha Card displayed the word *"LOVE."* Other cards had such words as freedom, patience, strength, creativity, kindness, grace and a whole stack of other clichéd spiritual lingo. On that specific afternoon, after I had taken position on a sticky blue yoga mat, the decks began to circulate. From each of the two piles I drew a single card, first permitting my hand to wander over the options and focusing "my energies" on the card that felt most intuitively accurate.

I laid both cards face down and passed the deck to Matt. Apart from the sound of wind blowing through the nearby foliage, the platform was hushed. I slowly flipped over the Angel Card, which read:

GRATITUDE.

A smirk crossed my lips. "Oh, the great divine is encouraging me to ponder the idea of gratitude. That's rich," I thought to myself drolly. Then I turned my attention to the second card, the Buddha Card, to see what other psychic sentiment waited. Like a cosmic slap across the knuckles, the same word appeared on my second card:

GRATITUDE.

"Okay, world," I whispered to myself. "I get it. I'm supposed to feel grateful." You don't have to be a statistician to understand that the odds of drawing the same card are highly improbable. It was a one-two appreciation punch.

The formal part of the class commenced, but before we dove into any downward-facing-dogs, we took turns sharing our words with each other. Julie was thrilled that I had mystically uncovered what she termed a "double." She clasped her hands together, eyes wide as she quipped, "Oh, wow! I love when this happens. You must have some interesting stuff going on!" I smiled, raised an eyebrow and nodded my head.

As we began to head deeper into the practice, I kept the word

GRATITUDE with me. I stretched my limbs and felt my body gradually become less rigid. And as my body relaxed, my mind also softened with the idea that maybe I'd been harsh, a bit too self-righteous. Rather than acknowledging the positive shift in The Farmer's perspective, I had remained indignant in my own frustration. Was there any benefit in that? If I were interested in preventing energy-draining frustration and tension, it might have been easier to have humbly said "thank you" and moved on.

But, like I said, humility has never been my strong point. ⭘

THE TIME CAME to leave the farm. I was groggy from a bad sleep, having spent the night with another unsettled stomach. This time it was indigestion or acid reflux or the beginning of an ulcer. With all the raw, fibrous foods I'd been eating — carrots, broccoli, onions, garlic, ginger, kale, tomato, lime and more — it was no wonder my belly had become acidic and my digestive system felt weary. I was salivating at the thought of eggs and toast, both dripping with the soothing goodness of melted butter.

For a fee, The Farmer agreed to drive Matt and me to the highway where we could hop buses to our respective destinations. Matt was eager to push east toward the Caribbean coast, whereas I had decided to go west to spend my remaining seven days near the beaches of Manuel Antonio National Park. Along with our backpacks, I sat in the bed of the pickup truck and watched the rural Costa Rican countryside bump past. The sun was just beginning to rise over the mountains behind us. I took one final glance over the valley where I had experienced what it meant to be "raw vegan." It was indeed a beautiful location, and the tropical swimming pools had been kind to me, but overall I felt unsentimental about my departure. In life, there are some struggles that can be helpful, as they build character and promote learning, and there are some struggles that are unnecessary and fruitless. My weeks at the organic farm provided me with the opportunity to grapple with both types of situations, and by that point I was merely ready for the experience to be over.

After 30 minutes on the back roads, the pickup pulled over where the dirt track met the paved highway, and I lowered the backpacks off the truck bed. Matt, with his cheerful disposition, gave The Farmer a hug and told him he'd be in touch. I hopped down, extended a handshake and simply said, "Good luck with things." He shook my hand. Our eyes did not connect.

Then The Farmer got back in his truck and drove away.

I turned to Matt. "Thanks, man. You really have been a beacon of sanity throughout the past three weeks." If the universe had encouraged me to express gratitude, I figured that Matt deserved it most. We exchanged a slightly awkward man hug.

"No worries, mate," he replied. "Come visit me in Australia!"

"Maybe I'll just do that."

I crossed the highway, sat down on a bench and waited contentedly for a bus bound for a beach. ☺

MARCH

Trujillo, Peru

The girl would not stop crying. She just sat there at her desk, tears streaming down her plump cheeks. With a snotty nose and hair in her eyes, she sobbed in waves, as though the apocalypse were upon us.

This was the first day of school for both of us. She was a six-year-old Peruvian student, just beginning her elementary school career. I was a 30-year-old Canadian English "teacher" who had never taught a lesson in his whole life. We were experiencing similar emotions — anxiety, confusion, trepidation — so I could understand her reaction. In fact, on some level, I also wanted to weep. But instead, my approach was to overcompensate, to be excessively animated and joyful, and to wiggle my eyebrows with enthusiasm. This effort, however, was a failure, and she looked at me as though I were a mutant hell-bent on stealing her lunch money.

The sobs only grew louder.

Oh, what to do? I scanned the classroom for my fellow volunteers, Lucy and Vanessa, in hopes that one of them might be able to use a feminine touch to help calm the situation. But they were already addressing their own respective disasters: Vanessa was

71

breaking up a wrestling match and Lucy was deeply involved in assuring a student that he did indeed have a first name. I could sense that they also felt overwhelmed, and saving me from Miss Waterworks was not high on their priority lists.

Crouching beside the crying girl, I put on my friendliest and most empathetic expression, wishing that she might see me as a human (and not a malicious monster). She paused momentarily, scanning my face one more time and deciding what to do next. Just when I thought that perhaps we had made an unspoken connection, she released a blood-curdling scream. Chernobyl was graceful compared to this meltdown.

The regular classroom teacher had abandoned us, probably in search of coffee or horse tranquillizers. I had no idea what to do with the hysterical little girl.

So I let her cry. ○

My destination for the month of March was Peru, a country I had been keen on for decades. My curiosity originated in grade school with the captivating illustrations of Incan peoples found in my social studies textbooks. You know, the kind of images that portrayed harmonious relations between brave European explorers and noble natives from the new world. Wow, did those Incan warriors ever seem welcoming! Many years later, glossy travel magazines seduced me with lush images of crumbling archaic mountain cities and friendly locals wearing well-crafted colourful hats. A month in Peru would provide me with insight into ancient local cultures, kick-start my stagnant Spanish skills (in a way that I hadn't managed to do on the raw vegan farm) and maybe give me the opportunity to nab one of those fancy fuzzy hats.

On a website called Workaway, which features work-exchange projects from around the world, I discovered Horizon Peru. The volunteer-based English school provides free lessons to an under-privileged community in Trujillo, Peru's third-largest city. (Trujillo is often left off the itineraries of foreign travellers, who customarily land in Lima before heading directly east to Machu Picchu for a photo op with a llama.) The organization accepts helpers for minimum one-month intervals and provides housing and home-cooked meals for $300 per month, an amount that I was starting to accept as standard. After reading many positive testimonials about the organization, and feeling excited about visiting a destination that I knew absolutely nothing about, I conceded once again to the idea of paying to volunteer. I completed an online application and was subsequently interviewed by the founder, a man named Manuel.

With two months of manual labour in New Orleans and Costa Rica under my tool belt, I was nervous at the thought of a very different role: teaching English. Back in Canada, I had tutored one-on-one, but I had no theoretical knowledge of how to create a lesson plan or guide a classroom of 30 children, let alone the pedagogy of language acquisition. Manuel approved my application and reassured me that to be successful with Horizon Peru, I would only need three things: a good command of the English language, an interest in working with people and a reasonable level of flexibility.

Check. Check. And check. ○

AFTER MY FINAL week in Costa Rica (with much of it spent filling my face with every baked good I could find), I embarked on a gruelling 24-hour marathon to relocate to Peru: sprinting through the Bogota terminal to catch a connection, attempting to sleep on an airport bench in Lima, having one flight entirely rerouted and being trapped in a plane on a tarmac for three hours in a random city named Chiclayo.

When my flight finally made it to Trujillo, I walked down the steps of the plane and into the airport, only to realize there was nobody waiting for me. If the pre-arranged driver had come, he was long gone by that point. Fortunately, a man who spoke a bit of English approached me as I picked my backpack off the carousel. His job, it seemed, was to act as the "taxi pimp" to a small horde of drivers. He asked where I was heading.

"I need to go to La Esperanza."

"Donde?"

"La Esperanza."

The taxi pimp raised his brow. Like that first night in New Orleans when I requested to be taken to the Lower Ninth Ward, I was once again destined for an area that few tourists venture to alone. He pulled a notepad out of his shirt pocket and motioned for me to write down the address.

"Es posible?" I asked, handing him a paper with the street name "José Martí" written on it.

"Sí ... " he acknowledged hesitantly.

The taxi pimp escorted me to a modern-looking car with frenetic Latino music pouring out of its speakers. He muttered something to the driver, and the next thing I knew I was in the back seat, barrelling down a freshly paved four-lane highway.

Whereas Costa Rica was humid and green, this new environment was desert-like, arid and pale red. On either side of the road were concrete estate walls and countless piles of dirt, while the cloud coverage was high and grey. As the car drew closer to the city, the buildings grew denser. Many of them were plastered with bright advertisements for various political parties, indicating an impending national election. The taxi slowed as we entered La Esperanza. The low concrete houses were weather-worn and the streets were empty apart from mangy, undernourished dogs and the occasional plastic bag. It was a world away from the well-manicured suburbs of Canada — or the verdant jungles of Costa Rica, for that matter.

Eventually, the driver stopped on José Martí Street at a blue building with the words "Horizon Peru" painted on the porch wall. With two levels, the house was taller than the neighbouring single-storey homes but was otherwise constructed in the same concrete style. The first floor had been coated in baby blue paint, while the upper floor was red brick. The door and windows were protected with iron bars.

I paid the driver in *soles*, closed the taxi door and stepped around a massive pile of trash positioned in front of the stoop. *Here goes nothing*, I whispered as I ascended the three steps that led to the front door.

Before I could knock, a short-haired woman, not an inch over five feet tall, opened the door. She had a pea-sized mole to the left side of her upper lip. Ever so slightly, it rose up her face as she smiled timidly.

"*Hola. Bienvenido,*" she said quietly. "*Soy Estella.*"

Estella motioned me to follow her into what appeared to be a schoolroom. White dry-erase boards lined the walls and a small assortment of desks and chairs were piled up on each other at the back of the room. The middle-aged woman led me up a set of stairs to the second floor of the building, where the smell of fresh, damp concrete permeated the air. Three young workers with trowels in hand turned to look at me.

"*Hola,*" I ventured. One of them pushed his chin forward in acknowledgment, and then all three immediately went back to their work. I followed Estella down a hallway toward the back of the house. She showed me into a bedroom with a single metal bunk bed, a child-sized wooden chair, a couple of shelves and a safety box that could fit a passport and a pocket camera.

"Okay?" she asked.

"*Sí.* Okay," I responded, not really knowing if there were any other appropriate responses. I wasn't exactly going to ask if they had a room with a mini-bar instead. She smiled again gently, pivoted and left me alone.

I put my bag down on the lower bunk. My initial inclination was to nap, but I decided that first I would explore the rest of the house and introduce myself to the others. Downstairs, I poked my head into a vacant dormitory room with three bunk beds, into a bathroom with a pink flush toilet and tiled shower, and then into a windowless living room. The only person I found was Estella. She was in the kitchen doing laundry while attending to something simmering on the stove. She grinned again and asked me a question in Spanish that I didn't understand. When she saw the puzzled look on my face, she waved her hand in a gesture that said "Oh, never mind. It doesn't matter."

Despite the minimal furnishings and the construction work, the house seemed functional — I mean, it had flush toilets, which was a step up from a buckoilet. And Estella seemed friendly enough. Yet something didn't feel right. My gut was struck with a familiar sinking sensation, similar to the one I experienced on my first day in Costa Rica.

Where were the other volunteers? ⟡

MY EYES FLUTTERED open. Hovering two feet from my face was an attractive young woman with glossy coal-coloured hair and an extremely pregnant belly. She was staring right at me.

"*Ho-la!*" she sang brightly. I rubbed the inner corners of my eye sockets and looked at her again. I had no idea who this woman was or why she was in such close proximity. In fact, in my grogginess, I wasn't entirely sure where I was or how I had gotten there.

"My name is Luz!" the woman continued, raising her eyebrows high above the rim of her wire glasses. "Welcome to Horizon Peru school!" Fortunately, Luz spoke in discernible English, which proved very helpful in jogging my memory: I was in Peru, in an upstairs bedroom of a schoolhouse. Luz was the wife of Manuel, and together they ran the project.

"You arrived okay?"

"Yeah," I replied, drawing myself up into a sitting position. "Apart from spending three hours trapped in plane on a tarmac in a city that wasn't on my itinerary and wondering if I'd ever reach Trujillo, I'm doing pretty good."

She looked confused.

"Forget it," I replied. "I was just trying to be funny. It doesn't usually work."

"*Ah, un humorista!*" she said as she laughed lightly and nodded.

For a moment, we both sat and smiled at each other. I wasn't sure if I was supposed to say something to spark further conversation or if there was some other local custom I should be adhering to. In other circumstances, it might have been appropriate to offer a compliment on the home, but between the stacked chairs and the renovations, the space was in disarray. And I didn't want to lie or offer up gratuitous sentiments. So instead I just kept a pleasant expression on my face, acutely aware of the awkward silence. Finally, after what felt like an eternity of uncomfortable cross-cultural grinning, I thought of a relevant question.

"Hey, where are the other volunteers?"

Luz explained that schools in Peru were in the final days of summer holidays. The organization's long-term volunteers had taught summer lessons at Horizon Peru, but they had left on a two-week break visiting Machu Picchu and Lake Titicaca. They were expected back in the coming days to prepare for classes, which would resume the following week. In addition, there were new volunteers scheduled to arrive, including a German woman and a Danish fellow.

"When you're ready," Luz said while adjusting her pregnant belly, "I'll take you to the *mercado* where you can have something to eat, and then we can ride a *colectivo* to the city. I'll take you to *el Starbucks*! We'll have the frappuccinos!" She beamed with enthusiasm.

I chuckled. The offer to see the market and learn how to navigate public transit was enticing, but the thought of going to Starbucks was comical. Peru is home to some of the world's most advanced ancient civilizations; the whole nation is an archaeologist's playground. I could only imagine what cultural and culinary opportunities waited around each corner. Low on my list of "Experiences to Have While in Peru" was to visit a generic North American coffee chain. Perhaps Luz was eager to prove that beyond the barred windows of the schoolhouse, Trujillo was modern and comfortable.

"Sure," I said, rising to my feet. "Let's go for frappuccinos." ○

OVER THE FOLLOWING days, the bunk beds at Horizon Peru filled as volunteers arrived (my roommate was the Danish guy — a polite 19-year-old with a penchant for reggae). As Luz had mentioned, a couple of longer-term volunteers returned from explorations in southern Peru. With the new recruits joining the ranks, we would be a group of six English "teachers" for the upcoming month. I use the term teacher with reserve because, like me, none of the other volunteers had any formal training in language instruction. For many of them, English wasn't even their mother tongue. Regardless of our lack of qualifications, we were asked to reorganize the volunteer house classroom and draw up logical teaching plans for the classes that would take place at the nearby public elementary school, San Francisco de Asís. The game plan we came up with was simple: first we would introduce the English alphabet and then progress to more complex lessons, such as colours and farm animals. It was almost as if we knew what we were doing.

Eventually Luz arranged us into two teaching teams. I was assigned to the crew that would spend mornings at the elementary school and afternoons tutoring at Horizon Peru's in-house classroom. My squad included Vanessa, a self-composed 24-year-old from Germany, and Lucy, a bashful 19-year-old from England. Despite her age, Lucy was the veteran in our trio, as she had already been with the organization for a month, offering tutoring sessions at the house.

On the day before the official first day of classes, we were scheduled to visit the elementary school and to meet some of the permanent full-time teachers. We followed Luz as she grasped onto her pregnant belly and waddled down the sand-strewn street, leading us past multi-coloured blockhouses and through the school's tall gates. Apart from a small group of girls skipping rope, the yard — which was the approximate size of two tennis courts — was empty. We crossed directly to one of the dozen classrooms and were invited to sit on chairs designed for bodies much smaller than our own. Above the blackboard at the front of the classroom was a framed portrait of a Caucasian Jesus.

Slowly the teachers began to trickle into the room. A few of them extended greetings and pleasantries to us, but most were uninterested in our presence. A couple of the men jostled with each other like school boys, while one woman flipped through what looked like an Avon catalogue.

Luz started the meeting by going over the class schedule, but many of the teachers ignored her completely and opted to gossip among themselves. At one point, the dull roar of the side conversations blocked Luz out completely, and her appeals for silence went ignored. I had been warned that the students of San Francisco de Asís could be unruly, and sitting in that teachers' meeting, I understood where they got it from.

When Luz finally adjourned the meeting, we walked back to the volunteer house quietly, the reality of the situation sinking in. Up to that point, none of the other volunteers had admitted to feeling nervous about leading a group. But if the students really were like the teachers — boisterous characters with little interest in the exotic English language or the exotic English teachers — we were in for quite the bumpy ride. ○

EVEN THOUGH ESTELLA and I couldn't string together a decent sentence in the other's respective language, we were intrigued by one another. Early each morning, she buzzed at the door of the volunteer house. Since I was still on that "up and at 'em" morning schedule from Costa Rica, I was always the one to unlock the front door for her. *"Como estás?"* she would say with a smile and a sideways glance before whooshing off to start her daily activities: cooking, cleaning, helping to care for Luz's three-year-old daughter and a multitude of other tasks that made the house feel like a home.

To the volunteers, Estella was an honorary Peruvian mother. She lovingly prepared our lunches, ensuring that we foreigners had the opportunity to sample local cuisine. One of her signature dishes was a warm potato salad called *papa a la Huancaina*, served with black olives, hard-boiled eggs and a white cheese sauce that had crushed saltines as a secret ingredient. (I never understood how she could transform coarse crackers into such an incredibly smooth sauce.) Estella's other specialties included a sweet purple corn beverage called *chicha*, a cilantro-bean concoction called *sarandaja* and, for a snack, an un-puffed popcorn called *cancha*, which was like the salty love child of corn nuts and popcorn. There were countless other dishes, such as chicken stews and fried rice recipes, that were nameless but just as appetizing. Estella's repertoire of culinary achievements reintroduced padding to my backside, which had diminished during my stint in Costa Rica.

At lunch, I was constantly the first person to shovel the meal down, leaving only a couple of chicken bones on my plate. Then I would wait patiently for the offer I knew would arrive as soon as Estella saw that my plate was empty.

"Más?" she would ask, with her eyebrows high, before offering me a second serving.

One evening, I decided to return the gesture. After a trip to La Esperanza's outdoor market, I took to the kitchen to craft one of my favourite recipes from back home: a lima bean and pumpkin stew. When Estella got word that there was a man mucking about the kitchen, she came to observe — in her world, men were more apt to use a skilsaw than a skillet.

"You want to taste it?" I asked her, gesturing to the simmering pot on the stove. Cautiously, she took the wooden spoon from my hand, extracted a few beans, blew away the steam and then pulled them into her mouth with her teeth. As she chewed, her eyes looked out through the barred kitchen windows.

Her eyes narrowed and she tilted her head to one side. Then she turned to me and gave me nod of approval.

"Es muy bueno."

At that moment, our friendship was sealed — brought together by lima beans and purple corn, and bound by respect for each other's abilities with a saucepan.

Who needs words when you've got food?

Perhaps I proved myself with the stew because when I expressed interest in learning how to make Peru's national dish, a citrus-marinated seafood salad, Estella immediately offered to give me a ceviche class at her house. My internal epicurean did a quick cartwheel of excitement — an invitation into a local's kitchen for a personal cooking lesson is the Holy Grail of travel experiences.

Major. Travel. Win. ○

THAT AFTERNOON, THE Peruvian sun was hotter than I had imagined. I was on a self-guided mission to explore downtown Trujillo: peeking my head into colonial churches, sampling slices of cakes from bakeries and taking photos of statues. Eventually I grew weary (read: I was a sweaty mess), so I began searching for a place where I could cool off and recharge. Outside of a small museum devoted to modern art, I heard the familiar sound of milk being frothed. Bingo. In less than 30 seconds, I was seated at the museum bistro, looking at a menu.

With a dated, elegant style, the café was different from the other restaurants and bars I had seen around Trujillo, which typically featured plastic patio chairs and pulsing music. The faded leather seats had been softened by a thousand cappuccino-seekers who had come before me. The walls were decorated with black and white photographic portraits of (what I guessed were) famous Peruvian artists. A six-foot mirror was framed in brass and adorned with playful cherubs at the top. Only three tables were occupied, including mine. By the window, a serious looking man and woman conversed in Spanish over cups of tea, while puffing on Lucky Strike cigarettes. The other table was taken by a group of chubby western girls sipping on sodas and exchanging stories about their travels.

After a sandwich and an espresso, I leaned back against the booth to contemplate my own travels. Peru had graced me with many new experiences: bartering for cheaper fares with taxi drivers, touring an ancient Chan Chan archeological site and, of course, getting a glimpse into a local elementary school. But my favourite activity so far was visiting the local mercado. The market was a small maze of individual vendors selling everything one might imagine: fruit, vegetables, fish, meat, grains and more. If only I had had more time, I would have spent hours sipping *sur-tidos* (fruit smoothies) and watching the people mix and mingle.

The previous morning at the market, as I was buying my mangoes and avocados, one of the vendors had flagged me over to his stand. He smiled brightly as he stood among barrels of rice, lentils and pasta. In broken English, he asked me if I was a Horizon Peru teacher. "*Sí!*" I replied, excited that someone wanted to talk with me. With pride in his eyes, the vendor explained that his son, Arturo, was taking lessons at the school.

Hoping to continue the conversation and wanting to reciprocate his social generosity by buying something from his stand, I asked him if he had *pepitas* (pumpkin seeds). I thought they'd be a nutritious addition to my morning oatmeal. But I obviously didn't convey my message well. Arturo's father looked at me with confusion, the same expression that most locals displayed whenever I attempted to speak Spanish. The wheels in his brain went into overdrive as he ran through the possibilities of what I might be asking for.

"*Qué?*" He scratched his temple with one hand and rubbed the other hand down his apron.

"*Pep-itas?*" I replied, this time switching the emphasis to the first syllable, in case that might help.

"*Papas!*" he exclaimed with enthusiasm. He took me by the elbow and guided me over to a neighbouring kiosk, where I was presented with four types of dirty potatoes.

I nodded my head. "Ah … *si!*"

Then I thanked him profusely and proceeded to buy a kilo of spuds. He could have offered up a three-legged llama with an incontinence problem, and I would have bought it. Arturo's father had taken the initiative to acknowledge that I was there. And, for me, that small gesture was significant, memorable.

In the museum café, I chuckled to myself as I replayed the interaction.

The chubby western girls continued to chatter. They were by no means obnoxious; as a matter of fact, I considered them rather respectful in their subject material and volume level. The girl with an American accent began to talk about a recent spell of homesickness. She missed her boyfriend.

Personally, I didn't feel homesick. Maybe it was because I didn't have a home to go back to: no apartment, no furniture and no fixed address. It was all part of a premeditated act to prevent longing for "home." Perhaps all these measures were working. Or perhaps it was because people like Arturo's father provided just enough warmth to keep the chill of homesickness away. Whatever the reasons, I was feeling grounded and capable.

I settled my tab and went back outside, refreshed and ready to continue exploring. ⚬

THE FIRST DAY of classes finally arrived. I got up early, showered and ate a big breakfast. Everything had been taken care of to ensure a successful day: the lesson had been planned, the activity sheets had been printed and the teachers knew we'd be coming. Before leaving the volunteer house, I went to the bathroom — twice. (There is nothing more embarrassing than wetting one's pants in front of a group of six-year-olds.) I was as ready as I'd ever be.

With teaching supplies in hand, Vanessa, Lucy and I marched down that same grimy street and knocked at the gate of the school, only to be greeted by a surly schoolyard bouncer who gave us an up-and-down with his eyes. After careful consideration of our broken Spanish and the glare of our pasty skin, he conceded that we were most likely who we claimed to be — *los profesores de inglés* — and let us in. The concrete courtyard was filled with young students dressed in matching uniforms. The girls wore white shirts and navy dresses, and the boys donned the same getup, but with slacks. But this wasn't an orderly highbrow boarding school where students marched politely in sets of twos. The Peruvian schoolyard was human pandemonium.

Projecting all the emotions that come with the first day of school — giddiness, exhilaration, sheer terror — the students fluttered like butterflies across the courtyard. Really loud, dishevelled, possessed butterflies. With unruly ponytails and untucked shirts, the students were playing a game called "I can make the loudest and most annoying sound in the world and I'm going to prove it!" From the sidelines, a handful of parents observed with indifference, looking like they had just rolled out of bed. No fancy cameras to capture the momentous first day of school. As one mother turned to leave, I swore I saw relief on her face as she put her hands together and offered a *gracias* in the direction of God. Meanwhile, teachers darted to and fro like newly corralled horses. No one greeted us.

The teaching schedule had us beginning the week with the first-grade students. As the weekdays progressed, gradually we worked toward the eldest of the elementary students, finishing with the sixth graders on Friday. Essentially this meant that on our very first day of school, we were teaching a group of six-year-olds who were attending their very first class. Ever.

Like gladiators waiting to enter the arena, Vanessa, Lucy and I stood outside the first classroom. It was eight o'clock in the morning, and the heat in the shade was shockingly intense. I wiped the sweat off my brow with my sleeve. *Why on earth had I worn flannel?* Did I honestly think that these Peruvian schoolchildren would see the delightful link between the fabric and my national heritage? *"Oh, the Canadian is wearing flannel! How charming!"* they would never say.

Finally, the teacher welcomed us into the class and then promptly left the room. We turned to face the six rows of students.

"Hello! My. Name. Is. Daniel. Today. We. Will. Practise. English."

I scrawled our names on the blackboard (which in retrospect was utterly pointless considering that first graders generally cannot read). Lucy used her modest Spanish skills to inform the kiddies of what we would be doing. I had hoped that our foreignness might hypnotize the students into a state of silence and that we'd be able to execute our lesson with grace and relative ease. Alas, that was not the case. Within seconds, total chaos erupted: a couple boys started throwing fists, a group of students pointed at us and sang some sort of mocking song, and one little fellow simply stood up and walked out of the room. It was all too much for the most sensitive soul in the group, a girl sitting in my section, who instantly began wailing.

Our strategy was to simply push forward. We distributed a manila folder to each of the students and instructed them to write their names across the front. It took us under a minute to realize that none of them could write. So we went from student to student, asking their names and writing them ourselves. Once that was complete, we proceeded to sing the English alphabet a couple of times. A few of the kids even joined in, but most realized that it was far more entertaining to use their manila folders as pointy hats. Others were less jovial, including the one girl who sobbed uncontrollably for most of the class. ○

ONE SUNDAY, WITH no English classes on my schedule, I strolled down José Martí Street with a very different type of class to attend. The day was cloudless. The mellow morning sunlight cast La Esperanza in a gentle light. I passed a man on a bicycle selling fish, a pair of older women carrying bags filled with limes and a well-dressed family walking to church. The mangy dogs, which were usually aggressive, were taking the morning off. The smell of freshly baked bread came from one of the corner stores.

From an address scribbled on a piece of paper, I located Estella's house without difficulty and rang the bell. Within seconds, the door flung open. I was greeted with a smile, which was becoming less timid day by day. The mole above her lip had become increasingly bouncy. In her pink T-shirt and spotless white capris, Estella grabbed my forearm and pulled me forward, a gesture that said "Come on, silly man. Don't just stand there gathering moss."

The large blue living room contained a pair of fluffy couches and a TV that was blaring a dubbed American action film. The walls were decorated with two posters of forest scenery and a single calendar that featured two blond toddlers hugging each other. A massive wooden table, with enough space to comfortably seat 10 people, stood in the middle of the room. By western standards, the style was sparse. An interior designer might have recommended painting an accent wall or adding some drapes over the barred windows. But this wasn't a suburb in upstate New York; this was La Esperanza. Comparatively speaking, the home was quite comfortable. There was even a desktop computer in the corner of the room, which attested to a higher standard of living than the neighbourhood average. I was relieved to see that Estella was not without basic elements of comfort and technology.

More surprising than Estella's relative comfort were all her relatives. Apart from her daughter, Karla, she had not mentioned the other members of her family (or if she had, I obviously hadn't understood). For some reason I thought that Karla and Estella lived alone, but to my surprise there seemed to be people everywhere. I almost stepped on a baby, twice. Introductions were made to her son, her daughter-in-law and her grandchildren. The horizontally splayed body on the couch was another son. And just when I thought I had met everyone, Estella's own mother and father descended slowly from a set of stairs. After a quick session of charting the family tree, I realized there were four generations under a single roof.

Estella insisted on serving breakfast and sat me at the large table beside her father. She served me a steamy cup of *avena con manzana*, a breakfast beverage of steaming liquidy oatmeal with apple. It was sweet and went down quickly.

Over breakfast, Estella's father and I played a game of charades about the food. I gave him a thumbs-up. He pretended to pour something into a glass, represented by his left hand. I did the same, clinked my "glass" against his, and we both downed our imaginary whisky.

As I was polishing off a chicken and olive tamale that Estella had forced upon me, her father excused himself from the table and started walking toward the stairs. But a few feet from the first step, he suddenly put his hand over his chest and collapsed against the side of a buffet hutch. I jumped up and raced over to him.

"Shit," I thought, offering a hand. "Is this man having a stroke or a heart attack? Did I arrive the day that Estella's father *dies*?"

He smiled and waved me off as he regained his balance. The other family members didn't appear terribly fazed. In fact, I'm sure I saw Estella roll her eyes. Other family members, including the limp body on the couch, failed to respond to the incident altogether. I was concerned about what had happened, but I took their lead and decided not to further intervene.

While I stood at the bottom of the stairs, ensuring that the old man made a safe ascent, Estella cleared my breakfast dishes. She refused my attempts to help with the cleaning, instead indicating that it was time to go to the market to buy ingredients for our ceviche. I had assumed that we'd be visiting the Mercado San Martín de Porres — the closest outdoor market to Horizon Peru — but Estella led us in the opposite direction, explaining with her hands that we were going to a much larger market. She rubbed her thumb and her fingers together, and then pointed downward. This was internationally sign language for "cheaper."

Mercado Nazaret was large and frenzied. We entered through the fruit and vegetable section, and I struggled to keep up as Estella weaved effortlessly through the mayhem. However, my curiosity interfered with my ability to maintain the pace. The mercado was an orgy of smells and sights, and I wanted to stop to taste, talk and take photos. We eventually paused at a booth to buy lemons and cilantro, and then at another for onions, potatoes and garlic. But my favourite stall was a fish stand where a woman wearing bright orange rubber gloves smiled serenely while violently chopping off fish heads with a sharp cleaver. She effortlessly skinned and filleted a bonito fish for Estella while maintaining conversation. Her ability to debone filets while chatting with those around her — without sacrificing any of her fingertips — was sheer performance art.

The other butcher stalls were also mesmerizing with their unapologetic presentation. Plucked chickens were piled in mounds, their heads and feet dangling limply. Eyeballs rolled off butchers' tables, landing on the ground where opportunistic dogs could nab them. Enormous sides of beef were strung from steel hangers large enough to hook a whale. It was a stark contrast to the sterile packaging of my homeland, where bacon and pig are considered separate entities.

An hour later, we finally had all the supplies needed to make ceviche. With arms full of purchases, including corn stalks for the pet rabbits and a massive watermelon for the grandchildren, we fell onto the back bench of a mototaxi and zipped up the hill, back to Estella's home and into her kitchen.

The ceviche lesson commenced. While Estella cleaned and portioned the darkish fish into grape-sized morsels, I sliced onions, shaved chili peppers, chopped cilantro, minced ginger and squeezed lemons. The fish was soaked in saltwater brine for 10 minutes, and then all the ingredients were combined. We topped the mixture with a generous sprinkling of cumin and cracked black pepper, and then set it aside to marinate. It all seemed far too easy.

Estella and I were washing up when her father came downstairs. He squinted in my direction and grinned, appearing in much better condition. Estella nodded toward him and then looked down and whispered *"Bebe mucho."*

The morning events suddenly became clear. Her father hadn't had a heart attack or a stroke; he had simply been drunk at nine o'clock on a Sunday morning. From Estella's body language, I sensed it was an issue of contention and my heart sank a bit.

But our attention soon turned back to the food.

The ceviche was now thoroughly marinated. We dished it onto plates alongside boiled potatoes, rings of corn on the cob, slices of purple *camote* (sweet potato) and strands of edible seaweed. And then we sat down with Estella's extensive family at their massive table and dug in. It was one of the most satisfying meals of my life — not only because it tasted so good but because of the moments that were part of creating it. ○

CLASSES AT THE elementary school progressed smoothly — well, as smoothly as one could hope. Teaching the younger students at the beginning of each week was more challenging, as many of them couldn't read or write. But by Thursday and Friday, we were able to create more complex lesson plans for the older kids. I learned various instructional approaches that were helpful: being animated generally worked, as did kneeling down to neutralize the height discrepancies. In many ways, I was less of a language teacher and more of an excitable clown who just happened to speak English.

In the elementary school's social hierarchy, volunteer English teachers ranked in an ambiguous grey zone between the measly student and the mighty full-time teacher. Because of this divide — or maybe for simpler reasons, such as the awkward language barrier — Vanessa, Lucy and I opted to bypass the staff lounge during recess and relax in the central courtyard. I've always thought that schoolyards are microcosms of society where you can gain insight into local culture. So I sat and I watched.

The kids of La Esperanza seemed quite healthy, apart from the odd rotten tooth, which was certainly linked to their incessant consumption of sugary popsicles. Groups of youngsters ran around screaming and laughing. Occasionally one of them would fall or be pushed down, and tears would surface. But in a matter of seconds, the madness would recommence. Children who had reached a certain age divided into gender groups, with the girls bumping volleyballs between each other and the boys kicking soccer balls.

One memorable morning, our volunteer trio was sitting on the hot cement steps when a group of 12-year-old boys approached, curious to discover what the heck these weird-looking *profesores de inglés* were all about. Upon establishing that we did not bite or smell like misguided hippies, one of them — the arms-folded-across-chest leader — began to hurl question after question in our direction. *Where are you from? What is your house like? How old are you? Do you like soccer? Do you have an amor?* I told him that he'd make a great customs officer. Vanessa and

Lucy chuckled, but the joke was otherwise lost.

We exchanged handshakes with the boys and then progressed to comparing hand size by matching palms against palms. Next they playfully requested to see how big my biceps were; the exploration of my differentness was also an analysis of my manliness. In response to their appeals, I jokingly displayed a mocked form of masculinity, flexing my muscles theatrically but allowing the boys to win arm-wrestling matches. The spirit of inquiry was playful, sweet and innocent.

Until it wasn't.

While I was busy enjoying what I considered a meaningful cross-cultural exchange, the leader of the group had taken the skin and scruffy hair of my forearm and folded it into a familiar reproductive shape. As the saying goes, it's all fun and games until someone non-consensually turns your forearm into a vagina and starts laughing directly in your face.

"*Puta!*" yelled the mischievous gang leader.

"*Puta!*" echoed his smutty posse of 12-year-old comrades.

My facial reaction was similar to that of unexpectedly inhaling a rancid fart, and I quickly retracted my arm.

"Game over, boys. I'm going to need my arm back now. Way to keep it classy."

The bell rang, and the boys ran off to their classroom. As we walked toward our next group of students, Vanessa and Lucy noted that no matter where you go in the world, 12-year-old boys seem to have a unique culture all to themselves. ☼

As SOON AS the renovations were complete, Horizon Peru house reopened for private tutorial sessions. The students were timid at first, including a set of six-year-old twins who absolutely refused to speak for our 45-minute lesson. After a couple of meetings, however, most of the kids were eager and willing to practise. My favourite student was Estella's 17-year-old daughter Karla, who was pint-sized like her mother but with longer hair and deeper dimples. Karla frequently hung out at the house, so she was accustomed to interacting with foreigners. This made our sessions far more relaxed. In addition to reviewing grammar and vocabulary, Karla and I often hit the streets of La Esperanza to pick up bread or popcorn while practising conversational English. Another fun activity was helping her understand the lyrics to her favourite Lady Gaga song:

'Cause I'm out in the club and I'm sippin' that bub
And you're not gonna reach my telephone

Together we tried to decipher the meaning behind words that the English-Español dictionary would never be able to explain.

"Dani-Daniel," she would call me. "What is 'bub'?"

"Well, 'bub' is the short form of 'bubbly,' " I explained, "which is another word for champagne. You see?"

Karla looked at me blankly. I did my best to explain the nuances of colloquial English, but there was rarely rhyme, reason or rule to the exceptions and variations — they just had to be accepted and memorized. Still, I often found myself apologizing on behalf of the entire English language.

Through my work with Karla, I discovered that I enjoyed teaching and that I could be more than a terrifying Canadian monster that made six-year-old girls cry.

Meanwhile, over at the elementary school, the classroom lessons were as hectic as always, even though the students became less frightened of the teaching team as time went on. And vice versa. On one particularly entertaining morning, I learned that magic occurs when a fly swatter and a set of flashcards are combined. As part of our lesson on animals, Vanessa divided our skeptical group of fifth graders into two teams while I tacked 10 animal flashcards onto the chalkboard. A volunteer from each team approached the board, fly swatter in hand, and waited for Lucy's call.

"Dog!"

The fastest student slapped the corresponding animal flashcard with her fly swatter and earned a point for her team. For the first round, we had to coax a volunteer from each team. By the second round, however, every hand was up in the air, vying to get access to the coveted fly swatters. That morning, the enthusiastic crack of animals being thwacked echoed through the school's courtyard.

When we weren't beating up bunnies and hitting horses at the elementary school, there were plenty of opportunities to explore different areas around Trujillo. On weekends, Estella organized day trips for the volunteers. A rusty old *cambio* (van) would pull up in front of the house early on Saturday morning, honking its horn, already bursting with most of Estella's family. With 12 bodies and no seatbelts, we'd endure potholed roads for the chance to hike a mountain or frolic on a beach beside the Pacific Ocean — destinations that foreign travellers might never discover on their own. During each excursion, there was a lunch-time pause when Estella would unveil her delicious dish of the day, which was greeted with a round of applause. These day trips always concluded with windswept faces, full bellies and plenty of smiles.

If my month in New Orleans had introduced a set of criteria for a successful month, then my experiences in Peru helped to solidify that list. Did I connect with interesting local people? Yup. Did I learn a new skill? Yup. Did I experience the area's geography? Yup. Did I manage to contribute in some sort of meaningful way? Well, I didn't manage to teach anybody the complete English language during my month-long stay, but I did have a great deal of fun standing in front of a classroom and acting like a duck. And when attempting to travel around the world for an entire year — this might sound obvious — having fun is immensely helpful. ☺

"HOLA," I WHISPERED to Luz as she lay napping in her single bed, but she didn't stir.

The tables had turned since my first day in Peru when Luz had eagerly coaxed me out of a siesta for a Starbucks expedition. Now, it was me hovering over her. The very pregnant woman had recently delivered a baby, and the news of the birth had reached the house where it was celebrated with a standing ovation. The volunteers had been invited to drop by the hospital to offer *felicitaciones* to Luz and to meet the newest member of the Horizon Peru family.

I didn't have the heart to wake her, so I slipped out of the private room to join a couple of other volunteers. Apart from an on-duty nurse, we were alone, three foreigners sitting in a sterile hallway. The soft beeping of a heart monitor came from a different room. As we sat and waited, I ran my hand over a soft hat that had recently become part of my wardrobe.

A few days previously, knowing that the baby could arrive at any time, Luz had proudly presented me with an early goodbye gift. I unwrapped a plastic bag to reveal a Peruvian wool hat: one side was brown and decorated with a traditional Chimu print, while the reversible side was beige and featured a series of proud-looking llamas. The word "Peru" appeared five times along the base of the hat, and long braided cords ran down from the earflaps. To top it off, a modest pompom decorated the tip. It was the Peruvian hat I had dreamed of finding. Only, it had found me.

"How did you know I wanted a Peruvian hat?"

"Everybody who comes here wants one," she responded, looking at me suspiciously, as though I were teasing her.

"Oh, yeah?" I chucked. "I guess that makes sense."

Luz's husband, Manuel, stepped into the hospital hallway. "She's awake!" he whisper-shouted. The other volunteers and I rushed into the room and huddled around her bed. Luz looked tired but calm. In her arms was a tiny boy child. The little fellow was an adorable bundle of wrinkled pink skin with a crown of jet-black hair, the picture of innocence. I offered an internal prayer that, despite the inevitable influences of the Peruvian schoolyard, he would remain sweet for as long as possible.

We had been cooing over the baby for a few minutes when Luz noticed my choice of headgear. "Oh, I like your hat," she teased.

"Oh, this old thing?" I said, pulling at one of the long braided cords. "It was a gift from a really lovely woman in Peru."

We both beamed. ☺

THE EVE OF my departure from Trujillo came sooner than I would have wished. At dusk, long shadows spilled across the colourful homes on José Martí Street. The sound of kids playing, interspersed with the occasional snarl of a mototaxi, drifted my way as I looked out the second-floor window of the house.

When I first arrived to La Esperanza, I saw it as unfriendly and impoverished: emaciated dogs that seemed ready to attack my ankles, dusty sidewalks strewn with plastic bags, and ramshackle concrete blockhouses whose inhabitants would stare suspiciously through iron bars. A month later, I saw the neighbourhood as, well, simply a neighbourhood. Unfriendly glances had been counterpoised with characters like Arturo's father. What I had perceived as "shabbiness" was contrasted by a strength of spirit. There, in the soft light of the setting sun and with the sound of children laughing, La Esperanza felt like many things. But "uninviting" was no longer one of them.

My experience at Horizon Peru had been deeply influenced by the people I had met there. Luz and Manuel had been supportive hosts. The students had been capricious and energetic yet also good-humoured and friendly. The other volunteers had been enthusiastic and easygoing. But there was one person who made La Esperanza feel like a home away from home. And I wanted to thank her.

Estella had been incredibly generous throughout the month, and I thought it would be fitting to reciprocate with a small offering. During the last days of my stay, I racked my brain trying to think of something that she could use, such as a fresh pair of hiking shoes or a new pot for her kitchen. But I didn't know the size of her feet, nor did I want to suggest that she should spend more time in the kitchen. Eventually, a practical but meaningful idea came to me.

94

Midway through the month, we had celebrated Karla's birthday at the volunteer house. All four generations of Estella's family had gathered to share a meal, eat cake and celebrate with lively salsa music. At one point in the evening, I snapped an image of the whole family posed together, and I figured that a print of this photograph would make a fine gift. I had the picture enlarged and printed at a shop in downtown Trujillo. I also bought a simple wooden frame, placed the print inside and wrapped it all together in newspaper. It wasn't glamorous, but it was personal.

That final evening, Estella was still at the volunteer house, fussing with the endless tasks to keep the house running smoothly. Once the sun had set, I left my perch at the window and grabbed Lucy and Vanessa to help interpret. Together we cornered Estella in an upstairs bedroom.

Without any pomp or ceremony, I awkwardly thrust the gift toward her. In my broken Spanish, I explained that I was thankful for all she had done for me. Estella looked at me hesitantly, uncomfortable being the centre of attention. She took the newsprint bundle into her hands, slowly pulled off the layers and stood for a moment, examining the photograph. Then she burst into tears, covering her face with her hand.

"Oh, no!" I thought to myself. "I've made *another* Peruvian girl cry."

After she composed herself, Estella gently placed the photograph on a bed and took me by the upper arms. Standing strong, she looked up into my eyes and began to speak a rush of sentiments. Spanish words flew forward in a current of emotion. Despite my best efforts to stay afloat linguistically, most of it went over my head. When she finished, Estella gave me a hug, picked up the photograph and left the room.

I turned to Lucy and Vanessa in a daze. "Did you catch any of that?"

"She's grateful," Lucy told me, smiling. "She said nobody has ever done anything like this for her before."

"Oh ... good," I responded, still a bit overwhelmed by the

response. I excused myself from the girls and shuffled off to prepare my backpack for the bus ride to Lima. ☺

ON THE FLOOR of my room, I gathered all my belongings: a ratty quick-dry towel, my paint-stained boots, a small set of toiletries, a couple of tattered books and my worn-out clothing. As I tucked the gear into the depths of my backpack, I thought about Estella's tears. I had done something good, right? Are tears a reasonable gauge? How do we ever really know? Goodness, it's a tough thing to measure.

I could say one thing, though, with relative confidence. Whether I was presenting a family portrait or getting a free cooking lesson, these acts of giving and receiving went beyond the transactional mechanics of "work-exchange" or the lopsided charity of "volunteerism." In that dusty neighbourhood, I found something that I was seeking intuitively but didn't even know it: the feeling that I had connected with another human being. ☺

APRIL

Buenos Aires, Argentina

Buenos Aires is fondly remembered as the city where, within five hours of landing, I was vomiting and crying alone on a bathroom floor.

Allow me to explain.

Before arriving, I was brimming with enthusiasm for Buenos Aires. I had heard countless rumours about the Latin American city that hinted at cutting-edge street art, succulent steaks and robust Malbec wine. But perhaps the biggest legend of all was the impassioned, dramatic dance — the tango. After a month in the Costa Rican jungle and another in a sleepy working-class neighbourhood in Peru, I looked forward to the promise of a city setting. Buenos Aires, I told myself, would be cosmopolitan and modern, emotional and amorous.

It was love at first sight and lust at first smell. As soon as I stepped off the plane, I noted a distinctive fragrance lingering in the sweet humid air. It was the kind of sultry aroma — notes of perfume and sweat — that could only come from a sexy population. Sure, I hadn't arrived with a specific objective to end up between the sheets with a local. But at the same time, I wouldn't say no to an unplanned love affair. If the theme of the year was

97

"try to be helpful," then I saw nothing wrong with a bit of extra-curricular missionary work, if you know what I mean.

Without delay, I headed directly to historic San Telmo — the oldest and most seductive *barrio* (borough) in the city. After conversing with the radiant receptionist at the hostel where I was booked for a few nights, I dropped my bags in a clean, modern-looking dormitory room. Back on the street, I wandered unhurriedly through cobblestone alleys, taking photos and soaking in the romantic colonial architecture and colourful, energetic street art. Along the sidewalk, the *porteños* — people of Buenos Aires — exuded a sensual confidence and creative style that referenced Paris, but with spicier Latino flare. Chins were held high. Dresses were cut above the knee. And any two individuals passing each other on the sidewalk risked breaking into dance.

As much as I'd like to believe otherwise, one cannot survive on romantic wonderment alone. My stomach started to growl, causing my attention to shift from the eye candy to the multitude of local cafés. It was difficult, however, to commit to one. Call me sentimental, but I wanted my *first* Buenos Aires bistro experience to be memorable. That's when an understated bar called La Esquinita caught my eye.

Like the *brasserie* in Trujillo, the café had a series of vintage photos on the wall. But it felt a bit more relaxed, with a long wooden bar, the sound of wistful accordion music pouring through a muffled radio and a floor that looked like an oversized black and white checkerboard. It was perfect. The café embodied a few of the qualities I prefer in a lover: classy and understated, with a never-ending supply of booze. And yet I felt shy.

With my lower lip between my teeth, I stood gazing at a menu in the window, occasionally glancing inside. There didn't appear to be any other touristy-looking individuals at the tables, which is why I hesitated. I didn't want to intrude upon a watering hole that was sacred territory for the locals.

"Bienvenido!" The bartender had caught me staring and called from behind the counter. He was an older gentleman with leathery skin, a moustache and a dishtowel over his shoulder.

Quietly taking a place beside the window, I opened a menu. But before I even had the chance to consider my options, the rugged bartender approached and asked what I wanted to drink.

"Algo de tomar, señor?"

It was a very logical question. I was, after all, in a bistro and people usually drink things in bistros. And yet I was caught off guard.

"Uh ... una cerveza por favor." I didn't know if I actually wanted beer, but I had blurted out the first thing that came to mind. Like a kid going in for his first kiss, I was nervous and wanted to appear suave or, at the very least, not inept.

"Litro o pequeña?" he inquired, motioning to the different sizes. A full litre seemed daunting, so I opted for the smaller option. And with that first drink order, I learned something important. In Buenos Aires, even the small beers are big beers. My *pequeña cerveza* came in a 650-millilitre vessel, along with a frosty mug and a selection of chips, nuts and other snacks.

Happily, I filled up the glass, inhaling the smell of lager. The first mug of beer went down easily, as did the second and then the third. Apparently I was thirstier than I thought. Within 10 minutes, the entire bottle of beer had been emptied.

Instead of staying for a second round, I thought I'd see what else the city had in store. I also wanted to find something more substantial than peanuts to eat for dinner. So, after settling the bill, I swayed out of the bar with my head feeling light. Dusk had fallen. "Oh, Buenos Aires, you minx!" I murmured into the evening air. "Where have you been all my life?"

After teetering a few blocks, I realized how worn out I was from the long overnight journey. The sweet embrace of my bunk bed gradually became more appealing than the romance of the streets. But before turning in for the night, I needed a proper meal. A block away from the hostel, I popped into a generic Italian diner. I devoured an enormous plate of ravioli with fresh homemade tomato sauce, mopping it all up with bread and butter. Then I paid the bill and headed straight for my hostel.

The gurgling in my stomach began as soon as I passed through the front doors and into the lobby. My hands suddenly turned clammy, and a recognizable halo of sweat formed on my forehead. Breathing deeply, I approached the front desk, where they kept the room keys. I needed the key to my room, and I needed it fast. The same radiant receptionist suddenly seemed less attractive as she chatted long-windedly with two new arrivals sporting Norwegian flags on their overloaded backpacks.

"Oh yes, you'll definitely want to check out the San Telmo antique fair tomorrow," she counselled, pointing to a square on the map. "And are you looking for any restaurant recommendations tonight?"

Oh God, no. The contents of my stomach began to claw at my esophagus. This *wasn't* the time for a tourist tutorial, especially one relating to food. The receptionist must have seen the agony written on my face. She kept talking to the Norwegians, but reached behind her into the cubbyhole marked "Room 508" and grabbed the electronic key. With a wink and a smile, she handed me the rectangular plastic card. I responded with a grimace and an audible stomach gurgle.

At the elevator, I jabbed the button for the fifth floor and waited a couple seconds. And then I pushed it again. And again. Why was this happening? What had I eaten? Why on earth was my room on the fifth floor? Finally the elevator arrived. With my eyes closed, I clutched onto the railing as it ascended. As the elevator doors opened, I raced forward and was swiftly outside the dorm room. I thrust the key card aggressively into the door.

"*BLEEP!*" The little lockbox flashed a red light, rejecting the key. I withdrew the plastic card, accidentally dropping it through my moist fingers. If I had been capable of speaking, I would have unleashed a violent stream of obscenities at the lock. But my teeth were clenched. Something was about to come forth, and it wasn't words.

I turned the key card around. I tried it upward, backward and upside down. After several failed attempts, the lock turned. I hurled the door open, darted directly to the bathroom and fell to my knees with my head over the toilet. The clean, white walls of the bowl became lined with a putrid mixture of beer and ravioli, infused with peanut chunks and the greasy shimmer of butter.

The silver lining of the situation was that I was alone. No other travellers were in the room to witness my sudden entrance and the subsequent echoes of a messy spewing session.

As I lay crumpled beside the toilet, I told myself to breathe. Tears streamed down my cheeks from the physical intensity of the vomiting. The cool tile of the bathroom floor provided comfort and relief to my burning face. ◌

OF ALL THE cities in the world that I dreamed of visiting, Buenos Aires was at the top of the list. Even from Canada, I could sense its sex appeal. I envisioned myself sipping full-bodied Argentine wine in smoky *milongas*, while heart-tortured couples acted out feverish tangos in front of my table. There was never any doubt that April needed to be devoted to excavating the quixotic mystery of Argentina's capital city.

The challenge, however, was finding a meaningful way to fit into the urban grandeur. How would I devote my time? Again, I turned to the Internet to research options. The obvious choice was to teach English. Most non-English speaking countries, I was discovering, were happy to have free assistance when it came to learning Shakespeare's language. That said, I didn't particularly want another month of teaching, despite the fact that I had appreciated my classroom experiences in Peru. Meanwhile, the other volunteer opportunities listed on work-exchange networks were essentially glossy pre-packaged voluntourism adventures and therefore out of my price range — and realm of personal interest. Finding a work-exchange arrangement in Buenos Aires was more difficult than anticipated.

Yet there had to be someone in the city interested in having an extra set of hands in exchange for room and board. Back in my day-to-day life in Canada, I would have been delighted to shelter a traveller in exchange for having a personal gopher. *You can cook me meals? Sure, here's a couch to crash on! You're offering to clean my toilet? Great, I'll make sure you have all the coffee necessary keep you fuelled! You're willing to walk the dog and pick up the dry cleaning? Wonderful, I don't have a dog and I don't own anything delicate enough for dry cleaning.* BUT YOU'RE HIRED ANYWAY! In my mind, it felt like a no-brainer.

With just days before my arrival to Buenos Aires, I had no host confirmed. So I posted an advertisement on the popular classifieds website, Craigslist. The ad highlighted some of my previous experiences, and I laid out my offer: I had 25 hours per week to allocate to a community-minded project or open-minded person in exchange for room and board. Within hours of posting, I received a response:

> *"Hi Daniel. I saw your ad, and I am looking for a volunteer to help me with the web development of my blog and to do market research in Argentina. If you want, you can come and meet me when you get here to Buenos Aires. I am in Almagro. Cheers! Carolina"*

Fantástico! After a few email exchanges, we established that Carolina's needs and my skills aligned perfectly. She was trying to develop a blog for hospitality professionals in South America, and I just happened to have experience in creating web content. Although blogging and market research weren't as stimulating as, for example, offering my amateur services in an Argentine wine-tasting focus group, Carolina's proposal was infinitely better than nothing. Plus, she invited me to stay at her home.

Perhaps the symbiosis sought in my travels would be found in Buenos Aires. ☼

AFTER SCRAPING MYSELF off the bathroom floor and washing regurgitated pasta and peanuts off the toilet seat, I brushed my teeth, put in some fresh earplugs and crawled dejectedly into the hostel bunk bed. What followed was a series of cold sweats, shivers, body aches and other flu-like symptoms. Eventually, I fell into a fidgety sleep that lasted a full 12 hours.

102

In Costa Rica and Peru, I had regularly been waking up at dawn. But that first morning in Buenos Aires, the sun was high when I finally felt stable enough to face the day. Moving very slowly, I headed down to the hostel cafeteria, wanting to take advantage of whatever remained of the free breakfast. (A low-budget traveller must stretch his peso!) Mercifully, my stomach accepted a small glass of water and a couple slices of fruit without an encore performance of the projectile-vomiting fiesta.

As I sucked on a juicy wedge of watermelon, I began to file through the events of the last 36 hours. What could have caused such a physical reaction? Did Argentine beer have some sort of super-potent effect? Had my dry months in Costa Rica and Peru made me a cheap drunk? Why did this exhaustion in Buenos Aires feel so different than normal jet lag? Three pieces of watermelon and two cups of coffee later, it hit me.

The relocation from Peru had been more gruelling than any of the previous transfers. In my quest to obtain the cheapest possible airline ticket, I had booked a flight path that included an eight-hour layover in La Paz, Bolivia. There I spent the night curled up in the fetal position on a concrete floor. And after I scraped myself off the ground to board my connecting flight, I read a placard on the wall that said the airport was famous for its altitude. At just over 4,000 metres above sea level, it was second only to an airport in Tibet for the highly sought-after claim as the highest commercial runway in the world. More savvy travellers will tell you that elevations of just 2,000 metres are associated with fatigue, nausea, light-headedness, vomiting and general physical malaise.

A little condition also known as "altitude sickness."

In other words, I had flown from seaside in Lima to 4,000 metres in La Paz then directly back down to sea level in Buenos Aires. My "*pequeña* hangover" was probably not the sole result of too much beer. Nor was it ravioli food poisoning. It was Bolivia's fault. Or better yet, the side effect of a discount ticket from a bargain-basement travel website.

With a diagnosis in mind, I researched the treatment options for altitude sickness. According to the Internet, the first thing that health professionals advised *against* was alcohol, as it slows the heart rate and subsequently makes the symptoms more severe. Well, I had already failed wonderfully at that. The best remedy for altitude sickness was basically time, rest and hydration. One source cited that indigenous cultures of South America used caffeine and a high-calorie diet to accelerate recovery. This suggestion appealed tremendously, so I decided to immediately implement a three-step treatment program:

1 *Refrain from moving, remain horizontal if possible.*

2 *Drink coffee.*

3 *Eat anything I desired, preferably large quantities of decadent treats.*

So that afternoon, apart from slowly wandering through the San Telmo antique market, I spent much of the day reclining and indulging in the occasional *café con leche* — now this was a therapeutic strategy I could handle! In fact, in my curative lethargy, I imagined the message that I would have needed to compose if I had arrived to Argentina on a work assignment:

"Hi boss! Buenos Aires is absolutely beautiful. But I've got a mean case of altitude sickness. I'm going to need to spend the day laying horizontally at the local café with an espresso IV and a steady supply of alfajores cookies. Have a nice day at the office!"

In hindsight, that disastrous South American flight path had taught me two invaluable lessons. Firstly, when it comes to air travel, the cheapest ticket is not always the best ticket. And secondly, when it comes to recovering from altitude sickness, I'm a champ.

Travel, such fertile ground for learning. ☺

WITH A BOX of baked goods in hand, I tapped on the large iron door of a grey brick building that was just one in a row of mismatched houses. I didn't know what I had purchased at the bakery, but the little pastry nuggets were colourful, so I assumed they'd make a nice first impression. A dog's bark acknowledged my presence, followed by the sound of someone's feet shuffling toward the door.

More than 48 hours had passed since my arrival, and I was back on my own feet. The symptoms of the unanticipated altitude sickness had subsided, and a renewed pulse of enthusiasm was coursing through my veins. I was in Buenos Aires — adventure awaited! One of my first exploits was to navigate the underground network of rails, known as the *Subte*. I needed to find my way from the hostel to Almagro, a neighbourhood located west of the central business district but still within the heart of the city. Compared to some of the other *barrios*, Almagro was less prominent, a middle-class blend of residential buildings and commercial spaces. After emerging from the busy Monday-morning subway, where my body was pressed against crowds of attractive Argentines, I stepped onto Avenida Corrientes. The street bustled with people performing their everyday activities: hauling grocery bags, riding bicycles, sipping coffee while reviewing last night's soccer scores.

The door creaked open, revealing a beautiful young woman with boisterously curly dark hair. She restrained a panting pit bull with a hand that flashed red painted fingernails.

"*Hola!* Are you Daniel Baylis?"

"No," I replied, "but I do play him on the Internet."

My attempt at humour drew a smile.

"You must be Carolina?"

"That's me," she responded. "Sorry about Rico. He's just eager to meet everyone. Please, come in." Through a short hallway, Carolina led me into an open living room with a high ceiling and ornate wooden doorframes.

"Welcome to my home. Would you like some yerba maté?"

"I've never tried it before. So, why not?"

"It's sort of like tea — but stronger, earthier. You are in Argentina, so you must try it."

"Well, then make mine a double."

Carolina smiled again and then motioned for me to take a seat at the dining table in the middle of the living room. She disappeared into the adjoining kitchen to boil water and fetch the dried yerba maté mixture. As I waited, Rico gave my hand a thorough tongue washing. A few minutes later, Carolina returned with a steamy kettle in hand. She proceeded to show me how to prepare and serve maté in the traditional Argentine method. The herb mix was poured into the customary maté gourd and then filtered through a metal *bombilla*. With caution, I sucked the steaming beverage through the straw and into my mouth. It had a bitter, herbaceous flavour. The experience was perhaps best compared to running through a dry, grassy meadow with my mouth open. I didn't hate it, but it would have difficulties competing with my daily coffee ritual.

"Well, that's ... *unique*," I said, trying to offer up something positive.

"For some people, it's an acquired taste," Carolina reassured me.

As we sipped our maté, we chatted about her project — a startup business devoted to students in the hospitality industry. After her own successful experiences working hospitality jobs in France and New Zealand, she wanted to help Argentine students develop their portfolios and even match them with international internships. When Carolina spoke, her whole body communicated: her eyebrows danced and her hands acted as if she might be directing traffic. This zeal quickly put her in my favour, and so I confirmed that I'd be willing to assist with photography, video shoots, web strategies and anything else that could help breathe life into her business.

After our gourds were drained and the conversation had reached a natural pause, Carolina rose to her feet and offered a tour of the rest of the house. With Rico at our heels, we investigated the rooms: an office with a communal work table where Carolina ran her business, a modest kitchen featuring a full-size fridge and propane stove, a tiled bathroom with a toilet and shower, and three bedrooms — two of which were rented to students, and one that was reserved for Carolina and her husband. The house was spacious and it felt social, although it was decorated minimally.

Before I arrived, Carolina had informed me that all the bedrooms were presently occupied, but she had accommodation available on the roof — an option that had piqued my curiosity. My own private rooftop abode nestled within the Buenos Aires skyline? Yes please! After seeing the rest of the house, we eventually made our way up to my sleeping quarters. Over in the far corner of the roof was a small, dilapidated shack.

"This is actually a tool shed," Carolina said. "But we've cleared it out just for you." She opened the little wooden door, and we ducked inside.

The space was not much larger than a dumpster. But it was equipped with ample shelving, a dangling light bulb and a single foam mattress. After surviving the disarray of The Shaft in New Orleans and managing just fine in a tent for several weeks in Costa Rica, I found the little rooftop hovel rather quaint. I immediately agreed that I'd return the next day with my gear and give it a try. There was something whimsically adventurous about spending a month sleeping on a rooftop — in a tool shed. ◌

AN EVENING BREEZE blowing from the Río de la Plata caused the treetops in Plaza Dorrego to sway gently. At street level, however, the city air was calm. Throughout the day the autumn sun had baked the cobblestones, and now they were gradually releasing heat as night took over. If I were a braver soul, I might have walked barefoot across the plaza, just to feel the warmth against my soles. The night in Buenos Aires provided beguiling opportunities.

During the daytime, the metropolis was your typical blend of concrete skyscrapers, aggressive taxicabs, colourful newspaper stands and balding men in business suits. After sunset, on the other hand, Buenos Aires stood in its own category. Like a flower that blooms at night, it became more awake, more enigmatic. Accordion melodies poured from cast iron balconies. The fragrance of grilled meat and cologne drifted in the air. Women's jeans weren't simply pulled on, they were painted on. The silhouette of two figures embracing in a narrow alley was a standard sighting. Buenos Aires — the urban manifestation of seduction.

And if Buenos Aires was the seductress, then the renowned Plaza Dorrego was the rose between her teeth. With cobblestone charm and stately trees, the square was debatably ground zero for classic Argentine cuisine and culture.

At one of the many al fresco bistros, I settled at a small wooden table for a grilled steak and a glass of Malbec. Despite the glow of streetlights, I could still see a star-speckled sky through the canopy of leafy trees. This was the Buenos Aires that I had dreamed of. At least a frame of it. A snapshot.

As if on cue, to punctuate the scene, the restaurant's three-piece jazz band began playing a smooth rendition of "What A Wonderful World." Had the song been included in a romantic film, I might have rolled my eyes at the clichéd soundtrack. But there was no need for cynicism at Plaza Dorrego — at that specific moment, the world felt exactly that: wonderful.

I took a sip, letting the smoky wine roll around in my mouth, savouring it and watching the legs roll down the side of the glass. Eventually, the band finished their set and the bass player toured through the audience with his fedora turned upside down. I dropped a few Argentine pesos inside. It seemed reasonable to give to people who made beautiful music, to those who were increasing the world's "wonderful" quotient.

With my plate cleared, I stood up, settled the bill and began to slowly wander back to the hostel. But before I disappeared down an alley, I paused and turned back for one more view of the plaza, of the dancing treetops, of the starlit sky. And, for a brief moment, I slipped off my sandals and took a moment to be still. The warmth of the cobblestones against my naked feet was as sensuous as a tender goodnight kiss. ○

With my backpack on my shoulders, I toddled out of the hostel and flagged the first taxi to come down the narrow street. The driver turned onto a main avenue that led us out of San Telmo and then eventually took a right onto a picturesque residential lane in Almagro. With the arrival of autumn, the trees had begun their annual transformation from green to several shades of gold.

In less than 15 minutes, I was knocking once again on the large iron door. Rico barked a friendly greeting. Before I knew it, I was sitting at the table with a gourd of yerba maté in my hand.

This time, Carolina's husband, a handsome Frenchman named Julien, was home. The three of us chatted leisurely about travel and life in Buenos Aires.

"I initially came here for work, but it wasn't long before work turned into pleasure," Julien said, winking at Carolina. "Years later, I'm still discovering new things about the city."

The two lovebirds had a hearty chuckle at the anecdote of my eight-hour stopover in Bolivia and its consequences on my digestive system. It's funny how disagreeable events can make for such entertaining stories.

Eventually Carolina and I got down to business. I cautioned her that there were no immediate magic tricks for establishing a successful online presence. But I did have some simple suggestions on how to use social media to help position herself as a leader in the hospitality industry. Throughout that first afternoon, I fired question after question about the direction of her business. *What is your purpose? Who do you want to attract? Where do you see yourself in five years?* Carolina's animated responses indicated that she was pleased to participate in the activity. By late afternoon, we had outlined some concrete steps to improve her website's content and consistency.

"Daniel!" she exclaimed jokingly. "You're making more work for me!"

I chuckled. "It's true. But it will all pay off."

When the sunlight outside the arched windows began to fade, we decided to call it a day. A lot of ground had been covered, and we were both tuckered out. Carolina was excited to learn more about online networking and search engine optimization. We agreed that I would lead a tutorial the next day on how to best use Twitter. Later in the week, we would talk about optimizing search engine results.

Over the course of the year-long journey, I figured that many of my tasks would be challenging or out of my ordinary routine — like painting ceilings or teaching English. And so far, they had been. Throughout much of the trip, there was an overarching theme when it came to my volunteer tasks: I often felt rather incompetent (and at times, not appreciated).

But there I was in my fourth month, doing something I had not anticipated: implementing my *actual* professional abilities. Most people would have been quickly lulled into a nap as I talked about Internet skills, but it was important information to Carolina for running her business. And after that initial session, I felt both competent *and* appreciated for the first time since leaving Canada. ○

IN THE LITTLE shack on the roof, I cut the light by pulling on the single bulb. Then I wiggled into my sleeping bag. With my hands tucked behind my head, I took a couple of long inhalations. *Penthouse living in Buenos Aires. I could get used to this.* Sure, there was an intensely chemical smell of paint fumes that I hadn't noticed when I hastily examined the shed the previous day. But I had a room all to myself. A bit of privacy was something rare for a budget traveller. And who did I know that had ever slept in a rooftop shed in Buenos Aires? Nobody, that's who. As such, I allotted myself five points for traveller bodaciousness (plus a bonus point for a rewarding first day at the new job).

After concluding in the office with Carolina, I had lingered briefly on the leather couch in the living room, waiting to see what my housemates were doing for dinner. Over the course of the afternoon, I had been introduced to the other residents: a Dutch woman living in Buenos Aires to study tango and an American guy taking a semester abroad. I wasn't waiting for anyone to feed me. It had been inferred during the first meeting that I would need to provide my own meals, and I hadn't tried to negotiate a better deal because I was simply happy to have a place to stay — but I was curious to see the procedure around meals. However, Carolina and Julien had reservations with friends, and the foreign students had retired to their rooms.

So I ventured out alone to the bustling commercial strip along Avenida Corrientes and settled at a cheap diner that served unexceptional grilled chicken. Next to me, a young couple with asymmetrical haircuts fed one another bites of cheesecake draped in *dulce de leche* as they gazed longingly in each other's eyes. After eating, I wandered further up the avenue to absorb the scenery: scaffolding, bakeries, dog poop, taxi horns, bookstores, faceless mannequins. The neighbourhood felt decidedly less trendy, but not in a bad way. Nobody was able to single me out as an outsider, so nobody harassed me. I was able to enjoy a certain anonymity.

Eventually I returned to the house, headed directly up to the rooftop and crawled into bed.

As weary as I was, the sounds of the city kept me from falling asleep. I heard traffic on the street, agitated dogs, heavy metal music from the next door neighbour. Then, around midnight, came the worst possible sound of all.

Bizzzzzzzzzzz.

I swatted at the air.

Bizzzzzzzzzzz.

For real?

Bizzzzzzzzzzz.

Bloody. Fucking. Mosquitoes.

In the jungle of Costa Rica, there had been the occasional mosquito, but they hadn't proven to be a terrible problem. I'd say the Costa Rican species of mosquito had been rather courteous compared to the vampire predators that began to swarm into that humble rooftop shed. Never in a million years would I have imagined that these pests would lurk in the urban sprawl of Buenos Aires. Dog shit and taxi horns? *Yes.* Mosquitoes? *No.*

111

One by one, they sunk their snouts into my flesh, maliciously draining not only my plasma but also the romance of my rooftop bungalow fantasy.

Not knowing what else to do or where else to go, I put in my earplugs to block out the buzzing and pulled the sleeping bag over my head in an attempt to create a protective bubble. Within minutes, I was roasting inside the sleeping bag but was too afraid to open the top of the sack. A long, suffocating night of sleepless agitation ensued.

The next morning, as the sun dawned over Buenos Aires, I unfolded myself out of the damp cocoon and staggered to the bathroom. I washed my hands at the sink and then casually glanced in the mirror.

I gasped in disgust.

Where my face used to be was a gory, pocked mask of ugliness. ☼

"WHOA!" CAROLINA EXCLAIMED with wide eyes as I walked into her office. "What happened to your face?"

"I think that rooftop shed is also an all-you-can-eat buffet for mosquitoes," I stated flatly. "Those guys were excited for some maple-flavoured blood."

"Oh no!" she exclaimed, pressing her hand over her mouth to suppress a laugh.

"Is this some sort of unspoken Buenos Aires initiation ritual?"

"No! We occasionally have mosquitoes in our room, but nothing as serious as this." Her eyes softened around the edges with sympathy.

"I'm really sorry," I continued diplomatically, "but I'm concerned about the potential for blood loss if I spend another night in that shed." By no means did I want to come across as whiny or ungrateful, but I also wanted to establish that I had my limits.

Carolina took a moment to think about the dilemma. "How about we pull a mattress into the office?" she eventually offered. "Each evening we can lay out a bed and then pack it up when we work."

The office was a high-traffic area, with people constantly passing through. This would mean a total loss of personal space: no naps if I needed one, no escapes to read quietly, no unpacking my bag and sprawling my gear. Nonetheless, it was certainly better than the little shed of horrors. Besides, I was still being hosted in an Argentine home and working directly with a local entrepreneur. On some level, this was accomplishing a personal objective.

The new sleeping arrangement, however, didn't address the mess that was my appearance. A few weeks prior in Peru, I had an unfortunate miscommunication with a barber that had left me practically bald. Now, adding insult to injury, my face was swollen and covered with ruby welts. I could easily pass as Voldemort's ugly brother. In one of the world's most seductive cities, I was on my way to becoming the antithesis of allurement. ○

CAROLINA PROVED TO be a very proud character. As we continued to develop business ideas and action plans that first week, she absorbed my recommendations with a non-expressive face. She quietly formulated her responses and then spoke with intent. Her back was constantly elongated and her chin was always elevated, not in a snobbish way but simply with nobility. If she ever decided to depart from the hospitality industry, she had just the right balance of elegance and danger for a successful career as a bullfighter.

Despite her dignified body language, Carolina was anything but hardened or inflexible. In fact, on most days she displayed her knack for hospitality by treating me to different Argentine delicacies, such as savoury *empanadas* and sweet *alfajores*. As the days passed, her persuasive abilities even managed to influence my taste buds on the merits of yerba maté. And toward the end of the first week, Carolina casually invited me to join her and some friends for a traditional Argentine *asado*, an outdoor meat-grilling get-together comparable to an American barbecue. Obviously, I accepted.

113

On the day of the party, I lost track of time wandering through the hip Palermo area where I sampled dumplings in Chinatown and got distracted by an impromptu tango event at an outdoor gazebo. When I finally returned to Carolina's house, I was exhausted. The party was in full swing without me. Up on the rooftop, a small yet boisterous crowd of folks mingled, with a merengue beat playing in the background. Having been handed a beer — from Carolina, whose crimson dress matched her lipstick and fingernails — I stood awkwardly, not knowing who to approach. Most folks were speaking in Spanish, leaving me unable to casually join the conversation. And when the guests switched to English I found myself too tired to think of clever chit-chat. Yes, I was tongue-tied despite the fact that 1) I was supposed to be a brazen world traveller, and 2) I make a living in *communications*. Eventually I grabbed a spicy chorizo and ate it by myself while flashing the occasional friendly smile. I was a socially awkward foreigner with the spotty complexion of a hormonal teenage boy.

Despite the lively atmosphere, the beer caused my eyelids to grow heavy. A short while later, I decided to call it a day. After excusing myself from the festivities, I went downstairs into the dimly lit office and prepared my makeshift bed: top sheet spread over the mattress, sleeping bag unrolled, pillow fluffed. But before seeking refuge in the bed, I convinced myself that I should go brush my teeth. I already had bad hair and bad skin, the last thing I needed was bad breath. However, as I stepped past the giant table in the centre of the office, my sandal came down on something that it shouldn't have, something unmistakably squishy. In flipping on a lamp, the source of the mushiness (and the subsequent funky odour) was revealed: a half-squashed turd muffin.

I groaned, staring at my poo-smeared flip-flop.

Are you kidding me?

Throughout the first week, I had noticed how the avenues of Buenos Aires were scattered with a higher than average amount of dog scat. But I had never imagined that the poop would find its way into a residential home — and onto the very floor where I was supposed to sleep.

I headed to the bathroom to deal with the situation. That's when I crossed paths with Carolina, who was talking to a tall man with long eyelashes and tanned, muscular arms. It was only then that I realized I was in my flannel boxer shorts, wearing one sandal and holding the other one, which was smeared with poo.

"Are you all right, Daniel?" Carolina's jaw dropped.

"Well, there's been an accident."

Employing a tone that fell somewhere between forced diplomacy and sheer humiliation, I explained what had happened. In some cultures it might have been normative to apologize profusely to a guest for the dog poop in his room. But no such apologies were offered. In her dignified way, Carolina explained that Rico would never do such a thing and that one of the visiting dogs must have been the culprit. She would ensure that the mess was cleaned up. Her composure seemed to say it all: Shit happens.

In the bathroom I rinsed off my sandal, cleaned the sink and brushed my teeth. Then I headed back to the office to finally crawl into the improvised bed. The sound of laughter from the remaining guests tumbled from the rooftop, and the office walls were repetitively illuminated with the headlights of passing Saturday night traffic. But perhaps the most notable disturbance was the sour, lingering smell of dog poop.

I stared up at the ceiling. The whole situation suddenly became painfully clear: my stay in Argentina was *not* going to be the poetic and seductive experience that I had dreamed of. It was time to re-evaluate the game plan.

Forget sexy times. I just wanted a decent sleep.

Of course I aspired to stick to my work-exchange ideals. But I also wanted to make this journey sustainable — I had to maintain my gusto for eight more months on the road. My personal objective to stay in the home of a local would need to be sacrificed. It was time to see what other sleeping options were available in the city.

Fortunately, I had a solution in mind. Just a few days previously, a friend from Canada had messaged me. Whether I wanted her to or not, she was coming to visit Buenos Aires (and me) for a few weeks. I figured I could stay with her and keep my accommodation expenses to a minimum.

My only concern was how to bring this up with Carolina. In her own way, she had been a wonderful host. If I were to pack up and go somewhere else, would I be insulting her? One should not mess with a matador. ○

OUTSIDE THE RESTAURANT, I sat on a metal chair and waited. I was jittery. I wasn't concerned about the impending video shoot; that seemed relatively straightforward. I was worried about telling Carolina that I would be moving out of her house. The issue had been gnawing at me, but I didn't know how to bring it up.

A woman strode by wearing a Burberry overcoat, holding a leash attached to a Dalmatian that had its nose thrust in the air. I rubbed my hands together and zipped up the top of my Gore-Tex jacket.

"Sorry I'm late!" called Carolina as she gracefully bounded down the opposite side of the street in high heels. She had been in meetings for most of the day, so we had agreed to meet on location. I stood up to greet her. But she stopped a couple of feet away from me. "Wait. Where's your camera?"

"It's in my backpack," I replied, pointing my thumb over my shoulder.

"Oh, good. Sorry. Ignore me. I'm just a bit nervous." It was her first time directing a video shoot. "You're not nervous, are you?"

I laughed … nervously.

"Oh, the video is going to be great. But I just wanted to talk to you about —"

"Good. No time for talking. The owner is waiting!" With that, she opened up the door to the restaurant and pushed me inside.

Indeed, the owner — a grandmother-like figure with a blond perm and a floral sweater — was waiting. Introductions were

116

made in Spanish. I smiled politely and then I got to work. The concept was fairly simple: a three-minute video interview, with some spliced B-roll to provide a visual tour of the restaurant, to be featured on Carolina's website. I could do this type of stuff in my sleep. Actually, the role of "videographer" suited me nicely because I could hide my spotty face behind the camera. From the sidelines Carolina asked the questions to the spritely granny. After we had sufficient spoken material, I wandered around the restaurant zooming in on sandwiches, napkins and artwork. Fifteen minutes later, we called it a wrap.

Back on the street, Carolina clapped her hands in delight. "That was wonderful — she invited us to come back at any time!"

"That's really great," I said, mustering up some enthusiasm. I was happy that Carolina was happy. And I figured it was my moment — or at least *a* moment — to break the news.

"My friend is arriving from Canada," I blurted out. "I've decided to stay with her in a hostel."

Carolina winced.

"What? Does this mean you want to stop working on my project?"

"No, no, no … I'm happy to help with your project. I just … well, I also want to spend time with her."

"Daniel. I understand. The floor of my office is not the best hospitality that Buenos Aires has to offer. I'm sorry I don't have something better to offer you."

"No, it's okay. You've shared what you could."

Before we could settle into any schmaltzy affirmations of our respect for one another, Carolina steered the conversation in a different direction. "Shall we go edit?"

"Sounds good."

We started walking, but she suddenly reached out and grabbed my arm a few steps later.

"Daniel, watch your step!"

I looked down. In front of me was a giant pile of dog crap.

Carolina had stopped me just in time. ☺

"Hey, Baylis!"

The voice chimed across the hostel hallway, and I turned to see a familiar face — my Canadian friend Chantal. A gush of warmth immediately shot into my heart.

"You made it!" I extended a hug.

Chantal was a big woman with a big heart. If she hadn't dedicated her life to advocating for displaced people as a refugee social worker, she was just the type of character who would have made an exceptional blues singer. Many years previously, we had been introduced through a mutual friend and quickly bonded over many similar interests: eclectic music, international food and, perhaps most notably, world travel. Chantal had voyaged extensively through Europe, Africa and Asia, but she had yet to visit Latin America. So when I told her about my intentions to spend a year seeing the world, she warned me she'd be joining for one of the legs of my adventure. Knowing that my first commitment was to the host organizations, I hesitated to extend an "open invitation" to friends and family. But Buenos Aires was a big city with plenty to offer visitors. I knew that even if I weren't always available, an independent world traveller would easily be able to keep herself occupied. And now that Chantal was standing before me, I realized how soothing it was to see a friend.

So there we were, two Canadian friends standing in an Argentine hostel. Compared to where I had stayed upon arriving in the city, this new place was closer to the central business district. Even though I was enamoured of San Telmo, I liked the idea of sampling different accommodations in various neighbourhoods. So I had no objections when Chantal had made the reservation.

We nabbed our key from the receptionist and ascended five flights of stairs to our room. With two narrow beds and mysterious stains on the wall, the room might have been described as dingy by someone with more refined tastes. But after what I had been through with mosquitoes and dog poop, it seemed perfectly welcoming to me. Plus there was a big window that opened onto a gravel rooftop, which provided an ideal vantage point to see the city.

"How was your flight?" I asked as I dumped my stuff onto one of the beds.

"Long. I'm exhausted. I just want to go to sleep." Chantal was never one to sugarcoat her true sentiments. "But first, can I just tell you how badly I got scammed in that taxi ride from the airport? The driver took some sort of weird route and ended up charging me 500 pesos!"

This was the equivalent of $100. The tariff from the airport shouldn't have been more than 200 pesos. "So what did you do?"

"Nothing. I paid the bastard. I was too exhausted to argue." She rolled her eyes with self-retribution, proving that even the most seasoned travellers were not immune to scams.

"Ouch. Well, it looks like all tourists get a special welcome to Buenos Aires," I stated. "I've got a personal list of initiations." She had heard about the altitude sickness and mosquito bites, but not yet about the dog poop.

"Let's hope that's the worst of it. This *is* my holiday."

For Chantal, the two-week trip to Buenos Aires was pure escapism. Back in Montreal, her average work day consisted of sitting in a small windowless office listening to first-hand accounts of rape, violence, political persecution and a myriad of other horrors that cause people to flee their home countries seeking amnesty abroad. (Like I said, she would make a wonderful blues singer.) A change of scenery in Buenos Aires was a well-deserved opportunity to recharge.

Before heading to bed, however, we climbed through the window and sat on the roof, chatting casually about the things we wanted to see and do in the coming days. Eventually, our conversation subsided and we simply sat in silence. Beyond us, at the edge of the rooftop, stretched an array of twinkling city lights. I bet if one were to look at Buenos Aires from above, they would see a sort of micro-galaxy of streetlights and neon signs. In a way, we were part of a constellation. ✛

I HAD BEEN sleeping for less than an hour when a fiery sting on my left shoulder woke me up. I switched positions and tried to go back to sleep but couldn't. It itched. I scratched. It itched some more. I scratched some more. Eventually, when I couldn't take the irritation any longer, I jumped out of bed and went to the hostel bathroom to inspect my body in the mirror. My arms and neck were covered in a bumpy rash of bright pink lumps.

"What's happening to me?" I exclaimed as I dashed back into the room and flipped on the light.

"Wha— what's going on?" Chantal said squinting, her eye mask pushed onto her forehead.

I turned to inspect the single bed where I'd been sleeping. To my horror, under the fitted sheet was a flock of little black bugs crawling across the mattress. Wobbly, Chantal rose from her own bed and joined me as I hovered over the menagerie of creepy-crawlies. She reached down and popped one of the critters with her fingernail. Blood burst forth.

"Dude, those are bed bugs."

"You're joking, right?"

She wasn't.

For a moment, we had no idea what to do. Like a couple of zombies, we stood over the mattress staring blankly. "I guess I'll go down to the reception," I finally concluded. I turned, left the room and descended the five flights of stairs to see what could be done.

The dozy fellow at the front desk seemed unfazed. He stated unapologetically that there were no other beds but that he could give us clean bedding. With fresh sheets tucked under my arm, I stomped back up to the room. In the meantime, Chantal had inspected her own bed and found a few stray bugs.

"What are we going to do?" asked Chantal in the most despondent tone I'd ever heard from her. In our dazed states of exhaustion and dread, we were officially the Tweedledum and Tweedledumber of the budget travel world. I suggested that we change the sheets, shower and then try to go back to sleep. We could deal with the situation tomorrow. But the ever-pragmatic Chantal pointed out that this Band-Aid solution would ultimately prove ineffective. Bed bugs do not, in reality, flee in fear of clean sheets and the smell of rosemary-mint shampoo. There was no option but to seek a room elsewhere.

I willed my brain to come back to life and figure out an alternative. The hostel where I had coped with my altitude sickness during my first nights in Buenos Aires had been clean and reasonably priced, and I estimated that it was only a 10-minute walk away. I rummaged through my backpack for their phone number and dialed. No such luck—fully booked. However, they were able to recommend another place just a few blocks away from our current location. So I hung up and called. Thankfully, this third option had rooms available.

At approximately 1:45 a.m., Chantal and I stumbled down the stairwell loaded with our possessions. After administering the evil eye to the remorseless receptionist, we exited the building and spilled into the night. The city's twinkling lights that had held our gaze just a couple of hours earlier seemed significantly less splendid now. Yet the freshness of the night air successfully cooled the fever of the situation. We even managed to laugh at the absurdity of our lot.

"I can't believe we had bed bugs," I stated, shaking my head as we walked down the dark street. "I feel sort of trashy, sort of dirty. But at the same time, maybe I've just qualified for some sort of hard-earned traveller's badge."

"Yeah, I suppose. But Baylis, do you know what's better than the bed bug badge?"

"What?"

Chantal stopped and turned to look directly at me, "Not having bed bugs."

I smirked. She was right.

Maybe the idea of a "bed bug badge" was a poor attempt at finding a silver lining. After altitude sickness and mosquitoes and dog poop, I'm not sure I needed any more badges. The better silver lining was the company. I don't mean to sound like a Hallmark card, but nothing cures the sting of bed bug bites like the company of an old friend. ☺

THE MONTH GOT better. The day after our bed bug escapade, Chantal and I contacted a local apartment rental service and managed to book the cheapest furnished flat we could find. It was a tiny studio apartment in the Retiro barrio that came equipped with a couple of single beds, a functional kitchen and even a small bathtub. The apartment didn't have rooftop views or a cast iron balcony overlooking an enchanting plaza. Nothing about its generic nature screamed "Buenos Aires." But it also didn't have insects or the smell of dog poop. And for the 10 days that we stayed there, I slept well. And this made a world of difference in how I was able to relate to the city.

In my leisure time, Chantal and I were eager tourists who simply surrendered to whatever possibilities came up. We wandered through the tombs of the Recoletta cemetery until we came across the resting place of Argentina's sweetheart, Eva Peron. We ambled through the colourful alleyways of La Boca to the classic sounds of Carlos Gardel pouring from shop stereos. We took a day trip across the Río de la Plata to the utterly charming town of Colonia in Uruguay. We learned about *gaucho* culture — the South American version of the cowboy — during a visit to an *estancia* in the grassy countryside. We rode bicycles, visited markets and ate well.

I was having an adventure, but it was not like what I planned or expected. During my first three months, I had been a volunteer first and a tourist second. Those roles became reversed in Buenos Aires. I honoured my commitments to Carolina, but the most enjoyable times of the month were not actually spent giving social media tutorials or talking about business strategy or shooting a video. They occurred while watching a gaucho waltz with a horse to the background music of a pan flutist playing a Celine Dion song (random, yet true). Or mistakenly ordering (and eating) cow's tongue at Bar El Federal. Or giggling to the point of tears after Chantal was accidentally sprayed in the face with the hostel's bidet. This gallivanting was a sea change. I had to remind myself that I was *allowed* to be silly and I was *allowed* to be a tourist. In one of the most beguiling cities of the world, I was permitted to find my "meaningful experiences" in the same way all the other foreigners did: following the advice of guidebooks, reading restaurant reviews, taking organized tours, sleeping in spaces that were not actual homes.

I loosened my grip on the reins. The downside was that April became more fragmented than the previous months. Over the course of my stay in Buenos Aires, I slept in eight different rooms, rarely ate a home-cooked meal and didn't give Carolina as much time as I would have liked. The upside was that the more I stopped trying to orchestrate a specific type of adventure — *where's my grand romance?* — the more content I became.

The second half of the month raced by. Before I knew it, Chantal was jetting back to Canada, and I had only a few days left to bid a final farewell to Buenos Aires. ○

By THE END of April, I thought I had received all the lessons that were in store for me that month.

I was wrong.

An important lesson about a very significant chapter in Argentine history happened on my second-last day in the country. I was strolling solo along Avenida de Mayo, one of the city's main arteries, in search of cheap empanadas. Distracted by midday hunger, I hadn't realized that I had crossed a street and entered into a plaza. In fact, I nearly bumped into one of Argentina's most famous buildings: the Casa Rosada (Argentina's pinkish equivalent to America's White House). This palatial mansion is better known as the famous building where Eva Peron opened the balcony window and asked the nation not to cry for her. Due to its importance, the stately building has been declared a national historic monument of Argentina.

This, however, was not my big lesson.

A protest of sorts was underway in the Casa Rosada plaza. But rather than the aggressive chants of sign-toting radicals that one might expect to see at a political demonstration, the protesters looked like they had taken a wrong turn on their way to the beauty parlour. A group of older women with white scarves wrapped around their heads were politely handing out papers. A little old lady approached me with a smile. She looked me in the eyes and offered a pamphlet with the words "Madres de Plaza de Mayo" written across it. I accepted and reciprocated with my standard means of Spanish communication: a polite grin and a nod. My stomach was growling, so I continued on my way — who has time for politics when they're hungry?

Later in the day, I came across the pamphlet when I was rooting through my backpack, so I decided to do a quick Internet search on these women with the white head scarves. The Madres de Plaza de Mayo, it turned out, were a legendary group of mothers who banded together to raise awareness about a dark chapter in Argentine history. In the 1970s and '80s, thousands of citizens vanished. People disappeared off the streets during a bleak era of state-sponsored terrorism now termed "The Dirty War." Many of the missing were leftist activists or self-identified communists, while others were government officials taken as prisoners by the left wing in retaliation. As the organization's title suggests, the Madres de Plaza de Mayo are the mothers and grandmothers of the thousands of individuals who vanished during this period.

Most historians would agree that The Dirty War is the dimmest part of Argentina's past. There have been reports of protestors and communists sent to government-led concentration camps, where cases of torture and sexual assault were widely documented. Pregnant women who were arrested were given caesarean sections and had their babies stolen from them. Other detained individuals were said to have been drugged, put in helicopters and thrown into the ocean. It was an intentional and systematic attack designed to decimate a segment of society. As such, it has officially been labelled as genocide.

I share these words, these nuggets of information, like I have become some sort of expert on The Dirty War. But I'm not. Google was there to spare me the embarrassment of asking someone about it and subsequently exposing my ignorance — even after having been in Buenos Aires for nearly a month.

At the time, I chastised myself. *How could you not have known about The Dirty War?* But as much as I would have liked to have offered myself a more valid excuse, my apologetic response was simple: *I'm sorry. I just didn't.*

One of my favourite university professors had a wonderful phrase that she used often in her lectures: "You don't know what you don't know." The ratio of what I know about the world versus what I don't know about the world bends exorbitantly toward obliviousness. For me, I had to literally be in Buenos Aires to learn an important lesson about Argentine history.

If I had learned about the Madres de Plaza Mayo in another manner, would the knowledge have resonated in the way it did? Is there anything more powerful than an elderly woman looking you in the eyes, requesting that you not forget? Little did that woman in the white scarf know, she hadn't simply provided a lesson about a tragic event but she also reminded me why I left home in the first place:

Travelling is vital because it exposes blind spots. ○

MY PARTING WITH Carolina was respectful but unsentimental. In her dignified way, she did not fuss or make a scene but sincerely wished me well on my further explorations. Although my volunteer working hours were diminished during April, I could see that my potential for personal impact had been perhaps the greatest so far that year.

Carolina might remember our coaching sessions.

Or she might not.

But she *will* remember me as that guy who spent the night in the shed of horrors and then interrupted her party with a poo-smeared flip-flop. And this made me realize there was something innately more potent when engaging one-on-one. My classified advertisement had been a whisper into the wind. It had proven, in its own little way, that the world's serendipitous workings could bring people together. ○

BUENOS AIRES IS fondly remembered as the city where, within five hours of landing, I was vomiting and crying alone on a bathroom floor. Then had my face decimated by mosquitoes. Then stepped in shit. And then got assaulted by bed bugs. I began the month with pep in my step, but my spicy strut quickly slowed to a shoulder-hunched limp. In Argentina's simmering culture, I had hoped to be a passionate protagonist comparable to the likes of Don Juan. But the universe had assigned me a different role. For most of April, I felt like the Quasimodo of Buenos Aires.

Yet I managed to scrape together a few minor lessons about travel from that early series of unfortunate events. From the layover in Bolivia, it became clear that the cheapest ticket is not always the best ticket. After walking through the streets in the middle of the night escaping from an insect-infested hostel, I was reminded that hardships are less hard when I have someone to suffer with. The Madres de Plaza Mayo inspired me to learn more about Argentine history. These elderly women taught me that simply being present in foreign lands had the potential to show me the stuff I didn't know.

By the end of the month, I had yet to sleep with anyone other than bed bugs. My clichéd fantasy of finding a Latin lover went unsatisfied. But with a bit of time (and a bit of wine), I grew to be pleased with what I did have. Yerba maté lessons. Warm cobblestones under my feet. Silver linings. And on occasion, a bed where I could sleep uninterrupted. I made my reckoning. What other choice did I have — to be bitter?

Nah. Who needs bitterness on top of bug bites?

Buenos Aires continues to be my half-finished love affair. The old flame that still flickers. The one where, in retrospect, you ask yourself nostalgic questions: *Could we be good together? What if we tried again? Should we?*

But this is the way things often transpire. Whether you're examining a city or a love affair or even a tango, there are always deeper layers to uncover. There are new territories to explore. There are different steps to master. And this all takes longer than a month. Perhaps a true love affair with a city lasts a lifetime. ☺

MAY

Cape Town, South Africa

It was good of Nelson Mandela to greet me as I stepped off the airplane in Cape Town.

I smiled back at him, casually tipping my tweed fedora (which I had purchased on my final day in Buenos Aires). As one of the world's greatest living legends, the man himself was reason enough to justify a visit to South Africa. Sure, the wild animals, stunning landscapes and world-class wines were also good reasons. But if anyone ever asks why you wanted to go to South Africa and you simply respond "Madiba" (Nelson Mandela's tribal name), there should be no further questions asked. And there he was, standing in front of me.

Okay, I should be more specific here. It wasn't the *real* Nelson Mandela who greeted me as I stepped off the plane. It was a life-sized poster of the celebrated man holding some sort of rugby trophy. And beside him was a sign that said "Welcome to South Africa."

But heck, that was good enough for me.

I was in Africa ... AFRICA! ○

THE AIRPORT SHUTTLE bus raced forward along a well-maintained freeway. I hadn't protested when the driver assigned me to the front seat, the optimum place to take in the scenery as we headed to downtown Cape Town. Yet despite my enthusiasm at having finally arrived on the continent, my immediate impression was anticlimactic — the South African landscape didn't appear terribly "African." My western stereotypes of a sunscorched, dusty, rural continent were confronted. Outside, the air was clammy and cool. The overall colour palate was an assortment of matted greys: drab multi-lane asphalt, low antagonistic clouds, and the darkness of Cape Town's mammoth landmark. Table Mountain served as a foreboding, angular centrepiece.

Despite the greyness and the ominous weather, the mood inside the shuttle was buoyant. The driver, a California-born man named Alan, took delight in pointing out various attractions to me and the other two passengers, a married couple from Alaska.

"I came here 10 years ago because I fell in love with a woman," Alan explained. "But now I'd say I'm fully South African. I stay because it's beautiful," he said as he casually pointed out some zebras on the side of the mountain.

After cutting directly through the central business district, Alan pulled over at a guest house where the Alaskan couple exited. But instead of continuing directly to the hostel where I was booked to stay for a few nights, Alan offered a quick detour.

"If you want, I'll drive you higher up the mountain for a view over the city."

"How could I refuse?"

A few minutes later, the shuttle van rolled to a stop along a road carved onto the side of the mountain. From our vantage point, we could see the waterfront and over the bay. I understood why Alan had decided to stay. The layout of the city was impressive, a contained urban sprawl of highrise buildings, winding highways and white houses with red roofs carved into hillsides. However, the man-made structures were inconsequential compared to the sheer grandeur of the elements. Tucked into a geographical nook, the city was cusped by two stunning natural barriers: a dramatic mountain range to the south and an expansive stretch of teal water to the north.

With its mountains to hike and history to learn about, Cape Town appealed to both my outdoorsy and intellectual interests. Was I nuts to have given myself only three days to explore it?

"I've always been a man who appreciated detours," Alan said, cutting the silence. "But now, let's get you to your hostel."

The van began to roll down the hill, aiming for the heart of the city. ○

THE SUN HAD set over my second day in Cape Town. I left the hostel to look for something to eat — despite my 36 hours in the city, I still didn't know exactly what South African cuisine entailed. I was determined to find out. The evening air had a nippy edge, a coolness that I had not felt since January in New Orleans. I plugged my headphones into my ears and strode down Buitengracht Street (one of the city's main thoroughfares) with 1980s hip-hop mash-ups flowing from my iPod.

Up to that point, everything had been agreeable. After Alan's generous detour, I squeezed in as much as I could: checking out the trendy boutiques and indie cafés on legendary Long Street and then strolling among the sculptures and street performers in the Waterfront District. Cape Town probably wasn't Africa's most emblematic city, but I saw it as a funky international metropolis with an African vibe. Apart from sightseeing, I had also managed to pick up extra supplies, such as long underwear and a sleeping bag liner, for my next volunteer project: an eco-lodge in the South African mountains.

As I continued down the street, there were suddenly fewer lampposts. The night became darker. The music flowing into my ears was making me feel energized, lively.

In fact, you might say I was too involved with the tunes.

That's why I didn't notice the two figures walking toward me until they were very close. They materialized out of thin air. My response to their rapid advancement was to step to my right to avoid collision. But then they mirrored my movement. That's when it dawned on me that this was not an impromptu sidewalk waltz.

They were coming for me.

A hit of adrenalin shot down my spine and into the far corners of my body.

My hands flew forward to block the impact. The two men seized my arms and yanked them over my head.

"Where's your fucking money?" one of them spat into my ear, not loud enough to attract attention but forcefully enough to indicate that they meant business.

"Okay. Okay. Okay," I blurted. "You … you can have my money."

I didn't have time to tell them where find it. The man on my right traced the line of my earphones into my pocket, reached in and ripped out my iPod. The guy on the left patted me down, discovered a bump and extracted my wallet. Still holding onto my wrist, he opened it with one hand and snatched the 800 rand I had in cash (approximately $100). Then he shoved the emptied wallet back into my hand.

And then I did something without thinking.

Looking at the guy with my iPod, I extended my free hand and shrugged my shoulders in a gesture that said, "Okay buddy, you got my money. Now, be reasonable and give the music back."

For a split second he hesitated. Pondering.

The guy quickly snapped back to the purpose of the mugging. He began running, with his accomplice following at his heels. The two assailants turned up the closest side street and were immediately out of sight. ○

I JUST STOOD there, dazed. Unaccustomed to being mugged, I wasn't sure how to respond. *Do I run after them? Do I start sobbing on the spot? Do I just continue on my search for a place to eat?* I did, after all, still have my credit card.

That's when a man stepped out of a nearby shop.

"What just happened?" he demanded.

"Two guys just mugged me."

"Where'd they go?"

"That way," I said, pointing up the street.

"Go inside my shop and close the gate!" he instructed and then ran off in the direction of the muggers.

Happy to take instructions, I did what I was told. I stepped inside and shut the cast iron gate behind me. In the middle of the loft-like room, there was a selection of armchairs, sofas and coffee tables. I sat on a velour couch and gently massaged my wrists, which had started to bruise. While a do-gooder chased after my assailants, I waited and willed my hands to stop trembling.

Minutes later, the gate creaked open, causing me to jump. The shopkeeper spilled into the store, panting, and then plopped himself on the couch across from me. In the light, I saw him clearly for the first time. He was tall and slender, with a caramel complexion, two hoop earrings, a goatee and a short Afro — a young, hip version of Morgan Freeman.

"I managed to catch up to them," he recounted with eyes wide open, "but then they split. I chased after the guy with your backpack until we got to a dead end. And then the fucking dude pulled out a knife!"

By the way the shopkeeper spoke, I could tell that he had found the chase exhilarating. But I'm not sure I would have been so amused. The guy had had a *knife* pulled out on him.

"He threw down your backpack and hopped the barbwire fence behind him. I couldn't get over the fence myself." He paused a moment to catch his breath.

I didn't respond because I was afraid he would hear my voice quiver. I was emotional. I had just been assaulted. My money and my iPod were gone. But that's not why I was crying. Bruises might hurt, but kindness makes my eyes water.

"Well," he continued, saving me from having to speak, "the bad news is that the muggers got away. The good news is that I got your backpack back." He proudly held out a green shoulder bag.

Again, I had trouble finding appropriate words. How could

I tell him that my backpack was actually still on my back? (Miraculously, the thieves had overlooked my bag, which contained a laptop and a digital camera.)

"Uh, thanks man. I really appreciate it … " I started saying, unsure if I should mention anything about the item he had rescued. Yet he would have soon realized I was actually wearing a bag and then I would have looked like a jerk for not telling him the truth. So I pointed my thumb towards the backpack that rested on my shoulders and spoke in an apologetic tone. "But it's not actually mine."

"Man, it was a decoy?!" the shopkeeper exclaimed, slapping his hands together and chuckling. He opened the bag. "Those fuckers! It's empty."

His laughter diffused my tension, and I smiled with him.

As the adrenalin slowly left my system, it dawned on me that I wasn't in your run-of-the-mill boutique. The esthetic of the space would best be described as vintage-chic. On the wall, a poster read "Calling all artists." Beside it was a clock made from a vinyl record. By the door, used clothing hung from a boudoir on wheels. A pile of faded books sat on the coffee table, while a tray of empty wine glasses waited at a bar. The concrete floor was painted burgundy. Billie Holiday was playing on the speakers. I had stepped off the cold, unfriendly streets of Cape Town and into some sort of bohemian diorama.

"By the way, I'm Dawie. Welcome to my clothing boutique and art space." He motioned around the room. "It's called Seventies-80s." ○

WHEN DAWIE ASKED if I wanted to call the cops, at first I wasn't sure whether or not it would serve any purpose. There was little the police could do at that point. The money was long gone and the iPod was probably already sold. But as I looked out the shop window and onto the narrow lane, I reconsidered. The people of Cape Town would probably want to know what happened on their streets; therefore, reporting the incident would be the right thing to do, at least for statistical purposes. So we called.

While we waited for the police to arrive, Dawie asked if I wanted a plate of food. Although the mugging had curtailed my hunger, I politely accepted, figuring that I should eventually eat something. He stepped behind the bar located in the corner of the shop and emerged two minutes later a steaming dish and a glass of red wine.

"I hope you like *pap*!"

"Sorry?"

"Pap."

"What's pap?"

"Brah! You never had pap?"

"Um … no."

"It's like porridge but made with corn." He was referring to the grainy substance under a curried vegetable dish. "Everybody here eats pap."

The smell of the food quickly made my mouth water, reminding me that at one point in the evening I had actually been quite ravenous. I took a small mouthful. It was savoury and fiery. As I ate, I became hungrier.

Halfway through my curry and pap, I looked up from my food and saw that another young man had quietly entered the shop. At first he hung to the sides of the shop, like a curious bird observing an unfamiliar creature from a comfortable distance. Dawie must have sensed my distraction.

"Oh, yeah, this is Moses. He works here."

"How's it going, brah?" Moses asked with a grin, exposing a gold tooth. He was bigger and darker than Dawie. His head was shaved and he wore an oversized sweater with baggy jeans.

"Well I … I sort of just got mugged."

"Oh, pappi!" Moses threw his head back and cringed but still maintained a big smile. "This'll be one evening you won't forget!"

Approximately 30 minutes later, a police sergeant strolled leisurely into the shop. He was tall and blond, with scars on his face. Without being invited to sit, he took a seat on the couch across from me. Dawie offered him a plate of pap and curry. The

Sergeant accepted. Before he asked any specific questions about the evening's incident, he ate. Between mouthfuls, he told Dawie, Moses and me about the time he got mugged. Or better yet, the time someone *attempted* to mug him.

"I ended up getting stitches because the guy pulled a knife on me," The Sergeant recalled in his thick Afrikaans accent, pointing to a scar on his arm. And then he sneered. "But after I finished with the fucker, he spent four months in the hospital."

Again, my eyes widened. We certainly had different approaches to dealing with muggers. Should I have been more resistant? Did this policeman think I was some sort of wimpy foreigner who allowed himself to get pushed around? Was he insinuating that I should have defended myself?

"Wow, I'll keep that in mind for next time," I replied.

After he had finished his curry and anecdotes, we got down to business with a full description of the details: where I was walking, how I was approached, the approximate time of the incident and what exactly was stolen from me. I shared the details to the best of my ability. The truth was that it had all happened so fast. I was a little hazy on the details.

"Now I'm going to ask you a strange question," The Sergeant warned. "These guys who attacked you, were they black or were they brown?"

Indeed, it *was* a strange question, primarily because all other racial options were omitted. Sitting on the couches, the three men gazed at me, anticipating my response — to my left was Dawie, who looked rather brown, and to my right, Moses, who looked rather black. Of course neither of these two guys were my assailants. But it did sort of feel like I was picking sides.

"To be honest, it was dark out. I couldn't say for sure. I'm sorry."

The one thing I knew for certain was that they had not been white. Nor did they appear to be Japanese or Mexican, for that matter. They had been darker skinned. And in the chaos of the moment, I hadn't made a point of noting where exactly the two guys fell on the pigmentation spectrum. In fact, if I were asked to pick them out of a police lineup, I'm not sure I could.

Eventually the police report was complete. The Sergeant flipped his clipboard closed and exchanged pleasantries with Dawie before turning to me.

"Take care of yourself out there." He pivoted and left the shop, returning to whatever else Cape Town would call in that evening.

Dawie and Moses offered to walk me back to the hostel. I was not about to refuse that. Along the way, they told me more about the shop, Seventies-80s, and the atmosphere they were trying to cultivate. The vision was to provide a home away from home, a space where people could come to drink a cup of tea, read a book, pick up a new vintage outfit and even perform music or spoken word. Dawie was heady and entrepreneurial, while Moses was grounded and playful. They both brimmed with optimism.

"Man, it's too bad you're leaving Cape Town so soon," Dawie said as we reached the hostel.

"I still have another day before I leave. Can I swing by the store tomorrow?"

"Ya, brah. Of course," Dawie replied.

"See you tomorrow, pappi." Moses bowed his head.

The two guys turned and headed back along the dark side-walks. I nodded at the hostel's security guard and then went directly to my room. I crawled into the bunk bed with sore wrists but a full belly. ○

THE MORNING AFTER the mugging, I headed to the hostel café for eggs and filtered coffee. I flipped through *The Cape Times* newspaper and waited for the caffeine to kick in. I had experienced whisky hangovers, and even an altitude hangover, but this was my first introduction to a mugging hangover. I knew that I wasn't in the best state of mind to make any brash decisions. And yet I felt like there was a new decision on the table.

The month of May was intended for quiet withdrawal. In fact, I had successfully organized a work-exchange in the Langeberg Mountain Range at an eco-lodge run by a Dutchman. It would be my first arrangement that required *no money*. A true exchange.

Sequestered among the hills, my responsibilities would include chopping firewood, clearing trails, hammering nails and scrubbing dinner dishes. After the urban bustle and challenges of Buenos Aires, I was eager for an outdoor setting, free of screaming sirens and swarms of citizens. Instead of people, the company would include wild porcupines, mountain tortoises, black eagles and maybe even a couple springbok antelope. The great South African outdoors beckoned, and I was eager to respond.

But the events of the previous night had caused things shift a few degrees. A completely different world had been presented to me — a side of South Africa that I never could have imagined accessing.

I felt pulled in two directions. The culture at the resort would be based around wilderness adventure, environmentally sustainable practices and space for personal reflection — all things that I valued. Yet I didn't want my experience in South Africa to suffer a similar disconnect that I had felt in Costa Rica. Specifically, I was concerned that I might miss out on the one thing I couldn't find anywhere else in the world: South African culture.

I downed the last of my coffee and then turned my attention back to the local newspaper. As I glazed over the articles, one headline immediately jumped off the page:

Cape Town Voted #1 Destination in the World

The article explained that the popular travel website TripAdivsor had recently unveiled its annual list of "Top 25 Destinations in the World." Beating out Paris, New York and Sydney, Africa's most southern city had been voted as the No. 1 place to visit. If I were looking for a sign, that headline was anything but understated. ⚬

OUTSIDE THE HOSTEL, the sky was an iridescent blue. I followed the same inauspicious route that I had taken the previous night. This time, though, I walked on the busier side of the street, not distracted by music.

As I strolled, I tried to figure out what exactly I would say to Dawie and Moses. It's not like I could walk into the shop and ask, "Hey guys, wanna be best pals for the next month?" I might as well write DORKFACE across my forehead. No, I didn't want to appear too needy or eager. These guys were cool, so my strategy would need to involve me being relaxed and carefree. Maybe they'd mention something they were working on. I could simply offer to help out. Yes, that would be the best scenario.

At Church Street, I rounded the corner and spotted Moses — in an Adidas jacket and oversized sunglasses — sitting outside the shop to oversee a sidewalk sale. On a small wooden table was an array of leather pouches. The mobile boudoir was now outside, teeming with vintage summer dresses and tracksuits.

Moses' face lit up when he saw me approaching. "Hey, pappi! How are you? Get mugged lately?" He laughed boisterously as he slapped his knee.

"Today's tally is at zero," I said with a smile. "But the day is still young."

I sat on the bench beside Moses and asked about his day. So far, in terms of sales, it had been rather quiet. But this didn't seem to bother him.

Moses asked if I would watch the merchandise. He went into the shop and returned with two cups of rooibos tea and an old atlas. For the next hour we sipped our teas and looked at maps of South Africa. Moses pointed to different areas, giving me a 101 lesson on the country's provinces. He told me about which tribal groups came from which area and what languages they spoke — Sotho, Zulu, Tswana, Xhosa and more. Moses stated proudly that he was able to understand eight languages and provided examples that displayed his abilities in linguistic gymnastics. When I tried to pronounce "Xhosa" with the correct clicking of the tongue, Moses just laughed.

Shortly before noon, Dawie arrived for his shift. Wearing a silk scarf and wingtip shoes, he sat with Moses and me to chat nonchalantly about the store. There were orders to fill. He might have to go up to Durban to find new stock. There were musicians to confirm for Friday's Love and Jazz.

"What's Love and Jazz?"

"People come to the shop for wine and live music. It's chill, man. You'd love it."

"Yeah. Well I was thinking of maybe sticking around Cape Town for a bit longer." This was my attempt to test the waters, to gauge a reaction.

"Cool."

Dawie perhaps wasn't picking up what I was putting down. So I pushed a bit further.

"Maybe I can find somewhere to help out."

It was bold as I was willing to get.

"You wanna be my bartender for Love and Jazz?"

"Sure." I responded with a grin. But then I remembered my keep-it-cool strategy and instantly wiped away the expression. I cleared my throat and spoke in a deeper voice. "I mean, if it's helpful … you know, if you don't mind."

"Mind?" he exclaimed and patted my back enthusiastically. "You just made my day!" ☺

AFTER RECEIVING THE invitation to help at Love and Jazz, I sent a regretful message to the eco-resort and explained the situation honestly. I felt guilty about backing out of my commitment. But I was navigating a tough conundrum: how often in my life would I be in the position to hang with a couple of groovy local guys in the world's top travel destination? I was fairly certain it was a "now or never" situation.

Granted, I had no idea if things would work out. You know, if I would *actually* find a way to be helpful beyond a Friday night bartending gig. But I was excited at the prospect of stepping into an entirely new realm, one where I'd get to hang out with my two stylish personal heroes. There was, of course, one drawback beyond the guilt of flaking out on the eco-resort. Once again, I was abandoning my ideals of a money-free work-exchange. I didn't want to ask anything more from Dawie and Moses, so staying in Cape Town meant paying for my own food and accommodation.

Sayonara budget!

By no regards would I be spending an exorbitant amount of cash, but for the second month in a row, I had to do some soul-searching regarding my expenditures. The money I had saved for this trip was really only enough to cover plane tickets and occasional extras; anything beyond that meant dipping into a line of credit. When making decisions that involved spending larger amounts of money, I was guided by the question "Is this worth going into debt for?" And more often than not, I couldn't justify extravagant add-ons or exploits.

By most travellers' standards, my budget was austere. There would be no gratuitous splurges on hot-air balloon trips at sunrise. I didn't even consider the popular shark-diving expeditions. Even a leisurely wine tour across the Cape Peninsula was out of the question. Whereas some people are guided by the traveller's paradigm of "I'll only be here once, so I better see and do everything," I decided to give myself permission to *not* see and do everything.

If I did splurge on something, such as a hostel bed for a month, it was because I wanted to invest in an experience that I felt I could not have in my non-travelling life back home. And this ultimately aligned with the larger goal of my trip to connect with people from around the world. My month in Cape Town became a primary example of deviating from the "work-exchange" structure to achieve something greater.

Indeed, I decided to stay and rent a room in a hostel, even if this meant incurring debt. It was a risk, an investment — and I didn't know what the return on the investment would be. But if you're going to break the bank, the best venture of all is friendship. ☼

"DANNY, CAN I ask you something personal?"

Moses had lifted off his oversized white sunglasses and was

looking directly at me. A few days had passed since the mugging. I had returned to the store each afternoon to help with menial tasks, such as rearranging displays, painting walls and holding down the fort when the guys needed to run errands. But oftentimes, Moses and I would sit outside on a bench in the sunshine and act as mannequins. We had developed a playful rapport, chatting about everything from our favourite musicians to religious beliefs. When posing questions, Moses would always look me dead in the eye, a habit that was both refreshingly friendly and uncomfortably intimate at the same time. Since our conversations always felt candid, I was taken aback when he requested permission to ask something personal.

"Um ... sure, Moses. You can ask me anything." My mind raced through all the potential subjects that he might be interested in broaching.

"Do you smoke the doobie?" he asked in all sincerity.

I chuckled. The question was far from daunting. Still, I took a moment to consider my response. *Was this an invitation to light up with him? Or a critical examination of my moral standards?*

"Well, my friend," I finally replied, "I have smoked a bit in the past. These days my drugs of choice are Merlot and espresso."

Moses smiled, his shiny gold tooth gleaming in the sun. "Yeah, brah. Red wine is good," he said, bobbing his head in approval. He brought his sunglasses back down over his eyes. A single car rolled slowly passed us. Otherwise the street was empty.

A few minutes later, I had a question of my own.

"Can I ask you something?"

"Yeah, brah."

"When the police sergeant was here, he asked me if the muggers were brown or black. What did he really mean by that?"

"Oh, Monsieur Baylis. That is a very good question."

Moses nodded his head up and down in approval of my inquiry, then took a deep breath and launched into an explanation. To be "black" meant that a person's heritage came primarily from an indigenous African group of people, such as Xhosa, Zutu or San. These folks usually spoke a native African language, as well as Afrikaans and/or English. To be "brown" was a bit more complex. It often indicated that one's origin was mixed, with roots, for example, in India or Malaysia — or even a blend of Black, Asian or European ancestry. These folks probably spoke Afrikaans and/or English, and possibly an Asian language. As he explained the racial nuances, I began to realize that, even if I had had this information before the mugging, I'm not sure it would have helped me make a more accurate assessment. These distinctions went beyond skin colour and over my head, to a certain degree.

"So you are black?"

Moses laughed, tilting his head back and clutching his stomach. "That's the first time anyone has ever asked me that," he replied. "Yeah, brah. I'm black."

My question, of course, was ridiculous. Moses was probably one of the blackest men in Africa. Yet I didn't want to make any assumptions.

Just then, a small group of college-aged white girls turned down Church Street, walking in the direction of the shop. With floral leggings and 1980s jewellery, they looked like they could have come from the streets of Brooklyn. The rack of vintage dresses and leather handbags caught their attention, and they paused to rummage as they chatted among themselves in Afrikaans. Moses greeted them with a welcoming "Hello ladies," and they nodded politely in response. A few minutes later, they departed without purchasing anything.

After the girls had disappeared down the street, I kept our conversation going.

"So what was it like growing up in rural South Africa?"

A smile took over his face. "Oh, it was wonderful."

Moses was a self-identified farm boy who grew up in the Free State, a central South African province driven economically by agriculture and mining. Most of his childhood days were spent in Hertzogville, a town where many people made a living growing maize and raising sheep. Zutu by origin, Moses had been raised as a Christian, like many black South Africans. When Moses was a boy, his father died from tuberculosis incurred from decades of working in the mines. After graduating from high school, Moses departed his hometown in search of greater opportunities. Following a short stint in Johannesburg as a welder, he came to Cape Town in hopes of bigger breaks.

One story I found particularly entertaining was how he and his friends used to kill porcupines to prevent them from eating the maize crops. They used the partially digested food from the porcupine's intestines to make medicinal tea, which apparently cured acne and other ailments. They used dogs to find the porcupines in their dens.

"Don't the dogs get quills in their mouth?" I asked, recalling a dramatic occasion when we had to rush our family pooch to the veterinarian after she had tried to pick up a porcupine with her face.

"Yeah, but the more that they get hurt, the more they learn." Moses had a way of concluding his stories with a nugget of wisdom that went far beyond his 22 years on the planet.

Wisdom, however, had yet to make Moses a rich man. While life in Cape Town provided more employment opportunities than in the countryside, it was no walk in the park. During his first year in the city, Moses lived in Khayelitsha, South Africa's largest and fastest-growing township. At nearly a half a million people, Khayelitsha is made up primarily of handmade shacks. By western standards, it would be considered a squatters' settlement — or, to use a less politically correct term, a slum. Moses' first job in the city had been as a parking station attendant, which required him to take the hour-long commuter train from Khayelitsha. This earned him just enough rand to keep himself fed. During a late-night shift at the parking station, Moses met Dawie, who eventually invited him to help out at Seventies-80s. These days, he slept under a set of stairs at the shop, hoping to earn enough commission to cover more permanent accommodations. If any money was left over, Moses intended to send it to his mother.

For a while we sat in silence, resuming our mannequin poses.

A biting wind zigzagged along Church Street. In the distance a police siren howled. The South African sun was intensely bright. But the harshness didn't seem to bother Moses. ☼

"HERE," SAID DAWIE as I walked in the door. "Wear this." It was a brown plaid clip-on bow tie. I snapped it onto my purple flannel shirt and hoped that I would look stylish enough to fit in. It was Friday night in Cape Town, and I had just arrived to Seventies-80s to begin my duty as the official bartender for Love and Jazz.

The store's lighting had been dimmed, and much of the merchandise had been pushed to the sides of the room. A crescent-shaped yellow pleather couch, along with a couple of corduroy seats, had been placed in front of a backlit curtain. Behind the curtain was an alcove that served as a performing area, where the musicians and spoken-word poets would soon begin. The wine glasses at the bar were ready to be filled. Beside them were two rotary phones with a small placard that read "Mr. President ... on hold."

Emulating that bartender I had seen on my first evening in Buenos Aires, I threw a dishtowel over my shoulder and took my place in the makeshift saloon. Eventually people started arriving, and I poured the two beverage options: Pinotage or rooibos tea.

(The evening supported my theory that outsiders always feel more included when given a task. My role of serving wine was exceedingly simple, yet important — at least to me.)

To warm up the crowd, Dawie spun a variety of jazz and disco tunes on the vinyl record player. Approximately 20 fashionably dressed students, artists and nonconformists began to gather: blacks, browns and whites. They chatted among themselves, forming little social pods that evolved as the music progressed. The event was open to everyone, but due to its niche market and limited advertising, I suspected that the people who attended were plugged into Cape Town's nightlife and artsy social scene.

Moses was working the door. When there was a lull at the

entrance, he poked his head back inside the shop.

"Lookin' good, brah!" He gave me a thumbs-up. "Almost like a real bartender!"

"Thanks Moses. You look spiffy yourself." He was wearing a coal-coloured tweed suit, complete with a trench coat that shimmered when the light hit it. On his head, he sported a grey felt top hat. And even though night had fallen on the city, his trademark oversized white sunglasses covered his eyes.

A few minutes later, the music was turned down and Dawie took the microphone.

"Welcome, friends, to another evening of Love and Jazz. Without further ado, let's get our first performer on stage."

The curtains were pulled open by hand to reveal a young man from Johannesburg dressed in blue jeans and a blazer, holding an acoustic guitar. He strummed a few chords and began to sing, but then he fumbled and stopped. He smiled bashfully and then explained to the small audience that he was nervous. Two guys in the front chided him playfully, encouraging him to try again. The singer started over, this time finding his groove and releasing a velvety melody. His voice quivered with vulnerability. It complemented the warmth of the acoustic guitar in the same way that two fragile ropes become stronger when intertwined.

The next performer was a beat-box master who produced vocal percussion with his mouth, lips and tongue. He bounced around the stage in a New Balance hoodie, taking moments to pause and close his eyes while his electronic backup track continued to pulsate a deep beat. At one point, the guy stepped outside the confines of the stage area and stood on a coffee table. The music was cut. Instead of rapping, he performed free-flow poetry, letting the lyrics alone hang in the air. On the occasions when he paused, either to catch his breath or for dramatic effect, you could have heard a pin drop in that shop.

In all, a total of six performers took their turn on the temporary stage. They ranged from soulful folk musicians to explicitly aggressive hip-hop artists to poets. All but one of the performers were male, all were black, and some performed in languages that

I could not understand.

From behind the bar, I watched in a mesmerized state. My month had been originally devoted to the great outdoors. I chose to stay in Cape Town on a gamble that I might find something that I'd never find anywhere else. And it was happening.

How bizarre and beautiful life can be. ○

WHEN I ANNOUNCED that I would be visiting South Africa, a couple of my friends back home put me in touch with their contacts in Cape Town, one of whom was a local woman named Ruth. When she heard that I was in town, Ruth immediately invited me to watch a rugby game with her crew of friends at a local sports bar. Despite the fact that I knew zilch about the sport, I happily accepted. What a perfect opportunity for an authentic South African experience: lager and rugby!

It was late in the afternoon when I ambled down Long Street in search of a place called Bob's Bar. Before I even saw the bar's signage, I could hear the blare of a television and the shouts of a boisterous crowd. Cautiously, I peeked my head through the doorway. A decent-sized crowd of folks had gathered. They stared intently at the large screen, occasionally yelling profanities at the players. Posted on a pillar was a list of 40 patented shots offered at the bar, including "The Pussy Bites Back" and "Bob's Ultimate Head Fuck." At the bottom of the shot menu, a small liability statement warned customers to drink the shots at their own risk.

"Daniel!" called a raspy voice. "Welcome to Bob's!"

I swivelled to see a happy blond woman with rosy, round cheeks. She grabbed me by the elbows and pulled me into her bosom. Then she administered a spine-cracking bear hug. I could only assume this person was Ruth. The thirtysomething Afrikaans woman was the unofficial social coordinator of a group of middle-aged professionals with an appreciation for rugby. Ruth sat me down at their table and slammed a Castle Lager in front of me within seconds.

"Listen up, you bananas!" she shouted to the entire bar. "This is Daniel! He's from Canada. He's travelling the world for a year, and on Tuesday he got mugged! Welcome to South Africa, dahhhhling!"

She hoisted her cocktail to cheers the gang and released a rowdy cackle. If the other patrons of the bar hadn't been paying attention, they were now looking to see why she was laughing.

"Hey, bitch!" a man yelled good-naturedly from the other side of the room. "Keep it down! There's a game on!"

"Fuck you!" she retorted, laughing loudly again.

"Thank you, Ruth," I said, blushing slightly at the attention, "for that detailed introduction." I wouldn't have personally introduced myself as Daniel-the-guy-who-got-mugged. But I'm sure it won me some sympathy points.

"You got the true South African welcome," said Tim, a mustachioed, copper-skinned man sitting to my left. He patted my back and continued. "Some people come to Cape Town and all they see is Table Mountain and a couple of vineyards. But getting mugged — ha! That's an authentic experience!"

"Thanks, man." I offered an honest smile and tipped my beer to him. And then I sought refuge in a bowl of potato chips.

The group's attention turned back to the game. The local favourites, the Cape Town Stormers, were playing against the New Zealand Crusaders. Because rugby is not as prominent in my corner of the world, Ruth's friends helped explain the rules to me, eagerly hoping to convert me into a Stormers fan.

From my foreign perspective, the atmosphere in the bar was equally as captivating as the rugby, if not more so. To the side of the room, some folks shot billiards. However, most were too busy hollering at the TV to focus on secondary activities. As the match continued — and as more of Bob's patented shots were consumed — the crowd grew more animated. Despite their commitment to the game, Ruth's gang made it their personal mission to ensure that my hands were continually occupied with a beer.

At halftime, Ruth dragged me outside for a cigarette and

offered her sentiments on rugby.

"Rugby brought us all together," she explained, referencing South Africa's massive World Cup victory in 1995. "It rallied every colour, every creed, every religion, everything. It made us one, and it keeps us one. And soccer, with the World Cup, has done exactly the same thing. Sport has got far more power than politics."

If Bob's Bar was an indication of the power of sport to bring people together, maybe Ruth was on to something. So far, it was the most integrated place I had visited in Cape Town. The hostel cleaning staff had been black folks, and the people at the upscale coffeehouses had been primarily white folks. But Bob's Bar was not only a mix of races but also of ages and genders and social classes. Perhaps the working-class sports bar is the South African equivalent of the healing circle.

After a second cigarette, Ruth and I headed back inside, where another fresh beer was waiting for me. Unfortunately, the second half of the game got messier for the Stormers. In every sporting match, someone walks away a loser. And on that ill-fated Saturday afternoon in May, the Stormers could not muster a win. The crowd at Bob's was less than impressed, and more expletives were hurtled at the screen.

To soothe the situation, I jokingly accepted all responsibility, citing that my rookieness to the game was clearly burdening the Stormers' ability to focus on their defensive manoeuvres.

"Well, he does have a point!"

"Blame Canada!"

"Somebody get this fool another drink!"

Outside, Front Street was becoming a melting pot of drunkards, night owls and rabble-rousers. My head was woozy from the beer, and I thought it best to excuse myself from Bob's Bar before I had any sudden craving for one of the patented shots.

"I'll see you bananas later," I said to the gang, experimenting with Ruth's lingo. They laughed at my tipsy attempt to incorporate local expressions.

"Now, let's get you into a cab," Ruth chimed. "We don't want you to get mugged again!"

She was right. The rugby game at Bob's Bar had been a riot and I looked forward to seeing Ruth again, but the charm of other authentic experiences need only be experienced once. ○

FOR THE NEXT few weeks, most afternoons were spent at Seventies-80s. I did not have a prescribed role. Instead, I would simply show up and lend an extra hand in a variety of capacities. Usually this involved hanging out with Moses and chatting about life. But I also did actual work: bits of painting, cleaning the store and taking photographs and video for promotional purposes. I tried to be helpful without being underfoot. Overall, the days were relaxed.

But not everything at Seventies-80s was picture-perfect. After a week, I began to see that the store was often empty, despite the cool concept. To its misfortune, the business was relatively isolated, a few blocks away from the bustling stores and restaurants on Long Street where most shoppers went to browse. The lack of customers was no sweat off my back. However, it did make me worry about the long-term future of the business — and for Moses' ability to earn himself a decent enough commission to help his mom or even get his own place.

In my free time, generally the mornings and the weekends, I visited many of the various low-cost attractions in Cape Town. I learned more about the apartheid area at the District Six Museum. I rode a choppy boat out to Robben Island and stood at the door of the cell where Nelson Mandela spent 18 years of his three-decade imprisonment. I wandered among the squirrels in the Company's Garden, pondered the exhibits at the National Museum, and read a copy of Mandela's memoir in the city's stately library. There was never a shortage of things to see or to do in Cape Town.

But make no mistake — hanging out with Moses was my favourite activity. ○

HALFWAY THROUGH THE month, I invited Moses to join me at one of Cape Town's theatres for a movie. He seemed enthusiastic about the idea and agreed to swing by the hostel later to pick me up. That evening I was in my room, absorbed in the task of writing to potential work-exchange hosts for July and August, when I looked at the clock to see it was 8:05 p.m.

I raced out the door.

Moses was already out on the sidewalk, waiting for me.

"Dude!" I stopped in my tracks and exclaimed. "You look *sharp!*"

He had dressed formally for the occasion, sporting a fine bowler hat, dark pleated slacks, a stylish button-up shirt and polished black loafers. The outfit was accentuated with a long umbrella, which he swung nonchalantly like a cane. It was as if he had somehow materialized from an era where people valued elegance and sophistication. Perhaps I shouldn't have been so surprised. Moses was, after all, a classy guy.

"Monsieur Baylis," he said in a sophisticated tone and motioned for me to start walking, "in my culture, it is important that a man have a nice outfit to wear. It's a tradition."

I was underdressed and unkempt, still wearing the same clothes I had randomly selected that morning: a flannel shirt and faded blue jeans. To make matters worse, my accessories were a boxy Gore-Tex jacket and Converse sneakers that were desperately in need of a cobbler — or maybe just a dumpster. I grew up on the West Coast of Canada where it is traditional to look like a dishevelled hippie. I thought about explaining this to Moses, but I feared the esthetic reference would be lost.

Our destination was only a few blocks away on Orange Street, at the oddly named Labia Theatre. (No, it wasn't one of *those* theatres.) The movie house, which was once the ballroom of the Italian Embassy, played independent local films and the latest in repertoire cinema from around the globe. It featured art deco detailing and a chocolate bar that sold homemade delicacies. The old-world ambience of the venue provided the ideal backdrop to Moses' dapper attire.

The cost for two tickets was 60 rand (approximately $9). Since I had extended the invitation, I insisted on paying. In the small theatre, we settled into a couple of wooden seats and waited for the show to begin.

"I haven't been to a movie theatre since I left Canada — over four months!"

Moses smiled politely and then said, "Yes, for me it has been around four years."

Oh, man.

Did I ever want to pull my foot out of my mouth at that moment. Judging by his sophisticated outfit, one might assume that Moses had the wherewithal to go to the cinema on a regular basis. In reality, his budget did not allow for frivolities such as movies — the fancy costume was simply borrowed from the shop. I wondered whether or not I should have brought him. *Was I dangling my own privilege in front of his face? Surely he knew that that was not what I had intended, right?* Before I could dig myself deeper into a pit of remorse, the cinema lights gratefully dimmed and the film began.

We had chosen a historical drama, *The King's Speech*, which told the story of an unlikely friendship between a man of means and a man with a lot of heart. On some level, this was apt. Occasionally, I glimpsed at Moses to see if he was enjoying himself. There was only a blank expression.

After the film finished, we headed into the warm glow of the lobby. Outside, it had started to rain.

"Brah," said Moses, "I love the movies. Thanks for that."

I was immediately relieved that he was happy.

"Now that you have taken me to the movies," he continued, "I would like to offer something in return. Before you leave Cape Town, I want to take you to Khayelitsha."

"Um … okay." It was an enticing offer, but I instinctively rubbed my wrists. "Is it safe for me?"

"Maybe," Moses paused. "If you want to see the real South Africa, it's not happening here." He motioned around the gorgeous art deco entrance to the theatre. And then he looked me in the eyes. "Danny, you need to see a township."

I nodded my head in agreement.

And with that, we pushed out of the theatre. An unlikely duo in the pouring rain. ☼

"CIGARETTE?" RUTH PUSHED a pack of Kent Special in my direction.

"Um ... sure," I responded. I've never been a committed smoker. But sometimes it can be beneficial to simply receive the gifts that people offer. "Only if you promise to tell me it will make me look more fashionable." I put my hand under my chin and posed.

"You banana." Ruth shook her head as if to disapprove of my attempt to imitate a model, but her glossy lips parted in a half-smile. Then she loosened the red silk scarf around her neck and reclined onto her elbows.

We were perched at the top of Signal Hill, one of Cape Town's prime vantage points, gazing across the southern Atlantic Ocean at a sinking auburn sun. Ruth had invited me for a ritual that she referred to as "sundowners" — a post-workday event associated with watching the sunset, but with booze. An uncorked bottle of Pinot Noir stood on the patch of grass between us. If I were to reach my arm out to measure with my fingers, the sun was about an inch away from the horizon.

"Daniel, are you religious?" Ruth tossed the question out of the blue.

I took a drag of my cigarette, exhaling a small cloud of smoke and briefly pondering the best way to answer. "Well, I went to a United Church growing up." The church I attended as a youngster, I explained, was among the more liberal forms of Christianity. "Now I suppose I'm a bit of a spiritual vagabond."

A decade ago, as I charged into my twenties with a self-righteous fist in the air, I would have responded that I was fundamentally against organized spiritual practice, that religion and the name of "God" were the root of every major war in history. Over time, however, my views of the world had softened, including those on religion. The world was mighty complex. As far as I could see, everyone had to etch out a path in this swamp of confusion that we call life. And the best that I could do for myself, I now believed, was to shift away from absolutisms and fundamentalist beliefs. I wasn't against Christianity — or cigarettes, for that matter.

"I'm a Christian," said Ruth, "but I have an appreciation for all religions. I take a bit from everything." She mentioned that she liked to participate in Ramadan. "The least I can do is give my body a vacation once a year from all the toxins I throw at it." Then she took another long drag on her cigarette.

The sun was now a quarter-inch from the horizon.

"What do you think happens to us when we die?"

This was the same woman who had yelled at someone to fuck off at Bob's Bar the previous week. Yet given the grand setting, the grand question seemed perfectly suitable. What better place to explore life's philosophical conundrums than on the side of a mountain, watching the sun sinking over the ocean? It was nearly impossible to *not* ponder the concept of eternity with the mystic glimmer coming off the boundless water. The post-mortality question was coming from a place of honest curiosity — and from a place of loss. During our first meeting at Bob's Bar, Ruth had shared that her mother had recently passed away.

I divulged to her that the question of "what comes after" derailed my life when I was a 16-year-old boy. My mind wandered to realms of existentialism, overwhelming me to the point that I could barely keep anything in my stomach for a couple of weeks. But as time marched unapologetically forward, I learned how to take any debilitating questions and put them on the shelf. (And while I'm in the pantry, maybe swap them for a top-shelf bottle of wine.)

"I believe there is something greater," Ruth said as she gazed out at the horizon. It was the final moment of the day when the sun becomes a half-circle, then a segment, then a sliver, and then is simply not there. The sun was possibly the perfect metaphor for the topic at hand: life. It is there, and then it is swiftly not.

"Yes," continued Ruth, "I believe I'll go to a wonderful place, where I'm with everyone I love."

She paused, wiping a tear from her eye with her scarf.

"And I'm fabulously skinny."

And then she released one of her heartwarming cackles. ○

AT VARIOUS PLACES throughout Cape Town, I had seen flyers advertising organized tours of Khayelitsha. I had been curious about visiting a township; however, I had reservations about participating in an organized tour. At best, these sightseeing excursions were community-driven initiatives that gave inquisitive foreigners the opportunity to gain a deeper understanding of life in a township. At the same time, they provided business opportunities for local artisans, cooks, drivers and tour guides. At worst, these tours were an opportunity for the privileged few to safely snap photos of "the slums" while participating in a tokenistic South African experience — a type of African safari, but instead of lions and elephants, there were poor people.

Admittedly, I was a lot like the average traveller in the sense that I was genuinely curious about what life looked like in a shantytown. And, yes, I was interested in taking photographs of what I saw. I probably would not have bought a ticket for an organized tour of Khayelitsha, but a personal invitation felt different. It felt more sincere — I would actually be welcomed by at least one person. Because Moses had lived in Khayelitsha and still had friends in the district, I figured that he would be entitled to a certain level of respect. Therefore, I would be relatively safe in his presence. In a way, it was in the same category of Estella guiding me through a local Peruvian market — a local taking a foreigner through the shared space of a community, a friend showing a friend a part of his life.

Yet I was still nervous.

It was the last Friday of the month when I picked Moses up at Seventies-80s. The sky was cloudless as we walked in silence down Long Street toward the commuter train station. Cape

Town seemed calm and collected. Moses was uncharacteristically quiet. His oversized sunglasses concealed his eyes, making it hard to fully read his facial expression. Numerous times he insisted that we stop at a pay phone to make a call.

"Hey Moses," I inquired after he hung up the third phone call, "is everything okay?"

"Yeah, brah," he replied. "It's just that I want things to go smoothly." He explained that he was trying to get through to his friend Mohapi, whom he wanted me to meet.

"If you don't think this is a good idea, I want to know," I told him in very serious tone. An influx of butterflies had taken over my stomach. The true risks of the excursion were hard to gauge. Strolling through a South African township is not the same as strolling through a middle-class Canadian suburb. But how much of my concern was valid? And how much of it was unwarranted nonsense? My heart rate increased. Was this worth the risk?

"Things are all good," he said as he lifted his sunglasses and looked directly into my eyes, holding the gaze. If he had blinked or glanced away, I would have aborted the mission on the spot.

At Cape Town Station, we hopped aboard a train bound for Khayelitsha and sat on firm plastic benches. I was the only white person in our carriage and possibly on the entire train. The engine kicked into motion and started crawling down the track. A busker with an electric keyboard strapped around his neck performed an upbeat gospel song as he walked up and down the aisle. He was blind, his eyes missing from their sockets. A preacher gave a 10-minute sermon in Xhosa. A beggar walked through the car with a club foot thicker than the trunk of a pine tree. Like a couple of old pals, Moses and I sat without speaking. The motion of the train, along with the distraction of the commuters, managed to take the edge off. An hour later, we disembarked at the Khayelitsha station, entering directly into a marketplace.

I stuck close to Moses' side as we navigated our way down a concrete ramp lined with vendors offering everything from bootlegged movies to handcrafted leatherwear, from barbershop services to recently severed sheep heads. The vendors' stands were crude constructions built out of wooden pallets and covered with various coloured tarps. For the vultures circling overhead, the market probably looked like a massive patchwork quilt. The atmosphere was somehow both chaotic and serene at once. Merchants occasionally called out to promote their wares, while small groups of men stood on the sidelines, quietly surveying the scene. Dressed in jeans and T-shirts, residents moved unceremoniously past the stalls as they went to and from the station. Eventually we stepped off the concrete ramp and onto a dirt road. We began the walk toward Mohapi's home.

With the bustle of its people, the market had felt relatively safe. But on the sun-drenched open street, I felt more exposed, more visible. Moses insisted on wearing my backpack as a precautionary measure to limit any link between potential wealth and myself. My skin colour was enough to garner me sufficient attention, to easily establish that I was a foreigner to Khayelitsha. There was no need to advertise that I was also in possession of a wallet and a camera. Perhaps our precautions worked because as we walked, nobody harassed us.

After 15 minutes, we ascended a sandy hill covered in shacks. We arrived in front of a one-room corrugated tin structure with rocks resting on the roof to hold it in place during stormy weather. Mohapi emerged from his house. He was a small, slender man with a serious expression and dark skin like Moses. His clothing was simple and western: a gingery orange sweater, faded blue jeans and brown leather sandals. Moses and Mohapi shook hands and spoke to each other in Zutu before they switched their attention to me.

"This is my friend Daniel," Moses gestured toward me.

Mohapi shyly shook my hand.

He looked at me and then looked away. "You can come inside."

As we ducked through the low doorway, Mohapi proudly told me that he built the structure himself. The walls appeared to be made of a thick cardboard material and were streaked from water damage. Light poured through cracks where the walls and the roof failed to fully meet. (Yet, considering the unavailability of building resources, he had constructed something far beyond what I could have done for myself.) The space was furnished with a double bed covered in a purple flowered blanket. The open windows were dressed with cobalt curtains that swayed gently with the breeze, and throw rugs covered the concrete floor. The kitchen area had a refillable gas-burning stove on a countertop and a microwave oven that was strictly ornamental, since there was no electricity — or plumbing for that matter. Several times a day, Mohapi had to walk a couple hundred metres to obtain water or to use a shared toilet.

Mohapi reached for a blanket at the end of his bed and unfolded it with pride. This was the tribal blanket presented to him after completing a traditional Zutu initiation ceremony. The details of the initiation were strictly confidential, he explained in a serious tone, but he confirmed that he had successfully transitioned into manhood. He modelled the blanket by throwing it over his shoulders like a stately cape and paused with a serious expression, indicating that the tribal ritual was not something taken lightly.

Moses, who had been standing quietly at the side of the room, finally spoke again, suggesting that we continue to explore the district. Soon we were out the door, walking the sandy alleyways. Along the way, Mohapi cautiously shared more details of his life. He hailed from the Eastern Cape and had come to Cape Town to make money to send to his wife. Working as a parking guard, he made 1,150 rand per month (approximately $120). Though I was curious, I thought it would be bad manners to ask how much of this salary he was able to send back home.

We stopped briefly at Mohapi's brother's house, another one-room corrugated shack. I was impressed with the spectacular view. At the very top of the same sandy hill, it overlooked the entire Khayelitsha district. Moses mentioned it was exceptionally beautiful at night with the glow of the lights below. The brother, a taller version of Mohapi with longer hair, was frying sausages over a propane stove for lunch. He invited us to join him.

Mohapi informed him that we would only stay for a bit, waving away the offer to share in the food. I asked permission from the brother to take photographs and was granted the go-ahead with a simple nod. While the guys chatted among themselves, I clicked a few shots. I paused, however, when I noticed a corkboard in the shape of the continent of Africa mounted on the wall. From the board dangled a sign with block letters that read "COMFORT COMES AFTER A STRUGGLE." This was a quick reminder that despite the scenic lights at night, life was not luxurious in Khayelitsha. After five minutes, we exchanged farewells and departed to continue our tour.

We walked down the other side of the hill and past a row of outhouses. Mohapi said that the government had erected them but failed to keep them serviced. Now many of the stalls were in disrepair and the community didn't know what to do with them. Beside the toilets were piles of trash, and beside the piles of trash a couple of children were playing contentedly. The sight of kids among rubbish didn't shock me. I'd seen similar images flash across televisions before. Except this time, there wasn't sad music playing in the background or an appeal to send money. Instead, there were people laughing, horns beeping and life functioning.

We walked past the hut where Moses used to live, and he insisted that I take his photograph. Although we only saw the corrugated home from the outside, I imagined that it was similar to Mohapi's place: minimal, crude, improvised. We then continued to a paved main road, which was lined with shops and stalls selling unidentifiable animal organs, mobile phone services and spiritual cleansing. Like what I had seen at the train station, one merchant had a table of sheep heads, each with newspaper stuffed up the nostrils as if to stop a nosebleed.

"They are called *smiley skop offal*," Moses explained, "because as they are roasted, the facial muscles contract and the sheep smiles."

He read the skepticism in my own facial muscles.

"They are actually quiet delicious, Monsieur Baylis."

"Next time I visit, let's get some," I teased facetiously.

"Well, you need to eat something from the streets."

At the following vendor, the guys insisted that I sample the meat that was steaming over the grill. To my relief, it wasn't some unidentified intestine or the face of a sheep. It was simply barbecued chicken feet, which seemed relatively appealing, considering the alternatives. Mohapi acted as a translator and ordered 10 feet. The woman vendor, with plump glistening cheeks and a purple head wrap, selected the juiciest feet off the grill and bundled them in a newspaper cone. Moses held the stack, and I cautiously picked up a dangly appendage and attempted to eat it like a chicken wing. The barbecue sauce was sweet and garlicky, but there wasn't much meat to be found. The vendor saw me struggling and released a belly laugh at my feeble nibbles. Moses intervened.

"Brah," he said, "you've got to throw the whole thing in your mouth and then spit out the bones."

With his advice, I shoved a full chicken foot in my mouth. It was a messy mixture of claws and bone and skin. I opted to chew for a few minutes and then just foolishly swallowed everything, bones and all. If nothing else, the people who had stopped to watch me were fully amused by my facial contortions. Mohapi cracked a joke to three boys sitting on a fence. They pointed and laughed. I smiled, intentionally exposing chicken skin caught in my teeth.

Next, we stopped at an open-air restaurant with wooden picnic tables, where we ordered a couple of steaks and three Cokes. I jokingly pretended to open the soda bottle with my teeth, feigning manliness. Mohapi, looking at me like I was crazy, brought the mouth of his bottle between his teeth and pulled the cap off with ease. Moses did the same. This actually *was* the normal procedure in Khayelitsha. So, for the first time in my life, I found the right angle and — to the horror of all dentists — successfully opened a bottle with my teeth. It was surprisingly satisfying.

As we ate the steaks (which I enjoyed *much* more than the chicken feet), Mohapi shared his philosophy on life.

"This is the hand that God has given me. It is up to me to make the best of it," he stated.

I wondered what he thought about me and the hand that I had been dealt. Did he see me as fortunate? How do two humans compare hands? Is that possible?

We left the restaurant, taking a different route back toward the train station. Along the way, we came across something I had not expected to see: an organic farm. Curious, I asked the boys if they wouldn't mind if we stopped for a minute. They agreed. An older gentleman named Sydney greeted us and gave a five-minute tour of the Masikhanye Food Garden — a vegetable nursery the size of a soccer pitch. He then offered a bowl full of their homegrown veggies — a curried medley of spinach and carrots. I never imagined that Khayelitsha would be home to an organic food project. In my defence, neither did Moses or Mohapi (though they both expressed interest in returning). I would have loved to stay longer at the garden, but in less than an hour it would be dark. Moses stressed that it would be unwise if I lingered in Khayelitsha after dusk. Despite the welcoming receptions I had received throughout the day, I figured there was no sense in pushing my luck.

At the train platform, I shook Mohapi's hand and thanked him for the opportunity to see his world. We had only known each other for a few hours, yet for some reason, I felt a pang of sadness at our parting. I offered him the same money that I would have paid to participate in an organized tour. He accepted it with a handshake and a smile. Then he turned and disappeared faster than I would have liked. Back through the chaotic market, among the people and the stalls. Back to making the best of his life in Khayelitsha. ۞

AFTER SPENDING A month at Moses' side, I refused to believe that he was standing me up. It was my final night in Cape Town. I had already finished my send-offs with Ruth and Dawie, but I had plans to hang out with Moses one last time. He had uncharacteristically not shown up at the arranged time, and I was worried that I would not see him again. My early morning flight was confirmed. My backpack was ready. My gift for Moses sat wrapped on the bed.

Just as I was about to brush my teeth and head to bed, the hostel manager knocked on the door of the dorm room and informed me that there was a man outside waiting to see me. I threw on my sneakers, grabbed my jacket and headed out into the evening.

Accustomed to being denied entry, he stood against the gate.

"Sorry I'm late, Monsieur Baylis," Moses began. "Dawie had me painting."

"No worries." My confusion immediately dissolved. "I'm just happy that you came."

We decided to partake in a final cup of rooibos tea and soon found ourselves at a generic fast food restaurant. Unlike our night at the Labia Theatre, this time there wasn't any type of pretention. Under the glow of fluorescent lights, I presented the small gift, something that Moses had mentioned wanting. His eyes lit up as he unwrapped the copy of Nelson Mandela's memoir, and he accepted it without making a fuss.

We chatted more about the future. Moses confessed that he was ready to move on from Seventies-80s. Considering the meagre clientele — and therefore limited opportunities to make commission — I found this news unsurprising. He stated that he might be able to rent a flat on the outskirts of town, somewhere closer than Khayelitsha. Maybe he'd take a waiter's course. He had also recently spoken to a welder, and perhaps there might be an opportunity to join him. His voice tried to sound optimistic. Occasionally his eyes would drift. Despite the various options he had mentioned, I sensed that he was still anxious about what was to come. As he sat there spinning his paper cup in his hands, I couldn't help but wonder if his list of possibilities was also his way of saying "Don't worry about me."

It was difficult not to be concerned. Moses radiated intellect and warmth and possibility. However, in world of arbitrary biases, even the shiniest people can still be at a disadvantage. This wasn't just a question of race — although race was an unmistakable variable, even in post-apartheid South Africa. But Moses also faced the challenge of being a country boy trying to make it in the city, compounded by the confusion that is inherent in being a twentysomething. For the first time in my trip, I felt tempted to reach into my pocket and give someone enough money to get them through the year. But I feared it would be awkward — or worse, insulting. What are the implications of handouts? Is the offering of friendship enough? At that table, under those florescent lights, I felt torn — guilty of certain advantages yet grateful for having made an uncommon connection.

After finishing our last swigs of tea, we marched slowly and silently back toward the hostel. At the gate, we paused. Moses admitted that he wasn't very good at goodbyes. The way I see it, though, a person who is comfortable with goodbyes is probably someone whose heart has grown callouses. And Moses was not one of these people.

"Keep being Daniel Baylis," he simply stated, extending his hand.

"Keep being Moses," I replied.

And there we stood, shaking hands. Both with tears in our eyes. ☺

JUNE

Marrakech, Morocco

The Islamic call to prayer was so loud that it momentarily muted the bustle of the crowd. The melody was both enchantingly exotic and perplexingly foreign. As far as I could tell, however, nobody was stopping to pray. In front of me, a man with tiny cymbals on his fingers suddenly sprung up and spun his head in a dizzying display of cranial dexterity. To my left, an irate monkey in a diaper was being pulled by a chain around its neck. To my right, a woman in tattered clothes reached for my hand and indicated that she wished to read my fortune. A mixture of incense and sewage scents lingered in the soupy night air. The taste of dust coated my tongue. This was twilight in Marrakech's legendary market square, Jamaa el Fna.

A young man named Brahim pulled on my arm and motioned for me to keep up with him. As a junior member of the cultural exchange organization where I was slated to volunteer for the month of June, he had been assigned to pick me up at the airport. Now it was his responsibility to make sure I didn't get lost or swindled — a job that would have been easier, no doubt, if I weren't so utterly exhausted from hours of plane rides and airport layovers. Originally, Brahim wanted to give me a tour of the market, but I kept lagging behind. Eventually he herded me into a restaurant.

On the second level of a café overlooking the plaza, Brahim and I exchanged formalities in broken French. I told him I was from Canada and that it was my first time in Morocco. The slick-haired 19-year-old responded that he was from the bear-bear culture.

"Bear-bear?"

"You've not heard of the bear-bear people?" he asked in disbelief.

"Um, no." I said apologetically. To be honest, I didn't even know there were bears in Africa. Brahim shrugged and looked away.

If I had been less drained, I might have felt bad about my cultural ignorance. But the transit from South Africa to Morocco had been the most demanding leg of the year — a 36-hour circuitous route that involved stops on two other continents. Yes, two other *continents*. Because flights between African nations are limited, I jetted from Cape Town to Johannesburg, up to Abu Dhabi, over to Paris and then down to Marrakech. The trek had left me emptied of energy, and the sweltering chaos of Jamaa el Fna did nothing to help my ability to think lucidly.

Brahim looked constantly into his mobile phone and provided regular updates on the situation. "The director should be here soon," he assured me at 10-minute intervals. Nearly two hours later, a well-fed man wearing wire-framed glasses and a three-piece suit arrived at our table. He looked weary, with his shoulders hunched as though the world itself was resting upon them. Yet he introduced himself with a warm smile.

"Hello, Daniel. I'm Abdul." He spoke slowly, revealing a mouth full of braces as he deliberately pronounced his words. "I am sorry I am late. I was called away to Casablanca today to take care of some business."

"No worries."

The wait had become tedious, but I was happy to see the guy. His presence meant that soon I could be horizontal. And at that moment, there was nothing I needed more.

We bid goodbye to Brahim. Then Abdul led me away from

the chaos of the market square to a taxi stand. As arranged before my arrival, I was to spend my first few nights with Abdul's family before being placed in a homestay. We sped far away from the city centre and into the sprawling suburbs of Marrakech. ☼

BELIEVE IT OR not, I've always been a bit of a book nerd. In elementary school, I was part of the Library Club, and I would scour the aisles for tales of adventure as I shelved books. I had a particular fondness for animal stories, especially those involving three specific creatures: dolphins, dogs or horses. One of my favourite childhood authors was Marguerite Henry, an American writer who penned exciting tales about racehorses and wild stallions. I read most of her stories, but the one that I recall most nostalgically is *King of the Wind*, a legend that opens in Morocco during the fast of Ramadan. The desert setting sounded remote and intoxicatingly mysterious, a million miles away from my cookie-cutter world.

Under the influence of Henry's writing, I began to dream about visiting my first foreign country — Morocco. In my mind, I could dig a really deep hole and be quickly transported to this faraway realm, where I would never again have to shovel a snow-covered driveway. In this mystical place, my principal mode of transportation would be an Arabian stallion named Sahara Breeze.

As I grew older, I became intrigued with the more sensual foundations of Moroccan culture. The savoury *tajines* and fragrant mint teas. The traditional bathhouses. The country's famous handcrafted products, such as fine-woven carpets, leather satchels and cast iron lanterns. The promises of Morocco seemed far too marvellous to miss.

When it came time to find a volunteer host in the North African nation, I identified several potential projects: an olive grove run by a French family, a babysitting gig with a couple of Irish musicians in Casablanca, a guest house led by an American organic gardener. All of these projects had their appeal, but all were managed by expats. Don't get me wrong. I have nothing against expats. However, of all the things I was learning from my journey, one of the most important insights was that few travel experiences are as meaningful as connecting with locals. My time in South Africa had just solidified the lesson.

Finally, I came across a community organization called Youth Association for Culture and Development (YACD). Their objective, as listed on their website, was "to promote peace, tolerance and solidarity, through helping young people acquire knowledge, skills and competencies." This sounded right up my alley. The icing on the cake was that they offered homestays — a perfect opportunity to really sink into Moroccan culture. After a surprisingly intensive application process that included a very long questionnaire, a scan of my passport and a nominal administrative fee, I received an official invitation from Abdul, the director. The document provided an authorized volunteer number and was imprinted with the organization's stamp of approval. This formal style was a far departure from the "just show up and we'll put you to work" approach of Common Ground Relief, for example, back in New Orleans. That said, there was something amusing about the formality of the application process. I deemed it my first foray into Moroccan culture!

My job for June would be to teach English and share Canadian culture with young adults at a community centre. Although I had already devoted a month to teaching English, the position in Marrakech appealed to me because it required a different level of classroom planning. I would be working with a more mature age group. It would also provide me with the opportunity to make new friends and maybe even get me an invitation for a free cooking class. At the very least, I'd get some home-cooked meals. In my mind, my days would consist of casually strolling through Marrakech's *medina*, making friends with the jovial shopkeepers, getting regular treatments at the local *hammams*, and then heading off to teach an English class full of fun-loving and eager students. I would be well fed and would maybe even get a desert tan. As far as I was concerned, Morocco could be nothing but *amazing*. ○

I AWOKE ALONE, in a concrete room that looked like a prison cell — feeling everything but amazing.

The previous evening's taxi had taken us down a dark highway, at least 15 kilometres away from the heart of Marrakech. We had travelled far further than I imagined going. It was well after midnight when we stepped into the tiled entryway of Abdul's three-storey concrete housing block.

"That's my father," Abdul whispered as he nodded toward a lone figure in front of a glowing television screen. "He's a retired general from the national army." Abdul spoke briefly in Arabic to his father, who responded without looking at us.

Quietly, I followed Abdul past a living room, through a short hallway and into a sparse bedroom where he had me leave my bag. He finished the tour of the house by showing me to a small bathroom with a toilet and hand sink, followed by a dimly lit mushroom-coloured kitchen. As we stepped into the cooking area, I noticed a petite woman wearing a *hijab*. She was sitting alone in the corner, without a radio or television to keep her company, and simply staring at a wall.

"That's my mother," Abdul stated. She turned in my approximate direction, nodded and smiled gently. And then she looked away again, her face returning to its original blank expression. You might assume that the kitchen of a Moroccan home would smell savoury (like a spicy lamb tajine) or sweet (like fragrant mint tea). Here the aroma was more like *eau de gloom*.

What had I signed up for?

Concealing my disappointment, I politely excused myself for the night. I shut the door to the bedroom softly behind me, removed my sweaty clothes and curled up on the single mattress on the ground. As I lay there, I was haunted by a sense of heaviness. So far this year, there had always been at least one other traveller around when I arrived in each country, whether it was at a hostel or project site (even in Peru, where I thought I was alone, another volunteer had arrived before sundown). This sense of isolation was a first for me. I was miles away from not only Marrakech but also other travellers — and in a house that lacked any discernible welcome.

Now morning had come and I lay in bed, blinking. My backpack was on a wooden desk. A small beige rug covered the grey concrete floor like a Band-Aid on an elephant's hide. High up the wall, a barred window allowed a bit of light into the room, but it also solidified the prison-cell motif. One thing was crystal clear: I did not wish to stay in this jail-like room, in this standoffish house, and in this far-flung neighbourhood for the next few days — and, if possible, not even for another night.

Eventually my bladder began begging for relief, so I got up, opened the bedroom door and tiptoed across the hallway to the bathroom. As I did so, I glimpsed into the living room, where I spotted Abdul sleeping on a bench lined with cushions. Had he given me his room? If so, why was it so minimal, so unlived in? Whatever the case was, seeing Abdul sleeping like a nomad actually made me feel even more self-conscious about being there. Like I was an intruder.

In the bathroom, I tried to make as little noise as possible. But I was confronted with a conundrum. *Do I flush the toilet or not?* I really didn't want to indicate to the household that I was awake. My ultimate desire was to disappear, to magically become invisible, grab my backpack and escape via taxi or bus or donkey back to Marrakech. Finally, I flushed and then dashed back into my prison cell.

An hour later, I heard Abdul moving around the living room. Accepting the improbability of turning invisible, I took a deep breath, got dressed and went to join him. There were things to discuss — the classes I would be giving and, more importantly, where I would be staying for the remainder of the month.

Abdul greeted me with a smile and invited me to sit with him at a table in the living room. He departed into the kitchen, where I could hear him exchanging words with his mother. A few minutes later, he returned carrying a tray of boiled eggs, pita bread and olives. As he poured us each a glass of tea, I kick-started the conversation.

"So when do I start teaching?"

"Don't worry. You will start soon," Abdul responded. He had a calm manner that reminded me of a skillful politician skirting a question.

And then, silence.

Abdul didn't say anything more. In fact, he didn't even look at me. He cracked open an egg and started spooning it into his mouth. So I did the same.

However, it wasn't quiet in my head. I was noisily formulating a polite way of stating that I wanted to head back to Marrakech as soon as possible. Information about volunteering could wait. The first priority was confirming accommodation. That said, my goal was to avoid another tense episode like in Costa Rica when I decided to leave the raw vegan farm early. Also, I didn't want to appear ungrateful, especially if Abdul had actually given me his room. So in order to minimize being rude, I decided that I would attempt to focus the conversation on my interest in exploring the attractions of the city.

"I think it might be more practical for me to stay closer to Marrakech," I said. "There's so much I would like to see and do while I'm here."

Abdul nodded, as if to indicate that he understood what I was trying to say. "I will contact Brahim. He will help you find a place to stay."

My shoulders immediately relaxed. I felt like I had dodged a catastrophe bullet. After clearing the table, Abdul indicated that he had work to do at home but that I could head back into the city whenever I wished. Unceremoniously, he gave me verbal instructions on how to return to the city centre. All I had to do was walk to the highway and get on a bus. So with my bag on my back, I bid farewell to him and exited the house without word from his parents, who were home but seemed to be avoiding me. After spending so much energy on wishing I could vanish, perhaps I had been invisible all along. ☼

BRAHIM MET ME as I stepped off the bus and escorted me directly to a cheap Moroccan guest house.

Commonly known as *riads*, traditional Moroccan guest houses are typically two-storey private residences with interior courtyards. The most opulent ones feature magnificent gardens and elaborate fountains. The riad where Brahim took me had a courtyard, but there was no garden. The closest thing to a water feature was the rubber hose that the cleaning staff had sloppily left lying outside the shared bathroom. With its plain walls, it could be optimistically explained as shabby-chic (with the "chic" part coming from the fact there were no bed bugs). Nonetheless, for about $12 per night, I had my own quiet room, complete with a sink, a mirror and a single bed with clean sheets.

Yet the most attractive aspect of my crumbling abode was its location. In the heart of the medina, I was now only a few steps away from the marketplace circus of Jamaa el Fna. It was a decent place to stay while Abdul arranged a homestay. ○

AT CAFÉ ALI, a slow-moving bistro on the fringe of Jamaa el Fna, I waited for Abdul in the shade of a patio umbrella. It had been four days since I'd arrived in Morocco, and I was finally scheduled to teach an English class. I was prepared for the first session, but I felt anxious. *Who are my students? What is their level of comprehension? Will they respect me?* In Peru, I had faced the first day of teaching with two other volunteers and a predetermined teaching plan, but this time I was on my own — alone in creating lessons and in leading the class, alone in my successes and in my failures. Abdul had assured me that there were other international volunteers with the organization. But where they were staying and what they were doing was still a mystery. As far as I knew, this was to be a solo venture.

In the park across the lane from Café Ali, rows of leafy trees were bursting with golden flowers. A gust of wind tore through the treetops, causing the petals to drip from the branches. They danced over the horse-drawn carriages like a shower of sunshine and landed softly on the dusty ground. It was whimsical moments like these when I was content to simply sit on the sidelines and be an observer. However, sitting on the sidelines was not what I had signed up for.

Thirty minutes after our arranged meeting time, Abdul appeared. Wearing an oversized business blazer and carrying a briefcase, he slowly plodded among the mopeds and donkeys as he made his way into the café.

"Hi Daniel!" Abdul said, sitting down beside me. "How are you?"

"Good, thanks," I replied politely, hiding my irritation over having been kept waiting. "Did you receive my lesson plan?" The previous day, he had sent a last-minute email informing me that classes would begin with a group of young men and that he wanted a plan submitted as soon as possible. I had stayed up late researching teaching strategies for adults and preparing appropriate activities.

"Yes." Abdul pushed his glasses up his nose. "It looks very acceptable." I didn't know what *very acceptable* meant, but I assumed it was better than *very not acceptable*.

"Okay, good. Should we get going?" As I began to stand, Abdul's chubby hand waved me back down into my seat.

"First, I will have a coffee. There is no hurry."

If circumstances had been different, I wouldn't have even needed Abdul to meet me at a café. We could have met directly at the community centre. I love finding my own way through foreign cities — it's like a large-scale treasure hunt. But even after four days, Marrakech was still an unfathomable maze. The streets signs, if present at all, were usually only written in Arabic. To make matters even more complicated, most of the city's routes were crafted long before linear grids became a municipal mainstay. My western-based logic did not translate here. Along with the occasional smell of donkey urine, part of Marrakech's charm — I would come to learn — was the architectural randomness and urban pandemonium. In my antsy, directionally-impeded state, I waited for Abdul to slowly drink his coffee.

When our respective tabs were paid, Abdul led the way to the same waiting area for shared taxis. After a brief negotiation, we boarded a communal beige sedan — with three people in the front seat and four in the back. Squished against the veiled woman beside me, I could feel the rise and fall of her chest cavity. The rhythm of her breathing reminded me to exhale.

We were dropped off in a residential neighbourhood where the surrounding three-storey apartment structures were built primarily with sand-coloured blocks. If one were to look at the city from afar, perhaps the only thing that would stand out from the desert landscape would be a sea of floating white satellite dishes.

Abdul and I walked a few blocks to a small, gated community centre. Leaning against the fence was a group of young Moroccan men in their late teens and early twenties, all dressed in western clothing. Abdul spoke to them casually in Arabic and motioned to me in what I assumed was an introduction. Like any teacher arriving to meet a new group of students, part of me had hoped for a hero's welcome, perhaps a brief session of jumping up and down while chanting "The Canadian teacher has arrived!" But the students just nodded politely, avoiding any direct eye contact.

"Hello. I am Daniel," I said with intentionally clear words, trying to gauge their level of comprehension. "How are you?"

"Hi," responded a short, clean-shaven guy in a T-shirt, blue jeans and flip-flops. "I am good."

I turned to a different young man, this time a tall, slender fellow with a goatee and a soccer jersey. "Hello. How are you?"

"Hi. I am good," he responded, grinning slightly.

This interaction happened five more times, each with the exact same response and similar shy smiles. Before I could begin another round of questions, Abdul corralled us into the building. In a peach-coloured room, a couple of tables were dragged together. Plastic chairs were placed around the perimeter of the tables and a dry-erase board was propped on the windowsill. This would be our makeshift classroom.

Our first activity was to create name cards so that I could address each student in a more personal way. There was Omar, Mohammed, Mounir, Badr, Noureddine, Tarik and Abdellatif.

"Ab-dell-a-teef?" I said hesitantly, looking for approval. It was an opportunity to highlight my own inabilities, an icebreaker to create an atmosphere where it would be safe to fumble with the difficulties of a different language.

After a rudimentary round of reviewing the English alphabet, we moved on to numbers. I wrote the numerical figures on the board. Then, for an extra challenge, I had each of the men dictate the spelling of the numbers. Moving around the group, each student had his turn.

"Oh – en – ee," said Mounir.

"Tee – duhb-uhl-yoo – oh," ventured Mohammed. And so on.

Eventually, we reached the number six. It was Omar's turn, and he was perhaps the most timid in the group. Tentatively, he said "es – ee – eks." Not one to shy away from lewdness, I wrote "sex" on the board. Judging by the laughter that ensued, it was evident that most of them understood the meaning of this word. Omar blushed and corrected himself. He chuckled as the other guys slapped him on the back.

After an hour of practice, I asked the group if they needed a quick pause. They nodded their heads in agreement. Just as we were breaking, the *adhān* — the Islamic call to prayer — rang loudly from the community centre's minaret, which was outside the classroom window. Perfect timing. Five of the students left the room to pray, while two others remained behind. In a mixture of French and English, I chatted with the two guys who stayed back. What type of work did they do? Or were they studying? How many siblings did they have? Were they married?

Ten minutes passed. And then twenty.

I wasn't sure how long a session of prayer normally lasted, but the delay seemed a bit extravagant. Self-doubt came creeping in. What if five out of seven students didn't return? How could I not take that personally? Perhaps what I thought was joviality had been interpreted as offensive.

Concerned, I asked the two remaining fellows whether we should resume the class. The most skilled student of the group, Tarik, shrugged his shoulders and said, "You in a rush to leave this place?"

"No," I smiled back. Tarik was right. What *was* the rush? His simple inquiry would be my second reminder that day to relax, to breathe.

And so we waited some more.

Thirty minutes passed and finally the other five young men wandered back into the classroom; there were no explanations, no excuses and no details. Their smiles indicated that they were still content. My fears were quelled. And, thankfully, the lesson continued without further incident. ○

PUBLIC BATHING IS a tradition as old as water itself. (Well, actually water is technically older, but you get my drift.) Many nations — including Japan, Finland, Turkey and North American indigenous cultures — have long histories of communal cleansing. Converging in steamy spaces offers individuals the opportunity to engage in personal hygiene and grooming activities in a subdued environment that enables gossip about misbehaving spouses and lunatic neighbours. These days, however, public bathing is more rare, at least where I come from. With complex plumbing networks and self-contained bathroom facilities at our disposal, the instances of good friends jumping into a tub together to scrub one another's hard-to-reach regions have plummeted to an all-time low. Luckily, the tradition of public bathing is still alive and well in Morocco.

An important part of Moroccan culture is a weekly trip to the bathhouse, or *hammam*, as it is better known. Existing in many Arab countries, the tradition of the hammam consists of gender-segregated steam rooms varying in their intensity of heat, with perspiring workers offering *gommage* (exfoliation) services. The philosophy is that one should maintain personal hygiene as a habit, but once a week, often on Fridays, an extra-intensive scrub-down at the local hammam helps ensure purity for prayers. A clean body correlates to a clean spirit, so the theory goes.

I decided to investigate the theory.

Strolling through Marrakech's medina, I quickly realized that Moroccan hammams basically fall into one of two discernible categories. The first type is for those who crave decadence. They advertise themselves as authentic bathhouses but in actuality are more like Moroccan-inspired western spas that cater to tourists with a penchant for pampering. These exclusive facilities also accommodate upper-class locals who have somehow beat the odds and have *dirhams* to squander on lavish escapism. The second sort of hammam is the layperson's public bath. These hole-in-the-wall establishments tend to be undecorated, murky saunas where local folks have gathered for eternities to maintain the aforementioned tradition of scrubbing skin and wagging tongues. There are generally no English adverts on the doors, which could be a hint that foreigners may not be welcome.

Across the alley from my riad was one of those local no-frills hammams. Its unassuming doorway greeted a regular flow of Marrakech residents, who came and went without any type of ado or excitement, dressed in traditional *djellabas* and hijabs. To them, a trip to the public bathhouse was an unspectacular part of everyday Moroccan life. To me, the hammam was enthralling and exotic. As my time in the city progressed, I often saw the grey-haired workers outside taking breaks: smoking cigarettes, sipping glasses of tea and talking softly together. Each time I set out from the riad, my eyes would wander across the alley to the hammam and to the workers. I would pause to watch people coming and going. Not wanting to be perceived as "that creepy, gawking foreign dude," I never lingered for more than a few seconds. (Deep within my flannel-patterned Canadian genetic material is a slightly debilitating fear of imposing.) After a week of surveying the hammam from a distance, I still hadn't bucked up the courage to even walk through its low archway to inquire about a treatment. Finally, in a moment of unbridled practicality, I decided to ask Mohammed, the friendly receptionist at my riad.

"Cet hammam," I inquired as I pointed across the lane, *"les tour-istes sont bienvenus aussi?"*

"Mais oui, tout le monde est bienvenu!" said Mohammed en-thusiastically, assuring me that everyone was welcome at the hammam. Before I could say anything else, he jumped up from behind his desk, grabbed the sleeve of my shirt and pulled me out into the brick-lined alleyway. He led me directly to one of the workers, a slender, grey-haired gentleman who was sitting on a rickety stool. The man sprung to his feet as we approached.

"Je vous présénte Mohammed!" Mohammed-the-receptionist said to me. It took me a second to realize that, indeed, both of these gentlemen were named Mohammed.

"Salaam alaikum," said Mohammed-the-hammamist. His small frame was dressed in what I imagined was a typical ham-mam getup: baggy T-shirt, rust-coloured swim trunks and damp plastic sandals. His twinkling eyes seemed trustworthy. *"Vous voulez hammam et massage?"*

"Yes ... uhhh ... *oui* ... *peut-être.*"

"On commence maintenant!" Mohammed-the-hammamist ex-claimed, lifting his hands into the air. To my surprise, he was ready to begin immediately. At over 30 ° C outside, a hot steam bath seemed counterintuitive. But then again, after a few hours of walking through the medina, I had become a sweaty mess. A scrubbing wouldn't be the worst thing for me. So I nodded in consent. And then I escaped from the friendly authority of the two Mohammeds to nab a different set of clothes and a towel.

In my room, I scrolled through my list of questions and con-cerns about hammam culture. I realized I didn't know a thing about local hammam protocol. What was I supposed to *do* in a hammam? Or, more aptly, what would be done to me? Is it polite to talk? Was I supposed to be naked? Topping my list of concerns was the same question that would plague most western males in this type of situation: *What if he tries to scrub me, you know, down there?* I'm a fairly liberal guy who's open to a wide variety of cultural experiences, but usually I require a couple of cocktails before I invite anyone to put their hands down my pants.

Five minutes later, I crossed the alleyway with a mix of anticipation and reluctance, and (perhaps most importantly) with baggy board shorts protecting my nether regions. I ducked cautiously into the hammam's reception area and turned left into a room that had a symbol of a man on the door. The change room smelled of soap and cigarette smoke. Mohammed-the-hammamist stashed my towel, sandals and keys, and then guided me into a muggy room. He warned me to watch my head as we ducked through another tiny door. The steamy space was lit by a single light bulb hanging from the ceiling. A man with a piece of fabric wrapped around his waist sat drenched in the corner, cleaning himself quietly. Mould speckled the ceiling, and a thick layer of rust covered exposed pipes along the wall. If the windowless hammam had been built for luxury, then time had transformed it into a dank cellar.

Mohammed instructed me to lie down on the slick tile floor. Then he began throwing buckets of warm water over my chest and legs. Once I was sufficiently saturated, he left the room without saying anything. I remained motionless, unsure of what to do. Had I missed an indication to follow him? Was I supposed to be washing myself? Or was this part of the experience dedicated to relaxation and absorbing the heat? The best strategy, I determined, was to wait for further instruction. That way, Mohammed might think I was a bit thick in the head, but at least it would limit my chances of doing anything uncouth.

A few minutes later, Mohammed returned, sporting a coarse blue glove on his hand. Without warning, the gloved hand reached for my upper thigh and vigorously began scrubbing. The exfoliating gommage had begun! I flinched at the sudden sting of the sandpaper hand. I had heard that the Moroccan gommage was not intended to be pleasurable, but this felt like he had strapped thumbtacks onto his palm and decided to unleash any bottled up aggression *on my flesh*. At one point, Mohammed paused to display the sausage-like coils of dead skin he had removed from my body. I wasn't sure if he was boasting about his abilities as a hammamist or delicately indicating that I was a filthy degenerate. Perhaps both.

If cleanliness is next to godliness, then I was on my way to divinity. The skin on my stomach blushed a bright shade of fuchsia, protesting as Mohammad attempted to sever off a couple of birthmarks. Finally, after what felt like an eternity, Mohammed mercifully stopped his assault. All around me, a thoroughly repulsive quantity of skin lay in small heaps. However, before I had the opportunity to grieve the loss of my epidermis, another deluge of water rushed at my face and body. The little chunks of membrane floated like miniature kayaks toward the drainage hole in the middle of the room.

With the exfoliation process complete and the tile floor rinsed of dead skin, the next phase was a nippy yet invigorating massage. Mohammed's poky fingers made my legs squirm in protest as he dug into the skinny muscles of my thighs. Indeed, the pressure was forceful but not malicious. As he bent over to massage my shoulders, I could smell tobacco on his breath. I told myself to soak it all in — to appreciate each rusty pipe, to embrace each painful jab and to savour the cigarette scent of my hammamist. Forget the wild stallions of my youthful imagination. This was a *real* slice of Morocco.

The last portion of the hammam treatment was the actual washing part. Armed with a couple of soapy washcloths, Mohammed came at me from a variety of angles: splaying me on my front, flipping me onto my back, and then sitting me up cross-legged. That's when he mumbled a soft, quick instruction that I didn't quite catch.

"*Pardon?*" I said with my best French accent, squinting through the blurry vapour.

Mohammed repeated himself just as quickly and pushed a washcloth into my hand. I must have had too much steam in my ears because I could not, for the life of me, comprehend what he was saying.

"*Désolé,*" I responded with a look of confusion. "*Je n'ai pas compris.*"

This time he made sure I'd understand.

"PÉNIS!" he instructed loudly, throwing in an English word. *"Wash PÉNIS!!"*

For good measure — and with abundant zest — he gesticulated a penis-washing action. Then Mohammed motioned to the washcloth in my hand and nodded encouragingly. His grandpa-like, twinkly eyes said, "Come on, young chap. You're a big boy now! Wash your penis all by yourself!"

The other men in the room turned and stared.

If I didn't already look like an overcooked lobster from the steam and scrubbing, Mohammed-the-hammamist would have certainly seen me blush. Yet, despite my mortification, I also felt a minor sense of relief. One thing was now abundantly clear: in the hammam, nobody but myself would be touching my delicate parts.

After a quick good-luck pat on the back, Mohammed rose to his feet and exited the vapour-filled room. The treatment was complete. I was left on the wet floor. And it was there that, beneath the cover of my shorts, I swiftly but subtly washed my own private bits. ○

"YOU DON'T NEED to worry," Abdul assured me. He was so close that I could see a partially chewed green olive in his braces. "Everything will be fine, *Insha'Allah.*"

We were squashed in the back seat of another shared taxi on the way to the second English lesson. The director of YACD had just finished telling me that one of the students had gotten into a fist fight with the manager of the community centre. If everything was indeed going to be fine, I wasn't entirely sure why he was disclosing this information. Was Abdul alerting me that fists could be hurled in *my* direction? The students had seemed timid and playful. I couldn't imagine that there'd be any problems of a violent nature. In fact, after the success of the first lesson, I was approaching the second session with more confidence — until he told me not to worry. When someone tells me not to worry, usually the first thing I do is start to worry.

When we arrived at the centre, I was surprised to see that there were no students waiting for us. We passed directly through the gates and went inside to set up the classroom. There were no posters on the walls, no audiovisual equipment, no fancy teaching tools. Preparing the class involved propping up a dry-erase board and arranging some chairs together. With a few minutes to spare, I took a seat near the front and reread my lesson plan.

As I reviewed, a tall figure walked into the room. I looked up to see a young man who hadn't been at the first lesson. He wore a pale blue djellaba — a traditional loose-fitting outer robe — and had cheekbones high enough to qualify him for the fashion runways of Paris or Milan. As I had done with the other students, I introduced myself in English and asked him how he was doing. He didn't answer. So then I tried a bit of French. Instead of communicating that he understood, his eyes darted from my face to the door. His hands coiled into fists. I wrote my name in clear block letters on a piece of paper, pointed to myself and pronounced my name. His firm expression softened slightly, and then I indicated that he should do the same. In shaky letters, he spelled out S-A-M-I-R. With only a minute left before the scheduled start of class, we practised the English alphabet together. His fists relaxed.

The other guys slowly trickled in, most of them with the same smiles that I had seen during the first class. To my delight, the seven guys had returned for a second session. But I was also happy to see new pupils among the group, including one young woman who spoke English relatively well. The class size had jumped to 13 students — a near 100-per-cent increase. That was all fine and dandy, except now a new challenge presented itself: I would need to cater to a wider range of abilities.

We began.

Only 10 minutes into the class, the adhān sounded. I looked at the 13 faces in front of me, trying to determine the best course of action.

"Would you like to pause for a few minutes?" I asked tentatively, wanting to be respectful.

They indicated that a break was not necessary. So I continued the lesson, yelling the conjugations of "to have" over the long and loud call to prayer. It seemed ridiculous to be competing with the adhān, but the other option was to stand silently like a muted buffoon, which would have been even more awkward. As I was shouting my way through a sentence, the call to prayer finally ceased.

"I *HAVE*! You *HAVE*! He *HAS* … ahem, has."

After a thorough verb review, we moved on to the vocabulary portion of the lesson: The Family. In my research, I had discovered a relatively simple worksheet from an ESL support website and had asked Abdul to print copies. Due to the unanticipated increase in class size, I asked the students to find a partner as I distributed the activity. They eagerly dove into the exercise. Within minutes, however, it became obvious that it wasn't going so well.

"What is *law*?" Badr asked as he pointed to the word "sister-in-law." I explained that it wasn't really important in this case. That's when it dawned on me that many of the terms were perhaps western constructs and didn't necessarily translate culturally — or worse, were inappropriate. Had any of their mothers actually been divorced and remarried? If not, then my attempts to clarify the concept of "stepfather" would be futile. My response was to remain positive and encourage them as best I could. Despite my best efforts, though, Samir became so frustrated that he got up and walked out of the classroom, not returning for the duration of the lesson. The room suddenly felt hotter, and the class morale melted faster than an ice cube in the Moroccan desert. The activity was a blatant teaching fail.

After struggling through a semi-successful class discussion around the subject of "favourite foods," the lesson mercifully came to an end. But before dismissing the students, I invited each of them to pose for individual photos with their name cards. Over the next couple days, I planned to memorize and perfect the pronunciation of their names. They took turns standing against the wall, posing for their mug shots. The students found this highly amusing and laughed while shouting "Prison Break!"

Abdul, who had been doing paperwork in another room, returned and asked us all to pose for a group photo for the Youth Association for Culture and Development website. The second lesson had ended on an energetic, playful note, indicating that perhaps Abdul was right when he told me not to worry.

Everything would be fine.

Insha'Allah. ○

NIGHT HAD FALLEN over Jamaa el Fna. With a full stomach and a sense of restlessness, I strolled through the market square in search of something. I didn't know what exactly I was looking for, but I suspected that I would recognize it if I found it. It wasn't sex or drugs or any other form of debauchery. Looking back, I'm fairly certain that I was searching for an emotion or a person or a story or perhaps an interaction.

Marrakech's marketplace was where the people went — a constant flow of locals and sightseers, snake charmers and beggars, families and thieves. There were no discernible traffic lanes or intersections. Instead, scooters and delivery vans pushed their way through the crowds, honking brashly to indicate their supremacy. A gang of teenage boys fired helicopter Glow Sticks high into the air and chased them to wherever they drifted. A group of gravity-defying acrobats tumbled for tourist donations. A crowd gathered around a young man dressed as a woman dancing to the dizzying melody of a screechy horn. How did a nation that seemed so clearly divided in terms of gender permit such a blatant example of deviance? If I had learned anything, it was that Morocco had an affinity for ambiguity.

As I walked past a vendor selling fried snails, I inadvertently locked eyes with a young man who took this glance as a signal to approach me.

"You want hashish?" he asked with his chin pushed forward.

"No thanks," I responded with a polite smile

I kept moving.

182

Beside the food stalls, a white woman was on her knees, vomiting. I stopped and asked her if she could use my assistance. She waved me away, stating that her boyfriend had gone to fetch water.

Earlier that evening, I had shared a meal at the food stalls with Brahim. He took me to Stall #53 where his friend worked. We sat along the back of the bar and sipped glasses of sweet mint tea. Brahim ordered two servings of their signature dish — *cervelle de mouton en sauce*. If I had any doubt about the translation, the sheep skull beside the stove provided ample clarity. The brain stew was a mix of meat and spices in a savoury bouillon sauce. The chunks were slightly rubbery but surprisingly tender. After eating, Brahim — who was "Berber," not "bear-bear" — regretfully told me he had to catch a bus back to his parents' home at the edge of the Atlas Mountains. So we bid our adieus and he departed.

I became a man of the crowd.

The square was renowned for its captivating performers. And perhaps the most celebrated and most magical entertainers of all were the traditional storytellers. People gathered in pods to listen to the raconteurs weave ancient Arabian tales of love and loss and magic and other subjects that I could only infer as an outsider.

At one of these storyteller circles, I paused. The audience's attention was on a weathered man with a white beard and animated hands. His words were not just spoken but given life through gestures, delivered in an oral tradition that is one part narrative history and one part performance art. The tales drifted hypnotically past the blazing kerosene lantern in front of him and into the ears of the people he had managed to attract.

The light from the storyteller's lantern was reflected in the eyes of those who huddled around. In unison, the attentive audience responded to his prompts, laughing at a punchline or raising their eyebrows during moments of drama. And at the most crucial moments, the spectators leaned forward as though the future of the world would be faintly disclosed or the meaning of life might be subtly divulged — if they only listened carefully enough.

I suspected that those able to understand him were rewarded with a message or moral that entered through the ears and fell directly to the heart. But the animated Arabic legends were lost on me; the lessons of the storyteller were not destined for my foreign heart. My consolation prize, however, was watching faces become illuminated and brought to life by words.

And so, on the outskirts of the human circle, I hovered like a ghost — present, yet not fully there. ○

ON THE THIRD day of classes, as instructed, I waited outside Café Ali for my ride to the community centre. Abdul had gone to Casablanca on business, so one of the students, Tarik, was scheduled to collect me at 9:30 a.m. on his scooter. I waited, and then waited some more. As the minutes passed, I grew displeased. Again, I had rushed to honour an agreed meeting time. Again, nobody was there to meet me.

A week had passed since my arrival to Morocco, but I was still finding it hard to adapt the relaxed attitude about time. I found myself running a repetitive pep talk through my head about respecting cultural differences. In Morocco, the *Insha'Allah* attitude reigned supreme. The only appropriate response to muster was this: *Hey white boy, deal with it.*

A half-hour later, Tarik pulled up with a smile. It was not a guilty grin for being late but rather a good-humoured expression that seemed permanent. His contagiously friendly demeanour confirmed that my firm western insistence on punctuality was my problem, and my problem only. I hesitantly positioned myself on the metal rack of his dilapidated scooter, and we were off.

The roads were cluttered with aggressive taxi drivers, bumble-bee-like scooters and the occasional enraged donkey. Therefore, the potential for calamity was substantial. But Tarik was a respectful driver, never speeding too fast and never carelessly passing over potholes. Throughout the 10-minute ride, we chatted about his studies in a semi-coherent mix of English and French. He was currently enrolled in a science program and hoped to complete his engineering qualifications in France. If he could navigate the coming years as successfully as the frenzied Moroccan roads, then his future looked bright. We made it to the community centre unharmed.

The students had already arrived and were lined up against an apartment building across the street. I walked over to them.

"Hi Omar," I stated, proudly displaying that I was well on my way to memorizing their names. "How are you doing?"

"I am good, thank you."

I practised basic greetings with a few of the other guys and was pleased to note that Noureddine deviated from the standard response of "I am good" to say "I am sleepy." Despite the glitches of the first two classes, perhaps we were making progress after all. As a group, we leisurely strolled across the street together to begin our third lesson.

But that's when things got ugly.

Standing in the doorway with his arms crossed, the director of the community centre blocked us from entering. Abdul had made it evident that he had been navigating a not-so-subtle tension over the past few days. However, I didn't really know any details. Could something as simple as an English class be drenched in politics? Or was there more at hand than the lessons? Did this have something to do with me being a foreigner?

The director threw his hands into the air and started yelling at the students — like they had intentionally burned down the community centre and then ran away with his daughter.

In defence, Badr and Omar started shouting right back. Their hands flew about, augmenting the size and scope of their frustration.

The men were suddenly standing nose to nose, like they were trying to push each other over using their foreheads.

If this type of argument had arisen back home, I might have been more willing to intervene. (But then again, in Canada, we would have probably opened a couple bottles of beer, sat down on a bearskin rug and begun the discussion using "I feel" statements.) Here, I was at a complete loss over what to do. I didn't have adequate language skills to help mediate whatever issue was at hand. And, for my own safety, I wasn't about to intervene physically. So I just stood there, frightened, watching the conflict escalate.

Not all of students had such visceral reactions. Abdellatif pulled out a mobile phone and started video recording the stand-off. Mohammed simply turned and walked away. Tarik, who was standing beside me, continued to smile despite the drama. He seemed the most level-headed.

"Is this because of me?" I whispered to him.

Tarik snickered, probably at the self-centredness of my inquiry. He reassured me that the skirmish had nothing to do with my presence, my westernness or even the English language. From what I pieced together, it was a dispute over membership fees.

I was somewhat relieved, yet still confused. Why would the students have to pay for what I thought were free classes?

The yelling persisted, and I continued to stand on the sidelines, paralyzed with inaction. Fortunately, that's when a young woman came walking down the block and approached me. She introduced herself as Abdul's colleague from the volunteer organization and stated that Abdul had requested that she come to the community centre that morning because he had feared there might be a conflict. The woman said it would be best if I left the premises. She would help me find my way back to the medina. I was happy to have someone from the organization to instruct me what to do. On the other hand, her explanation also provoked a greater question — why would Abdul knowingly put me in a problematic situation?

Before I was escorted away from the yelling men, I quickly noted my email address on a piece of paper and slipped it into Tarik's hand. I hoped he would have the gumption to contact me directly to arrange English classes for the group. To me, it didn't matter if we held lessons at a community centre or in someone's living room. I wanted the opportunity to continue to work with these guys. And even more so, I wanted to connect with them. I still wanted a cooking lesson. I wanted a personal tour in a neighbourhood where tourists never tread. I wanted an unknown and exclusive experience, something that I could never have planned but would ultimately reflect on with one clear and nostalgic sentiment: *Amazing.*

Instead, while the director and the students yelled at each other, I was being shooed away from the standoff and back to my riad.

Yet maybe it was for the best.

It's hard to build bonds when there are fists in the air. ☼

AFTER THE DISCOURAGING conflict at the community centre, I decided that a brief change of scenery was in order. The next scheduled English class wasn't for another two days. This delay provided an opportunity to escape the heat of Marrakesh and take in a bit of the Moroccan landscape on a getaway of sorts.

On the whole, prearranged tourism packages have never been my first choice. But with my volunteer project potentially in peril, my morale needed a boost — and an organized tour seemed like a sensible option. I found a tour company and booked myself on the cheapest overnight expedition: a two-day trip to the Valley of Draa to ride a camel and sleep in a Bedouin tent. (This did go against my "no perks" travel paradigm. Yet desperate times called for desperate measures. And if you're me, seeking solace in camels makes perfect sense.)

The next morning, I boarded a 14-passenger van filled with young international backpackers. A well-paved highway led us out of Marrakech and into the Atlas Mountains, where the road became kinked with slow hairpin turns. Curled up in a window seat, I was content to do nothing but look at the passing scenery: rivers that were a bloody shade of red from the sediment of the surrounding hills, fields littered with plastic garbage, women harvesting wheat and other crops, and mud-brick villages carved into steep cliff sides. The only thing more satisfying than the sweeping scenery was the figurative and literal sensation of someone else taking the wheel. All I had to do is show up.

The tour paused for lunch in Ouarzazate, a city famous for its movie studios (bonus fact: *Lawrence of Arabia* was filmed there). I was fed a steaming vegetable tajine dish, which I ate with a non-abrasive Japanese man who kept me entertained with anecdotes about his life in Finland working for a tech company. And then we pushed forward and reached a northern corner of the Sahara Desert where the tour leaders equipped us with *keffiyehs* (traditional Middle Eastern headdress). After that, we boarded a herd of unimpressed-looking camels.

At this point, I think it's fair to pause and make a wide-sweeping cultural generalization that goes something like this: westerners romanticize camel riding. With gallant, windswept icons influencing our perceptions on the big screen (such as the aforementioned *Lawrence of Arabia*), we have developed an adventure fetish for the unhurried plod of the humped beasts, the vastness of the desert, and the hot wind tousling our hair. And if you're me, you're the epitome of this generalization.

To be fair, the camel ride did fulfill my fantasy. For at least three minutes, it was actually pretty cool. The rest of the two hours were not bad, per se. But it quickly became apparent that camel riding was not the blissfully epic activity that one might imagine. For starters, the heaving strides of the camel paired with the minimally padded cloth saddle led to the unyielding crunching of my scrawny butt. And then there was the gaseous odour leaking from my creature's rear end that combined with an unfortunate wind direction, created a type of camel fart vortex. Furthermore, when the camel's fecal material fell to the ground, it went nowhere fast. The perfect blend of sand combined with the hot, dry weather made it nearly impossible to decompose. The Valley of Draa — at least the portion that we walked over — was like a giant camel litter box. It had been years since I watched *Lawrence of Arabia*, but I was fairly certain there wasn't that much camel crap involved in the movie.

The good news, however, is that I can legitimately now state that I "rode a camel across the Sahara." Well at least the tip of it. And if you're me, that's just the right amount. ☼

BY THE TIME I returned to Marrakech, I felt recharged and ready to teach again. I had just stepped out of the shower (to rinse off any lingering odour of camel fart) when I received a message from Abdul. He wanted me to meet him immediately. A few minutes later, I was sitting at my usual post in Café Ali, watching groups of rowdy young men parading toward Jamaa el Fna. They energetically waved Moroccan flags in allegiance to the national soccer team, which was playing against Algeria that evening.

In a record-breaking amount of time — mere minutes — Abdul sauntered into the café with a grin and ordered a glass of tea. His smile, I assumed, was indicative of good news. The students and director had come to the common realization that education was invaluable, drafted a peace treaty and couldn't wait for the next class to begin. *The Canadian teacher has returned!*

I've been told that my naiveté is adorable.

After a few sips of steaming tea, Abdul began. "Daniel," he said in a suddenly serious tone, "there is too much tension at the community centre." I instantly knew where the conversation was going, and it made my heart sink. "I don't like the way the students are interacting with the director."

"There's no way to move past the disagreements?" As I asked the question, a group of boisterous soccer fans approached, and my words were drowned in a maelstrom of team chanting. Abdul paused, letting the noise pass. If he heard my inquiry, he chose to ignore it.

"We will have to cancel the classes." Abdul's face was now pinched to emphasize his seriousness. "I am very disappointed."

"Yeah. Me too." This time I spoke loudly and clearly, looking directly at him. "Can't we just hold the classes somewhere else?"

"Don't worry about this," he stated, closing his eyes. He tilted his head back and waved his hand in dismissal. "I have another group for you to teach."

"Um ... okay."

"I'll get back to you in the next couple of days with the details." Abdul's smile returned. "In the meantime, just keeping enjoying Marrakech." With that, he put his glass down, wished me a good evening and headed to the station to catch the last train to Casablanca.

I remained at the café, watching the soccer fans and feeling tangled. Part of me, specifically the portion that wanted to be perceived as a "good volunteer," thought that it would be best to adapt to the new situation and to receive this new teaching assignment with as much optimism and vigour as I could muster. But another part of me, specifically the part that has a difficult time accepting unclear circumstances, felt entirely disappointed. I didn't want a different group. I liked the group I was with. I had names memorized. Names. Memorized.

Now, nearly halfway through the month, I was back to square one. Sure, I was quite capable of entertaining myself while Abdul organized this new group — the city was filled with uncharted alleyways and undiscovered hammams. Nevertheless, there would only be two weeks left in the month by the time classes got underway. The purpose of my year-long adventure was to become *involved* with different cultures from around the world. Chiefly this was achieved through building relationships, which needed a bit of time to develop, to ripen. There wasn't much time left.

Boisterous soccer fans continued to parade past, waving their red flags. And I was sitting where it was more comfortable yet less rewarding — on the sidelines, watching them. ○

OVER THE NEXT few days, I wandered with a sense of aimlessness around Marrakech. I visited the famous Majorelle Gardens. I got swindled into a tour of a nauseatingly odorous leather tannery. I browsed through the photos at the Maison de la Photographie. I even splurged on a massage at one of the more exclusive hammams.

Yet I felt like I was biding my time, waiting for my Moroccan *raison d'être* to reveal itself. As the days began to stack up, the heat and constant bartering started to wear me down. In the eyes of the locals, I was clearly a tourist. This knowledge commonly came with the assumption that I was visiting Morocco to amass a small fortune of beautifully handcrafted products to decorate my life back home. My unwillingness to purchase Berber rugs, exotic spices or clay tajine dishes inevitably sparked disappointment from merchants. I would wander on, hoping to come across something more meaningful, across a situation where the exchange of dirhams was not the key objective.

One morning late into my second week, I wandered through Jamaa el Fna and stopped briefly for my daily glass of freshly squeezed orange juice. As I sipped the cool nectar, a man cycled past, balancing a tray of steaming mint tea goblets with one hand and steering with the other. The recurrent clink of coins from a cigarette seller provided a percussive beat for a waddling group of German tourists who snapped photos and then hastily returned to an air-conditioned coach. A veiled woman zipped by, sitting sidesaddle on her husband's motorcycle. Whether night or day, the square was in constant motion, a continual undulation of scooters and donkeys, dervishes and tourists. I returned my empty glass to the vendor, who had cracked brown fingernails. The acidity of the juice had taken its toll over the decades.

After stopping to buy a small bag of dates, I retired to a café. When alone (which was always), my preferred destination was the shady terrace of Café Glaciers, where I had a view of the busy square. I took a seat on the terrace, planning to read a book. But that's when a gentleman to my left casually mentioned how hot the wind was.

"It sure is," I replied. "It stings if I look in the wrong direction." The wind had the ability to instantaneously dry the eyeballs. For protection, I found myself constantly squinting.

Little did I know that the wind would catalyze an hour-long conversation with this gentleman, an older character named Olhour. He wore a faded yellow polo shirt and straw hat. The

191

way the skin creased around his eyes suggested that he had spent many years smiling. After learning I was from Canada, he told me he had been to California in the past, but his new dream was to see the Rocky Mountains. We made our way through a variety of topics: democracy, travel, Morocco.

"We are a country that is at a unique geographical and cultural crossroads," he proclaimed. "We are Africa's closest point to Europe. We are western and eastern. We are modern and Arab. We are diverse."

I nodded, appreciating the genuineness of the impromptu conversation. And then Olhour volleyed the exchange into my court.

"How have you enjoyed your time in Morocco?"

If this had been a more superficial chat, I might have glazed over the question and offered up something about the beauty of the Atlas Mountains. But Olhour had proven to be an attentive conversationalist. I figured he could handle my honest sentiments.

"To be frank," I responded, "it's been challenging." I explained the lack of success with my volunteer venture. My intent wasn't to complain but rather to determine if he had any insights about my difficulties. Or to see if he could lift the veil off Moroccan culture ever so slightly, to offer me a glimpse of something I had overlooked or simply not seen in the first place.

Olhour sat silently for a moment, rubbing a wrinkled hand over his clean-shaven chin.

"We are in the Coca-Cola epoch," he stated, nodding his head in agreement with himself. At first I assumed that he was referencing the westernization of the world, of international megacorporations and perhaps even the irreversible decline of centuries of indigenous wisdom. And, to a certain degree, perhaps he was.

"You know how you become energized when you take a sip of cola? The sugar and caffeine do magic in our bodies, and there is a period of euphoria." Olhour lifted a hand to illustrate his analogy. "But what happens after that? We crash. We enter a valley that is lower than where we began." He let his hand fall, smacking the table. "Well, right now, as a global community and here in Morocco, we are at the end of our peak. A crash is imminent. It has happened to each civilization before us."

This was really not the response I had anticipated.

His anecdote politely dismissed my own self-centred woes by placing them next to a planet-sized predicament. In no uncertain terms, he was stating, "Of course you're going to feel dissatisfied! Look at the world around you!"

And so I took a moment to do just that. The first thing that caught my attention was across the plaza: Café Argana. The renowned restaurant was concealed in scaffolding, hiding the damaged remnants of a terrorist's bomb that had exploded just a few weeks previously.

Olhour was silent for another moment, potentially to let his final words accumulate potency. And then he spoke.

"My only hope is that we can fall gracefully … *Insha'Allah*." ○

A PEBBLE WHIZZED by the tip of my nose like a bullet, launched inadvertently from the wheels of the car in front of us. I clung onto the motorbike with a sweaty grip and attempted to hide my head behind Abdul's shoulders, hoping that whatever god presided over Moroccan traffic would be kind enough to spare me from a fatal collision.

For the impending meeting, Abdul had dressed professionally, complete with a business suit and briefcase. I was wearing khaki shorts, my favourite plaid shirt and a pair of tattered flip-flops. Before I boarded his motorbike, Abdul mentioned that I looked weary. This subsequently made me wonder how he perceived me. In his eyes, was I a tired-looking vagabond? Or was he insinuating that I had been riding the Marrakesh Express to hashish heaven? Sure, I was underdressed. But even if I had wanted to wear more sophisticated attire, professional outfits are compromised in sake of portability when one lives out of a backpack for a year. And if my eyes were tired, it was the result of dealing with ambiguity. It was the fatigue that comes from two weeks of not knowing what was going to happen each day.

This was a Friday afternoon. We were on a highway outside of Marrakech, heading to where I was set to volunteer with a new group. After many days of dwindling hope, Abdul had finally emailed to inform me that we would visit the facility where the new English classes would take place: a woman's centre for artisans. I was immediately intrigued and somewhat daunted by the thought of a class full of Arab women. Would they be motherly and hospitable to an eager English teacher? Or would they greet my foreignness and maleness and whiteness with distain and suspicion?

Abdul eventually slowed the motorbike and turned onto a side street. We crawled down an unpaved road, entering into a newly constructed community. From an outsider's perspective, the dusty neighbourhood was not unlike where Abdul lived, with its empty sidewalks and three-storey apartment buildings in various phases of development. I wondered how on earth I would get to this corner of the city by myself — or would I have to continue to rely on Abdul? It was much farther away than the first community centre. To my untrained eyes, it lacked any decipherable landmarks. Finally, Abdul pulled the bike over in front of a single level whitewashed building. I hopped off and looked around.

In my mind, I imagined that we would be greeted by a group of shy women with headscarves who would extend generic pleasantries and formally invite us into the centre. Perhaps they would even guide me to the work areas where they made their handcrafts.

But there wasn't anybody in sight — no one at the centre, and no one in the entire neighbourhood. A plastic bag drifted by. The only sound was the distant drone of the highway. My temples began to sweat.

"Where is everyone?" I asked. The door of the women's centre was closed tight, barred with a chain and lock.

"I'm not sure," Abdul responded, and then he looked into his mobile phone as if it might provide the answer.

"What do you mean you're not sure?" I asked, trying to keep my cool.

"They must have gone on strike." He raised his head to look at me and then shrugged his shoulders.

"On strike?" I didn't understand how he arrived at this conclusion so quickly.

"Yes. Sometimes people go on strike," he stated nonchalantly.

The obvious question ran through my head: *Why had you bothered hauling both of us out to this women's centre without confirming that there would actually be people present?*

As I stood there looking at Abdul looking blasé, my hopes of being helpful in Morocco disintegrated, once and for all. All those lesson plans and all those concerns about being accepted became suddenly irrelevant. Teaching English lessons was as likely as finding a horse named Sahara Breeze.

If I were a more compassionate person, I might have been able to cultivate sympathy for Abdul, recognizing the challenges that come with community organizing. But I was tired of pep talks, of rational attempts to dismiss my own agenda and my own desires. I was exhausted with the continual self-assurance that certain experiences were culturally normal and that I should simply roll with the punches. I wanted to participate, to offer students something they might find useful, and inevitably be rewarded in the process. If anything, that trip to the women's centre confirmed something I was learning about the reality of volunteering with organizations: I could only be as helpful as an organization would enable me to be.

Abdul looked up from his phone and shrugged his shoulders again. "Let's get going. I have more meetings this afternoon," he stated. "We'll try again on Monday." We rode back to the city in silence and, at the entrance to Jamaa el Fna, bid a quiet goodbye to each other.

That was the last time I saw Abdul. ☉

IN EVERY GAME of cards, there's a point where a player's wisest move is to simply cut his losses and leave the game. This is how I came to view my time in Marrakech.

After the disappointing trip to the women's centre, I spent the weekend pondering my options. I didn't want to wait around in the stifling heat *hoping* that Abdul would facilitate a volunteer experience. I could no longer twiddle my thumbs while trusting that some opportunity would miraculously fall at my feet. After a week of scouring through my junk email, I had also given up hope that Tarik would reach out to organize classes at a different space.

The highs and lows had left me too exhausted to face the draining crowds. To avoid the relentless heat, I hid in my riad and tried to block out the chaos. I finally arrived at the exotic land of Morocco yet lacked the motivation to get out and appreciate it. Consequently I felt remorseful. The decision became clear — it was time to politely bow out, to walk away from the table, to cut my losses. There'd be no lessons. No homestays. No opportunities to build bonds.

I sent an email to Abdul thanking him for his time and informing him that I would be moving on. He replied, expressing disappointment. I didn't respond. I didn't know if there was anything else to say.

For the second half of the month, I decided I would alter my approach and give myself permission to simply drift across the country. At that point, I was nearly halfway through my year-long journey. Apart from the final week in Costa Rica, I had more or less stuck to my original game plan of spending each month in a single geographical location. But this time, things hadn't worked out as planned. I felt like the situation warranted some "escape."

So I became a classic backpacker: riding trains, wandering through cities and sleeping in crowded dormitory rooms. In the capital city of Rabat, I was overcome with a severe case of stomach flu, which led to me vomiting into a gutter, alone. The city of Fez was an intense, confusing labyrinth where my most pronounced experience involved a man with crazy eyes who spat in my face as I walked past him, for reasons unbeknownst to me. However, there were good moments too. The coastal town of Essaouira was a cooling seaside retreat, and its backpacker hostel provided a familiar social scene. The blue-walled mountain village of Chefchaouen was rejuvenating. Those three days of fresh air helped alleviate the tired look that had become embedded in my eyes.

As I drifted through these towns, I experienced the nation from the sidelines. And I grew to accept this external position, comfortable with my status as an outsider. In fact, there was something beautifully simple about drifting. The stakes were lower. If I didn't like the hand that one town dealt me, I could easily bow out. Head on down the road. Onward, to the next point on the map.

Yet I never found the one thing I wanted. Despite shaking that sense of despondency that I had felt in Marrakech, I never crossed a threshold into a realm of "connection." I never felt fully welcome.

As the months were unfolding, I began to realize that sometimes I would have the opportunity to feel connected to a nation — or at least an individual from that nation — and sometimes I would not. I was going to win some. I was going to lose some. For the meaningful experiences to happen, the only thing I really knew how to do was show up and try to remain open.

On the final day of the month, I boarded an airplane. I bid farewell to a nation that still remained aloof, still remained a mystery.

Yet, who knows? Maybe I'll return to Morocco someday. Maybe I'll have the opportunity to truly discover the inner workings of this nation that infiltrated my childhood dreams. Maybe I'll get the chance to return to the land where "exotic" and "challenging" are precariously synonymous. And maybe I'll be dealt a different hand — I'll find the *amazing* that I sought.

You know, *Insha'Allah*. ☺

JULY

Ruffepeyre, France

One of the greatest ways to gauge the value or "success" of each monthly arrangement was my emotional reaction upon departure. As I bid farewell to certain places, my cheeks had become damp with the emotions of parting. Other months, however, had left me more than ready for the next leg of the journey to begin. Intriguingly, a pattern seemed to be developing: every amazing month of strong friendships and great hosts was followed by a month of trials and tribulations.

The year had started strongly. My time in New Orleans had been rich with interesting people and learning opportunities. From the highs of Louisiana came a dramatic decline in personal morale at the raw vegan farm in Costa Rica. In March, my experiences in Peru were replenishing — not only in the dietary department but also from the laughter in the classroom, the adventures with fellow volunteers and the general delight of being under Estella's wing. And then came April in Buenos Aires. The passionate metropolis and its people were beguiling, but one unforeseen challenge after another — altitude sickness, mosquitoes, dog poop, bed bugs — thwarted my best efforts to seduce and be seduced by the city. My visit to South Africa commenced ominously, yet the friendship and kindness of Moses, Ruth and Mohapi softened the country's rough edges. Then there was June in Morocco, and, well, it had been an exercise in adjusting my expectations.

Now I was officially halfway.

Setting out on my year-long quest, I had fully expected the peaks and valleys — that's what budget travel (and life, really) is all about. I was grateful that the first six months of the year had not been one giant demoralizing experience and that the lowest of the lows were never too low to actually compromise the journey. I hadn't contracted malaria, lost a limb or forced my family to relinquish their entire life savings to rescue me from an international kidnapping fiasco. Overall, I had been extremely fortunate and I knew it. Yet acknowledging my good fortune did not equate to a sense of perpetual travel bliss.

In fact, a psychological force quite the opposite of ecstasy was taking root. Six months of travel had begun to take their toll. The constant new settings and the constant adjustments, the regular introductions and the regular goodbyes, the changing diets and the changing dynamics, it was all wearing me down. At the half-way point of the expedition, I had symptoms of too much adventure and stimuli — a condition one might call "traveller's fatigue."

This affliction goes beyond simple drowsiness or the usual indications of jet lag. It's a consequence of long-term travel and can manifest different behaviours and internal sensations. Or lack thereof.

For starters, numbness sets in. You might expect that an international voyage would spark a certain amount of wonderment. But after six months on the road, I was finding myself feeling apathetic to new sights and experiences, and even to the prospect of meeting new people. Did I really want to spend the afternoon wandering alone through another food market? Would I regret retreating to an air-conditioned café instead of visiting that historical site? Oh, you're a twentysomething British girl who wants to volunteer at an African orphanage? Yawn.

Self-imposed isolation is also a telltale sign of traveller's fatigue. In South Africa and Morocco, I had opted for private accommodation, a decision that permitted counterproductive seclusion. It is a vicious circle. The budget traveller isolates himself to escape the overstimulating setting. But then there is no new inspiration to lift him from his funk. So he waits for something to happen. Nothing does. No one knocks on his door to offer those free private tours or cooking lessons that he wants. Although solitude might help a person to recharge in the short term, isolation can make the situation worse if it becomes a habit.

Perhaps the saddest symptom of traveller's fatigue, however, is dreaming of home while living out one's international fantasy. Though I never truly considered out-and-out cancelling my trip — at least not at that point — I noticed a tendency to internally fade from a foreign location and become absorbed by ideas about my post-travel lifestyle in Canada. *Where might I live? Where would I work? What projects could I undertake?* It's an unfortunate paradox. There were countless people, I was sure, who would love to be in my shoes travelling the world. My subsequent reaction to traveller's fatigue was also a blend of remorse and self-reproach.

There's nothing more pathetic than feeling bad about feeling bad.

Fortunately, I had a good idea of what might remedy my disorder. What I needed was a calm location with less stimulation. A gentle situation that would encourage me to socialize. An organized project with a routine structure. And so, with hopes of offsetting my traveller's fatigue, I marked the halfway point of my journey by arriving to a little nation called France. And the great thing about France is that it can be just so darn lovely.

Le sigh. ☺

DAMN, TOULOUSE. YOU looked *fine*. Compared to the other urban strongholds of Europe, such as bohemian Barcelona or historical Rome, some might find the southern French city rather humdrum. But after having spent most of the past six months in less developed corners of the world, I was relieved that Toulouse immediately felt organized, refined, even elegant. There were no aggressive taxi drivers outside the airport vying to nab my business. The streets sparkled, free from the plastic bags and stray dogs that I had witnessed in Trujillo and the outskirts of Cape Town. The tap water could be consumed without fear of a gut-punching intestinal parasite. Toulouse had all the comforts of home but with far better croissants and more stylish citizens.

My departure from Morocco, like any good breakup, wasn't without a minor setback. As a final goodbye-brouhaha, a Moroccan airline had delivered me safely to France (great work!) but also decided to leave my backpack in Casablanca (not so great work!). My knee-jerk reaction was bitterness — was Morocco really throwing a last-ditch curveball? I tried to frame things in a different light, to give the nation the benefit of the doubt. *Morocco was so sad to see me leave that they desperately tried to cling to a memento.* (In times of powerlessness or frustration, I become blindly delusional about my own importance.)

At the airport customer service desk, I addressed my backpack casualty with a reassuring young man.

"Monsieur, your bag is still in Casablanca. We will do our best to get it back."

Then he winked at me. I wasn't sure if it was flirtation or just gratuitous French charm. Either way, the situation seemed to be under control.

With no real options but to keep going without my gear, I hopped aboard a public bus bound for the local train station. From downtown Toulouse, I rode the rails northeast to Averyon, a sub-region of the Midi-Pyrénées corner of France. While the other passengers of the train routinely checked their watches, I was absolutely in no rush. Outside my window, the landscape rolled like a silent French documentary film with no real plot, instead offering multiple frames of stunning cinematography: lush linear vineyards, meandering rivers, tree-lined country roads and the occasional quaint brick village adorned with its own ancient Catholic church. An hour before sunset, the train traversed a deep ravine and crawled into the mid-size town of Rodez.

I stepped off the train and immediately saw the person I was looking for. Nico was taller than the average man, with a pronounced French nose, dishevelled hair and glasses that were held together with a bit of duct tape. Limestone scuffs stained his clothes, but he had a tidy smile and his eyebrows wiggled when he spoke.

"*Bienvenue*, Daniel!" he exclaimed, offering a tough-skinned hand to shake. "Welcome to Rodez!"

"Thanks. It's really good to be here." I wasn't offering any false banalities. Despite my fatigue, I was always energized by a fresh project in a fresh country.

"I see you're a minimalist!" he said, referring to my lack of luggage.

"Yeah, I guess Morocco is offering me some complimentary lessons in non-attachment," I joked back, shrugging my shoulders.

"Don't worry about your stuff," Nico assured. "We have lots of work clothes for you to wear. Let's get going."

As we exited the station and headed over to his car, Nico didn't really walk as much as gallop. Within minutes, we had departed Rodez and were whizzing on a narrow two-lane highway in a compact sedan best described as a tin can on wheels clinging to its final moments of functionality. Nico drove the vehicle with the same gusto with which he walked, and at one point we may have rounded a corner on two wheels. The destination was a few kilometres west, to a small village called Ruffepeyre with a population of 75.

"Tomorrow's going to be a busy day," Nico shouted above the roar of the engine, "as we'll be getting ready for this weekend's big event."

"Oh?" I raised my eyebrows. "What's happening?"

"A party!" Nico exclaimed, widening his eyes. "There will be drinking and dancing and performances." He paused from his explanation to zip across the centre lane, passing a slow-moving truck and narrowly missing a head-on collision with a delivery van. "Everyone's invited ... friends, neighbours, volunteers. You're going to love it!"

As he was telling me more about the party and the platform he needed to construct for the live performances, a weather-worn red brick tower became visible on the horizon. It was, by far, the most distinguished structure across the rolling countryside, dwarfing the other buildings and the trees in the same fashion that the Eiffel Tower dominates the Parisian landscape.

Minutes later, in a cloud of dust, Nico pulled the car to a stop at the base of the tower. Happy to have survived the wild ride, I stepped out the vehicle, eagerly taking stock of my new surroundings. Ruffepeyre was green and lush, strikingly different from the intense heat and redness of Morocco. The faint aroma of wheat fields and plum trees lingered in the air. The sun cast a warm, gentle glow on the village. Larks chirped leisurely. It was a giant French countryside cliché, yet I was not immune to its charms. And if everything went according to plan, this was going to be my home for the month. ☺

WHAT IS IT exactly about France that makes people sigh? According to the United Nations World Tourism Organization, France is consistently the most visited nation in the world, beating out both the U.S.A. and China year after year. Tourists are drawn to the Mediterranean nation for a multitude of reasons, not the least of which is its cuisine. Some of the mainstays include decadent cream sauces, crusty baguettes, bold cheeses, perfect *pâtisseries* and the most sophisticated wines in the world. And if delicious food's not your thing — I'm looking at you, raw vegans! — the country offers incredible vistas, including the beautiful French Alps and the rolling hills of the south. There is also the romance of the language, the rich history of dramatic revolutions, the medieval architecture, the contemporary art and the most coveted bicycle race in the world. And let us not forget the people of France, a special breed of humans that are branded as broody, arty, snobby and, above all else, carnal. Many people love to make fun of the French, but I suspect that those same people are jealous because they were not born *Français*.

When deciding which countries I wished to visit in Europe, I put France at the top of the list. To be honest, I had already visited *la République*. A previous trip had taken me to Paris, which I had *adoré énormément*. However, I had a sneaking suspicion that there was more to France than goofball poses in front of the Eiffel Tower and lounging lazily beside the Seine River (with cheap bottles of Bordeaux, of course). The southern regions beckoned with verdant vineyards, fresh baked bread and that patented *joie de vivre*. My inner romantic begged for the opportunity to experience it all first-hand. So the month of July was bequeathed to France.

Throughout the journey, my tactic was to research host sites a few months ahead of time (as most organizations weren't able to plan too far in advance). I began to notice something initially counterintuitive: There seemed to be a correlation between a nation's economic development and its call for international volunteers — with wealthier countries offering *more* work-exchange opportunities than their developing counterparts. When I thought about it more deeply, the skewed presence of "richer" nations made sense. Industrialized countries had better Internet access and literacy, which, in turn, translated into more online postings. Not to mention the fact that countries such as France and Australia had significantly higher labour costs than, for instance, Peru or India. Incorporating helpers into a project was not just an amusing way of meeting people from around the world but also a viable strategy to keep operating costs to a minimum. The greatest challenge in finding a host project in France was simply sifting through the masses of options: farms, wineries, guest houses, campgrounds and more. My strategy was to filter the opportunities according to geographic location, personal interest and reviewer testimonials.

One listing specifically piqued my interest. A renovation venture in the southern *département* (territory) of Averyon summoned ambitious volunteers to participate in a manual labour project. It had glowing reviews and also promised leisure time to explore the region. What appealed most, however, was the uniqueness of the task: the restoration of a 13th-century Cistercian monastic tower.

With fingers crossed, I sent a message to the host expressing my interest, sharing the story of my travels and attesting to my recently developed skills. If he needed a kitchen floor tiled or wanted his chickens to improve their English language skills, I could be the man for the job. Nico replied, asserting that his chickens were already fully bilingual. Nonetheless, I'd be more than welcome to help for the month of July. ☼

Inside the monk's tower, the lights went dim. In centuries past, this might have been an indication that it was time to pray. But on that particular night in Ruffepeyre, prayer was the last thing on anyone's mind.

Who wants to be holy when there's a massive disco ball hanging from the rafters?

The first few bars of synth and drums pulsed over the stereo. Behind a velvet curtain, a man stepped forward. He was wearing a black leather miniskirt that failed to conceal his thick hairy legs. With two small cantaloupes under his shirt, he circled the stage with his head held high. And then he stopped to tap his foot to the beat and adjusted his perky fruit breasts.

In the audience, the woman beside me — who was dressed as Björk — released a catcall whistle.

Finally, the skirted man raised a vacuum cleaner hose to his mouth.

"I want to break free … I want to *break* free!"

This flamboyant lip-sync performance marked the beginning of the annual Ruffepeyre talent pageant.

After 48 hours in the south of France, I had become smitten with the alluring elements: the bucolic landscape, the adorable top-heavy resident dog named Dolly and the patisserie truck (which was more or less a bakery on wheels that rolled through

206

the country lanes, showering rural-folk with velvety éclairs and fresh baguettes). Plus the other volunteers were difficult to dislike. Chip from New Orleans fired question after question about my time in the Big Easy. Natalie from Nigeria immediately brought me an unopened toothbrush when she learned that my luggage was lost. And Hanna from Sweden blushed each time she spoke. As for the rest of the volunteers, well, they didn't stop smiling.

That morning, the crew had been conscripted to help build a performance stage, to clear the property of its scattered renovation gear and to ensure that the grounds were sufficiently manicured to host a crowd of 50 visitors. Like a group of *castors occupés* (that's French for busy beavers), we darted about in preparations for the gathering. By the time the evening arrived, the wooden table in the courtyard drooped with a mountain of steamy quiches and an endless selection of cheeses, plus the plethora of booze options, including some very potent dandelion wine.

Guests started trickling through the property's stone archway — not just residents of Ruffepeyre but visitors from all over the region. Nico's sister drove in from Toulouse. A group of volunteer helpers came from a farm project in a neighbouring valley. Many people arrived in costume. At one point, I observed a three-way conversation between Audrey Hepburn, Will Smith (circa *Fresh Prince of Bel-Air*) and a man dressed as an old woman carrying a leek like a purse.

Then we all headed into the monk's tower. One by one, the bravest of the guests took their turn on stage. A grey-haired woman with high cheekbones sang the French standard "Tous les Garçons et les Filles." An Israeli couple performed a choreographed dance routine to Hindi music. A 10-year-old local girl and her little sister sang an a cappella rendition of "Part of Your World" from *The Little Mermaid*. Nico, dressed as Elton John, performed a stirring karaoke version of "Crocodile Rock."

The crowd was lively and intoxicated. I cheered supportively.

But I was also hesitant. Despite the seemingly good elements of Ruffepeyre, I was having a difficult time leaving precautionary mode.

My specific modus operandi was this: when the other shoe dropped, I'd be ready. If the past months had taught me something, it was to not let my guard down. When I had been too optimistic or too carefree, that's exactly when I had been mugged or had stepped in dog poop or had my karma attacked by a hungry farmer. I don't mean to sound fatalistic, but I feared there would be a catch. Nico would reveal some hideous hidden Jekyll and Hyde characteristics. An angry militia of fire ants would suddenly overtake my mattress. I'd accidently step into an abandoned well and break my femurs — yes, *both* of them. An anvil would fall from some great height (which, because the tower used to be owned by a blacksmith, was actually not entirely impossible).

Something was bound to happen.

That night, however, the most serious incident was when one of Freddie Mercury's cantaloupes took a tragic fall out of his brassiere and cracked open on the floor. ○

As THE DAYS progressed, Nico continued to prove his consistency of character, despite my concealed suspicions. Parallel to my first impressions, he was a bundle of energy and dishevelled clothing and boyish grins. In fact, his relaxed approach to managing the various work projects quickly situated him as one of my favourite hosts of the year. But Nico had more than an agreeable personality; he also had an interesting personal history. In fact, to lead a more self-determined lifestyle, he had recently made some big life changes.

Born in the early 1970s in the town of Mont-de-Marsan, Nico was raised in the southern suburbs of Paris. In his twenties, he left for London, where he spent most of his professional life working for an international corporation. After nearly two decades of being a businessman boxed into a desk, Nico decided that he needed a drastic lifestyle change. He abandoned the business world with a specific objective: to actually appreciate his life.

So he returned to his homeland of France in search of something more sustainable, more communal, more meaningful.

One fateful afternoon, Nico was casually driving through the back roads of the Averyon region with thoughts of rural relocation germinating in his head. His wandering eyes drifted toward a crumbling tower that was stamped with a sign: À VENDRE. The structure was intriguing to him — it was neither barn nor church. Different from the other edifices in the region, it was a *mélange* of citadel and silo. Nico stopped the car and stood before the deteriorated tower. At four storeys, it looked like a piece of architectural Jenga. The corner edges were composed of large slabs of stone, while the exterior walls were a patchwork of grey, pink and white rocks that must have been replaced over the years as required. There were holes where windows used to be.

He imagined the history of the site and where he could steer its future.

"We need a young man to renovate this place," a voice floated into his ear.

Nico turned to see someone behind him. The man wore a tweed cap and had the lines of many decades etched into his face. He introduced himself as Yvon and stated that he lived across the street with his wife, Renée. It just so happened that Nico was standing in the little town of Ruffepeyre, a French hamlet small enough to fit into a snow globe. The historic tower stretching before him was for sale. It simply needed the right person for the job. For many years, Yvon had been waiting for this right person to arrive.

Over the next few days, Nico researched the history of the tower. The structure, it turned out, was constructed in the 13th century to serve two main purposes. Firstly, it was built to house a Cistercian abbot, who used the space to render justice over the region. The second purpose was as a traditional farmhouse. The surrounding land was quite fertile, and the Cistercians used the tower to shelter animals and store food from the harvest. As the centuries rolled forward, the stewardship over the tower and the surrounding land changed hands. But the primary usage of the edifice remained consistently based around agriculture. At the beginning of the 20th century, a blacksmith took proprietorship over the tower and constructed attached living quarters. The remnants of his vocation, such as a cast iron stove, continue to decorate the space today. After the blacksmith passed away, the tower fell through different hands and was not adequately maintained. It had survived wars and revolutions and plagues, and even the most destructive element on earth — time itself. But time was coming dangerously close to winning another battle. The tower was a historic mess.

Nico had a distinct sensation burgeoning inside: renewed purpose. His father had been a woodworker and had bestowed him with the skills of construction and renovation. Plus Nico had an appreciation for history and archeology. It would take years of work to repair the tower, but with a bit of endurance (and the right help), he was certain that the place would be restored to its previous glory. Could this be the new direction his life would take?

As Nico stood on that gravel road, it was perhaps Yvon's sentiments that told him he had not simply found a new project. He had also found a new home. The elderly countryman delivered a powerful message that most of us crave to hear: "We've been waiting for you."

"WELL, MR. BAYLIS," stated the icy administrative voice on the telephone line, a far departure from the flirtatious Frenchman at the airport, "it appears that your backpack is still at the airport in Casablanca."

A week had passed in Ruffepeyre, and my lost luggage had yet to depart Morocco.

"Correct me if I'm wrong," I bounced back, trying to keep my cool, "but there is a flight each day from Casablanca to Toulouse, no?" I didn't want to sound like a jerk, but the sheer ridiculousness of the situation was corroding my sense of diplomacy.

The voice paused and then spoke again. "Yes, Mr. Baylis."

"Well, do you think that someone — anyone really — could just put it on one of those planes?"

"We'll put in another request," the voice responded dryly. "Have a nice day."

"I will have a nice day when you return my backpa—"

CLICK.

Since arriving at Ruffepeyre, I had developed an eight-step morning ritual: 1) Dial the third-party lost baggage company. 2) Inquire about the status of my backpack. 3) Establish a verbal tango session. 4) Experience a deep sense of powerlessness. 5) Become frustrated. 6) Hang up or be hung up on. 7) Feel as though nothing had been accomplished. 8) Go feed the chickens.

To be fair, I was functioning just fine without my backpack. On the night of my arrival, Natalie had given me that new toothbrush. During an evening trip to Rodez, I had purchased two new pairs of boxer shorts. Nico had a whole wardrobe of extra work clothes for helpers to wear. Life seemed to march forward. Perhaps if I had been in any other location, I might have grown frustrated with the limitation of my fashion choices. But the fresh French country air, in conjunction with the regular consumption of Beaujolais, had a certain placating effect. I was well fed, working hard and in the company of great people. If a missing backpack was the worst of my troubles in life, things were looking pretty good. The only motive fuelling me to continue tracing down the backpack was a basic sense of customer entitlement — I pay to fly with you, you deliver my luggage. Simple.

Yet as the days ticked by, as much as I curmudgeonly cursed their disorganized existence, that Moroccan airline enabled an important travel nugget: I could survive fairly well with relatively few possessions.

With part defeat and part liberation, I began to accept the grim probability that I was never going to see my backpack again. ○

To my astonishment, the days passed and nothing horrible happened. Nico continued be quite sensible and benevolent. I found all the other volunteers to be rather pleasant. I didn't even catch herpes from a contaminated leather work glove. Somehow I had stumbled upon a winning work-exchange project. This nook in the south of France had a harmonious balance of all things a traveller could desire: good food, great accommodation, interesting people, the opportunity to be truly helpful, and care-free leisure time.

The meals were often the most enjoyable part of the day. The food was not extravagant, but in most instances it was home-grown and it was fresh. Nico's garden was just beginning to offer a bounty of beets, tomatoes, broad beans, carrots and potatoes. By mid-month, a zucchini pandemic was upon us, and our re-cipes often revolved around the creative usage of this squashy green vegetable. In the root cellar under the kitchen, a large bin of unshelled walnuts (from the backyard tree) supplied another source of nourishment. When my hands were idle, I'd often grab a nutcracker and start building a pile of raw walnuts, which would be incorporated into frittatas and salads. The half-dozen chickens produced eggs. The grandiose rosemary bush provided a go-to seasoning. The plum and peach trees offered dessert. At a grocery store in Rodez, Nico purchased whatever wasn't grown or harvested, such as dried pasta or roquefort cheese or these enormous French-style bacon bits called *lardons*.

The food might have been local but the help wasn't. My arrival brought the grand total of on-site helpers to eight. Together we formed a fun-loving motley crew representing various corners of the world from Sweden to Nicaragua to Japan (and a few places in between). Our assembly in Ruffepeyre was like a United Na-tions summit but with less grey hair and more Merlot. Instead of isolating myself, I was willingly coaxed into card games and bicycle rides and stories around the campfire.

You'd think that with all those people, it might get a bit crowded, but there was enough space for everyone. The accom-modation in Ruffepeyre was rustic yet comfortable. Although

Nico slept in the living space above the kitchen, which itself was attached to the monk's tower, most of the volunteers were lodged across the gravel lane in a separate building called *le castel*. With plaster crumbling off the walls and with resident bats, the 350-year-old three-storey chateau was also in dire need of maintenance. However, the large home had a fully functional bathroom with a flush toilet, a contemporary shower and a washing machine. Each morning, I swung my feet out of a bed onto a lavish Turkish rug in a building that was older than Canada itself. The castel would go down as the most idyllic accommodation I had all year.

During the first week of July, the task was to reinforce an exterior wall of the castel. After decades of erosion from wind, rain and sun, the mortar between the pink stones had crumbled away and left the structure progressively vulnerable. Therefore, the maintenance objective was to replace the mortar in a process that Nico called "pointing." For this to occur, there were primary tasks to address first: making trips to the quarry to source sandstone, crushing lumps of rock into sand for the mortar, and constructing scaffolding (which was like a life-sized game of Lego). That first week of work was an unglamorous blend of banging rocks and getting covered in mortar goop — a slightly modernized procedure that the monks of Ruffepeyre would have used to build and maintain the structure in previous centuries.

After months of using more knowledge-based skills, such as teaching English and blog strategy, I welcomed the physical labour. I even became the go-to mortar-guy, thanks to my ability to concoct the perfect soupy balance (an expertise that I had initially acquired while tiling in New Orleans). I wouldn't say I learned any life-changing new skills that first week, but the consolation prize was that Nico was always fair with his work-exchange expectations. The helpers were scheduled Monday to Thursday, with a half-day on Friday and a full weekend to explore the surrounding region or to simply relax.

On the weekends, we were able to use the bicycles to visit a farmer's market in the neighbouring town of Valady or to meander down country lanes. On special occasions, Nico took us on little excursions around the region, such as visiting the picturesque stone village of Belcastel and celebrating Bastille Day in Rodez. During the week, when the working hours were complete, the evening activities would vary. One of my favourite diversions was to kidnap Dolly the dog and stroll through the fields at dusk. Or I'd take my turn at transforming whatever ingredients were available into dinner. Whatever the activities, they usually included a few bottles of wine, which I never protested. Not once.

After the logs on the fire turned into embers or the card players folded their hands and excused themselves from the table, I would wander back to the castel — always with my head tilted toward the night sky, contentedly searching for stars. ☼

THE FRENCH AIR was crisp that morning. A ray of sunlight crawled across the milky walls of my rustic bedroom and bounced toward the exposed wooden ceiling beams. Faint whiffs of lavender from a nearby field pirouetted through the open casement windows. Outside, a choir of sparrows gossiped ferociously while pecking at dangerously ripe peaches dripping from an overburdened tree. By all accounts, the castel was a sublime setting — the type of tender location where one could remain all day to serenely write poetry, casually strum a guitar or, if in the company of a romantic partner, to make unhurried love until the body required sleep again. However, poems about peaches and soft moans of ecstasy were not on the schedule that morning.

Nope, there was a farmyard animal to slaughter.

Behind the monk's tower, a poultry coop contained six egg-laying chickens and an increasingly rotund guinea fowl, whose singular purpose was to end up in the oven. Destiny would be fulfilled on that lucky day — or unlucky day, depending on perspective. After many weeks of helping, a volunteer named Jesse (from Vancouver!) was set to depart that afternoon. In honour of his time and energy devoted to the restorations, Nico

214

had suggested that we celebrate with a lunchtime feast of roasted guinea fowl.

The slaughter of the fowl, I figured, was something that I ought to watch. Participating in the killing of the bird would definitely augment my street cred among the agrarian crowd. And so, after slipping myself into the same dirt-crusted wardrobe that I wore each day, I reluctantly left the room of sunbeams and birdsong to head up the gravel road to a traditional red stone house, the home of Yvon and his wife Renée. This is where the murder was scheduled to take place.

Nico and Jesse had already arrived and were chatting casually with the elderly French couple. The fresh-faced Jesse vigorously rubbed his hands together. This action might have been to ward off the morning chill but was more likely a physical reaction to the element of excitement in the air. I could feel it too. In all my three decades of life, I could not recall ever having been present at the killing of an animal. (Once, on a late summer's night while driving with friends in the nether regions of Wisconsin, we accidently mowed over a raccoon. But I'm fairly certain he had suicidal tendencies based on the way he darted in front of the vehicle. So it was an innocent accident, not intentional slaughter.) The killing of the guinea fowl would introduce a new level of premeditated butchery to my roster of life experiences.

Nico and Jesse made space for me to join them, and together we formed a naïve yet curious audience. My hands also began to rub together.

The small-statured Renée was silent. Burgundy-dyed hair spurted from the crown of her head. She wore a simple blue and purple plaid dress covered by an avocado green vest that appeared to be home-knit. The crow's feet around her eyes attested to years of staring across the region's many wheat fields. When looking into these eyes, it was difficult to know which one to focus on. The right eye was milky blue and the left was dark with a loose eyelid drooping overtop, and the two eyeballs did not function in unison. To those who knew her, she was a cuddly French grandmother. But in centuries past, Renée might have been mistaken for a mystical town sorceress. The double-edged knife in her hand did nothing to dispel her witchy veneer.

"She has been killing poultry for 61 years with that same knife," whispered Nico, motioning to the blade. "It's been the death of at least a thousand birds."

We began walking around the house to the wooden barn where the guinea fowl was about to meet its demise. Beside Renée strolled her equally pint-sized husband, the poster boy for adorable antique French gentlemen. Upon Yvon's white hair casually sat his grey flap cap. Over a thick collared shirt, he wore a red wool sweater that was thin at the elbows. He smiled more than his wife. Neither of them talked much — possibly because of the language barrier, possibly because they were unsure why a crowd of people would gather to watch the killing of a bird.

When they did exchange words, the elderly couple spoke French with hearty farmland accents. French, however, was not their mother tongue. Renée and Yvon came from an exceptional cultural and linguistic lineage known as Occitan, whose closest language-relative would be Catalan. According to UNESCO, Occitan is classified as an endangered dialect, which means that it is not being transferred to new generations. In contemporary French society, Renée and Yvon were uncommon characters, the last expressions of a disappearing culture. Being in the presence of the aged couple was the anthropological equivalent of stumbling across a couple of rare mountain gorillas while trekking through central Africa.

On the dirt floor of the barn sat a cardboard box. The box bounced a little in protest. Did the guinea fowl know that the end was nigh? Perhaps there was a prayer to be said or a quick ritualistic dance of gratitude to the gods for enabling lunch. The correct procedure around the slaughter of animals was foreign to me. So, like a lighthouse, I stood and simply watched.

Yvon reached into the box and extracted the guinea fowl by the feet. *"Elle est jolie. Elle est lourde,"* he stated tenderly, noting the weight of the bird.

By hanging poultry upside down, I learned, gravity becomes

the most appreciated ally of a soon-to-be-slaughtered bird. The blood rushes to the brain, and the animal is unable to comprehend what is happening. I took a mental note of this technique, in case I ever find myself on an airplane plummeting from the sky. (I'll be the guy with his feet in the overhead compartments.)

"*Viens ici, ma petite*," coaxed Renée. She took the bird's head in her hand. Without delay or melodramatics, she skilfully punctured her vintage blade into the vein that ran along the slender neck of the bird. The guinea fowl was surprisingly calm. Its eyes blinked as the blood trickled out of the neck and into a bucket below.

Drip. Drip. Drip. The life literally began to pour out of it.

Renée glanced in my direction and raised her eyebrows in a look that seemed to say "*C'est la vie.*" Or, maybe in this instance, "*C'est la mort.*"

The guinea fowl no longer protested. As I watched the bird's final moments, a combination of remorse and inquisitiveness and sadness rotated in my heart. Internally, a question surfaced: *Do I really need to eat animals?* However, as I began weaving my way into a complex ethical debate, Renée distracted me with a surprising next move.

After a minute of dripping blood, the guinea fowl appeared sufficiently dead. But from out of nowhere, the diminutive elderly woman produced a thick wooden stake and began striking the fowl over its scrawny birdy head, conking the life out of any remaining cranial cells with the tenacity of a professional baseball player going for a home run. After three high-pitched, echoic blows, the neck of the fowl swung limp. Renée looked conclusively satisfied with her work.

During the commotion, Yvon had left the barn. He reappeared with a large steel pot of boiled water. The limp bird was taken by the neck and submerged in the scalding bath. After 20 seconds of blanching, it was placed on a newspaper-covered table. The heat from the tub was enough to cause the feathers to flake away as Renée used her wrinkled hands to massage the chest of the guinea fowl, alternating from left to right as necessary to prevent cramping. All the while, Dolly the dog sat watching at the barn door with her head crooked to one side.

When the feathers were sufficiently stripped, the next step was to clean out the innards. Renée invited us to gather in her kitchen. As she walked by en route to the house, I could see a glimmer of sweat on her forehead and a thin streak of blood smeared across the skin of her neck. She swung the guinea fowl casually at her side, as if it were the latest Louis Vuitton handbag. Killing fowl wasn't glamorous work, but she seemed to do it with a certain *je ne sais quoi*, unburdened by sentimentality.

The inside of Yvon and Renée's home was country-themed, though not in an intentional or staged country-kitchen sort of way. It was a reflection of their actual rural life. The appliances and décor had probably not changed much in the many decades that they had been married and living in the same house. The only modern exception was a flat screen TV that blared the morning news at a volume appropriate for the hard-of-hearing. The sunshine yellow walls of the kitchen were decorated with an old clock, a couple of silver serving platters and a painting of a medieval castle. At the centre of the room, a six-seat rectangular table was decorated with a plastic floral tablecloth. On a faded wooden hutch were time-worn photographs of loved ones. The room smelled of dust and fruit pies.

Renée commenced the next part of the proceedings. The kitchen table was lined with newsprint, and the scrawny feet and limp head of the guinea fowl were clipped away with pruning sheers. Then Renée made a wide incision into the lower region of the chest cavity with a paring knife and began disembowelling the naked bird. A string of lungs, heart, stomach, esophagus tubing and other pea-sized internal organs were extracted by hand with a familiarity that attested to many years of preparing poultry. In less than 60 seconds, the table became an anatomical cornucopia of yellow, crimson and pale grey organs. It was the type of scene that, in my pre-travelling days, I was more likely to witness as part of a modern art installation at an *avant-garde* gallery. But this was Friday morning for Renée.

In a playful display of boyishness, Yvon pulled the bird feet off the table and scratched at the air. He chuckled softly and asked Nico if he wanted to keep the extraneous parts of the fowl. *"Non merci,"* Nico courteously responded with a smile.

Now thoroughly eviscerated, the guinea fowl was rinsed with water, placed on a small red tray and pushed to the end of the table. Renée's role as poultry executioner was formally over.

Before departing to start our own working day, we loitered for a couple more minutes in the kitchen. While Yvon cleared the newspapers and their squelchy contents, Renée shared some photographs of her mother-in-law, a religious woman who had diligently recited the rosary until her final days. At the age of 97, she dropped her head quietly at that same plastic-covered table.

I imagined that Renée and Yvon would also be blessed with long lifespans. They maintained a type of lifestyle that correlated with the ability to endure decades: austerity, humour, physical work and uncomplicated cuisine. Unlike younger generations, they did not have much use for mobile phones and fashion trends, or even sunbeams and poems about peaches. Theirs was an unpretentious and traditional existence — where food came from the field and barn, and death was simply a part of life. ○

AFTER THE SLAUGHTER of the guinea fowl, the morning work consisted of mixing more mortar, finishing the crack-filling reparations on the exterior of the castel and subsequently dismantling the three-storey scaffolding. After a week of focusing our attention specifically on repairing the wall, we viewed the completion of that specific phase of restorations as a substantial accomplishment. Not only would we be honouring Jesse's departure at the lunchtime feast, but we'd also celebrate another item checked off the lengthy "to do" list for the restoration project.

In the kitchen attached to the monk's tower, Natalie, Chip and I eagerly gathered to prepare the midday celebration. The guinea fowl was slathered with a rosemary butter rub, nestled into a cast iron casserole dish and placed into the propane oven to roast. While the beast was baking, the vegetable patch was raided for additional items to complete the menu. It was one of our finest culinary assemblages: a salad of garden tomatoes and buttery heirloom lettuce with a mustard vinaigrette, boiled baby potatoes topped with chopped rosemary and rich *crème fraîche*, and sautéed zucchini with cracked walnuts and cream sauce. Finally, to mop up all the flavours, a homemade whole-wheat loaf was sliced and arranged into a bread bouquet.

With the food underway, our next mission was to create an ideal dining ambiance. The long wooden table in the courtyard was set with an assortment of mismatched cutlery, antique plates and wine glasses of various sizes. Purple and white onion flowers were snipped from the garden and arranged erratically in a vase, forming a decorative centrepiece. The indoor stereo speakers were tilted outward and light jazz piano filled the country airwaves. The main musical entertainment, however, was from the trilling of the birds in the walnut tree, which also provided the perfect amount of shade from the hot summer sunshine.

Before we left the home of Renée and Yvon earlier that morning, we had invited them to join in the lunchtime festivities. They had been, after all, an important part of the production of the meal. The couple accepted the invitation, and they came sauntering from across the lane shortly after the spread was laid upon the table. Renée clutched a freshly baked sugar tart in her hands. Once everyone had assembled — Renée, Yvon, Nico and the handful of volunteers — we settled onto the rickety chairs around the table. Our glasses were filled with walnut wine and raised in honour of good food and good people.

"*À votre santé!*"

We saluted and clinked glasses, expressing gratitude to Renée and Yvon for being part of the day and wishing Jesse safe travels as he headed back to Canada.

Then we eagerly dove into the food. Like floats in a Mardi Gras parade, the different dishes circled the table. They were showered with spectator approval. The produce from the garden had that "an-hour-ago-it-was-still-in-the-ground" level of vivid, sweet crispness. The music was lovely. The company was warm. Everything was downright perfect. Except for one thing: the guinea fowl.

Something had gone drastically wrong. Having never had previously tasted the flesh of guinea fowl, I had no concrete basis to make comparisons. But I was confident that the meat wasn't supposed to taste agonizingly chewy and flavoured like the bird had been reared on a steady diet of snail manure and battery acid. What *was* guinea fowl supposed to taste like? Had we overcooked it? Had the slaughter soured the flavour? Where had things gone awry? How does a fowl become so — errr — foul?

A hush slowly fell over the table. Normally this might be taken as a sign that guests were too busy enthusiastically stuffing food into their mouths to speak. As I looked around at the various young and old faces to gauge a reaction, it was clear that people were indeed eating — just not in a voraciously satisfied way. Nobody made eye contact. Most were taking bites of zucchini or buttering pieces of crusty bread. Jesse had taken a regrettably large portion of guinea fowl. He stabbed a piece on his fork and stared at it with the keenness of someone attempting to pass a kidney stone. If I had been able to steal into the unspoken thoughts of the guests at that table, I'm fairly certain I would be privy to a common assessment: *What on earth is this vulgar, rubbery substance on my plate?* Yet nobody spoke up. The taste of the bird was becoming the elephant in the room (or, as I now label unacknowledged awkwardness, "the guinea fowl at the table"). I wondered if anyone would have the gall to speak up.

"Daniel, please have some more!" encouraged Nico as he picked up the plate of guinea fowl and passed it in my direction. I was not sure why he was putting me in such a prickly position. Was he trying to show Renée how much we appreciated her work? And that we would not let any of the bird go to waste? I endeavoured to be a people-pleaser, but I had my limits. At that moment, guarding my stomach trumped any attempt to make a sweet elderly Frenchwoman feel cherished.

"I couldn't eat another bite," I politely responded. I forced a

221

smile and avoided gazing longingly at the small mountain of flaky baby potatoes and that tasty tub of *crème fraîche*, which I would have happily spooned directly into my mouth.

Nico grinned and pushed the platter insistently in my direction. His eyes widened, as if he were using mind-control to force me to accept the bird. "There is plenty left!"

"Well, for obvious reasons ..." I stated between my teeth, in a moment of brazenness. I paused because I didn't know what exactly I was going to say next.

All heads turned to look at me. Even Renée and Yvon, who did not understand English, turned merely to see what everyone else was looking at. It was my moment to state what was on everyone's mind, to end the awkwardness, to take my honourable place as a speaker of the truth.

And I happily let that moment zip right on by.

"Because everyone is saving room for the sugar tart!" I exclaimed after scanning the table, luckily finding the perfect diversion tactic.

"Who wants dessert?" Natalie chimed in, quickly picking up on the strategy.

A chorus of responses chimed forth: "Oh, me!" and "Yeah, I'd love some!" and "Don't be shy with my slice!"

The sugar tart saved the day.

Whatever was left of the guinea fowl was pushed aside to make space for a pot of coffee, along with a selection of mugs and smaller dessert plates. The meal ended without further drama. The sugar tart was devoured and the table was cleared. Then Renée and Yvon shuffled home across the lane, Nico drove Jesse to the local airport and the rest of us retired for an afternoon siesta.

Yet, to this day, the mystery of what went wrong with the bird remains unsolved. Perhaps we had overcooked her or maybe she had truly eaten something that affected her flavour. Whatever the case might have been, I figured there was a good chance that, if a poultry heaven existed, she was up there looking down on that lunch scene and hooting with sweet revenge. We beat her over the head. She assaulted our taste buds.

Well played, guinea fowl. Well played. ○

"DANIEL, THERE'S SOMEONE here for you!" Nico shouted across the courtyard.

I poked my head up from the chicken coop. For the past hour, I had been entrenched in the mucky pen, scraping manure off the wooden planks and dreaming about what we'd prepare for dinner. The garden was practically throwing zucchinis at us.

"Okay, I'll be right up!" I yelled back. I put down my trowel and scraped a layer of poultry poop from the soles of my shoes onto an unlucky rock.

"Sorry, rock," I murmured as I darted up a set of stairs toward the entrance to the property.

But despite my capacity for playful repartee with a rock, there was an uneasiness in my gut. In the middle of the French countryside, I was certainly not expecting any visitors. It's not like an old friend could swing by for *croissant et café* and a brief *tête-à-tête* on the various techniques of slaughtering poultry. My mind immediately raced to the worst possible scenario: someone at home had died and, to deliver the news, they had sent one of those frightening French mimes to re-enact the tragic situation. So far that month, everything had been going so well. *Was something bad finally about to happen?* I took a deep breath and braced myself for the worst.

Instead of a silent performance artist, however, a tired-looking taxi driver stood waiting at the gate to the courtyard.

"*Vous êtes Monsieur Baylis?*" he inquired with the rasp of 10,000 cigarettes.

"*Uh ... oui ... c'est moi.*"

"*Signez ici, s'il vous plaît,*" he growled, forcing a clipboard into my hand. "*J'ai ton sac à dos.*"

They say that one should never shoot the messenger — but what about kissing him? What is the social etiquette around celebrating the courier of good news? I wanted to wrap my hands around his smoke-stained face and plant a big smooch on his wrinkled forehead. He popped the taxi trunk to reveal my faithful backpack. It had somehow escaped Moroccan airport purgatory and had been dispatched nearly 200 kilometres from Toulouse to Ruffepeyre. The bag was slightly scuffed but in one piece.

"*Merci!*" I grabbed for his hand but landed somewhere between his wrist and forearm. I shook his limb vigorously a couple times. He looked at me like I was crazy and withdrew his arm. Then he got in his taxi and produced a shower of gravel as he drove away.

A few rocks hurled at my shins didn't dampen my spirits. Twelve days had passed since my arrival in France, and I had conceded that I would never see my backpack again. My morning ritual with the third-party baggage company was proving to be futile. I had reluctantly — yet successfully — passed through the four emotional stages of luggage loss: frustration to anger to despondency to the final state of acceptance. The backpack was not coming back.

But there it was — the resurrection of my stuff. For me, the bag was significant not because it would increase my fashion options and reintroduce the practice of applying deodorant. The backpack was important because it was filled with memorabilia. I am not one to amass many souvenirs, but over the course of six months, I had collected the odd map, a couple of books and even a few new T-shirts. My Peruvian wool hat was in that backpack, as were my red bikini-style manbriefs. That stuff had sentimental value. In a way, the reunion with the backpack was exactly like seeing an old friend again — a warm-hearted buddy who gave me a big hug and then presented me with a plethora of clean underwear options. ☺

WITH MY BACKPACK returned, life in Ruffepeyre was practically perfect. Yet it wasn't simply the good elements, such as the wine and company, that made the month pleasurable. It was also the lack of other specific travel-related challenges. Questions and difficulties that I constantly navigated in my previous months seemed to take a welcomed sojourn. *Is it safe to walk the streets at night? Do I feel confident about this water source? Should I lock my backpack to my bunk bed? Has this stew been cooked sufficiently? If I switch to a cheaper accommodation, will I end up with bed bugs? If I go out, do I know how to communicate sufficiently with a taxi driver to be able to return to where I'm staying?* These questions were constantly swirling in my head as I navigated my day-to-day interactions from New Orleans to Marrakech and all the stops in between. But in Ruffepeyre, the living was easy. I had nothing to complain about.

Well, almost nothing.

Even in the little village with its population of 75 people, there were a handful of situational hazards that threatened both my emotional and physical well-being. Perhaps the greatest single menace was the conspiratorial trickery from the six chickens. Those scallywags were constantly plotting emancipation from their pen, driven by a singular mission: to mutilate the veggies on the vine. One day, they destroyed approximately eight tomatoes. Those tomatoes could have been in my belly. Also, I recall an incident early in the month — during one of the many crazy quiche blowouts — when we poured the last drop of wine, only to discover *no more bottles* of liquid happiness remained in the cellar. What an exceptionally horrific situation, a foolishly overlooked predicament! Furthermore, after an intensive rock-lifting session while attempting to construct a wall around the herb garden, I developed a *mid-size callous* on the upper region of my right palm. This injury could have been detrimental. Thankfully, by that point in the month, I had learned to maintain an apocalyptic supply of vino. I was able to manage the pain of my wound and circumvent further discomfort by drinking — wait for it — *with my left hand.*

Genius, I know.

Apart from the aforementioned incidents, the weeks drifted by without drama. But the nature of the project did shift slightly. After a productive period of hosting volunteers and accomplishing many restoration-related tasks, Nico decided that he wanted to relax for a couple of weeks of vacation at the beginning of August. This meant that I was the final volunteer to arrive in Ruffepeyre. The other helpers eventually wandered on, continuing with their travels or taking on different work commitments. For the second half of the month, there were only four of us: Nico, Chip, Natalie and myself.

The dynamic was quieter but still agreeable. With fewer people on site, the tasks also evolved. There wasn't the labour force for the heavier reconstruction endeavours, so other projects took precedence: maintaining the garden, cleaning the inside of the castel, sanding wooden planks for kitchen cabinets and digging a pond for the backyard.

Due to the smaller number of volunteers, I had an entire room to myself with a big double bed for the second half of the month. In the evenings, I often took long walks through the fields (with nobody except Dolly the dog). At first, this might seem like another form of self-isolation. However, the big difference was that I wasn't avoiding anything. I was quietly appreciating it all. ○

WITH PLENTY OF free time and more personal space — and without the typical risks that came from solo travel in other destinations — my mind wandered farther, to philosophical landscapes. For the first time in my travels, and also perhaps in my life, I was immersed in a community-based project that was both rural and well managed. Nico and his restorations in Ruffepeyre provided me with an excellent example of how first-rate rural living could be achieved. It was social, creative, sustainable, contemplative and downright delicious. I asked myself: *What more does one need than a quiet lifestyle and bucolic elements? Could a rural life be a life for me?* A non-urban existence came onto my radar as a viable option for the future. Possibly the greatest peril of July, apart from the wine shortage and the hand callous, was the desire to scrap the entire year-long travel project and to remain indefinitely in the south of France.

As much as I was tempted, though, I couldn't stay. Despite

finding my own work-exchange heaven in Ruffepeyre — a situation where I did *not* pay to help for the first time that year — curiosity once again began nipping at my ankles, pressing me forward.

Those weeks in the south of France had been what I needed: the perfect remedy for traveller's fatigue. Throughout the beginning of the month, I had waited for the other shoe to drop: a brick to fall on my toe, a surprise bout of diarrhea, a devastating baguette shortage. However, the closest thing to a double-edged sword was Renée's poultry knife. There was no reason to believe that accepting bountiful blessings would incur some sort of karmic debt. Sometimes life is complicated. But sometimes it's not. Sometimes there's a fine balance of rain and sun, and the crops simply grow in abundance.

So at the end of the month, I continued on my journey, feeling stronger. I said goodbye to Nico and Dolly, to Renée and Yvon, to the chickens and zucchinis. I offered a simple *au revoir* to a little place called Ruffepeyre — and to a restoration site that was, well, exactly just that.

Le sigh. ☺

AUGUST

Edinburgh, Scotland

I pulled the pillow off my head and glimpsed out the window over a vacant parking lot. It was raining, again. With all the moisture in the air, how long could someone stay in bed without dying from dehydration? Everything they say about Scottish weather is true. During the entire month, I'm not sure a day passed when it didn't rain. Even my brain felt wet. The national tourism bureau might want to try a new slogan: "Scotland, a delightful location for the despondent."

With only a few days left in August, I was supposed to be amusing myself at a massive fringe festival in Edinburgh. But after three weeks of unfulfilling volunteer office work, I had found the experience rather unamusing, rather unfestive. So I had run away to Glasgow, where I was spending most of my time alone in a stale university dorm room. It wasn't glamorous accommodation. It was the best I could afford. The small chamber was comfortingly institutional, void of any stimulation such as artwork or fresh air. The fluorescent light had two settings: off or depression. At this point, I couldn't tell which it was switched to. The locks on the window added to a certain psychiatric-ward esthetic. In a way, it was all fitting.

My month was a mess. I was a mess. My bones had turned to lead. I was hooked up to an IV of exhaustion, with little drops of depletion trickling into my body. Peeling myself off the plastic mattress seemed like an impossibility. All the personal restoration that had occurred in France was gone. Like a marathon runner who hits the wall during the final 10 kilometres of a race, I had reached an eight-month emotional roadblock. Unlike the weariness that I had felt when I left Morocco, however, this rut wasn't a normal bout of traveller's fatigue. This time, the problem was compounded by an acute case of human jadedness.

Over the previous three weeks, a series of events had culminated in a month-altering decision based on two mutually exclusive options: I could continue to trudge away with an unsatisfactory volunteer position at the Edinburgh Festival Fringe or I could attend a Dolly Parton concert. Like any sensible human being, I chose the country-singing superstar. And it had been a grand concert. But now I was left with the Dolly-aftermath and the remnants of a fractured month weighing on my mind.

The path forward seemed unclear. I couldn't conceive of getting out of bed, let alone continuing with my travels.

Yet, I couldn't cancel the rest of my trip. And what? Crawl home with my tail between my legs? Only to have to explain to the people in my life why my plans didn't work out? Calling it quits on my year-long travel plans would mean acknowledging that I had failed to achieve one of my life goals. This was not an attractive option. Of all things to fear in the world, I dreaded my own self-reproach the most. Besides, I didn't even have a home or a career waiting for me back in Canada. I had intentionally quit my job and given away my apartment so that *I couldn't turn back*. I hadn't burned my bridges as much as snipped the suspension cords, just enough to make retracing my steps difficult.

I had to keep going.

But at the same time — how? How would I summon the energy needed to navigate new countries? To fully appreciate the journey?

For the time being, the only thing I could do was to remain

horizontal, to take comfort in hiding. So I fell back against the mattress and repositioned the pillow over my head.

Outside the dormitory window, the rain just kept on falling. ○

DESPITE THE DREARY weather, there are many reasons a traveller might be drawn toward Scotland. The nation is, after all, the birthplace of golf. The sport was invented at some point in the 15th century as a complementary activity to the other national pastime — indulging in a wee drink called whisky. For centuries, both locals and visitors have flocked to the various distilleries and corner taverns across Scotland to experience the magic effect that occurs when barley and wheat are transformed into that special golden alcoholic beverage. (And by "experience," I mean "get hammered by.") Travellers are also lured by the geographic appeal of Scotland, such as the famous Loch Ness and her mysterious monster, or the opportunities for multi-day trekking adventures through the dramatic highlands. While some folks are attracted to the screech of bagpipes, others come to sample a unique Scottish delicacy: the noble haggis. Finally, some men go to Scotland simply because they seek emancipation from pants.

I, however, chose Scotland for its famous August festival.

The Edinburgh Festival Fringe is the world's largest arts festival. Also known as "The Fringe," the festival dates back to 1947. That's when a rogue group of performers took advantage of the freshly formed Edinburgh International Festival (a highbrow performing arts event) to showcase their own alternative theatre. Around the fringes of the official festival events, these rebel theatre companies staged their performances and successfully nabbed the attention of the crowds — and the nation. Every year thereafter, more and more like-minded performers followed the example of this original gang, and in 1958 the Festival Fringe Society was created. Since then, the concept of fringe theatre has caught on outside of Scotland and has become a worldwide phenomenon. The ethos of the international fringe movement is an unapologetic mix of edginess, technical simplicity, affordability

231

and accessibility. Oh yes, and a healthy dash of anarchy.

These days, the Edinburgh Festival Fringe has reached proportions unimaginable to the original impromptu group of theatre revolutionaries. Every August, thousands of dancers, comedians, actors and musicians take to stages all over Scotland's capital city. For performers — whether unknown or internationally acclaimed — the festival is an annual celebration of anything that can be performed on stage (as well as a few things that don't actually need to be performed on stage). Many of these shows are free or pay-what-you-can. But the majority are ticketed events, and upwards of two million tickets are sold over the course of the month. There's no question that today's Edinburgh Festival Fringe is big business. And where there is money to be made, the innocence of the venture inevitably becomes compromised.

What was once an impromptu gathering of performers is now a massive beast, one colossal carnival of performers. And everything that follows in its trail. ○

LANDING IN EDINBURGH, I was a man without a plan. For the first time that year, I arrived at a new destination with no concrete host or work project confirmed. This was both exciting (in the sense that there was an entire city of potential to explore) and slightly anxiety producing (in the sense that there was an entire city of potential to overwhelm me). I had no idea how the month would unfold. But I did know one thing: it was *the* time of year to be in Scotland's capital.

The biggest question was never *if* I should go to Edinburgh. With its bustling art scene, gothic architecture and stunning landscape, this historic capital was up there with Buenos Aires and Cape Town as one of the world's most alluring destinations. And I hankered to be part of the thrill of its festival. The biggest question was how I might fit myself into the pandemonium of the city during the massive event.

The roots of my involvement dated back to March, when I was in Peru. I had mentioned to Lucy from England (my fellow volunteer English teacher) that I was considering going to Edinburgh for The Fringe. She suggested that I look up a reputable theatre company named Pleasance. The company had a long tradition of programming quality acts during the month-long festival, and they provided room and board to 200 volunteers during August. Their website had a rousing call-out for team member applications: "If you are driven, ready to do your bit, and able to keep a smile on your face all day long—we want you!"

From the other side of the world, this looked to be the perfect work exchange opportunity. Something that would—pardon the pun—fit the bill. On my end, I could offer motivation and eagerness, and even a ready smile. On their end, they presented a once-in-a-lifetime opportunity, as well as room and board. So one quiet evening in a hostel in South Africa, I completed an online application to volunteer with Pleasance.

Much to my chagrin, these volunteer positions were highly sought after. In June, I was among hundreds of applicants to receive a polite rejection letter. To be honest, I was a bit disappointed. As a 30-year-old with both professional and volunteer experience, I had figured I was a shoo-in.

So I went back to the Scottish drawing board. As the eighth month of my journey approached, I decided to experiment with a different methodology. Instead of trolling around for potential hosts on the Internet, I decided to take a step back and let the hands of fate determine what this leg of the journey would look like. What would happen if I simply showed up in Edinburgh and said, *"Can I help ye, lads and lassies?"* Would I find opportunities? There were hundreds of venues, with a couple thousand shows happening throughout the city. I presumed that there had to be someone, somewhere, who could use an extra set of hands. To my advantage, I was willing to do anything: wash dishes at the scuzziest of restaurants, pour Scotch until all hours of the morning, walk the Royal Mile to promote performances, or star in a one-man show about the psychological dangers of bed bugs. All I needed was a chance. With a mixture of faith and trepidation,

I bought a plane ticket to Scotland and opted to let destiny run its course.

However, the day before I departed from France, I did something to tinker with fate in a pang of 11th-hour jitters. It was an action that would deeply steer the course of my month: I sent a message to Pleasance.

"Just a quick note to let you know that I'm still available as a volunteer, should there be any last-minute positions available. If not, wishing you a wonderful festival. I'll be around for the month!"

The next day, shortly after arriving in Edinburgh, I received a reply from the assistant to the director:

"We have just had a late dropout. Are you in Edinburgh? Are you able to come and meet us? Please call as soon as possible!!"

It was wonderful news. I did a quick Scottish jig of joy and then called to confirm a time and place for an interview. A couple of hours later, I met with two friendly yet frenzied Pleasance staff members. On the spot, they offered me a volunteer position in the Press Office.

Within 24 hours of arriving in Edinburgh, I had secured a volunteer job and was provided with a modest single dormitory room. After an initial rejection, fate had delivered a surprising resolution to the unknown direction of my month, ultimately inviting me to take a leading role with Pleasance. ☼

THE NEXT MORNING, I wandered down to the edge of Edinburgh's Old Town neighbourhood to the Student Union's courtyard on Pleasance Street. The stately grey stone buildings that surrounded the courtyard were typical of the district's medieval-looking style and dated back many hundreds of years. The name of the street, and subsequently the theatre company, originated from the Scottish word *plesance*, which denotes a park or garden. For the month of August, this historic location would function as the primary headquarters for Pleasance shows and administration.

The atmosphere in the courtyard, however, did not have the peace and tranquility you might associate with a park or garden. The scene was comparable to the first day of school — except instead of a typical run-of-the-mill school that taught math and social studies and biology, this was a special institution where everyone was majoring in drama. Important-looking people were running in each direction. Others, those who appeared slightly less important, were arranging their hair or staring into their mobile phones. One big-man-on-campus walked by, deeply engaged in a walkie-talkie conversation. He then swivelled theatrically and returned in the direction he had come from. It was the type of environment where the busier you looked, the more prominent you probably were. In my hiking boots — which were still smudged with the red dirt of Ruffepeyre — I stood unobtrusively on the edge of the courtyard, attempting to stay out of everyone's way.

Clearly, I would need to shift gears. I felt like the friendless country bumpkin who had just moved into town and had worn the wrong shoes to the first day of classes. I would have to stuff any residual slow-food, farm-loving French mentalities deep inside my proverbial bagpipes, as these mindsets were not going to help me cut it as a Pleasance volunteer. In fact, if I moved too slowly, I was liable to be mowed over by some stage lighting.

The curtain would be rising, both figuratively and literally, in a matter of days. Much work remained to prepare the venues for the thousands of festivalgoers who would be marching into Pleasance sites.

There was, however, a hint of camaraderie in the chaos. From the expressions of excitement and the exchanging of hugs among volunteers (mainly the less important-looking ones), I deduced that many of the other folks in the courtyard had been involved with Pleasance in previous years. The joy from the reunions was mildly contagious. It helped soften my sense of reluctance. To effectively execute a string of 200 shows, it had to take a certain amount of solidarity. I figured there was a good chance that *I'd* be hugging everyone by the end of the month.

As I stood on the sidelines wondering what I should be doing, a young blond woman with a megaphone stepped up onto a small tower of black stage-equipment boxes. She introduced herself as the General Manager and began directing the less-important volunteers up a set of stairs and into one of the seated indoor venues. As a rookie volunteer, I merged with the herd, entered the auditorium and took a chair. The important people were on stage (I knew who was important because they were speaking into a minimum of three mobile phones at any given moment). Each head honcho was given a few minutes to talk about his or her respective domains of importance. After a brief pep talk, we were instructed to head back into the courtyard and split into our respective volunteer teams.

When I had been applying for a position many months previously, I had researched the various Pleasance teams and the volunteer positions available. The folks assigned to the Street Team were the organization's cheerleaders, hitting the pavement to energetically promote the various shows. This was a mucky rain-or-shine gig that required a can-do attitude and a good pair of galoshes. Those appointed to Front of House were like mobile information booths. Their job involved directing people to the toilets, ensuring that ticket holders found their way to venues and ushering the masses into mannerly queues. The Box Office volunteers got to sit in little booths and dole out tickets. And finally, the Technical Crew was responsible for, well, technical stuff, like turning lights on and off. I had been assured during my interview that each job was exceedingly important.

Back in the courtyard, my eyes wandered across the sea of volunteers until I saw someone holding a small sign: Press Office. The yard proved to be an obstacle course that had me ducking under scaffolding, dancing over coils of extension cables and dodging jets of spray paint. Somehow I made it to the other side without incurring an injury or getting trampled by one of the mobile-phone-toting important people. There I joined a group of other individuals who looked as bewildered as I did. ☼

"Hɪ," I ɢʀᴇᴇᴛᴇᴅ, summoning a bit of moxie. "I'm Daniel."

The members of the Press Office team took turns briefly sharing individual introductions. We were a group of seven, including volunteers from New Zealand, Australia, England and Canada. But before we had the opportunity to chit-chat about our Commonwealth origins, we were whisked off to our working space.

While much of the festival action would take place around the courtyard where we had congregated, the Press Office was located 10 minutes down the road at Pleasance's other main venue called "The Dome." One of the other volunteers, a friendly bearded fellow named Matt (yes, another Matt!), struck up a conversation with me as we walked to our office. The early-twenties man was an aspiring theatre critic from London and looked something like the human incarnation of a teddy bear.

"So, have you been to the festival before?" I asked, mining for a bit of insight on how the next few weeks would unfold.

"Oh, yes," Matt responded. He was dressed like a proper English gentleman, with a collared shirt and well-polished shoes. His cheeks became increasingly rosy as we walked the narrow cobblestone avenues. "But only as an audience member. I haven't really volunteered before. I'm interested in getting a bit of work experience."

"I just came on board yesterday," I confided. "They told me I'm the 'Broadcast Liaison' — and I don't have a clue what that entails."

"Oh, don't worry. I haven't the faintest idea of what I'm supposed be doing either," Matt said, reassuring me. "I can guarantee you one thing, though. This is The Fringe, and that means it's going to be one hell of a ride!"

I wondered what exactly he meant by that. But I had just confessed that I didn't know what my job was, so I held myself back.

I didn't need to appear even greener.

We were led into a University of Edinburgh building on Potterow Avenue. We went up a set of stairs, down a corridor and into a room the approximate size of a wrestling ring. Seven desktop computers sat on seven squeezed-together desks. This space would be the press headquarters for the next month. Our first task was to transform the plain walls of the office into a visual smorgasbord. The activity was like putting up wallpaper. But instead of the typical flower print that you might see in your great-aunt's bathroom, we used posters featuring the faces of up-and-coming comedians, dance troops and singers from the United Kingdom and around the world. We were told that every single show had to be visible on some surface area. Posters dangled off desks, and even the back of the door was wrapped in smiley signage.

At first, I thought this team exercise was a bit tedious, slightly unwarranted. Didn't we have more important tasks to do than decorating the walls? Shouldn't I be learning about what my *actual* volunteer role demanded? Was there no volunteer orientation manual to review? Little did I know that the act of postering the office was an informal yet important tutorial for the uninitiated newbie (such as myself). I would come to understand that being constantly surrounded by the glossy faces helped us to memorize the names and venues of that year's roster of shows. Plus, having the Pleasance posters on the walls of the Press Office helped performers feel important.

"If it's anything like I imagine," explained Matt as he passed me a long piece of Scotch Tape, "performers and PR representatives will come in here and look for their own poster." He paused to step back and admire his work. "If they don't see their own faces, I'll bet they get whiny."

After a few hours of decorating and subsequently making alterations (based on which acts were more important), we had successfully adorned the stark walls with the faces of that season's Pleasance program. One thing was for sure, the posters had instant effect: they brought me into the festival mindset. And by

238

the end of that first day, I felt an immediacy in the air, like the show was about to begin. ○

OF ALL THE volunteer positions at Pleasance, those in the Press Office were the most sought-after. Beyond being an administrative hub, the locale was a hotbed of the who's who in British theatre and the entertainment biz. Through the doors of that poster-strewn office would walk the most notable BBC presenters, the most respected and feared theatre critics and the most acclaimed performers. However, I had absolutely no idea who any of them were. For a Canadian dude who can barely keep up with Hollywood performers, all that British fame was lost on me.

My official title at Pleasance was Broadcast Liaison. Initially, I was confused about what that actually meant. I figured that any job with the word "liaison" in the title would be tremendously significant and terribly secretive. Initially, I hypothesized that my role would involve intense negotiations with a dash of perilous espionage. I would have to become like John Malkovich in *Dangerous Liaisons*. Except, instead of seducing beautiful Victorian women, I would need to seduce members of the BBC.

Lucky me.

But, as they say, beggars cannot be prudes. I had arrived in Edinburgh as a man without a plan, and Pleasance had offered me an opportunity to achieve a dream — to be involved with the world's greatest fringe festival. Who was I to complain? So I dove in and got to work.

Well, sort of.

First, I had to find out what my job actually entailed. During the first day of postering our workspace, I had ascertained a few key responsibilities. For instance, I knew that I had to show up every day to the Press Office and sit behind an antiquated computer. This was helpful because understanding where to physically present oneself is basically half the battle of most tasks. And so I sat at my desk and tried to look occupied — much like when I donned the leather tool belt in New Orleans to look like

239

a handyman, I figured that the appearance of capability could be mistaken for capability itself. To help with my masquerade, I even got myself a clipboard on the second day. Everyone knows to trust a man with a clipboard.

Nevertheless, as the days passed, I slowly managed to wrap my head around the concrete responsibilities that came with broadcast liaising. My job was essentially to coordinate the communication between three important festival stakeholders: the broadcasting media (such as television, radio and photojournalism), the public relations representatives (of the 200 Pleasance shows), and the 30 Pleasance venue managers (who, for liability reasons, needed to be informed of anyone recording a show).

Through trial, error, guesswork and a smidge of luck, I eventually decoded the general procedure. Someone from the media, such as an ITV network television program, would contact the Press Office with a request to film at a Pleasance show. Let's use Irish chanteuse Camille O'Sullivan as an example. I would contact Ms. O'Sullivan's PR representative to see if she was interested in coverage from ITV. (The usual response to media requests would be an enthusiastic "Yes!") If I received the green light from the PR representative, I would check where the performance took place and then contact the corresponding venue manager to see if a television crew could enter the site. If everyone agreed that recording could occur, I would proceed to reserve media tickets, reconfirm with each party involved and, if necessary, arrange wireless microphone frequencies with the technical department.

This might seem like a straightforward procedure. In reality, however, it was often laced with unforeseen landmines. For instance, the PR agent might not be answering his mobile phone. Maybe the venue manager wasn't out of bed yet. Or, my personal favourite, the show was starting in 30 minutes and I would have to summon the theatrical spirits to help me hastily confirm with all stakeholders. Plus, I had to battle against my own ignorance. As an unenlightened foreigner in the land of the Scots, I had no idea which publications or TV presenters or medias were important. Therefore I had no way of knowing which requests were worth bending over backwards for.

This is where Matt saved my skin numerous times.

"Hey, Matt," I called as I emerged from behind my computer. "*The Telegraph* — are they actually important?"

Matt scratched his beard, pondering for a second. "Well, it's sort of a big newspaper. One of the biggest ones in the U.K. I don't read it, though." In proper British form, he wasn't shy about subtly adding his own editorial comments.

"Okay. What about the BBC's *The Culture Show*? Does anybody watch that?"

"A few people watch it, I think." Matt confirmed. "It's a highbrow arts program that tries hard to be trendy. But it often has good stuff on it."

"Finally, Lyn Gardner," I read the name on a printed email that for some reason had come onto my desk. "Should I care about her?"

"Yes," Matt's eyes widened. "Lyn is a hero. Probably the best theatre journalist in the U.K., maybe the world. She champions the unusual and alternative quite a lot."

"Ah … " I concurred, nodding my head. " So, yes, I probably *should* care about her. Thanks, Matt."

"Just doin' my job," he replied before stoically turning back to his computer screen. If it weren't for Matt, I might have let some generic loser with a blog into a sold-out event and then turned away the Queen of England.

To reciprocate, when I wasn't deeply embroiled in my own dangerous liaising, I would try to help Matt and the rest of the office process the non-broadcasting ticket requests and allocations (for critics, dignitaries, et cetera). When the curtain lifted on the festival, a tsunami of demands descended upon the press office, with each media source wanting to be the first to expose the hottest acts of that year's festival. Almost all media who asked for tickets got them. But occasionally a fanatical talent manager would ixnay a reporter from a publication that wasn't reputable enough. Or, early in the month, he might simply sigh in exasperation and say, "We're just not ready for reviews yet." (Sometimes the PR representatives were more exaggerated than the performers.)

To respond to the requests, a rigid protocol needed to be followed and it inevitably led to a mountain of administrative work. Consequently, we were all overworked and overwhelmed. We came in early. We stayed late.

In that claustrophobic office in rainy Edinburgh, I learned quite quickly that The Fringe wasn't just about jokes and amusement. It was the platform where fresh talent was revealed and careers were launched. Stars would be born that month. And it was our job to make sure that nothing stood in the way of the business of star-birth.

A significant portion of the people who walked into the Press Office took their roles quite seriously. This was a side of The Fringe that I had not anticipated. Many outsiders perceived The Fringe as fun and comedic, but the festival was no laughing matter for those behind the curtains. ⌂

MY FAMILY, TO my great fortune, has always been supportive of my often-nutty endeavours. When I was in my early twenties, for example, I moved 4,000 kilometres across the nation without a job or a plan, merely to marinate in Montreal's artistic splendour. My family did not protest. They even made pilgrimages to visit. When I returned home and flaunted my freshly discovered vegetarianism, they politely accommodated my experimental morality and provided a steady supply of tofu. They suffered patiently through my career blunders, bad haircuts and broken hearts. And when I announced my plans to travel the world for a year, there were no signs of disapproval from my next-of-kin. In fact, the general sentiment was "Go for it, Danny!"

My sister — bless her loyal soul — had been the captain of my cheer squad throughout the year-long journey. When she got wind that one of my favourite country musicians, the iconic Dolly Parton, was scheduled to perform in Scotland during my visit, she figured that a couple of tickets would make for a fun mid-trip surprise. I don't exactly know how she managed to fandangle it from the other side of the Atlantic Ocean, but my sister secured two front-row tickets to see the self-described "Backwoods Barbie" in concert.

I was informed about these tickets a week into my stay in Edinburgh. Needless to say, I was thrilled. Dolly Parton was up there with Leonard Cohen and Bob Dylan as rare-touring musicians who I desperately hoped to see in concert. When it comes to seeing aging music legends, hesitancy is a grave mistake. Sure, Dolly might look like a million bucks, but that's only because she has seen more injections than a needle exchange site. The truth was that she was no spring chicken anymore. The time to see her in concert would be now.

The only concern was that I would require a half-day break from "liaising" to zip away to Glasgow for the concert. If I worked hard and proved myself to be a reliable volunteer, I assumed that a short absence in the context of a month-long commitment would not be a major issue. It all seemed perfectly reasonable in my mind. ○

A MINUTE BEFORE the curtain was scheduled to lift, I flashed my official Pleasance ID card to the Front of House volunteer and snuck into the back row. The lights dimmed. The audience members hushed. A single spotlight came on.

It was late afternoon, I had kept on top of my emails, and there was no broadcast recording slated for the rest of the day. That's why I had decided to finally enjoy the kickbacks of volunteerism, so I snuck off to see my first show: *A Celebration of Harold Pinter* starring Julian Sands.

As I sat upon the wooden pew waiting for the show to begin, I realized I hadn't the faintest clue of what I was about to see. Who was this supposedly famous actor Julian Sands? And why was he reading the poetry of some Nobel Prize-winning fellow named Harold Pinter? Oh, it didn't even matter, really. With all the buzz the performance was receiving, it was sure to be a safe choice. The fact of the matter was that I was just content to be there — at The Fringe, in Edinburgh, finally seeing a show!

One of the perks of volunteering at The Fringe, I had presumed, would be free access to a variety of ticketed events. And this was not a false assumption. When volunteers were not scheduled to work, they were given the opportunity to attend anything not sold out. We could simply flash our executive Pleasance photo-lanyards and parade into most events. However, being a spectator was a bonus reserved for those volunteers who had had less "official" responsibilities. For example, those working Front of House or with the Street Team had specific scheduled work hours and the rest of their time was for leisure. In contrast, my role as Broadcast Liaison required me to be *always* on duty. This lack of off-time made seeing shows rather challenging. I had to capitalize on the quiet moments.

The performance commenced.

A balding middle-aged man with fair features strolled onto the stage and took his place behind a lectern. The half-full house instantaneously broke into applause. This was Julian Sands. He spoke directly to the crowd, welcoming everyone to his performance. And then he opened up a binder and began what he was there to do: read poetry.

At first, I was into it.

At least, I told myself I was into it. This was poetry, after all, and I am a writer. I should have a deep appreciation for all things literary. In fact, wasn't there some sort of old-school charm to performing poetry aloud? Some sort of artsy-fartsy legitimacy?

I ought to have been into it. Really.

But shortly into the third poem, my eyelids grew heavy. I found myself plagued by a series of tonsil-revealing yawns.

My average day had had me clocking out of the office shortly after the sun had set, around nine o'clock. And since I'm not much of a night owl, my typical evening ritual involved grabbing a bite to eat and then trudging back to my allocated dormitory bedroom. Bone-weary, I would collapse on the cigarette-smelling mattress and prepare myself psychologically to repeat the whole volunteer rigamarole the next day.

I began shifting in my seat.

Luckily there were no other audience members sitting next to me as I attempted to find a comfortable position on the firm wooden bench. Finally, I slouched so low that the beam of the pew supported the back of my head.

Yeah, that felt better. *Much* better.

At some point, the inevitable occurred: I accidentally slipped away.

The next thing I remember was the sound of applause. I was horizontal on the pew, with my cheek soaking in my own drool.

Sitting up abruptly, I saw Mr. Sands bowing on stage.

His performance had ended, and I had slept through nearly the entire thing.

And that's how I came to discover that the perks of being an Edinburgh Festival Fringe volunteer are only truly valuable if you can remain perky. Or at least conscious. ⬡

BY THE END of the second week, I had become an expert liaison. I'd go far enough to say that liaising became not just a function of my volunteer role but also an innovative and stylish lifestyle. When I needed an energy boost, I no longer ordered coffee. I would reach into my pocket, extract a couple of pound sterling and use that money to liaise with the barista to negotiate the creation of a latte. Crossing the busy streets of Edinburgh was an incredible act of liaising prowess. Sure, no words were exchanged with drivers, but I could cause double-decker buses to come screeching to a stop, just using my expert liaison eyes. I no longer had bowel movements. I liaised with porcelain.

One might assume that, having mastered the art of liaising, I must have been drunk with power and contentment. Yet I wasn't. Outside the Press Office window, one of the world's greatest carnivals was roaring, and I longingly pressed my ear to the pane as it marched on by. I wasn't seeing any shows. I was constantly exhausted. And worst of all, I began to find myself bumping up against aggravated individuals, even becoming a whipping boy for built-up personal tensions. For instance, there was the whole cable-in-the-alley incident.

During the first week of the festival, one of the Pleasance variety shows was set to grace the cover of a local nightlife magazine. I had liaised with the PR agents and arranged to accompany a photo crew around the courtyard to help them find an appropriate location for the five-minute cover shoot. The photographer seemed relatively important, so when he asked permission to snap a couple of portraits in an alleyway, I gave him the green light. Space was tight, but the brick walls provided a good backdrop for portraiture. The photographer started setting up his lights and tripods. He also stretched an extension cord across the lane.

In a case of unfortunate timing, the Pleasance Site Manager happened to be walking by.

"That is a massive safety hazard!" he hissed, yanking me aside. Then he ordered that the photo-shoot be stopped and relocated immediately.

As the photographer was repacking his gear, the lecture continued.

"The safety inspector was standing 20 metres away from you!" The Site Manager growled through his teeth and exposed the whites of his eyes. "Running a cable where people walk? You could have got us shut down!"

"Um ... sorry?" I replied, unsure of what a more appropriate response would be.

It had never crossed my mind that a thin cable dropped over an alleyway would trigger such outrage. I wanted to explain that I was new at the job and that the learning curve was steep. Instead, I saved my breath.

Was there any point in being defensive? Probably not.

In another instance, I received a verbal pounding when a camera crew was spotted using radio microphones in an open-air venue without permission. This crew had not followed proper

246

festival protocol by seeking authorization with the Press Office *before* shooting. Therefore, I was unaware of their intentions to record. The sound engineer caught wind of their presence before I did and urgently phoned me. Using a tone that inferred that I had an intellectual impairment, he lectured me about how the world could cataclysmically implode if radio frequencies somehow got crossed. Boy, did I learn an important lesson that day. But it wasn't how to do my job any better. I learned that interpersonal skills were not a prerequisite to work in the technical department.

Departmental supervisors were strained and on edge, and this tension trickled down to the employees and volunteers. As a result, certain luxuries, such as civility, were starting to fall off many priority lists.

My personal theory is that if folks don't have the energy to treat others with respect, they should remove themselves from the situation until they are ready and able to be respectful again. My ideals and what was actually occurring, however, were two separate entities. The unspoken festival motto seemed to resonate like this: *To hell with diplomacy! The show must go on!* Which was weird, because the call for applications said something about permanent smiles being a must.

The days were often 12-hour marathons of trying to ensure that other people were happy. And there were no days off. To be fair, I *had* been forewarned that the position would be demanding. What I hadn't expected, though, was that a death-race mentality would take hold so quickly. It all started to take its toll on me. I found myself thinking that volunteering at Pleasance wasn't all that pleasant.

Yet, in my most frustrating moments, I imagined a rhinestone cowgirl standing backstage, calling out to me in her Southern accent: "Keep yer chin up, Danny!"

And so I kept going. ○

It was 4:30 on a Friday afternoon when my experience at The Fringe reached its dramatic climax. I was sitting at my desk, responding to a last-minute request from the BBC to film in the courtyard. Despite some bumps in the road, the Press Office team had reached the end of its third week of operations, and we had mercifully come to a smooth patch. By this point, I was on a first-name basis with many of the journalists and media reps covering Pleasance productions. Plus, a week had passed since I had last been lectured for an error. I was starting to feel competent at my job.

The atmosphere in the Press Office was refreshingly buoyant. Matt was feeling excited about his recent email correspondence with a wistful Glaswegian indie rock star who had contacted the office to see if there were any hidden tickets for a certain sold-out show. The tickets had become harder to get than tiger milk. But Matt, a major fan of the aforementioned rock star, successfully made two seats appear at that evening's performance and was giddy at the thought of personally handing over the tickets. The rest of us were feeling more keen simply because we had finally caught up with all the backlogged press requests. And with a bit more time on our hands, we could finally start seeing some shows.

The following evening I was scheduled to see the show that I was most excited for: country music's kitschiest queen, the incomparable Dolly Parton. And this was not going to be some nosebleeder experience in the back bleachers. No siree! I had tickets for the *front row*.

The Press Office coordinator, my immediate supervisor, had granted me permission for a half-day absence to see the concert. Matt would take over the Broadcast Liaison responsibilities for the afternoon, enabling me to duck out at approximately 2 p.m. This was enough time for me to ride the two-hour train to Glasgow and party with Ms. Parton. I'd stay overnight and then hop the rails early in the morning to be back on duty for my liaising responsibilities before the Press Office even opened. Everything was settled.

That was, until the General Manager of Pleasance marched unexpectedly into the office.

The diminutive blond woman walked through the doorway and sprinkled some cordial greetings to the other volunteers in the room. Then she crouched down beside my desk. It was clear that she had come to talk to me and me only.

"Hey, Daniel," she said, tilting her head to one side and administering a faux smile. "How are you?"

"Good."

I swivelled my chair to face her. For a manager, she was quite young. Somehow she had quickly ascended the professional ladder to an impressive position with Pleasance. Despite her young age, she had cheeks that were faded to a washed-out shade of grey — that's what three weeks of troubleshooting and putting out fires and bearing the brunt of anything that went wrong with the theatre company does to a person. And her eyes had that glazed-over look that comes from spending too many minutes glued to the radiating screen of a mobile phone. If they ever start a makeup brand called *Defeated*, she would be the right spokesperson.

"What's up?"

"I just wanted to touch base about your request to take a half-day off tomorrow." Her faux smile quivered.

"Um ... Okay."

"So, as you are aware, the commitment to Pleasance is a full month. Ultimately, we can't have volunteers dashing off!" The General Manager's forced tone was unfittingly peppy. Still crouching, she elaborated on their policy, stating that volunteers in past years had missed family weddings and other important events because they made the month-long commitment.

"We just don't have the capacity to manage requests like this."

My jaw clenched. In retrospect, I'm thankful for this subconscious physical response, as it kept me from blurting out all the things that were running through my head. That I thought their blanket approach to managing volunteers was counterproductive. That being denied a half-day vacation was preposterous. That they didn't own me. That this was a *volunteer* position.

For theatrical purposes, I wish I could paint the woman as a vile witch who was hell-bent on sabotaging my Dolly-dream. But she wasn't. I could tell by the way her eyes consistently drifted from my face that she was uncomfortable delivering the news. In other circumstances, we probably could have been friends. However, she was the General Manager, and as such, she had responsibilities on her shoulders. When it came to processing broadcast requests in the Press Office, I had a procedure to follow. And when it came to managing volunteers, she had protocol as well. And she wasn't deviating from her duties.

For a brief moment, our eyes locked. During that instant, we waged an intensive unspoken battle, waiting to see who would make a next move. Eventually, the General Manager blinked and looked away. Then she ended our silent power struggle with a final statement.

"We don't really do this type of request, okay?"

The choice to punctuate her phrase with an "okay?" was both irritating and comical — as if I would suddenly acknowledge my subordinate position, reciprocate her fake smile and continue forth as an emotionless android.

"Um ... Okay?" I pulled my chin back and shrugged my shoulders. My words weren't offered in agreement. If anything — and I'm not proud of this — I was mocking her.

The General Manager smiled one last time.

Then she rose to her feet and left the room. ○

AT MY DESK, I sat trying to process the new information: Pleasance would not permit a half-day absence. I felt sick to my stomach. I had spent the past three weeks toiling at this role — accumulating nearly 250 volunteer hours — yet my request for six hours away was denied. This did not make sense to me.

Despite my befuddlement, I felt certain of one thing: there was no way that I was sacrificing front-row tickets to Dolly Parton for a thankless volunteer job. The situation was ludicrous. Surely there had to be some sort of flexibility or middle ground. Yet the General Manager had just explained in very clear terms that the organization did not offer such privileges to volunteers. Was it really coming down to two mutually exclusive options — Pleasance or Parton?

Oh, cruel twist of fate!

When I finally gathered my wits, I glanced over my computer to make eye contact with Matt. I knew he had seen the General Manager crouching beside my desk and was aware that something was unravelling. With a slight nod of my head, I signalled him out of the office. We stealthily stole away to an adjoining outdoor patio. It was surprisingly bright out.

"So, as you saw, the General Manager just paid me a visit." I was squinting, unaccustomed to the sunshine. "She just pulled the guillotine on my Dolly Parton concert."

"Whoa!" Matt replied with wide eyes. "What are you going to do?"

"I dunno. I just feel so disappointed at the moment."

Although the past few days had been better, Matt also struggled at various moments throughout the month to keep his morale high. He had previously confessed that there were times when he thought of simply picking up his personal items and walking out of the Press Office forever.

"If you quit, I would completely understand."

"Really?"

My greatest worry was not about broadcasters or PR agents or even the outcome of the shows with Pleasance. Everything would function without me. My main concern was that I didn't want to fracture the friendships with the other volunteers in the Press Office, especially with Matt. In a similar way that hostage victims form friendships, we had established a bond essential to surviving an intense experience. Quitting felt like a betrayal.

"Yeah. It's valid," he stated. "You're not asking for too much."

"Thanks, Matt." He gave me a pat on the back and then returned inside to honour his own commitments.

After a few minutes of composing myself, I also returned to

the Press Office. I proceeded to robotically perform any broadcasting tasks that needed immediate attention. But as I attempted to keep myself busy, it dawned on me: this was bullshit.

I briefly pondered a dramatic exit. This was my opportunity to go down in a burst of flames, to perform the greatest impromptu show at that year's Edinburgh Festival Fringe. In a symbolic gesture of freeing humankind from the shackles of thankless administrative work, I would stand up on my desk and take my turn at some hysterical anarchist broadcasting. The whole fringe movement had begun with a gang of rebels — it was time to summon the spirit of its ancestors.

"Fuck you. Fuck you. You're cool. Fuck you," I would yell, while pointing at any obnoxious PR agents within my vicinity. "This is supposed to be a comedy festival. But nobody is laughing! The only joke around here is this job! *I QUIT FOR DOLLY PARTON!*"

And then, in a fit of madness, I would rip off my shirt and run cackling uncontrollably from the building just to remind everyone what the sound of laughter actually sounded like.

But I didn't do any of this. Obviously.

I had no energy left for theatrics.

Instead, at the end of the working day, I quietly gathered all my belongings from my workstation. Then I politely bid my colleagues a lovely evening and left the office.

My exit was simple, as if a trap door opened beneath me: I was there, and then I was not. ☼

IN SOME RELIGIONS, it is believed that service is the path to the divine. Selfless deeds are considered the highest form of human action. Not only does service benefit others, it also produces a feeling of self-worth while winning karmic points for future lives or securing a fine piece of real estate in heaven.

But, between you and me, I've never been one to search for sainthood.

Heaven sounds boring.

The purpose of my journey was not to save the world or sign

up for a year of indentured servitude. I was nothing more than a guy going door to door, looking for reasonable opportunities to help out. I was testing an age-old system of good-natured exchange. I never felt indebted to any one person or any organization just because they chose to engage with me.

At the same time, as much as I did not feel a sense of debt to Pleasance, I also really disliked the act of quitting. Call it personal pride or an inflated sense of dignity, but I took each of my commitments seriously. Something had to be very wrong for me to pull the plug on a work project. So far that year, I had left early from the raw vegan farm in Costa Rica and walked away from the volunteer project in Morocco. If I threw in the towel in Scotland, it would become my third "failure." And this weighed heavily on my mind as I deliberated over what to do. I didn't want my actions to be interpreted as ditching out on a commitment when presented with a sparkly distraction.

Still, I couldn't help wondering if I should have handled the situation differently. There were, after all, alternative courses of action. For instance, I could have avoided a conflict altogether by staying mum about the concert and then simply calling in sick. Or I could have ducked out and had my colleagues cover for me. But I had no desire for such cavorting. I had given Pleasance a mile, and all I was asking for in return was an inch. I never anticipated that the organization would be so unwilling to compromise. And that, ultimately, was the deal-breaker.

I took action the morning after my interaction with the General Manager, the same day as the Dolly Parton concert. In a regretful yet firm tone, I composed a letter of resignation expressing my disappointment in the lack of flexibility of the volunteer position. I made clear my intentions to leave my post as Broadcast Liaison, effective immediately.

I hit "Send" with a mixture of sadness and anger. Why had I been put in a position where I had to choose? And, my dearest Pleasance, what did you think I'd actually pick? ☺

NEITHER BILLY CONNOLLY nor Sean Connery responded to my invitations for them to join me in the front row at the Dolly Parton concert. So I invited an old high school friend, Erin, who just happened to be living in Edinburgh at the time. As planned, we rode the afternoon train from Edinburgh to Glasgow. There we honoured our country roots by partaking in some pre-show Budweiser action. Then we went to the concert.

The evening was magnificent. For the sake of everyone's time, I will not provide a minute-by-minute recapitulation. But I will say this: the country vixen sang all of her classic tunes, as well as a couple of new ones. Her voice was clean and fresh. She also sported a selection of gloriously tacky outfits. (Experts have determined that, due to Dolly's world tour, the sequin manufacturing industry had the most lucrative year since Cher was relevant.)

I especially appreciated her song called *The Sacrifice*, which lyrically summed up a human conundrum: sometimes you have to surrender certain things to gain others.

"You don't drink the water if you don't dig the well."

Or in my case, Daniel Baylis doesn't get to a Dolly concert without quitting a job.

(So let's all assume she wrote the song for me.) ☺

SOMETIMES WE DIVE into situations only to realize that they are not quite as ideal as we had imagined. In retrospect, I view the events with Pleasance similarly to those of closing time after a night spent drinking at a bar.

We were a case of two slightly desperate parties grappling with the sad reality of "last call" — our respective options were becoming limited. After administering a blurry up and down, the prominent (and slightly promiscuous) Pleasance said to me, "You'll do."

I had stars in my eyes, excited that someone was willing to accept me, a Fringe virgin. We threw caution to the wind, quickly hailed a taxi and jumped into the sack together.

But then the morning after came.

The brightness of day cast a sobering light on the situation. We pulled away from each other. One of us had an unexpected rash. The other was wondering why their bum hurt. (For the sake of everyone's dignity, I shall refrain from extrapolating on this analogy. You get the picture.)

I will say, however, that one person's drunken mistake is another's dreamboat. The volunteer positions offered by Pleasance are good opportunities for folks, such as Matt, who are interested in gaining work experience in the entertainment and arts industries.

During the weeks spent in the Press Office, I was informed that many people who have volunteered with Pleasance have gone on to secure excellent positions within the industry — many crediting Pleasance as having played a major role in this. I think the theory might be that if you can survive the volunteer experience at The Fringe, you can survive anything in the business.

Still, my advice to future applicants is simple: Don't expect any fringe benefits. ۞

AND SO IT was that I found myself in Glasgow, sequestered in a sterile university dorm room. Lying in bed. Unable to get up. My only plan was to avoid Edinburgh completely. The wounds were too fresh.

Part of me had thought that a departure from Pleasance paired with the Dolly Parton concert would be enough to rapidly restore my energy levels. But instead of the emotional rebounding that I had forecasted, I bounced like a soggy sack of compost. I was lost in a sea of seconding-guessing and jadedness.

During the days that followed the Dolly Parton concert, my morale hit the lowest point of my entire year. Eight months of travel paired with the Fringe Fest dejection was like a double whammy. I had reached a saturation point. This might have been the end of the journey. In fact, if it weren't for something entirely mundane, something totally ordinary, I'm not sure what would have happened.

I spent a few days walking.

After nearly 48 hours locked in that sterile Glasgow chamber, I emerged and blinked at the bright, overcast day. Fuelled by many cups of coffee, I put myself on a double-decker tour bus and sat there watching the Scottish city roll past the window. Rather than hiding in bed, I forced myself to at least pretend to be a tourist. I took photographs of things I didn't particularly care about. I attempted to listen to the babbling commentary about the history of Glasgow. Eventually, I disembarked from the bus and wandered like a zombie through an art gallery. Then I strolled along the banks of the River Clyde. This felt right.

I walked until my legs felt heavy.

I walked until my lungs felt renewed.

I walked. And walked. And walked.

For four full days, I roamed around the city. The action of moving forward somehow began to dismantle the metaphoric rain cloud hovering above my head. And during this process, I clicked — I came back online, so to speak, emotionally and mentally. I didn't become cheerful or feel suddenly appreciative of the month that had passed. But I summoned just enough battery life to continue.

And then, much like my exit from the Pleasance Press Office, I quietly disappeared from Scotland. Ready for the next month. Ready for the next chapter to begin. ☺

SEPTEMBER

Galilee, Israel

"Yodfat Junction!" yelled the bus driver.

I disembarked from the green intercity bus and collected my backpack from the lower storage compartment. Then I watched the rundown vehicle sputter away, leaving me in a cloud of diesel fumes.

Alone on the side of an Israeli highway.

The sun had set a couple of hours previously. This meant that I was not only alone but also alone in the dark. Wasn't this the premise of most horror films?

Most of me was scared. I had a preconceived notion that the average Israeli was as tough as nails. Because of mandatory army training, any citizen of the nation, should they have the urge, could sneak up and kill me silently with nothing but a pomegranate and some dental floss. I surveyed the area, looking for potential perils, wishing I had stayed enrolled in those childhood karate classes.

How did I manage to get myself into these positions?

Despite my uneasiness, a small part of me — the foolish part — was entirely amused by the situation: on the side of a road in the Holy Land, I was waiting for a man named Yacob about a venture with some milking goats.

This type of random exploit makes a guy feel exceedingly alive. Or it kills him. ✧

MY HOST FOR the month of September was an organic farm in the Galilee hills called Goats With the Wind. As much as I looked forward to checking the place out, my first mission was just getting myself halfway across the nation to find the darn farm.

Earlier that day, I had departed Tel Aviv on the bus. Throughout the ride, I sent a steady stream of text messages to Yacob, the Israeli goat farmer, who was supposed to collect me at a place called Yodfat Junction. I had saved his number in my mobile phone and thought it might be helpful to update him on my estimated arrival time. But I received no messages in return. Now I had arrived and there was nobody waiting for me.

A half moon hovered shyly over the low hills. The air was dry and warm. Once the diesel fumes dissipated, I noticed the aroma of sage. A hundred metres past where the bus had stopped was the start of another road, a junction. I walked toward the intersection, stashed my bags inside a bus shelter and strategically positioned myself under the glow of a street lamp. It was at that point I decided to stop texting and try a real phone call.

The line rang and rang.

Finally, at the eighth ring, someone picked up and I heard the faint sound of breathing. But nobody spoke, so I began.

"Uhhh ... hello? Hello, is Yacob there?"

"Sorry?" responded the distant voice of an older woman.

"My name is Daniel. I'm the Canadian volunteer. Is Yacob there?"

"Who?"

"Yacob."

"Who?"

"Yacob!" I over-enunciated loudly. "I'm standing on the side of a highway. There is a man who is supposed to pick me up."

"What?"

"I'M TRYING TO GET TO THE GOAT FARM!"

"I don't know anything about goats!" said the confused woman, her thick Israeli accent reminding me that I was in a very foreign place.

"There's no Yacob there?"

"No!"

Click.

Crap. This was *not* good. I had assumed that the logistics of getting to the goat farm would be simple: get on bus, hop off bus, greet whoever was eagerly awaiting my arrival, drive to the farm, be embraced by a sea of affectionate goats. But clearly my optimism was paired with a heavy dose of naiveté. I didn't know what to do next. What *is* the standard protocol when stranded on an Israeli highway, trying to find a goat farmer named Yacob?

I spent the next few minutes pacing up and down the side road. Occasionally a car roared along the highway, but none turned. According to a street sign, Yodfat was another few kilometres further down the lane. Apart from the pounding of my heart, which had manifested itself in my eardrums, the only sound was crickets.

That's when I had my moment of clarity. I realized that maybe, just maybe, I had the wrong phone number. I dug to the bottom of my bag to extract my journal. Sure enough, Yacob's phone number was there, scribbled on a piece of paper alongside a sandwich receipt and some unwritten postcards. I quickly saw what had happened. When I had saved the number in my mobile phone, I had mistakenly put a "0" where a "9" should have been. Consequently, I had been sending text messages to that poor confused woman all day long.

I tried the correct number. It cut to a voice mail service. The recorded Hebrew message was indecipherable, but at least this time I had reached a male voice, which was a step in the right direction. Without a moment to think, I spewed out an unrehearsed soliloquy:

"Um, hi. My name is Daniel. I'm trying to get a hold of Yacob, regarding the goat farm. To be honest, I don't really know where I am. Well, other than on the side of a highway. But if you could help me, that would be … uh … really great."

I hung up. And then I slapped my forehead — how despairing and ridiculous. Whoever received that message would ascertain this information: weirdo foreign-guy standing on a highway, looking for an animal farm. Who in their right mind would rush out into the night to rescue a character like that? Nobody would. At that moment, there was one solid word to describe my situation: SCREWED.

I started examining the bus shelter, which was becoming my most viable option for refuge that night. It wasn't glamorous, but there was a roof and a relatively level slab of cement on the ground. If I could survive the rooftop mosquito shack in Buenos Aires, I could survive this, right? But wait. Weren't there some terribly poisonous snakes in the Holy Land? I vaguely recalled a story in the Bible about someone dying from snakebite. My best approach, I strategized, would be to crawl in my airtight sleeping bag and form my patented safety cocoon. I'd walk into Yodfat the next morning.

But just when I was about to construct a mattress out of dirty socks and unfolded maps, my phone sprang to life.

"Hello, Daniel here!" I shouted with desperate hopefulness.

"It's Yacob. I'll be there in 15 minutes."

Click.

Sure enough, 15 minutes later, I saw a pair of headlights in the distance. They weaved along a crooked road and illuminated the shrubby hillside. A rusty red pickup truck rolled to a stop at the bus shelter. The window jerked down. A stern young man with a shaved head and a robust nose leaned his head out.

"Are you the volunteer for the farm?"

There was nobody else within sight. So for a split second, I thought about cracking a joke and saying that I'd ask around. But I bit my tongue and went for cordiality.

"Yup, that's me!"

After heaving my backpack into the bed of the truck, I hopped into the cab and offered my friendliest smile. "You must be Yacob?"

"Yeah."

"Thanks, man. I am *very* happy to be saved from the side of the highway."

He reciprocated with a brief nod. But he said nothing as we shifted into motion and began to retrace the road to Yodfat.

The truck was immediately filled with an awkward silence. Yacob didn't ask me about how the journey from Tel Aviv had been or even if I had been to Israel before. I considered striking up a conversation, but I didn't want to be that guy who chats to fill space. Besides, maybe he didn't speak much English.

Eventually we turned onto a dirt road.

We stopped at a stone building that looked to be some type of farmhouse. Without saying anything, Yacob got out of the truck. So I did the same.

"This is where you sleep," he announced, opening a barn door and flicking on a light. "You settle, then go down to the kitchen." He motioned down the lane, which was lit only by the truck's headlights. Yacob pulled out my big backpack, lifting it with the ease of someone accustomed to throwing hay bales. Then he got back into the vehicle and pulled away.

With my gear under my arms, I stepped into the stone shack. It smelled of straw, and a chorus of tinkling bells suggested that farm animals were my neighbours. With eight months of travel now logged, I had managed to lower my lodging expectations to little more than a mattress and a roof. That's basically what the room offered. But as a bonus, there was also a gritty sink, a concrete shower and an uncovered light bulb. As I stood there, a mouse poked his head from a pile of blankets. Across a ceiling rafter, a monstrous spider walked on legs so long they could wrap themselves around a deck of cards. Home sweet home.

Figuring that the other volunteers would be in the kitchen, I ditched my things and trekked down the gravel driveway in search of lights and voices. The half moon was now covered in clouds. Without any source of natural light, it was impossible to see past my toes. As I walked, guided by the glare of my mobile phone, I sensed a series of animal pens to my left. From inside these cages came the shuffling of hooves and the occasional bray. Wanting to investigate, I paused and shone the light toward the pens. A hundred sets of eyes gazed back. I walked a bit faster.

The path curved, and ahead was a sliver of light shining from the crack of two swinging doors. I entered and found myself standing among clay pots and piles of herbs in an open concept kitchen that led to a patio.

"Uh, hello?" I called tentatively, loud enough to be heard but quiet enough to not be invasive. Nobody responded. Nobody was around. Not even Yacob.

The situation was perplexing. *Where was everyone?* And more pressingly, was it okay to help myself to food? Unsure of what to do, I decided to sit and wait. And as I waited, I reviewed the situation thus far.

The welcome had definitely not been gracious. In fact, the interactions with Yacob had felt standoffish, perhaps even frosty. This was a source of concern. After a handful of work-exchange experiences, I had learned something important: first impressions can be telling. The initial 24 hours at any project was often enough to predict how the following weeks would unfold. On the raw vegan farm in Costa Rica, for instance, I had smelled outlandishness shortly after arriving. But in France, Nico's warm welcome set the tone for the entire month.

My main reason for staying optimistic was that true wackos don't have the capacity to keep farm animals alive. Yet the lack of people, especially volunteers, made me very concerned. *Oh, Jesus of Nazareth, was I really in for another sufferable experience?* I was barely over the agonies of Edinburgh.

Just as I was about to head back to the stone shack and go to bed hungry, I heard the sound of footsteps on gravel. ☼

"You're not actually thinking of going to Israel, are you?" The question hung uncomfortably in the air. It was December.

I was sitting with a friend and chatting about my upcoming trip around the world. We had rambled through the destinations I had dreamed of visiting, such as Buenos Aires and Morocco. Now we had shifted our focus to the Middle East, specifically to which nation I would visit.

"Um … well … maybe?" I explained that I had heard about Israel's history of exchange-based volunteerism. Agricultural communities known as *kibbutzim* and *moshavim* accepted foreign helpers. These types of projects fit perfectly with the structure of my trip.

"Well, you might want to reconsider visiting an occupied state," he challenged, making it clear where he stood on the topic of Israeli-Palestinian relations. "Some compare the situation in Israel to South African apartheid."

"Oh …" I paused and looked away. I didn't really know how to respond to his challenge, primarily because I didn't have an educated standpoint on the topic. So, to avoid further confrontation, I moved the discussion forward. "Anyway, that'll be September, which is a long time from now. Heck, I don't even know if I'll make it that far. But if I do make it that far, then in October, I'll head into Asia …"

Like a burr to a woolly hiking sock, my friend's question latched onto me. It began to dawn on me that a trip across the world couldn't *not* be laced with implications. The 12 countries that I chose to visit would inevitably reflect my personal politics and priorities — or lack thereof. I began to feel self-conscious about my itinerary. In my mind, my agenda seemed quite harmless. But is there such thing as travelling innocently across the planet?

During the months that followed our conversation, I vacillated about which Middle Eastern nation I would visit. I felt certain that omitting this corner of the world, with its deep history and distinctive cultures, would be a disservice. Yet which state would offer a meaningful experience and the political stability to make it safe enough to enter? I wanted experiences that would be noteworthy, just not the "look out for the bombs" type of noteworthy.

From what I had heard, Israel was relatively stable and actually had a booming tourism industry. But perhaps it would be wise to steer clear of such a politically charged state. If I didn't have well-informed politics, or at least an objective opinion regarding Israel, would it not be best to hold off until I was more educated? Eventually, Israel was displaced from my list of "must-visit" destinations.

As I began to make my way across the world, I continued to toss around some important travel questions. *Does a visit to a nation equate with support of its political actions? In any given country, who is affected by my presence as a foreigner? Is "boycotting" a state an effective form of protest?* I came up with no easy answers.

And as the year progressed, I began to meet travellers from all over the world. Some of these people ended up steering the course of my journey. And, serendipitously, two of them just happened to be from Israel.

One of my first evenings in France, during that *grande fête* in Ruffepeyre, I met a good-natured Israeli couple (the same duo that wowed the crowd with their India-inspired dance moves). Sun-drenched and earthy, Yonatan and Neta were volunteering at a nearby farm project. Over the course of July, our paths crossed frequently and soon we became friends. One evening, the Israeli couple joined us for zucchini quiche and glasses of Bordeaux in the monk's tower. I explained the work-exchange premise of my travels to Yonatan. He put down his glass of wine, ran his hands through his curly hair and then spoke in his demure tone.

"My friend, you must visit Israel."

"Oh, I'm not sure ..."

"I know some places that take helpers."

My ears perked up.

Off the top of his head, Yonatan mentioned three no-cost volunteer projects: a charming Arab mansion in Nazareth, a traditional *kibbutz* near Be'er Sheva and an organic goat farm in the Galilee. They all sounded interesting, but one stood out. The prospect of milking goats in the Holy Land was almost too rich for my little heart to bear.

So my plans to visit Israel were reinstated, catalyzed by a connection with gentle and well-travelled Israelis. And through my process of grappling with some of those philosophical travel questions, I came to a simple reasoning: having undefined politics about a nation is a valid and rational reason for a traveller to visit. Ultimately, I wanted to move from feeling complete ignorance about the Middle East to being able to form my own views based on what I saw and experienced first-hand. With that in mind, I proceeded, hoping that a month in Israel might offer a morsel of awareness into a complex situation.

Oh yes, and insight into goats. ☼

THE KITCHEN DOOR creaked open. A tanned Asian woman with a wide grin on her face stepped over the door frame. A gangly blond man with thick-rimmed glasses and a blank expression followed her.

I quickly stood up from the stool.

"You must be the new volunteer!" the woman exclaimed, cocking her head to the side to examine me. "I'm Seungjoo. I'm from Korea!" I shook her outstretched hand and introduced myself, confirming that I was indeed a new volunteer.

"Welcome to the goat farm! It's a *special* place," she added, slowly enunciating the word "special."

"Thanks. I'm happy to see some other volunteers," I added and then looked toward the guy in her company.

"Hi. I'm Benjamin," he said, also offering a handshake. "I'm from Manhattan. Don't hold it against me." His tone was dry, but I could see a smirk in his eyes. "When did you arrive?"

Briefly, I recounted my transfer from Tel Aviv, including the stress of being stranded alone on a highway and arriving to the kitchen only to be greeted by nobody.

"Sorry we weren't here," said Seungjoo. "We walked 30 minutes into Yodfat to check our email."

"Yeah, and don't take the lack of welcome personally. That's typical," added Benjamin. "You're in Israel. Don't expect anyone to pander to you."

I nodded, absorbing the cultural pointer.

"You hungry?" asked Seungjoo with wide eyes. Without waiting for an answer, she began to raid a cooler that held a variety of goat cheeses. Then she arranged them on a plate with some leftover cabbage salad and pita bread. Much to my delight, it was the finest goat cheese I had ever tasted. The soft *labneh* was yogurty and tangy. The firmer varieties crumbled on my tongue, unapologetically sharp. Others simply melted with sweetness, smooth as butter.

As I ate, I posed more questions about the farm and, more specifically, the host family. Benjamin gave me a brief "Goat Farm 101." The matriarch of the house, Daliah, was in charge of running the kitchen. That evening she was away on business with her husband, Amnon, who was the founder and head honcho of the farm. Rounding out the top three central characters was Yacob, the son-in-law of Daliah and Amnon, who led the milking and participated in much of the general maintenance.

"And don't worry about Yacob," assured Benjamin. "He's a good guy."

Eventually, Seungjoo, Benjamin and I cleared up in the kitchen. Then we walked together back to the stone shack beside the goat pen. With the bounty of goat cheese for dinner, the company of other volunteers and the reassurance that my hosts were not socially isolated eccentrics, my morale took an instant upswing. I pulled down one of the mattresses propped up against the wall, grabbed a blanket and tucked myself in. ☼

THE NEXT MORNING, I awoke to the sound of goats clomping around the stables. I rose and stumbled out of the small stone shack to see the sun breaking over the sand-coloured eastern hills. Stretching my arms toward the sky, I gnashed the air with a monstrous yawn and took in my surroundings. In the daylight, the property was a different world, far more welcoming than in the shadows of night. The hut where I slept was essentially part of the barn, with only a thin wall between me and a large herd of goats. The barn was attached to the farm's main building, and together they formed a boomerang-shaped bungalow. The whole property — which included a couple of yurts, some out-houses, a wine cellar and a hayloft — was nestled halfway up the end of a U-shaped valley, with thinly treed hills acting as a perim-eter. A single dirt track cut through the farm, zigzagging its way out from the homestead and back toward the highway — and eventually the rest of Israel.

Benjamin came out to join me. Squinting into the sun, he informed me that there would be coffee waiting. Together we moseyed to the kitchen in sleepy silence and arrived to a steam-ing pot of percolated espresso. Yacob and his brother were seat-ed at a small table on a veranda overlooking the goat pen. We pulled up wicker footstools to join them and were greeted by close-mouthed nods.

A bit of caffeine was exactly what I needed to kick-start my day. However, as I was about to dive into the coffee, I noticed that the two Israeli men hadn't yet served themselves. Instead, they were simply sitting in a state of non-motion, staring over the goats. The blankness on their faces perplexed me. If their eyes had been closed or if they had been humming some sort of mantra, then I would have assumed that they were observing a type of reli-gious ritual. But their postures and actions didn't suggest prayer. If anything, it was more like a stoic stiffness, a Clint-Eastwood-looking-over-the-Wild-West sort of moment, like they were gaz-ing across the pasture and telepathically informing the goats that they *owned their goaty souls*. I followed Benjamin's lead, sitting there unobtrusively yet wondering what was happening.

At last, Yacob made a move toward the coffee pot and poured some thick black java into a tiny cup without a handle. Any type of mannish stoicism quickly vanished as the weathered Israeli goat farmer, with his husky forearms, took a delicate sip from his thimble of coffee. With goblets the size of shot glasses, we looked like four grown men gathering for an early morning Disney Prin-cess tea party. If I had been with friends from back home, the situation would have warranted some sort of cheeky jab about our collective masculinity. But I bit my tongue, knowing that the two men had probably been through Israeli army training. If I said the wrong thing, they could likely snap my neck like a carrot.

I waited for my turn and then served myself a shot. I didn't see any sugar on the table, just a small bottle of warm milk. I coloured my coffee with the cream and took a swig.

Damn!

My face puckered in disgust.

Yup, that was definitely *goat's* milk.

Despite my long-standing affinity for goat cheese, I have failed to develop even the slightest appreciation for the repulsiveness that is raw goat milk. The downside was that my morning coffee tasted horrible. The upside was that I was now abundantly awake.

When the brothers finished a couple rounds of diminutive coffee shots, they got up and left the table without a word.

"All right," Benjamin said. "Ready to get started?"

"Sure, but what am I supposed to do?" I was surprised that there wasn't a more formal orientation or briefing from the hosts.

"The guys are going to do the milking, and Seungjoo usually helps with that. So I'll show you how to feed the animals."

"Sounds good to me." I had secretly hoped that milking a goat would be my first lesson, but I figured I would just learn it later.

Although the goats were the main attraction on the farm, there was also a small menagerie of other animals: sheep, horses, cows, chickens, ducks, dogs, cats and one old donkey that might well have been around when Jesus was roaming the very same hills. As we went over the responsibilities, I listened attentively, trying to memorize all the details. What I had imaged would be a simple two-step process was actually a multi-faceted maintenance algorithm.

EXPECTATIONS

1 *Select animal.*

2 *Give animal food.*

REALITY

1 *Select animal.*

2 *Ensure said animal has water.*

3 *If it's hot, check water levels multiple times during the day.*

4 *Give the donkey the same feed as the sheep, but don't give it to the horse.*

5 *Give the baby goats alfalfa, not hay.*

6 *Give the lambs hay, not alfalfa.*

7 *Don't feed the geese.*

8 *Shut the chicken pen tightly or a dog will run off with a hen in its teeth.*

9 *Female goats get more than the male goats because they need to produce milk.*

10 *To avoid the dominant heifer stealing the entire meal, adequately partition the feed for the cows by tossing hay in a variety of directions.*

11 *Occasionally, you'll come across a dead puppy. Take the initiative to bury it.*

12 *The cat's name is Carla. She's the queen of all the farm animals.*

I asked Benjamin how he kept track of everything.

"It's not rocket science," he replied in his New York City accent, gazing over the rim of his glasses. "Just stay out of the way ... and make sure nothing dies."

"Got it." ☺

DURING OUR INITIAL introduction in the kitchen, Seungjoo mentioned that Goats With the Wind was a "special" place. At first, I didn't really understand why she chose that word or why she continued to use it as the days went by. Maybe, due to her limited English, she couldn't think of a better adjective. But the more time I spent on the farm, the more I came to realize that every person who visited had his or her own reason for believing that the place was "special."

For Amnon, the founder of the farm, the place was special because it was his life's work — his personal history was embedded in the geography of the land. Many decades previously, he roamed the hills nomadically with his flock of goats and slept under the night sky. As the years passed, he grew familiar with each rocky outcrop. He memorized the shadows of each tree. He knew where to find water when the rain was sparse. But as more and more land across Israel was allocated for settlements or agriculture, his roaming space began to dwindle. So Amnon solicited the government to conserve a small parcel for collective farming usage and received permission to establish a more permanent facility, a family-run farm. As opposed to a *kibbutz* or *moshav*, which generally involve multiple families or a larger community, the farm remained a small-scale venture over the years. And to this day, in that humble stone-strewn valley in Galilee, goats outnumber people by an approximate ratio of 20:1.

For many Israeli youths, Goats With the Wind was special because it was a refuge from a complicated world. During my time on the farm, I met numerous young adults who popped by for a visit. Many of these friends were actually volunteer alumni who had helped with the goats for longer stints, some of them spanning several years. I noticed a common theme among many of these individuals: they had completed their mandatory army service and weren't quite sure what to do with themselves next. Goats With the Wind seemed like an ideal post-army refuge. A place with a reliable pulse to mark the moments of each day. A haven where — in direct contrast to the military — serenity and autonomy were weaved into the farm's culture. That little valley in Galilee was special because it was the antithesis of what one might associate with an army: a safe place, a home.

And then there were the international volunteers, like

Seungjoo and Benjamin, who had their own definition of why the farm was special. Goats With the Wind offered foreign visitors the opportunity to experience life on a functioning goat farm and to be involved with a microcosm of Israel, a pocket of the nation where the average tourist rarely treads. Tucked away in the Galilean hills, it was not just off the beaten path, it was nearly impossible to find.

Over the weeks I spent at Goats With the Wind, the farm would come to feel like a special space for me as well. But I had my own reasons. ☺

"DANIEL, COME," SEUNGJOO called as she poked her head into the stone shack. "Yacob has returned. We're going to help with the afternoon milking."

It was an hour before sunset on the first day. I was quietly reading, occasionally distracted by a couple of farm puppies who enjoyed chewing on my flip-flops. The morning had been spent helping Benjamin with the feedings and other odd jobs. But since Daliah and Amnon had still not come back, and Yacob was nowhere to be found, even Benjamin wasn't sure what we should do next. All of the animals had been thoroughly watered, so we opted to relax, to lie low.

With the prospect of milking goats at hand, I jumped to my feet, changed into my hiking boots and followed Seungjoo into the station. My single biggest goal for my month at the goat farm was about to be achieved.

Sure enough, Yacob and his brother had arrived. They were hauling coffin-sized sacks of grain from the pickup truck into the station. Neither of the brothers greeted me, but that didn't mean my presence was unacknowledged: through an iron gate, countless goat faces peered in my direction. In the adjacent pen, the 160 lady goats had returned from their daily jaunt through the Galilean hills and were staring curiously at the milking platforms, aroused by the smell of grain.

Twice daily, the goats were milked — by hand. You might

271

assume this would take all day, that by the time the first round was complete, it would be necessary to corral them up again for Round Two. But Yacob and his brother were highly skilled with their hands. What would have been a milk marathon for the average inexperienced schmuck (such as myself) took less than an hour when the Israeli brothers were working in unison. It helped, however, that they had an effective system in place.

The way to a goat's teat is through its stomach. Motivated by the allure of food, the goats were marched single file onto one of two waist-high platforms. There they wedged their heads into individual stanchions (slots) and began devouring their mixture of oats, buckwheat and barley. A wooden bar was lowered across the back of their necks, locking them into place yet leaving their back ends exposed. The older goats were accustomed to this routine. They munched away unconcernedly while the brothers walked behind them and administered an efficient yanking of their teats. The younger ones, however, were a bit fussier, often kicking or jumping to avoid the mammary molestation. But resistance was futile; no lady goat ever escaped a milking.

What made the system extra efficient was having two platforms, each accommodating 12 animals. So as the brothers tackled the goats on one platform, Seungjoo and I prepped the other side. First, each stanchion was sprinkled with a half-scoop of grain. Once the feed was administered, the gate was hoisted to enable exactly one dozen goats to come scrambling, single file, toward their rations. But occasionally an overly eager (or overly hungry) goat dove into the first available stanchion and began crunching the grain. This would cause a goat backlog by obstructing the others from proceeding forward along the narrow feeding platform. The solution was simple: the offender was encouraged to keep moving via a swift kidney poke with a wooden staff. Once 12 goats were in position, the restraining bar was brought down. This process took approximately four minutes, just enough time for the brothers to milk the 12 goats on the other platform.

And then we switched sides.

The restraining bar was lifted, and the ladies escorted themselves out the other end of the platform and into a secondary pen to avoid mixing with the not-yet-milked goats. They knew the drill. The only time intervention was required was when one of the gals paused at a different stanchion to nab leftover grain. Again, a gentle jab to the abdomen or a loudly yelled *"yalla"* (Arabic for "let's go") would prove most effective in reminding her that the show was over and that she should proceed to the yard without further delay. Once the platform was cleared of goats, the routine commenced again. Fresh grain was placed in each stanchion. Then 12 new goats aligned.

Call me simple, but I *adored* the whole system.

There was a rhythmic pulse to the procedure: goats in, goats milked, goats out. I loved the sound of the metallic scoop as it ripped into the grain. I loved the feel of the coarse goat hides as I nudged them off the platforms. I loved watching the silver buckets as they became frothy with gallons of harvested milk. But perhaps most of all, I loved being involved with the milking because there was an immediate sense of achievement. Apart from the ability to move quickly and the willingness to slap goat bums, the preparation of the platforms required little actual expertise. Thus, I was able to be helpful.

Despite my rapid learning curve and dazzling abilities as a milking assistant, Yacob continued to display a cool detachment, letting Seungjoo show me how to prep the stanchions and abstaining from interaction. However, after I performed a string of successful platform preparations, ensuring that each goat was perfectly lined up and ready to be milked, Yacob paused and pivoted in my direction.

"Daniel," he said as he looked me up and down with his bushy eyebrows furrowed, "how long will you be here on the farm?"

"Uh, a few weeks," I replied tentatively, unsure if a shorter stay or a longer stay would be a more appealing response.

"Oh," he said apathetically. "Then I won't teach you how to milk the goats."

"What? ... Why?"

Before responding, he wiped his upper arm along his forehead, dampening his threadbare T-shirt.

"You're not worth the investment."

With that, he went back to milking.

And I was crushed. ۞

THE FIRST TIME I met Daliah, the matriarch of Goats With the Wind, she was in her territory: the kitchen. Judging by her thick mass of salt and pepper hair and by the weathered creases on her face, I'd say she might have been in her early fifties. But she had a "women who run with wolves" sort of motif that made it hard to gauge her actual age. Holding a pile of plates in her left hand, Daliah wiped her right hand on her floor-length skirt and extended a soft handshake.

"Hi Daniel." Daliah smiled wearily and exposed a missing premolar tooth. "You made it to our farm."

I was about to tell her the funny anecdote about my misdialed phone call from the side of the highway when she pushed the pile of plates into my chest and nodded toward the veranda.

"Please help set up for the meal." And then she turned her attention back to a tajine dish, which was simmering over the gas stove. Dinnertime had arrived, and there would be no time for chatting about how I was enjoying my stay thus far.

On the veranda overlooking the goat pen, Benjamin was arranging brightly patterned Turkish rugs over the wooden surface and then positioning colourful seat pillows in a circle. Dinner would be served on the ground, Bedouin-style. As I set the "table," Yacob walked onto the veranda, heavy in conversation with a long-haired man in a beige collarless shirt. They slipped off their sandals and sat beside each other on the cushions, their conversation continuing in Hebrew.

A minute passed. Then the long-haired man paused and looked across the veranda — in my direction — as if something was slightly different with the scenery.

"*Shalom.* I'm Amnon."

I knelt on the vacant cushion next to him, shook his hand and introduced myself. But as I was about tell him how I was eager to help out around the farm, especially with milking the goats, he turned back toward Yacob. Their conversation continued with a display of arm movements and energetic eyebrows.

Soon after, Daliah and Seungjoo came to the veranda, their arms teetering with various dishes. The food was positioned on a large silver platter in the middle of the circle. Eventually, six of us — Daliah, Amnon, Yacob, Benjamin, Seungjoo and myself — were seated for dinner.

As always, my knee-jerk reaction was to dive in and start serving myself. Thankfully, I noticed that everybody else was patiently holding back. So I waited. All eyes turned to Amnon, who picked up a loaf of bread, closed his eyes and spoke a string of words in Hebrew. He cut off a piece of the bread and ate it, and then passed it to Yacob, who also tore off a piece. The loaf went around the circle and ended at me. I took a small morsel and popped it in my mouth, mimicking what the others had done (and hoping that I wasn't making any grave social blunders).

With the blessing complete, Amnon reached for the food. And then Yacob. And then the volunteers. Daliah insisted that everyone else fill their plates before she served herself. The meal was a spread of sautéed potatoes, labneh cheese drizzled with olive oil, tender stewed lamb, cabbage salad and a bottle of Merlot made from grapes grown on the farm's own vines. The stew was eaten directly from the large clay pot, and the drippings were sopped up with chunks of bread. Throughout the dinner, Amnon and Yacob talked between themselves. Daliah occasionally offered a sentiment. Benjamin, who was able to follow a bit of Hebrew, engaged sporadically. Seungjoo smiled attentively, turning her face to each person who spoke. I also attempted to politely remain attuned but found myself drifting in thought.

Overall, I can't say that it was unpleasant. The food was scrumptious. We were sitting outside in the mild evening air. I even had a glass of wine in my hand. In many ways, the situation had all the ingredients to rival the splendour of those communal meals I had shared in France. But something was different. Whereas in Ruffepeyre I had promptly felt like part of the experience, here I was just *observing* the experience. From the outside. ☼

A TRIP AROUND the world is filled with countless learning opportunities. In New Orleans, I became interested (and somewhat skilled) in the art of laying tile. In Argentina, I learned about the Dirty War, and the industrious actions of the Madres de Plaza de Mayo. In Morocco, I learned that a man with a loofah sponge could inflict more pain than most medieval torture devices. In Israel, I also learned something very significant: goats are the coolest creatures on earth.

No, seriously.

Goats are affectionate and curious, stubborn and playful. They produce raw material for the most wonderful products, such as wool for cashmere sweaters and milk for bold cheeses. Goats function as low-emission lawn mowers. They have the most extraordinary horizontal pupils. And let's not forget that male goats make sounds reminiscent of Chewbacca. Goats are the most overlooked and underappreciated beasts of the animal kingdom.

On that Galilean farm, I discovered that each goat had its own disposition. And some stood out from the herd. For instance, there was no mistaking the four male goats. They were larger in size and did not hesitate to display their manliness through non-consensual advancements on the females and the occasional premature ejaculation. (Tip: If you appreciate dry shoes, don't walk too close to a male goat.)

The ladies, however, were far more refined. There was Deborah, the young gal with a long buttery coat and charcoal ears. She seemed to reject her goat status. Contrary to the herd mentality of her peers, she would constantly attempt to escape the pen and join the realm of humans. There was a goat I nicknamed "Ginger Spice" because of her auburn colouring. Ginger Spice had droopy eyes, which made her constantly look like she had smoked too much marijuana. Then there was old Beatrice, a white-coated gal with a dented bell hanging from a pink collar and one lopsided horn (or one frisky horn, depending on which way you looked at it). While her colleagues could become skittish at milking time, Beatrice always exuded a sense of wisdom and serenity, assuming her position at the stanchions with dignity and a greater acceptance of the whole arrangement.

But what if I had to choose one goat above all others? The fairest of them all? Now, *that's* a difficult task. My first inclination would be to diplomatically proclaim that there were too many lovely goats and to choose one would be like selecting the most cherished of one's children.

However, if I were pressed hard enough, I would admit that indeed I had a favourite goat, a beloved young lady whose disposition was like the pleasant aroma of orange blossoms.

Her name was Juliette. ○

A SEMI-PREDICTABLE ROUTINE developed on the farm. The early mornings were pleasantly banal: as the sun peeked over the horizon, I would awake to the tinkling sound of goat bells, shuffle like a zombie to the kitchen, sit in uncomfortable silence on the veranda, hammer back coffee in dainty cups, and then assume my role as co-master milking assistant (a job that I shared with my mentor, Seungjoo). Afterward, I scrubbed down the milking area and helped with any additional animal feeding that needed to be done. When these morning chores were complete, it was time for mid-morning breakfast, which usually consisted of tomato salad, browned potatoes with fresh parsley, crusty bread, goat milk yogurt and, if the chickens had been motivated, a couple of fried eggs. I enjoyed this portion of the day. After breakfast, however, things became less foreseeable.

Unlike the early morning, the hours that followed breakfast and preceded the late-afternoon milking were the most variable and erratic part of my day. Sometimes I was pleased with what

I was assigned to do, other times I was uninspired — or worse: totally clueless. In general, any job in the garden was enjoyable, such as harvesting grapes for winemaking. Plucking the juicy bundles of dark blue fruit from the vine had an intrinsic quality comparable to popping bubble wrap or cracking the crust on *crème brûlée*. I could have picked grapes all day.

But the vineyard was small, and other less glamorous jobs tended to take precedence. One day, the bulk of my time was spent collecting large rocks to help restore a garden wall. Another time, I found myself teetering on a rooftop, carefully wiping the dust off the farm's solar panels. Toward the end of the month, I assisted a tradesman from Yodfat with upgrading the water pipes (and by "assisted" I mean "handed him wrenches and fetched him water"). On the whole, I didn't mind the grunt work or the support tasks, especially when I was in the company of other volunteers or one of the many locals that would come to spend a day helping on the farm.

But I did have a few grievances.

First, Yacob wouldn't teach me how to milk goats. In his defence, I hadn't broached the topic with him since our first day working together. He had made his sentiments about the topic copiously clear, and I didn't see the point of making an issue out of it. But it did leave me a bit disgruntled.

Next on my list of whinges was the fact that I could be called to duty at any point. One of the components I appreciated most about my experiences in Ruffepeyre and Trujillo was the well-defined project working hours. I knew when I was on the clock and I knew when I was off the clock. Call me a wet rag if you must, but I'm the type of person that appreciates knowing when nap time will be.

And my final gripe was that I often found myself wondering what I should be doing or how I should be doing something. In my non-travelling life, direct communication was my broad strategy. But I was not in Canada, or even France. I was on a goat farm in the Galilee. Certain approaches that work in one culture don't necessarily translate into another. Perhaps I could have *asked* for more clarity, but that would put me at risk of inconveniencing my hosts. Hence, as Benjamin suggested, I tried to stay out of the way, to wait to be told what to do, and to tackle my chores to the best of my ability.

Such as when I attempted to construct a fence.

The sun was oppressively intense that morning. Shortly after breakfast, I strolled over to the baby goat pen and pulled the watering hose across the gravel lane to ensure that the trough was adequately filled for the searing heat of the day ahead. Down the lane, I could see Amnon slowly approaching with purpose. His lengthy grey hair, billowy white shirt and pair of leather sandals created the sort of style that denotes leadership in an obscure spiritual sect. To be fair, the patriarch of the goat farm wasn't overly kooky or even religiously enthusiastic. But he was firm, maintaining a rigid posture and speaking with his head constantly cocked back. There were a couple of occasions where he scolded me specifically for generic farm occurrences: "Why do the chickens have no water?" and "Who left that gate open?" If I had known the answer to these rhetorical-type questions, the problem wouldn't have existed in the first place. To cope, I developed an effective tactic called "avoidance." But on this day, he was coming for me. So I braced myself.

"Daniel," he started slowly, with his eyes squinting, "today you will construct a fence around the bamboo."

On a recent trip to the city of Haifa, Amnon had acquired three waist-high bamboo plants. They had been planted directly under the grey-water drainage pipe outside the stone shack, with the intent to create a type of eco-friendly filtration system. The problem, however, was that the bamboo was vulnerable to nibbles from any goats that happened to escape from their pen.

"Uh ..." I responded cautiously. "Okay." I didn't have any fence-building experience or expertise, but I figured I'd give it a shot. How complicated could it be? Besides, I was eager to prove that I wasn't a totally incompetent fool.

"There is fencing material near the compost pile." And with no further instruction, Amnon turned back down the lane.

As soon as I finished filling the water troughs for the baby goats, I got to work gathering metal lattice, tracking down a pair of pliers from the workshop, and hunting for thin metal cable to use as industrial-strength twist-ties. Now, with the ingredients laid out in front of me, it was time to start baking.

How to proceed?

First things first: get an architectural game plan. To make matters simple, there were a series of pre-existing posts around the bamboo. If the lattice were positioned in such a way that it tilted outward from the posts, I reasoned, the bamboo would ultimately have more space to develop and expand. Plus, the enclosure would also appear less cagey and hopefully encourage a spirit of openness and natural growth. (Unlike the goats and the bamboo and anything else living a confined existence, the brilliance of my design sensibilities had no boundaries!) After patting myself on the back for such cutting-edge vision, I began to section off pieces of the metal cable. One by one, I attached the pieces of lattice.

An hour later, as I was bending my last metal twist-tie into place with the pliers, I heard the sound of hooves on gravel. Amnon, who had taken the horse to survey the surrounding hills, had returned. As he drew nearer, I stood proudly beside my freshly constructed feng shui fence, waiting to be commended on a job well done.

Amnon dismounted and put his hands on his hips.

"This is no good," he said bluntly.

"What? ... Why?" He was clearly missing the cleverness, the intentionality of my work.

"Look. Someone might hit their eye on this corner." To illustrate his point, he walked directly toward the angular fence and pretended to be maimed by one of the protruding corners.

He had a point.

"Build it again," he instructed. Then he got back on his horse and rode away.

I spent another hour repositioning the pieces of lattice so they tilted inward. Sadly, this design meant the bamboo would be caged in. But a cage was better than the alternative: certain death by goat nibbling.

When I had finished my second attempt on the fence, I sat on a stone at the edge of the gravel lane and took a big drink of water. It was nearly noon, and the sun overhead had transitioned from pleasantly warm to painfully unforgiving.

Once more, Amnon came strolling past my project, this time with a shovel in hand. I jumped to my feet. He paused to give the fence a strong shaking.

"No, no," he stated. "Too flimsy! Even a baby goat could knock that down."

I took a deep breath and got back to work. This time, I attached even *more* metal twist-ties, ensuring a solid construction. While the fence did become stronger, it also started to look like an oversized porcupine with all the protrusions of the metallic ties. The bamboo had gone from thriving in a spacious plant condominium to living in a snug (but relatively safe) cage to, finally, enduring a hostile barbwire prison.

Shortly before lunch, Amnon returned for a final assessment of my work. This time, he didn't touch the fence, didn't even bother to test its durability. His face was written with dissatisfaction.

"You've done enough with this, " he said and then dismissed me with his hand. "Go give water to the cows or something."

I put down the pliers and walked away without saying anything. ☼

THERE WAS ONE exclusive job on the farm that I have yet to mention. A job that I was *actually* good at. In fact, this task was so pleasant that I almost regretted experiencing it because all future jobs — on the farm or elsewhere — would seem lacklustre in comparison.

After their morning milking session, the lady goats were released into the hills to forage for food. Wild fodder comprised a significant portion of their nutritional intake, which helped to ensure them an organic diet while reducing the farm's feed costs.

In the surrounding territory, the ladies would graze on whatever flora they could stretch their necks to reach. Later in the day, any time between noon and three o'clock, they returned of their own volition. A giant, slow-moving, amorphous furry flock would be seen descending through the valley. And as it advanced, we ran to open the gate just wide enough so that we could count them one by one as they entered. For some reason, as soon as they reached the top of the zigzag driveway, those ladies switched into high gear and hightailed it toward the freshly scattered alfalfa waiting in their troughs. Anyone in their way was liable to receive a horn in the abdomen. In fact, each afternoon was like a mini-version of the Running of the Bulls, only goatier.

(Incidentally, the male goats never left the pen. The men just sort of hung around, waiting to be fed and ejaculating on stuff.)

Along with the milking goats and the male goats, the farm also had 40 baby goats that had been born in spring. By that point in the season, the kids had been weaned from their mothers and were now kept in a separate pen. This allowed them to develop a sense of independence while maximizing the milk yield from the moms. Eventually, the male baby goats were sold and the female baby goats were reintroduced to the rest of the herd. Then the adult males would make themselves useful by providing sexy times at sunset. Pregnancy, and thus milk production, would occur. And the whole husbandry/circle-of-life thing would be sustained.

In preparation to rejoin the milking goats, the baby goats needed to become habituated to a daily walk. They had to learn to stick with the herd, especially outside the confines of a pen. Therefore, a volunteer was selected each morning for a very special task: to guide the baby goats on a stroll.

Out of all the roles I assumed during my year of travelling the world — mason, farmhand, teacher, blog mentor, cook, painter and broadcast liaison — the single post that I adored the most was baby goat herdsman.

The chore involved a three-hour promenade. The main responsibility of the human guide was to ensure that the herd did not break into sub-groups or that succulent shrubs didn't prove to be too distracting as the bunch moved forward. Because the baby goats had been following a specific route for the weeks before I arrived at the farm, they more or less knew where they were going. All the herdsperson really had to do was to keep up with the little ones.

Late into my first week on the farm, I was bestowed with the coveted role of guiding the baby goats. The previous day, I had joined Benjamin on his final baby goat walk, since he was scheduled to depart the goat farm for greener pastures. (He was leaving to volunteer at the Arab mansion in Nazareth, which just happened to be the same guest house that Yonatan had recommended to me.) On our walk together, Benjamin shared all the wisdom he had amassed in regards to herding.

"Just use a stick and keep everyone together."

Guided by a simple tenet — *No kid left behind!* — it was now my turn to take the leadership role of solo baby goat herdsman.

At the entrance of the pen, I stood overlooking a sea of long furry faces. I had prepared myself for the jaunt by bringing a small backpack with water and a book. In my hand, I held a wooden staff. Apart from a cloak sewn out of potato sacks, the only thing missing for this shepherd was the herd.

I opened the gate cautiously, bracing myself for a surge of goats.

But instead of rampaging, like they had done the previous day, the herd just stood there staring at me. Their heads tilted to one side in unison, as if to say, "Who does this bearded, dirt-covered fellow with the aura of incompetence think he is? Jesus?"

"Okay, kids," I spoke rationally. "Let's go." I motioned up the hill with my staff.

Nothing.

"It's time to go for our walk!"

Zilch.

"*Yalla!*" I yelled and slammed my staff on the wooden fence, creating a loud crack that echoed across the valley. The baby goats must have finally understood my supreme authority because that's when they charged. Kicking their hind legs into the air, the little munchkins tore past my knees, nearly knocking me off my feet. They ran up the hill and began barrelling down the dirt road. I sprinted to catch up, fearing that they might take advantage of my newness and make a break for eternal freedom.

Fortunately, the embarrassment of being a grown man chasing baby goats lasted only a few minutes. A water trough near the entrance to the farm provided a thirst-quenching diversion for the wee goats. As they paused to drink, I managed to catch up to the pack. I waved my staff like a madman to make it clear that I was actually in charge and that any radicals in the group could easily be turned into a savoury dinner stew. I did, after all, have peripheral experience in the slaughter of farm animals. My posturing must have worked because, from there, the herd walked behind me at a relatively polite pace. That remained the case until the kids were distracted again, this time by potential snacks.

Approximately two hundred metres further down the gravel track, we passed a fenceline. The goats made a beeline for a carob tree, hoping that the wind had knocked some sweet pods from the tall branches. Jumping over rocks the size of small cars, I used my shepherd's staff to round them up again — back onto the road and toward our goal destination: a gated field at the far edge of the property.

Once I had them all corralled into the grazing field, I blocked the entrance. The baby goats were free to roam and scrounge for whatever foliage they could find. In addition to the assortment of green bushes to munch, there were dried grasses to sample and thorny shrubs that only their goaty little mouths could process. (Whereas other animals are often selective about what they eat, goats will munch on basically everything.) For the first few minutes, I attempted to guide the kids around the rocky pasture to where tasty plants were plentiful. But then I thought "Why am I bothering?" and opted for a different strategy — a little policy you might call "baby goat empowerment." Soon these babes would join the big goats, and they wouldn't have a doting Canadian mentor to guide them to the greenery. So I let the kids sort it out for themselves.

Positioned on a comfortably shaped rock under another carob tree, I stretched out and extracted my book. The tinkle of little bells on the goat collars allowed me to know where the herd was wandering. As long as I could hear them, I was a happy herder. And so I read, occasionally pausing to look out over the valley or simply to listen to the wind.

I had been sitting for an hour when I heard bells approaching. The baby goats were coming to investigate why on earth I was just sitting, given that there were so many twigs waiting to be munched. At first they remained at a reasonable distance, but then, one by one, they grew bolder: gnawing on my backpack, tugging on my T-shirt, scratching their heads on my hiking shoes and even attempting to rip pages out of my book. Forty curious four-legged creatures surrounded me in what was essentially a baby goat cuddle puddle, an experience that could melt the most hardened of hearts. But before I dissolved into an emotional mush, they wandered away again. Disappointed in my lack of edibility, the kids sought out more digestible options. But that afternoon, the most exceptional goat of the herd hung back.

At first glance, Juliette didn't look any different from all the other baby goats. She sported a simple white pelt with a greyish mohawk running from her head down along her neck, oversized floppy ears that she had yet to grow into and little knobby horns sprouting from her head.

But she was distinctive.

You see, Juliette had been tragically rejected by her mother shortly after birth. To prevent her inevitable demise, she was subsequently hand-fed by humans. Although the other goats might nudge or nibble me, they were always a bit distant and skittish. But Juliette was affectionate. That day, she curled up at my feet and rested her little goatee on my outstretched legs. She was uncommonly warm, and I was a willing victim of her affections.

Without a doubt, I had attained an ultimate traveller experience. In fact, that moment — I'm proud to announce — I set the global benchmark for work-exchange preciousness.

   In the rolling hills of Galilee.

   Sitting under a carob tree.

   With the company of a beautiful gal.

   As a baby goat herdsman. ○

BESIDES THE SWEETNESS of the baby goats, another much-loved aspect of life at Goats With the Wind was a string of individuals that I labelled the "Israeli drifters." This set of locals had all volunteered at one point or another on the farm. They would stroll down the dusty track, often arriving without notice, toting a knapsack and an artillery of fascinating stories. One afternoon a tall woman with a brush cut arrived on a horse and was greeted with warm hugs from Daliah. I found out that this woman's parents had kicked her out of the family home many years ago (for undisclosed reasons). If Daliah and Amnon hadn't given her a place to live, she would have turned to life on the streets. On a different occasion, a young man with a curly Afro and the most peculiar sole-less leather shoes (which he purchased on a recent trip to Turkey) arrived late in the evening. He joined Seungjoo and I on the veranda for tea and shared his insights about the hidden corners of Jerusalem.

The Israeli drifters were often in their twenties and spoke English well. They would spice up an otherwise solemn dinner with adventurous anecdotes. The regular presence of these ex-volunteers suggested that the farm had a legacy of strong relationships, especially within Israel. And the fact that they stayed in contact and returned regularly conveyed a particular bond — both with the farm and the family that kept it running.

Late in the month, a notable drifter appeared.

Following an intensive session as a milking assistant, I entered the kitchen for dinner and noticed a new figure talking to Daliah. By this point, I was accustomed to random people arriving unannounced; it was just part of the farm's culture. But this guy was different.

"I'm Slava," he said as he greeted me with a firm but gentlemanly handshake. I was immediately struck by how ridiculously handsome he was. Wide cheekbones and chocolate eyes. Shoulder-length hair and a bit of scruff over a defined jawline. A working man's tan. Testosterone levels off the chart. Just the sort of guy I would never take to a party because next to him I'd be rendered invisible. So, obviously, my first reaction was to mildly resent him.

Throughout the course of dinner that night, I learned that he was born in the former Soviet Union and had immigrated to Israel with his mother at the age of five, shortly after the collapse of the communist state. In his late teens, he was conscripted for his three years of mandatory Israeli military service. He served an additional year in the army and then retired. Through word of mouth, he heard about the goat farm, and it became his on-again, off-again home for many years. Daliah and Amnon had become parental figures to him.

As he spoke, I hoped he would get a bit of parsley stuck in his perfect teeth — something to prove that he was a mere mortal like the rest of us. But to no avail.

The next morning, Slava and I were partnered on a mission to restock the feeding sheds with hay bales from the barn. He was familiar with the ins and outs of the farm — and was able to flawlessly reverse the tractor-trailer into the barn, which even Yacob botched from time to time. While my delicate hands required leather gloves to avoid being slashed and my nose dripped with a messy case of hay fever, Slava made the physical work seem effortless. His time spent working the fields had given him the strength of a rancher and the classic sun-soaked mouldings of a Galilean farmer. To his credit, he was patient and accommodating about my lack of strength and skill. In fact, as we spent more time together, it became difficult to dislike the guy — despite his unfair facial symmetry and inhuman physique.

By mid-afternoon, we took a break and reclined on the veranda beside the kitchen — a welcomed rest after much physical exertion. With a pot of black tea and some chocolate wafers sitting before us, the atmosphere was finally calm enough for me to broach a topic that had been on my mind all morning.

"What did you do in the army?" I asked, hoping that I wasn't being inappropriate or insensitive. I was simply curious. Being told you *had* to enlist in your nation's army was a truly foreign concept to me.

"Have you seen the film *The Hurt Locker*?"

"No. But it's about a military unit that dismantles bombs, right?"

"Yeah. Exactly," he replied casually. "My job was basically the same."

I pulled my chin back, nodding with consideration. I couldn't recall ever having spoken to anyone who had been in a combat situation, let alone dismantled a bomb.

"So where were all these bombs that you had to deal with?"

"There are some things we are not permitted to share," Slava stated matter-of-factly with a half smile. That was a hint to steer the conversation in a different direction.

So I posed a broader question. "Overall, what do you think about your years in the Israeli army?"

"It was a positive experience that was also horrible. I lost one crew member every year during my service. That's four good friends who were killed."

I poured us more tea. After several minutes of munching on biscuits and watching the clouds roll by, I succumbed to my curiosity again.

"Would you go back if you needed work?" I asked, since Slava had mentioned that he was trying to figure out what his next move in life would be.

"I'm glad I did it. It made me stronger. I don't want to do it again."

By that point, we should have returned to work, but we continued to talk for nearly two hours. I sensed that Slava was not just patiently tolerating my questions, but he might have even enjoyed the interview. Sometimes relative strangers make perfect confidants.

Having tipped back many cups of tea and emptied the cookie tray, we stood up and wandered down the dirt track. As we walked, I decided to share a challenge that I was facing. I felt the right balance of distance and comfort with Slava to tell him my honest opinions.

"At times, I love being on the farm. At other times I feel like a constant fuck-up." Given that he knew Daliah, Amnon and the farm so well, he seemed like the right person to field my concern. I told him about my dismal attempt to construct a fence around the bamboo. "I'm not always sure what I'm supposed to be doing. Then, when they give me a task, they don't tell me how they want it done."

He stopped in his tracks, smiled and raised his eyebrows in congratulations, as if I had suddenly had a major breakthrough.

"That is the beauty of it!"

"What's the beauty of it?"

"Here on this goat farm," he said as he gestured to the surrounding hills, "there is no mommy to hold your hand. There is no army sergeant to tell you what to do."

Slava hesitated, then added nine words that suddenly reframed my entire month.

"You have the opportunity to learn things for yourself." ○

"LET'S GET THESE goats milked," Slava announced, yanking me from my personal epiphany and motioning toward the milking station. I hadn't realized that this was where we'd been heading.

"What? Just the two of us?"

"Yeah, the sun is starting to set." This time he nodded to the western hill. "And Yacob and the others aren't back yet from working in Yodfat."

"But I've never actually milked the goats," I admitted.

"So?"

"So ... I'll just prep the stations for you."

"As you wish." He shrugged his shoulders and rolled up his sleeves.

We hopped into the milking station. I organized the platforms, shovelling grain into the feeding troughs and exhibiting my finesse as a master-level milking assistant. When the feed was in place, I pulled up the gate. The first set of 12 eager lady goats came jousting forward, stomping their hooves across the wooden platform and angling their horns into the stanchions.

While Slava got to work with the first set of goats, I quickly prepped the other platform. Not to toot my own horn, but at this point in the month, I was moving fast and could prep the stanchions in under two minutes. This speed was required when the brothers did the milking. In fact, with the two experienced milkers on the job, I barely had enough time to dismiss the goats who had already been milked, fill the troughs with grain and then get a new set of goats lined up. That afternoon, however, Slava was working alone. Even if he could milk as fast as Yacob, it would still take him twice as long to tackle solo. After getting the second set of goats ready, I stood there for a few moments, watching him work.

That's when it dawned on me that I could be helping.

With a surge of gumption, I grabbed one of the extra steel buckets. Then I approached the rear end of the last goat on the platform — an older gal with a grey coat, a blue collar around her neck and an engorged udder. I had no idea what I was doing, but I figured I might as well try.

"I'm sorry if this doesn't feel exceptionally pleasant," I whispered.

Like a hormonally charged teenager on prom night, I went for a breast. The goat seemed to smell my inexperience and was resistant, squirming away from my amateur advances. I reached back in, but she pulled one of the classic goat avoidance tricks by sitting on the bucket, concealing her teats. I pulled the bucket away and forced her to return to her feet. Using my forearms to pry her hind legs open, I repositioned the bucket. Finally, I wrapped the fingers of my right hand around her long nipple and squeezed hard, expecting milk to come rushing forth.

Nothing happened.

With my left hand, I clutched vigorously on her other teat and squeezed hard.

Nothing happened.

Milking a goat, I discovered, was harder than it looked.

I gritted my teeth, focused all my attention and channelled my inner farm boy.

Moving my hands slowly, I mimicked the motion that I had seen from Slava and the brothers. By closing off the top of the teat with my thumb and the knuckle of my index finger, I trapped a small amount of milk at the bottom of the nipple. Using my remaining fingers, I forced the pressure down toward the valve at the bottom, like pushing water through a pinhole of a miniature balloon.

That's when the magic occurred.

I got milk!

The warm liquid missed the bucket entirely, squirting me straight in the chest.

In most cases, a shot to the heart is usually bad news, but for this city slicker it was a definitive win. I was elated. However, there were no triumphant fist pumps in the air or victorious karate kicks. In the presence of Slava, the living definition of virility, I opted to bottle up any urges for animated celebration. Besides, I still had an irate goat on my hands. Literally. So I continued milking, gradually readjusting my technique and aim. Sure enough, I began to produce the beautifully distinctive sound that I sought: the ping of milk shooting into a steel pail.

Much to the detriment of many lady goats, I continued to practise my milking skills, pausing regularly to prep the stations for the next batch of sufferers. By the time we were finished with all the goats, I had contributed a single litre of milk at most to the session's 40-litre yield. My hands were cramped and my chest was damp with rogue milk. But it didn't matter. Underneath that mucky shirt, my heart was proud. ○

"WHAT ARE YOU doing here?" I exclaimed with my eyes wide open.

The enticing smell of dinner had summoned me to the kitchen, where I found Benjamin casually chatting with Seungjoo as she frantically hovered over a number of steaming dishes on the stove. It had been nearly a week since Benjamin had left for the Arab mansion in Nazareth, and I didn't think I'd see him again.

"I came back," Benjamin stated nonchalantly. In his dry New Yorker way, he explained that the guest house had been pleasant enough, but after a couple of days he realized that the farm was where he needed to be.

"Well, it's good to have you back," I replied, "because Juliette missed you." I was just about to share my afternoon goat-milking breakthrough when Seungjoo cut in.

"Dinner will be ready in five minutes!" She had volunteered to prepare a traditional Korean-style dinner. Judging by the aromas drifting from the stove, we were in for a treat. The gathering was the largest to date with the usual suspects, plus Slava and a few folks who had been invited from Yodfat specifically for the Korean meal.

On the veranda, I took a seat beside Daliah. Her flowing cotton skirt — which was typically in constant motion, waltzing with the food she was preparing — was tucked motionlessly around her legs. She looked more relaxed than I had ever seen her, perhaps because she had the night off from her duties as head chef.

With the return of Benjamin, the presence of Slava, the extra guests and the delicious Korean food awaiting us, the atmosphere was cheerful and celebratory. A couple wine bottles were uncorked, and glasses were passed around the circle. Then we toasted each other in three languages: *"Cheers! L'chaim! Gun-bae!"*

Seungjoo presented her multicoloured meal, a traditional Korean dish called *bibimbap*, which consisted of fried vegetables, grilled meats, steamed rice and poached egg. The ingredients were presented in individual piles on one giant serving platter. Each food mound provided its own distinct realm of flavour.

"Now this is the best part. We must mix everything together!" Seungjoo exclaimed enthusiastically.

One of the guests from Yodfat was given the honour of stirring the ingredients before they were served. The flavours came together. Something greater was achieved.

While plates were being filled, Daliah turned to me and asked how my day had been.

Now this was a pleasant surprise! No one in that farming family was in the habit of fussing over my welfare. Initially, I found their detachment jarring, but I eventually grew accustomed to it. In fact, I could see how Slava found the lack of coddling to be liberating. Yet when Daliah gave me some attention — and the opportunity to talk — I jumped on it.

I proudly told her about my triumph, that I had finally jumped in and learned how to milk a goat. As she listened to my story, she nodded her head. When I finished, she shared a wise but simple sentiment stemming from her many years on the farm.

"Ah ... this is how we all begin."

"Oh, yes. I'm a beginner, all right," I added, pointing to the stains on my chest. "I'm wearing half of the goat milk harvest on my shirt!"

Daliah was not one to grin gratuitously. So when she tilted her head back and released a hearty laugh, I knew I had accomplished something special. Significant personal progress was made that day. Not only had I extracted milk, but I had also extracted a smile. ☉

As with my arrival to the farm, there was no pageantry on the day of my departure. The friends that I had met in France, Yonatan and Neta, were scheduled to pick me up and put me up for a couple of days. But before they arrived, I did my own round of goodbyes. I sat in the dirt with Juliette, offering some carob pods that I had plucked especially for her. I exchanged contact information with Seungjoo and Benjamin, excited to have friends from Seoul and Manhattan in my traveller's Rolodex. I would have said adieu to Slava, but he had disappeared from the farm as mysteriously as he had appeared. For Slava, perhaps no goodbye was the simplest goodbye.

Yonatan's truck rolled into view, weaving its way down the gravel lane. With my backpack slung over my shoulder, I stood before Daliah and Amnon, who offered me a handful of cheeses and a quick hug. After many months of hellos and goodbyes, my capacity for mawkishness was running low. I was coming to see that a lack of sentimentality could also be a gift in disguise.

During my final days on the farm, my perspective shifted. What I had initially interpreted as a lack of cordiality was perhaps better summarized as an absence of affirmation. For example, Yacob's words had been harsh — "You're not worth the investment." But the statement wasn't necessarily an accusation of personal ineptitude. In fact, it had little to do with me. The man had 160 goats to milk and needed to have them milked correctly. His words were a straightforward communication, a blunt yet realistic cost-benefit analysis. However, never was I specifically told *not* to milk the goats. The only thing stopping me had been, well, myself.

"You are always welcome to come back," Daliah said without schmaltziness or tears.

For all those times when I wasn't sure if my presence was appreciated, this was a surprising stamp of approval. ☼

As I PULLED out of the farm to head back to Israel and the rest of the world, I glanced at the stone shack and the goat pen and the scrubby hills. I understood more deeply why Benjamin and Slava and all the Israeli drifters kept returning. I understood why Seungjoo and so many others characterized the place as "special."

We all had our reasons.

But for me the goat farm was special because it skipped over pretences and preciousness to pose a direct challenge: *Here is an opportunity for learning. Now what are you going to do about it?* ☼

OCTOBER

Goa, India

The Indian train rounded a bend and then suddenly crossed a trussed bridge. Without warning, my bare feet were dangling over a deep gorge lined with emerald foliage and divided by a slender red muddy river, 50 metres below. I gasped — half out of terror, half out of delight.

I needed fresh air, so I had left my cabin and found an open doorway at the end of the car. Due to a little thing called "liability," this would never happen on a train in Canada or in any other country with a strict set of safety policies. But this was India. And people don't go to India to stay in their comfort zones. Hence, I took my chances and sat on the lowest step.

Earlier that morning, I had arrived late to Mumbai's Chhatrapati Shivaji Terminus. The train to Goa had already started rolling when I spotted it from the other side of the station. It quickly became a classic run-to-catch-the-train chase scene, which had me leaping over bodies on the ground and nearly tipping a samosa cart. I jumped into the first car I could. It was, of course, the wrong cabin. I had to awkwardly tiptoe through a steamy kitchen and trudge across a few cargo cars with my backpack while I searched for Car 1A — better known as "First Class."

It's true. For the one and only time that year, I had purchased myself a first-class ticket. Approximately $15 got a person from Mumbai to Goa on a 12-hour train ride. Or for those with a bit more cash, $35 secured a top bunk in a first-class sleeper berth with air conditioning. When booking the trip, I took approximately 0.02 seconds to make the decision. Because I was in a developing country, I figured there would be plenty of challenging experiences waiting to toy with my own comfort zone. So why not take advantage of a bit of pampering when the opportunity arose?

After I found my berth, I tossed my backpack onto the bunk bed, hoisted myself up and then stretched out, amazed that I had managed to catch the train.

A throat cleared. It was only then that I realized I wasn't alone. On the opposite lower bunk, a well-groomed Indian man with grey hair and a crisp white shirt was sitting cross-legged and staring up at me. Beside him, a woman in a teal sari was curled up, reading a newspaper.

"Hello," said the man, with a smile half-hidden under his moustache.

"Oh, hi," I replied, propping myself up on elbow.

"Where do you come from?" His head bobbled back and forth.

That simple question was enough to trigger a long conversation. As the urban sprawl of Mumbai gradually switched to pastures and dense green forest, the elderly Indian couple administered the standard Indian interrogation: *Where does your family live? What is your job? Do you have a girlfriend?* I willingly answered their questions and fired a few of my own. They responded in broken English and hand gestures. Their son lived in Mumbai. They resided in Goa and thought it was the most beautiful place on earth. Chatting with the couple was entertaining — it was as if a friendly welcoming committee had been included in my ticket price.

The only reason we stopped talking was because we became distracted by food. Once the train started moving at full speed, the staff began to wander up and down the corridor hawking their delicacies: *Chapati! Chicken loli! Chai!* The sweet and delectable spiced tea was dirt cheap and was superior to any chai I'd ever had at a café in Canada. Inspired by the tea, I took my chances with the various food choices. Each dish cost next to nothing and was served piping hot. The breaded chicken was crispy yet tender. The fried rice was lemony in colour and savoury in taste. And despite the legends of explosive diarrhea told by western travellers who test out local Indian food, the only discomfort I suffered was an overly stuffed belly.

After gorging myself and then indulging in a catnap, I ventured out of my first-class berth to explore what else the train had to offer. Making a pit stop in the bathroom, I noticed the railway ties passing under the hole in the floor. Whatever was deposited into the "toilet" fell directly onto the tracks. After the bathroom experience, I decided to get some air. That's when I suddenly ended up in a position with nothing between myself and the possibility of falling 50 metres into a tropical ravine. If I hadn't been worried about frightening other passengers, I would have yelled at the top of my lungs, a visceral response to the thrill of the moment. Instead, I momentarily shut my eyes and tried to imprint the sensation into my emotional data bank.

I felt more refreshed, more alive than I had in months. The motion of the train. The friendly travel companions. The delicious food. The stunning scenery. The simple knowledge that I was in India. It all added up to a sense of balmy satisfaction. Nothing was required from me, I received no unwanted attention, and the biggest decision I had to make was whether I should eat *dhal* or fried rice, or simply order both.

I sat back and watched the countryside roll by. As the train trundled south from Mumbai to Goa — running along open fields of sugar cane and crossing rickety narrow bridges, passing through dark tunnels and pausing at open-air stations — I felt like something was being accomplished. I was progressing toward the next project. I was advancing toward the next adventure. ○

INDIA!

The land of spices and swamis, of mountains and maharajas, has summoned adventurous spirits for millennia. For years, I had also been a distant admirer seduced by its charms. In fact, for a variety of reasons — such as its geographical splendour, daring cuisine and reputation for being the birthplace of spiritual enlightenment — India was my No. 1 country crush (even surpassing my boyhood fascination with Morocco). As such, including India on my year-long itinerary was a no-brainer.

All that said, the problem was this: India is a big, messy nation. How does a traveller find an interesting place to be helpful? Or even an average place to be helpful? Or even just an average place to be? (And ideally a place that wouldn't lead to a bowel-bombing case of dysentery.)

A popular choice for many visitors to India, especially the spiritually inclined, is to seek out an *ashram*. As places of divine hermitage, ashrams provide transformative experiences for the existentially starved, primarily through the practices of yoga and meditation. An ashram seemed to dovetail with the ethos of my journey. Didn't most sites of devotion accept wayfaring volunteers? It's part of the whole "enlightenment mandate," no? Although I had zero experience with meditation, I figured it couldn't be much more difficult than a nap, and I was good at naps. Plus, I was already a yoga convert.

Like many frazzled westerners, a few years prior I had turned to the practice of yoga — or at least what we call "yoga" in the West — to bring some balance into my life. The endorphins from an hour on the mat had comparable properties to a bottle of wine, but without the hangover. And it was far cheaper than seeing a therapist. As I began to think about what I might do in India, naturally I had visions of myself draped in white cloth, stretching out my arms in warrior pose and plugging into a high-speed connection to the divine. Heck, maybe the month would even present me with an opportunity for a deep transcendental flogging from a wise Hindu guru. And in reciprocity for his generous holy abuse, I could milk his goats.

As October drew nearer, however, I started to second-guess my Indian fantasy. *Was I ready for a full-blown ashram experience? Did it even fit with my goal of "participating" in each community I visited?* Throughout the year, I had been on the hunt for culture, social exchange and new skills. Would I find these things at a retreat? In my mind, an ashram was an epicentre of internal work — not exactly the place to pass around a bottle of whisky or learn how to kill a guinea fowl. Besides, I was fairly certain that my mind would implode if I were suddenly secluded in spiritual solitude after nine months of travelling, working and processing new stimuli. I needed to keep the lens focused outwardly — to stay buoyant and perky. Less Dalai Lama. More Dolly Parton.

So I started looking at other possibilities. Across India, there was certainly no shortage of farms, schools, tea plantations and guest houses. Some of them were even listed on work-exchange websites. The tricky part was figuring out which project would give me the opportunity to immerse myself in a community, to experience the real India — or at least *a* real India.

After scouring through a couple different online networks, I came across an attractive option called YogaGypsys. The description on their official website brought me to a full halt:

> "Imagine a tropical paradise just yards from the warm Ara-
> bian Sea, nestled beneath palm groves with a constant cooling
> breeze. Visualize traditional Indian huts, Portuguese villas,
> tree houses and tipis set amidst lush gardens. Experience
> calm and serenity as you wander around the temple complex
> with yoga devotees, tai chi and other holistic arts practition-
> ers. Hear the music of ancient and modern. Taste the food of
> many traditions. Journey to YogaGypsys, the best that Goa
> has to offer."

To this adventure-loving yet fatigued soul, the write-up was blatant travel porn. The retreat was accustomed to hosting foreigners and had received a glowing review from a fellow who had had a successful work-exchange experience during the previous season. In addition to the "palm groves" and "serenity" — which were clear selling features — the project presented the opportunity for volunteers to take yoga classes. Even though I didn't want the confines and seclusions of a traditional ashram, I figured that a few casual yoga sessions would help rejuvenate my mind while stretching out my muscles. YogaGypsys promised to be the perfect initiation to India, a sort of "Spirituality Lite" that came without transcendental flogging — and all at no cost to the volunteer.

So I wrote to YogaGypsys to inquire about a stay. A British woman named Cati replied, explaining that volunteers were needed for basic manual labour: painting, moving furniture, erecting tipis (yes, for real!) and other random jobs. The chores sounded reasonable to me, so I expressed my definitive interest and was given the thumbs-up to help out.

A week before I was set to arrive, Cati messaged me from England:

> "I most likely won't be back to YogaGypsys until mid-October. My partner Baba G is there. He'll be happy to assist you, and we'll meet later. By the way, do you ride a motorbike? It's a small 125cc Yamaha. It would be very useful for you."

So, let me quickly summarize the prospects for October: One month in India at a yoga retreat beside the beach *with access to a motorbike?*

Why, yes. Don't mind if I do! ☺

AT PERNEM STATION, I stepped off the train into the muggy air. The train had arrived two hours late, and it was now nearly midnight in northern Goa. Given the delay, I was unsure whether Baba G, the co-manager of YogaGypsys, would be there to greet me.

The chaotic bustle that I assumed was a mainstay of all Indian rail stations was nowhere to be seen or heard. The "station" was little more than a single tin-roofed office building and a small gathering of people. From the head of the train, I walked in the dark along the uneven concrete platform toward the building's flickering florescent lights. I began scanning people, searching for a face that was searching for me. One by one, they exited the covered platform. Only a handful of people were left as I headed under the office's awning. Just as I was wondering if I would need to devise another one of my notorious survival strategies — perhaps a bench to sleep on for the night — I heard a voice to my left.

"You are Daniel."

I turned abruptly to see a man sitting cross-legged on a platform bench. He had wide mocha cheeks, long corkscrew hair and a round stomach. Under the bench was a pack of scrawny stray dogs.

"How did you know?" I joked. As far as I knew, I had been the only white person on the train. I stood out like an arctic rabbit at a tiger carnival.

Baba G smiled, but not in a way that indicated that he understood or that he was amused by the rhetorical nature of my question. Instead of standing to greet me, he shook my hand and motioned for me to sit with him. I unfolded myself out from under the weight of my backpack and joined him on the bench. Baba G had a small packet of cookies in his hand. He took one out and gave it to a dog, who accepted it cautiously and then scurried away to eat it alone.

"Welcome to Goa," he said, while continuing to look at the dog. "How was your journey?"

"It was *really* enjoyable." I opted not to divulge the part about travelling First Class, out of fear that he might think I was snobbish or indulgent. "I think I may have drank my body weight in masala chai."

"These dogs," he said, not acknowledging my response, "they have nothing. Yet they still wag their tails."

My goofiness — a default setting when chatting with someone I've recently met — would clearly have to be substituted for a different approach. As we continued to chat casually on the platform, I noticed that Baba G had a tendency to look off into the distance, like he was seeing something I wasn't. Throughout the conversation, he had a relaxed expression in his eyes and continued to show sympathy toward the dogs.

Eventually, Baba G unfolded his legs, rose to his feet and nodded toward the parking lot. Soon we were in his Jeep, heading directly west to the coast. As he steered, Baba G shared some of his history. He was born in Rishikesh (the world capital of yoga) and had travelled as a vagabond across most of India before taking a job as a professional chef in Mumbai. How lucky was I? Here was a man with all the qualities of an ideal Indian host: experience in budget travel, expertise in Indian cuisine and, most likely, a profound knowledge of yoga. If Baba G was a bit spacey, I figured it was because he had achieved expert levels of non-attachment. He was probably operating at some uncommon divine frequency, unaffected by the irrelevant earthly details that burden the rest of us. As we progressed down the narrow winding road, I couldn't help but wonder: *Would Baba G become some sort of guru to me over the course of the month?*

The Jeep sped through the night, occasionally passing over a single-lane bridge or slowing around a sharp curve. The road was bordered with dense vegetation. Occasionally the vehicle's headlights would illuminate a concrete shop on the side of the road, branded with the logo of a mobile phone company. At that time of the night, there wasn't much traffic, but at one point we came screeching to a stop to avoid a cow on the road. As the Jeep navigated around the cow and slowly regained speed, a motorcycle zipped past us. It reminded me of the offer Cati had made in her note.

"Can you teach me to ride a motorcycle?"

Baba G turned and flashed another loose smile.

"Yeah, Danji, no problem." ☼

A ROOSTER CALLED me from a dream about milking goats. It took me a moment to realize where I was. Under a mosquito net. In a tool shed. At a beachside yoga retreat. In the state of Goa. In the nation of India. My foggy morning brain was stuck in first gear. *Why do I always end up in a shed?*

After arriving in the dark the previous night, Baba G had given me a quick tour of the grounds: the Portuguese cottages, the kitchen, the path to access the beach, and the place where I would be sleeping. Although I tried my best to appear gracious when he opened the bamboo door to the rickety structure, he must have sensed my disappointment by my sudden silence. Don't get me wrong; I wasn't ungrateful. It was just that the online description of YogaGypsys had specifically urged me to "visualize beach huts, villas, tree houses and tipis set amidst lush gardens." I had expectations.

"Volunteers normally sleep in a tipi," Baba G had reassured me, trying to read my blank face, "but monsoon season was longer than usual this year." And then he explained that the maintenance guys hadn't had the opportunity to set up the tipis or even take the protective tarps off the beach huts. It sounded reasonable, so I swallowed the setback and went directly to bed.

Now it was morning. I crawled out of the mosquito net and perched on the side of the bed. A mountain of cardboard boxes was piled upon the concrete floor, along with a couple of unplugged portable fans, an ironing board and stacks of empty soda bottles. The roof was made of woven palm leaves attached to slender bamboo slats. A ceiling fan turned leisurely, circulating the warm air.

My stomach growled, so I threw on a grubby shirt, a pair of shorts and my rapidly deteriorating hiking boots to wander down to the kitchen. The yoga retreat was on the side of a hill and was split into two levels: upper and lower. The top portion of the property had access to the main road, a small parking lot, a series of storage sheds and three charming Portuguese-style cottages. On the lower level was the open-air kitchen, the cement yoga platforms, five bamboo beach huts, a few tipi bases, a couple of rickety shower stalls and two other cottages. Most of the buildings were still covered in large blue tarps that safeguarded them from aggressive rains.

The welcoming smell of simmering chai hit me as I walked

into the kitchen. Stirring the pot was the site manager, a slender young Indian man named Ganesh. I had met him briefly the previous night. He smiled and handed me a steamy cup of the tea.

"How do you sleep last night?" Ganesh inquired as his head bobbled in the same fashion as the friendly moustachioed man on the train.

"Not bad," I replied in half-truth and blew on the edge of the cup to cool the chai. My sleep had also been "not wonderful." Ganesh and some of the other employees were housed on the other side of the storage shed, and I had heard their TV blaring Bollywood dramas long after I had turned out my own light. Again, this was quite contrary to the soundtrack of crickets or the crashing of waves that I had associated with a beachside yoga retreat. Still, there was no need for an over-privileged hissy fit.

"So where are the others?" I inquired.

Ganesh looked at me blankly.

"Like, the other volunteers," I clarified.

"You first volunteer of the season!" he said with a beaming grin. "Together we make YogaGypsys ready for first guests."

I reciprocated a polite smile, but a familiar warning signal went off in my head. I knew that happy helpers were signs of a good exchange host, whereas a status of "no volunteers" was open to interpretation. On one hand, being the only westerner on site might provide me with the perfect opportunity to connect with the staff. On the other hand, there would be no other "outsiders" to assist with the adjustment to the new environment. Still, regardless of whether or not I had people to connect with, wasn't there a fine stretch of beach waiting for me? It was hard to be overly alarmed with a cup of chai in my hands and the sound of the ocean only 50 metres away.

"So what do we have to do to get ready for the guests?"

"Oh, many things. Much work to do!"

Just as Ganesh began to elaborate, three maintenance workers walked into the kitchen, served themselves chai and then dragged some plastic patio chairs into a semicircle. The site manager paused and quickly made introductions. There was

Ganesh's stern-looking older cousin. Next was a middle-aged Nepalese groundskeeper who appeared to be containing a giggle. And lastly, there was the groundskeeper's nephew, a stocky fellow who resembled a young Jackie Chan. The men greeted me with a collective nod.

Ganesh grabbed my forearm and pulled me away from the group, explaining a painting assignment that he wanted me to start. But we were interrupted once more when Baba G strolled into the kitchen, wearing a sarong, a T-shirt and string of wooden beads. In a surprisingly gruff tone, he barked an order at the maintenance guys, who begrudgingly got to their feet and shuffled into the sandy courtyard to begin their work. And then Baba G turned to me peacefully.

"Good morning, Daniel."

I nodded.

"Excuse my tone," Baba G said. "If I don't discipline those guys, they would probably fall asleep on the job."

Ganesh didn't acknowledge Baba G. Instead, he waved for me to follow him and led me to the middle of the yard where he pointed out a jamboree of creatively named paint buckets: mochaccino brown, wispy sea breeze, harvest orange. The monsoon rains had muted the vibrant colours of the Portuguese cottages, and we needed to bring them back to life.

My task was to paint the window grates. So I got to work, quietly on my own, painting iron bars with a thick coat of sunshine yellow. Like on the goat farm when I assumed the role of milking assistant, I immediately relished my job at the yoga retreat. The act of painting was simple, achievable, meditative. Even on the smallest of scales, things were becoming brighter. ○

DURING LUNCH ON that first day, Ganesh informed me that it was customary for the maintenance team to rest after eating, avoiding some of the most sweltering hours of the day while permitting time for digestion. A daily siesta was just the kind of ritual I was happy to respect. Following the meal, which involved using my fingers to scoop savoury dhal and sweet white rice into my mouth while sitting under a palm tree, I headed to the kitchen to wash my plate. There I found Baba G finishing his own lunch.

"Daniel, what will you do during the afternoon rest?"

"Well, I was thinking of taking a quick nap," I responded, "and then maybe spending some time on the beach." The water was begging me to dive in.

"If you're interested, I have a friend to see in Arambol." He paused to pull his long, wavy hair into a ponytail. "We can take the motorbike. You can swim at the beach there." I had no idea where Arambol was located or what was there to see. But since it sounded like an adventure, I happily consented.

Around mid-afternoon, we piled onto a rusty Yamaha motorbike and began moving northward up the coast. The landscape consisted of a patchwork of rice fields, overgrown forest groves and sleepy beachside villages. As the bike rushed over hills and around sharp corners, we entered different realms of odours: a sultry zone of floral fragrance, a salty blow coming directly off the open water, a charcoal-scented patch wafting from a field where sugar cane was burning. With each new aroma and with each vantage point over the shimmering Arabian Sea, I felt more and more optimistic about my month in Goa.

Ten minutes after departing, we pulled into a bustling beachside village. The bike decelerated to a leisurely speed. We rolled past a series of colourful corrugated iron shacks that functioned as roadside merchant stalls. They offered a range of beach-friendly merchandise: rainbow hammocks, billowy yoga pants, fake designer board shorts and Bob Marley beach towels. Interspersed among the vendors was an assortment of Internet cafes, travel agents, youth hostels and karaoke bars.

"Welcome to Arambol," Baba G announced as he slowed the motorcycle to a walking pace.

The place had the refinement of a hippie's basement. This was clearly the Goa I had been warned about. When I had told friends and fellow travellers about my destination, a thematic string of sentiments had been thrown my way and generally

306

included a tone of voice that seemed to say "Are you sure you want to do that?" In an online forum, one traveller accused Goa of not being the real India, while another reminded backpackers not to forget their bongs.

I had dismissed most of these sentiments as backpacker snobbery. But after a quick glance around Arambol, I understood where Goa's infamy had perhaps originated. At best, the town was a suitable place to make travel arrangements, send some emails and take a quick dip in the sea. At worst, Arambol looked like a gritty beach-town drug haven catering to that special breed of westerners who have dropped out and washed up.

As the story goes, Goa's golden era was in the 1970s, when it became a utopian destination for counterculturists and rainbow warriors. Although the influx of flower-power pilgrims escaping the confines of western society tapered off in the 1980s, Goa has continued to suffer the effects of a beatnik bomb. Many decades later, psychedelic radiation still ripples through the area.

Baba G downshifted to the lowest gear and then stopped completely, putting his feet on the ground to balance us. I dismounted, and he rolled the motorcycle to rest among a long line of parked bikes.

"Daniel, you can go swim over there." He pointed down a lane leading to the beach. "I'll be at Chili's Guest House with my friend." He pointed in the other direction to a large yellow building. "Come and find me when you're finished."

The lengthy beach was speckled with a mixture of foreigners and locals, some playing in the water and others relaxing on lounge chairs. The sand was firmly packed, not the soft and sinking grains that I preferred. But it was pleasant enough. As I walked toward the waterline, I chuckled at my own beach snobbery. Truth be told, I've never seen a view of the ocean that I didn't enjoy.

The first item on my beach itinerary was to dive into the sea. I shed my flip-flops and T-shirt, lunging gleefully into the warm water. I swam out through the bobbing waves until my toes lost contact with the ground below me. After a few minutes of floating on my back, I returned to shore and gave myself a poor man's exfoliation by rolling around, covering myself in sun-baked sand. In my sand suit, I sprawled out starfish-style, hoping that someone, somewhere, would receive my telepathic request for a cocktail served in a coconut. Tragically, 20 minutes passed and no drinks materialized. So I headed back into the water, rubbing my skin with the dried sand to remove any grime that had accumulated since my hammam experience in Morocco.

Scrubbed and re-energized, I retraced my steps along the beach. Eventually, I wandered back along the alleyway where the motorcycle was parked and popped into one of the shops to pick up a soda and a couple of postcards. I scanned the creaky card rack looking for the most provocative pictures: photographs of naked *sadhus*, images of Hindu deities engaged in coitus, psyche-delic *Sri Yantra* paintings (basically everything that was over-the-top cliché). The joke to the folks at home would be that I had finally come to India and was having non-stop tantric sex while dropping a shitload of LSD.

As I approached the cashier, I chuckled to myself, imagining my mother's face as she opened her mailbox.

"Two hundred rupee," said the woman, with one eyebrow raised and her lips pursed tightly together.

I handed over some bills with a smile, hoping to receive one in return.

"Must be nice to be so close to the beach!"

Nothing.

Tough crowd.

As I sat sipping my cold drink on the step outside, I wondered why the shopkeeper had given me the sour face. Did she assume I was *actually* part of the sleazy drug tourist crowd? In examining my attire, I realized that I certainly fit the description. On my feet was a pair of rainbow flip-flops that I had picked up in Costa Rica. Around my waist hung a faded pair of cheap board shorts, the same style as those available at the roadside merchant stalls. And, to top it off, my jaw was now covered with a scruffy beard that hadn't been trimmed since it took root in early July. Essentially, I was the grand marshal for burned-out-hippiedom.

The irony was rich.

Despite my ragamuffin stylistic flair, I had little interest in taking drugs while travelling. Some people travel specifically to experiment with mind-altering substances in exotic locations: weed in Amsterdam, cocaine in Colombia or acid in India. I'm just not one of those people. Besides the solid arguments that drug tourism is problematic for local economies and can cause cultural erosion, my reasoning is more self-centred: I can't afford to have a bad reaction to a narcotic while I'm alone on the other side of the planet. It's less of a value judgment regarding the morality of drug usage and more of a rational decision to mini-mize hazards while navigating foreign spaces and unknowable variables. A classic case of harm reduction methodology, you might say.

I finished my soda and returned the glass bottle to the woman in the shop — a gesture that finally earned me a smile. Then I headed up the lane to Chili's Guesthouse. From the other side of the street, I could see Baba G sitting on the third-floor balcony, chatting with a small group of people.

"Hey, Danji!" he bellowed boisterously as he saw me approaching. "Up here!"

Inside the guest house, I made my way up a staircase and stepped onto the tiled terrace, which overlooked the low roofs of Arambol. I was introduced to a couple of young men from Israel and a girl from Canada. They quickly resumed their conversa-tion about an electronic music party scheduled for the following week. A plastic table in the corner was littered with empty beer bottles, an overflowing ashtray and a set of portable mini-speak-ers attached to an iPod, which blared tinny trance music.

One of the Israeli guys rolled a joint. It was passed around the group, quickly arriving at me. The cigarette posed an un-fortunate conundrum: I really didn't want to smoke it, but then I didn't want come across as a killjoy either. I tried to dodge the offer in the most non-judgmental way I could think of.

"Oh, I'm taking a break."

"No way, man!" countered the woozy guy who had rolled the joint. "You can take a break in Canada, but you can't take a break in India!" He nodded at the spliff before pushing it in my direction.

"I'm good." I insisted, apologetically raising my hands to decline his offering. He shrugged his shoulders and turned to the Canadian girl. She resolved the ganja standstill by taking the joint and inhaling deeply.

The minutes ticked by. Soon an hour passed. The sun was beginning to set, and I started to feel restless. The group of travellers was friendly enough, but the adventurous afternoon I had imagined having had, well, gone up in smoke. And now my host — and only ride home — was baked out of his tree. Things had gone from mildly uncomfortable to downright dodgy. I had spent nearly all my rupees and now had insufficient cash for a taxi. I didn't know how to drive the motorbike. Walking was a non-option because the day was quickly fading into night. And even if it were light enough, I had no idea how to get back to the yoga retreat.

Finally, Baba G rose. He bid goodbye to his hazy-eyed comrades, and together we headed down to the street. As I walked, I assessed the situation: old rusty motorcycle, blitzed Indian man, confused traveller. Ugh. Given that Baba G and I had just met, I was worried about the implications of refusing to return with him. If I rejected the ride, would I be branded as the uptight westerner who was too self-righteous to do as the locals do?

The situation was lose-lose.

"Please take care of me," I whispered to Krishna, Lakshmi, Vishnu or any other god who might be willing to help. Then I reluctantly got on the two-wheeler.

As we left Arambol, my knuckles gripped the motorbike rack. Baba G tilted his head to the sky and laughed wildly. Then he yelled into the evening air.

"Whoa, I'm so stoned!" ☺

BY SOME STROKE of luck, Baba G and I made it back to YogaGyp-sys safely. I got off the bike and walked away without saying anything. On the exterior, I kept my cool. What sense was there in expressing frustration to a man higher than the Himalayas? Internally, though, I was muddled with emotions. Topping this list of feelings was a sense of foolishness. Who was the more reckless and unwise person in this situation? The man who drove a motorcycle under the influence? Or the sober guy who knowingly accepted a ride from him? It was perhaps the most imprudent thing I had done all year.

And on top of feeling foolish, I was disenchanted. Not simply because I had ended up in a no-win situation and had made an irresponsible decision, but also because I now had contrary evidence to my first impressions. Unless I was looking for some type of Cheech and Chong-inspired spiritual guidance, Baba G was *not* the wise guru I had hoped he might be.

That night, I crawled under the mosquito netting and sprawled across the single mattress. As I lay in the sticky night air, I told myself to take a deep breath and relax. That day I had done a bit of painting, seen more of Goa and even had a swim in the ocean. The whole "drugged and driving thing" had been unfortunate, but nobody had been hurt. All's well that ends well, right? If I had signed up for a month of getting to know the culture of India, maybe that was exactly what I got — sort of like getting mugged in South Africa. Nobody promised that participation in local communities would only include heartwarming experiences. Nobody promised that authentic experiences would be fun.

And as for Baba G, well, I decided not to write him off completely. Perhaps he still would be able to lead a yoga class or provide a lesson on how to prepare a perfectly balanced *garam masala*.

I would, however, keep him at arm's-length. ○

THE DAYS THAT followed the stoned motorbike episode lacked comparative drama. I worked at my tasks, which usually involved brushing vibrant colours onto various surfaces. During the afternoon break, I wandered the abandoned beach. The tourist season hadn't swung into full gear, and oftentimes I could walk a mile without seeing anyone. Most days, I'd jump into the warm waters and body surf in the shoulder-high waves or I'd bury myself in mounds of sand. Or I'd sit and watch (in amazement) as wild Goan cows came strolling down the beach and meandered past me, as if I were a stump to be avoided. In general, I wasn't unhappy. How could anyone be unhappy in paradise? Yet I wasn't tucking lotus flowers behind my ears and skipping through the palm grove in a state of ecstasy either.

Many of the elements at YogaGypsys had a double edge. Because there were no other volunteers or westerners, I was having the truly immersive experience I wanted. Yet I often found myself shut out of conversations, which were primarily in Hindi (as they naturally would be). The assigned chores were always doable, which meant that I never felt incompetent. But then again, I wasn't acquiring any new skills either. The location was magnificent but not magnificent enough to offset the cramped dynamic with Baba G.

Perhaps the most incongruous, and even ironic, part of YogaGypsys was that there was no yoga happening. Heading into the month, I had assumed that I would have the opportunity for regular guided practice. But because there were no guests at YogaGypsys, there were no scheduled yoga classes. If I wanted to do yoga, I'd have to lead my own session. To be fair, one evening Baba G did suggest that the two of us wake up early to practise together. The next morning when I showed up on the yoga platform, I was greeted with a gorgeous sunrise and also the sound of snoring drifting from Baba G's room. As for the maintenance guys, they demonstrated zero interest in *asanas* or meditation. They were into yoga the same way that New Jersey construction workers are into Jazzercise. In fact, I began to suspect that the average Indian was far more concerned with the bliss derived from Bollywood blockbusters. Posing like a tree? Nah, that was for chumps. Consequently, I shied away from grabbing a mat and practising alone on the yoga platform. I didn't want to seem even more different from the group than I already was.

I badly wanted to connect with the maintenance guys, who were polite but standoffish. Cross-cultural charades can be fun. The feeling of transcending language barriers is one of the great joys of travel. Yet on the occasions when the charades didn't succeed, I was left feeling more isolated than when I began. I tended to eat my meals alone because the others dispersed from the kitchen, opting to watch Hindi dramas in Ganesh's room. I suspected that they were hiding from Baba G.

Personally, I didn't avoid Baba G, but I didn't go out of my way to be chummy with him either. I tolerated him in the same sort of way that you accept an irritating drunk uncle. In our interactions, he treated me with respect. I was never greeted with hostility, never snarled at in the way he barked at the maintenance guys. As a matter of fact, occasionally I sensed that he sought company or conversation — but maybe "social interaction" wasn't necessarily his strong point. For instance, there was the time he possibly gave me a compliment.

Shortly before dinner one evening, I was sitting on the tiled floor of the open-air kitchen, wrestling with a stray dog named Lovely that had adopted YogaGypsys as her home. Baba G walked in and lifted the lids off the pots one by one to inspect dinner. He paused, as if deep in thought, and then he tilted his head in my direction.

"Danji, you have a very old soul."

People throw around that expression frequently. But I've never been sure what "old soul" really means. It's like a blanket label for people who aren't douchebags. So I offered up a joke.

"Actually, those are just wrinkles from squinting too much."

As usual, my attempted witticism was lost.

"When you remember all your other lives, you will be very wise."

"Um, thanks?" I replied. I wasn't sure if he meant it as an optimistic compliment, as in "Damn, white boy, you're sitting on a spiritual goldmine!" or a reprimand, as in "Why are you playing

313

on the floor when you *should* be remembering all your other lives?"

So I smiled in confusion and kept on playing with Lovely. Meanwhile, Baba G started making himself a salad.

With standoffish coworkers, a socially awkward stoner host and no yoga classes at the yoga retreat, I can't say that this was the experience I had imagined for my month in India.

I suppose sometimes there's the lesson you expect to receive in life.

And then there's the lesson you get. ☉

YOU MIGHT ASSUME that because I was on the trip of a lifetime, there would be no temptation to fantasize about other adventures. Ironically, that was not the case. If I am guilty of anything, it's that I have an insatiable appetite for daydreaming. When I'm passing time in a monotonous situation — such as painting grates or waiting for a hot cup of chai to cool — my mind automatically wanders to idealistic thoughts. For example, I'd like to spend a couple months on a sailboat, drifting around the Mediterranean. It would be my pleasure to drive a beat-up caravan through Namibia and Botswana. I get giddy at the thought of riding the Trans-Siberian Railway from Moscow to Beijing. If I could make a dollar off of each dream, I might just have enough cash to fund my favourites!

The achievement of one dream, I've learned, does not quell the desire to tackle others.

Near the top of my list of starry-eyed adventures: India on a motorcycle. There is something inherently audacious yet classically romantic about exploring the world on two wheels. From Che Guevara's journey across South America to Ewan McGregor's circumnavigation of the globe, a motorcycle has been the chosen transportation for many of the world's contemporary nonconformists. In his popular novel *Zen and the Art of Motorcycle Maintenance*, Robert M. Pirsig talks about the immediacy of being on two wheels. In a car, the driver is removed from the surroundings. But on a bike, one becomes vulnerable to the environment: the wind, the rain, the temperature, the smells. The world becomes more tactile. What better way to explore a sensual nation than on a vehicle that allows the explorer to experience the odours of cinnamon and elephant dung while suntanning his arms?

In my mind, combining the two elements — motorcycling and India — was a recipe for amazingness, a phenomenon waiting to happen. A double rainbow.

Now I found myself in India with access to a motorbike. The serendipitous alignment of these two elements did not go unobserved. I was also aware that addressing two contrasting dreams at the same time — focused work versus blatant adventure — was not merely improbable but also incompatible. To start with, I had already begun a work-exchange project. Even though it hadn't lived up to all of my glamorized expectations, the situation wasn't so bad that it merited jumping ship. Sure, I'd opted for short tourism breaks in Costa Rica, Morocco and Scotland, but only after reaching a breaking point with the volunteer projects. That wasn't the case in India. Besides, there were practical reasons to consider, such as the fact that YogaGypsys owned the motorbike that was so central in my dream getaway. Or that biking across India would take much more than a month. Or that I would need to — ahem — know how to ride a motorbike.

Details, details.

Despite all the reasons a motorbike trip wasn't realistic, I couldn't seem to shake my curiosity, my longing. It was impractical and selfish and risky, but part of me began to think that maybe, just maybe, I could just sample the dream. It might be good for me. I'd gain extra insight into Goan geography while feeling like a cast member from *Easy Rider*.

It didn't help that I had plenty of mental space for daydreaming. If I had been giving English lessons to schoolchildren, for example, there wouldn't have been time or energy to let my mind wander. But I wasn't teaching. I was painting. As I coated iron gates with a shade of yellow that made turmeric seem dull,

I slowly convinced myself that a "test drive" of a motorbike adventure was not unthinkable. I could justify a few days to dabble with a dream, couldn't I?

As Oscar Wilde famously stated, "The only way to get rid of temptation is to yield to it." ☺

ONE EVENING, AFTER a day of smearing gallons of pink flamingo paint across the exterior walls of one of the Portuguese cottages, I was sitting alone on the beach. The sun, a giant flaming mango, was sinking over an unusually choppy sea. From down the beach, I spotted the youngest of the maintenance men (the stocky fellow who resembled a young Jackie Chan) approaching. Naresh moved slowly, making shapes in the sand with his big toes as he walked. Eventually, the young Nepalese fellow plopped down on the sand beside me. With paint splotches and armpit stains, his shirt was messy from a day's work. His signature wad of tobacco was tucked into his lower lip.

"Danny! Sun setting!" he said. None of the other maintenance guys had tried to engage me in conversation, but Naresh was different. It was only his second season working with YogaGypsys, and perhaps he was still intrigued by the idea of foreigners willing to work for no pay.

"How are you?" I asked. It was the same introductory question that I used with Peruvian school children and young Moroccan men, the magic three-word conversation starter.

"Oh, fine."

"You like swimming?" I gestured to the large body of water before us. I was surprised that none of the maintenance guys ever went into the ocean.

"No swimming," Naresh responded, shaking his head rapidly and squinting his eyes — insinuating that I had posed a ridiculous question. He paused and then spat a glob of spit from the chaw marinating in his mouth. "Waves big. Crashing on head. No good."

Until coming to Goa to work, perhaps Naresh had never

gazed over a body of water that had no visual end point. Maybe it looked like an infinite toilet bowl that would flush any fool who dared to venture too deep. I had a small realization that Naresh and I had something in common: Goa was a foreign land to both of us.

I continued to dig for conversation. "You like working here at YogaGypsys?" I asked, curious to know more about how the maintenance crew perceived the work they did.

He brought his shoulders to his ears and turned his palms upward in that universal expression that means there is no easy answer.

"Cati-mama good boss. Cati-mama nice woman."

He then paused.

"Baba G bad boss. Acting big and important." He puffed up is arms and imitated a gorilla. Judging by the tone Baba G took with the maintenance workers, I didn't doubt Naresh's assessment.

Then we fell silent.

The sky erupted into autumnal shades of butter yellow and burnt orange. The palm trees bordering the sandy beach swayed in the gentle but persistent breeze off the water. The sound of the sea was a singular sort of sonata. Any conversation would have been an unnecessary distraction from the offerings of the natural world.

Once the sun had disappeared below the horizon, we trudged off to the kitchen together. Up to that point, I had yet to witness the preparation of a meal, and there were notes to take on how to prepare traditional cuisine.

"Can you teach me how to make chapati?" I asked as we walked through the narrow sandy lane that led to the resort.

"Okay, Danny making chapati!" Naresh replied, adding a playful cadence to his words.

In the kitchen, Naresh gathered the ingredients for the Indian staple and began a wordless demonstration. He mixed flour and water to create a sticky type of dough and then massaged it into a malleable sphere on a floured surface. Then he separated the dough into egg-sized balls and used a wooden rolling pin to transform them into thin discs, adding a bit of vegetable oil and extra flour along the way to help prevent tearing. He folded his circles into little triangles and rolled them flat again before tossing them into a hot frying pan. The dough browned and blistered, producing a warm bready odour that made my stomach claw at my rib cage.

All in all, it was tremendously simple.

With Naresh looking over my shoulder, I began to create my very first chapati, scooping up flour and then moistening it with water. The process was not as easy as it looked. I struggled to find the right balance of water and flour. Instead of a smooth ball, mine was an uneven beige globule. And even after semi-successfully rolling out the dough and then frying it in the pan, I did not achieve results that were nearly as appealing as what Naresh had effortlessly produced. My chapatis could be optimistically described as the Salvador Dalís of the bread world — eccentric, surreal, anarchistic. But I ate them nonetheless, proud that I had completed my first authentic Indian cooking lesson.

After dinner, Naresh followed me back to the storage shed, cheerfully reciting the English alphabet as he walked along. He seemed happy to have the chance to practise his language skills, and I was all too happy to help. We sat on the floor in my room and chatted for a while, until his eyes fell on my laptop computer. Curious, Naresh asked me to pull it out.

I hesitated. I didn't want to flaunt my technological possessions — not out of fear of having anything stolen by the maintenance guys but because I was worried that the item might sabotage our burgeoning friendship through the disparity that it represented.

"We look at my village!" Naresh pleaded, with eyebrows nudging encouragingly. It was a difficult request to refuse, both because of his honest yearning to feel connected to home and my desire to understand what "home" looked like for him. I conceded.

I booted up my computer, inserted a wireless Internet key and opened a browser to look for his Nepalese village. Using a satellite map to zoom directly over the region where he grew up, Naresh was soon able to recognize the landscape. His eyes lit up at the sight of the river that ran through his homeland. He pointed to a fuzzy figure that was supposedly his house, a second fuzzy figure that was his school and a congregation of fuzzy figures that made up the nearest village. I watched his face watching the computer.

After touring through his Nepalese valley, I was about to close the computer when Naresh insisted that we continue surfing.

"Search for 'Nepal music!' "

Whether or not Naresh knew how to navigate the Internet, he was certainly aware of its splendours. So we found a couple of Nepalese artists and listened to some energetically fluty tracks.

But it didn't end there.

"Search for 'Nepal video!' "

We discovered short video clips, including one from the streets of Kathmandu showing women in traditional Nepalese garb and another with mountains set to the soundtrack of more energetic flutiness. The video recordings weren't the most modern I've ever seen, but it didn't seem to matter. Naresh was enthralled with the virtual access to a familiar world.

After nearly half an hour of browsing through Nepal's music, images and video — interspersed with long waits due to the slow connection speed — I took a deep breath, trying to politely hint that it was time for me to close the computer and for him to leave the hut. I was ready to head to bed.

But Naresh had one final request.

"Search for 'Nepal sex!' "

"Oh, no thank you," I replied with a smile. "Sleeping time for this guy." I pointed a thumb to my chest.

Perhaps he thought I had not understood.

"Nepal sex, you search?" he asked again. This time he wanted to make sure I fully comprehended, so he inserted his right index finger into a pseudo-vagina made by his left fist, and he thrusted it back and forth in a surprisingly vigorous fashion. Then he nodded his head zealously, as if to say "Come on. Everyone loves sex!"

319

I laughed out loud at his sign language.

And then politely declined, again.

Naresh shrugged his shoulders in a way that communicated, "Well you can't blame a guy for trying!"

Then he bid a polite goodnight and trudged out of the bamboo shed. ☼

AFTER THE QUESTIONABLE episode with Baba G on my first day, I realized that learning to drive a motorbike was not just about chasing a dream. It was about acquiring an extra life skill. If there were an emergency at the yoga retreat, for instance, I might need to take the bike to summon help. Or if anyone ever decided to cast me in an action film, I'd obviously want to do my own stunts.

My game plan had been to keep any mingling with Baba G to a minimum. When I did interact with him, it was usually to ask him for a lesson on how to drive a motorbike. Despite my appreciation for self-empowerment and Slava's claim that "learning things for yourself" was a great way to acquire a new skill, motorcycling wasn't exactly in the same skill domain as goat milking. I needed the assistance of someone who knew what they were doing. So each morning as I picked up my cup of chai from the kitchen, I would ask Baba G if today was our day for a motorbike tutorial. I was usually met with dismissive assurance: "Yeah, sure Danji. We'll have a tutorial in the afternoon." But by the time the siesta rolled around, Baba G would be nowhere to be found. Maybe he had gone to a neighbouring town to buy paint or had zipped off to pick up some extra ingredients for dinner or was in his room with the door closed "meditating" and "burning incense." I began to accept that a motorbike lesson would probably never actually happen. After 10 days of harassment, however, a breakthrough inexplicably occurred.

With about an hour left before sundown, I spotted Baba G wandering across the sandy yard. I put down the bedside lamp I was painting and yelled over to him.

"Hey, Baba. Isn't it time for our motorbike lesson?" By this point the question had become a personal running joke, a little something I used to entertain myself.

"Okay, Danji. Let's go."

"Seriously?" I put down my paintbrush. "Okay!"

Before I had time to think twice — or switch into appropriate footwear — we loaded onto the bike and headed down the highway, searching for a quiet country road. I was tingly with excitement.

Back in Montreal, I had driven a scooter during the summer months, so the motorized two-wheel universe wasn't unfamiliar. Nor was operating a manual transmission. At the age of 14, I had learned to drive my Dad's car, a reliable five-speed Subaru station wagon. With the horsepower of a leaf blower, my Montreal scooter was only single-speed. A real motorbike had gears, and therein was the challenge. What I needed to do was combine the knowledge of driving a manual transmission with the equilibrium required to remain on two wheels. Simple enough.

Baba G pulled down a dirt side road and brought the bike to a stop.

I hopped off and examined the machine. I wish I could dazzle you with my impressive knowledge of motorbike makes and models, and how I was standing before a rare gem of a bike. But I can't. I can confirm that it was a Yamaha and it was from the 1980s, judging from the maroon and silver panelling.

"Okay," Baba G began. "Riding a motorcycle is all about balance. What you need to do is discover the relationship between the clutch and the throttle."

"Clutch and throttle. Got it."

"And once you give it a bit of gas and the engine revs, you have to slowly release the clutch."

"Rev and release. I can do that."

As I straddled the bike, a surge of energy rushed through me, and I hadn't even started the engine yet. I put my flip-flop on the kick-start and stepped firmly. The two-wheeler came snarling to life. I gently turned the throttle, and the bike revved eagerly. Those who have ridden a motorcycle know that there are few sensations in the world that rival the vibrating of an engine between the legs. (Well, I suppose I can think of something else. But let's stay focused here.)

Baba G got on the bike behind me. I cautiously released my grip on the clutch while increasing pressure on the throttle. To my surprise, we lurched into motion and started rolling forward along the dirt track. My nostrils flared. I grinned.

"Go easy!" Baba G cautioned.

I kept the bike in first gear. We wobbled forward, with just enough speed to keep us from falling over.

For the next few minutes, I guided the bike up the back road, bravely venturing into second gear and then third. It was treacherous learning terrain, but if I could navigate a rocky path with sandy spots, I could handle the bike almost anywhere. At the top of a hill, we took a quick break and then turned back to retrace our steps. On the return, I was feeling more confident and had the bike screaming along at a brazen 40 kilometres per hour.

And that's when I nearly hit a cow.

Just as I was riding with a sense of competence, I rounded a corner and suddenly a herd of bovine appeared. I slammed on the foot brake. The engine stalled. I braced myself for impact. And as the back tire skidded across a patch of gravel, I planted my left foot and caught the weight of the bike before it tipped, just two feet from a monstrous brown heifer with a camel-like hump on her back.

The cow stood there apathetically, looking at me as though I had rudely interrupted an exhilarating session of cud chewing.

Baba G had managed to stay on the motorbike until the very last second when he had pulled a graceful (and somewhat miraculous) pirouette by pivoting on his right foot and dancing away from both the bike and the cow. I looked to gauge his reaction.

"Well done!" he exclaimed, returning toward me. He patted my shoulder in congratulations. "You've survived your first Indian speed bump."

My easygoing instructor got back on the bike and let me drive all the way back to YogaGypsys. By successfully swerving away from the obstinate cow and not dropping the bike — all while wearing flip-flops — I felt like I had successfully passed an unofficial Indian road test.

When we merged back onto the main road that led to the yoga retreat, I allowed speedier vehicles to pass as I hugged toward the side. To the west was a low copper sun. In the air was a faint odour of chapatis being fried. In my ears was the hum of the motorcycle engine. On my face, the wind. Despite the concentration that the bike demanded, I made a mental note of the magnitude of the moment.

"I'm riding a motorbike in India!" I repeated to myself, smiling. ✪

THE SHIFT WAS so gradual that I barely even noticed it: I fell into a comfortable groove.

Each morning I'd arrive to a vat of masala chai in the kitchen. After pouring a cup of the delicious creamy elixir through a strainer to catch the chunks of ginger, cinnamon and cardamom, I'd walk down the path to the beach. There, I'd savour my steamy beverage while gazing at the ocean. Essentially, I was a tea advertisement waiting to happen.

Much of my working hours were spent painting the exterior and interior of the Portuguese cottages. As I slathered the walls with bright colours, I'd often listen to music and fall into a state of un-time, that unique psychological dimension that comes with doing repetitive tasks. Other chores involved sanding and refinishing items for the cottages (such as lamps or ceiling fans), oiling the teak furniture or other odd jobs around the site, none of which were mentally or physically taxing.

During my afternoon break, I would go for my ritual jump in the ocean and subsequent roll in the sand while the maintenance guys napped in the shady corners of the grounds. Or I'd wander up and down the shoreline, peeking into tide pools and watching baby crabs waltz with the waves. In a way, afternoons became my opportunity to energize, to decompress, to receive Mother

Nature's specific brand of therapy — the sun, sand and surf de-toxification treatment. Perhaps a tropical beach is all the yoga anyone actually needs.

After sunset, I showered off the day's salty combination of sweat and ocean water before I headed to the kitchen to help with dinner. The meals were consistently centred around the same basic ingredients: onions, tomatoes, peppers, potatoes and lentils mixed with cumin, coriander, ginger, garlic and chili peppers. Occasionally chicken or fish would be added, and rice was served as an accessory to each meal. I usually helped by chopping vegetables, washing dishes or making my surrealistic chapatis. Despite the recurring ingredients, I never found the food redundant or uninspired, and not once did I miss the formality of eating with utensils.

Because the weather grew stable, the blue tarpaulins were pulled off the beach huts, freeing up a new option for accommodation. Gleefully, I bid farewell to the cramped storage shed and moved down the hill into a bamboo bungalow. My evening soundtrack of Bollywood gunfights was replaced with the lulling white noise of the Arabian Sea meeting the Indian shoreline.

As the days passed, the maintenance guys became progressively friendlier. Perhaps I had passed my cultural quarantine. Perhaps the Internet surfing had solidified my friendship with Naresh. Whatever the case might have been, the men started to include me in their exclusive lunchtime eating circle on the dusty yoga platform. One afternoon, I was invited into Ganesh's room to watch television with the guys, a gesture that was similar in appeal to the invitation to go to Starbucks in Peru. However, I accepted the offer. Instead of my customary beach frolic, I joined the guys to watch television in a language I couldn't understand, solely because I was honoured to be included.

My attitude toward Baba G changed. The motorbike lesson helped balance my perspective on him. He had taken the time to help me, and for that I was grateful. Indeed, the guy was a bit of a stoner, in addition to being socially awkward and potentially classist. But he wasn't *evil*. At a bare minimum, I felt certain that he was not bent on intentionally sabotaging my happiness.

The situation in Goa became borderline blissful when I got my own set of wheels. With only 10 days left in October, I decided to indulge myself — as if a first-class train ticket hadn't been enough! — by renting my very own motorbike. The leasing process was surprisingly efficient via a system called the "Indian Societal Network of Motorized Vehicles." In other words, Ganesh called a guy he knew who rented bikes. In no time, I was mounted on a sporty red Honda that had twice the power as the old YogaGypsys Yamaha and cost a mere seven bucks a day.

The monsoon season had ended. My relationship with the maintenance guys had improved. I had access to my own bike. Things had evolved. The only thing that hadn't changed was my desire to beta-test a dream of experiencing India on a motorcycle. And, to top it all off, I even had some spare time coming up at the end of the month. You see, after some less-than-inspiring volunteer experiences that year, I had learned an important work-exchange lesson: whenever possible, under-commit oneself. (It's so much easier to ask to stay longer than apologize for leaving early.) During my initial contact with YogaGypsys, I had only offered to volunteer for three weeks. And now those three weeks were nearing an end. So, there I was in India with a motorbike, the ability to drive it and a few days of leisure on my hands. ○

FROM A BAR stool in the kitchen, Baba G looked up briefly from his notes to see me in the doorway with a small duffle bag. After a quick up and down, he returned to reviewing his mess of papers, which were spread across a table. At the centre of the clutter was the official calendar of the yoga retreat. The first guests were scheduled to arrive in a matter of days. The tipis still had to be erected, but the Portuguese cottages looked vibrant once more, and the bamboo beach huts smelled fresh. Even the sand in the palm grove had been manicured into a visually pleasing design. YogaGypsys was more or less ready for the high season. Although I knew that the yoga retreat would run seamlessly without me, I felt a twinge of guilt, a sense that I was abandoning my crew. The call of the bike, however, trumped any feelings of remorse.

"All right. I'm outta here for a few days."

"Okay, be safe," Baba G responded, still sitting on the other side of kitchen. He didn't look up.

"I'll do my best." I pivoted to leave but was caught mid-stride.

"Hey, Danji," Baba G called. I paused and glanced over my shoulder. He was staring directly at me.

"I hope you find what you're looking for."

I nodded a wordless thank you. Then I walked up the hill and started my motorbike. ☉

I DON'T KNOW what possessed the scorpion to dart across the highway. Perhaps the intense heat had made him suicidal. With his coiled tail and deadly pinchers, he scuttled across the asphalt, acting more like a drunken butterfly than a dangerous arthropod. Straddling my hot red motorbike, I had milliseconds to make the decision — swerve or turn him into a scorpion pancake. Thankfully, I had already established a successful track record in avoiding wildlife. I leaned ever so slightly to the right and ripped past the little fellow without sending him on a one-way trip to the divine. As I continued to race down the highway, I yelled into the face shield of my helmet: "Whenever I ride a motorbike across Goa, I dodge venomous creatures!"

I realized how much risk was involved in my pipe dream. Having only a week's worth of riding experience, I knew it was crazy to embark on a rented bike and navigate unfamiliar side roads (and do it all alone). But maybe that's why I loved it. I was riding on a personal edge. And the scorpion incident, however brief, was significant. For that fleeting moment — at least in my own eyes — I was a hero.

That first day, I didn't exactly know where I was heading. Following the coastline, I zigzagged my way down from the northern corner of Goa into the southern regions of the state. And as much as I would love to be perceived as a two-wheelin' daredevil,

326

the truth of the matter was that I rarely went above 50 kilometres per hour. By nightfall, I had managed to reach the town of Goa Velha, a historic Portuguese colony turned tourist hot spot. Exhausted, I found a cheap hotel and went to bed early, wiping a cockroach off the pillow and lying uncovered on the mattress, damp from the humid air.

The next morning, I visited a few of the Catholic churches and noted the Jesus statues draped in wreaths of Diwali marigolds. Then I placed the key into the motorbike ignition, pressed the "start" button and struck out again. Baba G had mentioned that Palolem was one of the most popular beaches in Goa. I decided that my plan — and I use that term lightly — was simply to keep going south in the hopes of discovering what made it so remarkable.

Over the next few days, I continued to sample my Indian motorcycle fantasy. I ate plenty of appetizing meals. I slept in quaint seaside huts. I drank chai from roadside vendors. I dug my toes into the sand of many different beaches. Many aspects of my expedition lived up to my expectations. The air against my forearms and chest. The vibration of the bike between my thighs. The back roads. The sunshine.

Like any beta test, however, my adventure was not without encoding glitches. On the second day, my rear tire suffered a puncture. (Thankfully, I was able to find a motorbike mechanic who quickly addressed the issue.) I also got lost. In fact, I discovered that becoming disoriented is a part of any solo two-wheel navigation, since it's impossible to read a map and drive a motorbike at the same time. I crossed Goa's biggest bridge five times — not because it was scenic but because I kept missing my correct turnoff. Also, my forearms got sunburned.

Just like my first few days at YogaGypsys, I was back to being content but not elated. As each day passed, I began to question whether going on the motorbike trip had been a wise decision or not. Was the sand on the other beaches any softer than the beach at the yoga retreat? Was the food that I ate on my getaway any more flavourful than what came out of the YogaGypsys kitchen?

Was I having a grander adventure?

But perhaps the question that surfaced most often during my five-day motorbike trip through Goa stemmed from Baba G's final words in the kitchen: *What was I actually hoping to find?* ⚪

IT WAS MY final evening in Goa. I had returned to YogaGypsys, unscathed from my motorbike trip. Back to the beach for one last sunset. The palm trees were swaying with a familiar leisurely rhythm and the baby crabs were playing peekaboo in the sand with their typical shyness. But things had changed.

Couples romantically walked hand in hand, often stopping to take photos of themselves with the tropical twilight as their backdrop. An Indian lifeguard was now on duty, and he roared along the beach on an all-terrain vehicle, leaving the sand scarred with tire tracks. A white girl with an "Om" tattoo between her shoulder blades was doing sun salutations. In my five days of absence, tourist season had descended on Goa.

Not only did the beach feel different but so too did YogaGypsys. For starters, the yoga retreat now actually offered yoga classes. Big boss Cati — a frazzled yet friendly middle-aged blond woman with impeccable posture — had finally returned from England. The first set of international guests had arrived, transforming the palm grove into a more formal, more intentionally "spiritual" space. Baba G faded into the background, no longer barking orders. Ganesh seemed to have an extra spring in his step. Along with the guests, another volunteer had arrived. A long-haired, glassy-eyed Czech kid had moved into my beach hut. But perhaps the most notable change was that Naresh had departed suddenly for Mumbai to visit his father in the hospital. The fact that I didn't get to say goodbye caused a pang of regret.

But did I regret the bike trip?

Well, whether I had gone on my motorbike trip or not, the tourist season would have still arrived. Things would have changed nonetheless.

Plus there's the inevitable learning that comes with a beta test.

They say that there's no such thing as failure because even "un-success" provides practical information. You learn what *doesn't* work. With that logic, my little two-wheeled sojourn — excuse the double negative — *couldn't not* be beneficial on some level. Indeed, I had learned a few things about the reality of travelling via motorbike, especially in India. First of all, watch out for cows and scorpions! The most important takeaway from the test drive, however, came from the glitches. The flat tire, the constant sense of being lost and, yes, the burnt forearms — they all taught me that I was really *not* ready to embark upon a full tour of India. And I may never be.

Finally, I can't say that I regretted those five days of absence because they enabled the most valuable lesson of the month: YogaGypsys had been a magical place all along. I had a stoned anti-guru who taught me a practical skill. I had a TV-loving maintenance team that came to accept me as one of their own. I had simple work. Cups of tea. A beach. Everything one could hope to find.

I gazed across the water.

The waves on the Arabian Sea were gentler than I had seen all month, and a soft breeze blowing from the south carried notes of pineapples and brine. The sweet and the salty. The seemingly contradictory. The handsomely paradoxical. ☺

NOVEMBER

Luang Prabang, Laos

I only had one objective: the cockroach must die.

In the sleepy town of Luang Prabang, I was standing in the middle of a hostel dorm room armed with a flip-flop. The region was known for its tranquil Buddhist ambiance and stately green hills. I, however, was behaving anything but Zen. It was late on a Friday afternoon. You'd think I'd be seeking out a beer or searching for a riverboat tour. But no. I was far too busy with murder on my mind.

THWACK!

My sandal came down mere millimetres from the cockroach's torso, prompting him to scurry under my pillow. Yes, not only was the insect in my room, but he was also on my bed. And he was a nimble sonofabitch.

I had landed just three hours prior. After enjoying one of my patented arrival naps — curled in the fetal position around my backpack, like spooning a familiar lover — I awoke groggy and disoriented, unsure of what to do with myself. A shower seemed sensible. I opened my backpack with the hope that I might find something clean to change into. But as my hand reached in, surveying for fresh underwear, I felt the distinct tickle of little insect legs on my palm. Shocked at the sudden realization that there was something *alive* in my bag, I leaped from the bed. From a few metres away, I stared back to see what would crawl out. Seconds later, the cockroach swaggered over the zipper, pausing a moment as if he were stretching his arms and saying "Where's lunch?"

And, thus, the *cucaracha* dance began.

THWACK!

Missed by a long shot. The cockroach simply bounced off of my bag and scuttled around the white bedsheet.

It wasn't that I thought the walnut-sized insect was particularly disgusting or distressing. In general, I have never suffered from the debilitating fear of cockroaches that plagues many of my fellow westerners. On the farm in Costa Rica, for instance, roaches with a leg span wider than my passport wandered through the kitchen. Those guys didn't really bother me. They didn't sting or bite or attempt to hijack my raw vegan pizza. If anything, cockroaches have a certain entertainment value. They're sort of cute, especially when they fall on their backs and do that spastic dance as they attempt to flip over. Furthermore, you've got to appreciate their sheer ability to survive. Is there any other species on earth more eager to exist?

With all that said, I couldn't let this particular cockroach live for the simple reason that he was a stowaway from India.

THWACK!

Missed again.

His little antennae darted back and forth teasingly, with the same sass that a spoiled child might display. You know, the type of kid who raises his hands to the sides of his head to form moose-like antlers and sticks out his tongue to blow a fart sound when you ask him to clean his room.

"I'm sorry, you little brat, but you will *die*!" I muttered between clenched teeth.

Whereas other cockroaches might have warranted a straightforward flick out the door, this foreign cockroach had to be exterminated. Any species that originates in India should stay in

India. And since I wasn't about to take him back to the airport and book him a ticket to Goa, the best solution was annihilation.

I needed a new technique. Instead of another direct swing, I flung the pillow back. From a side angle, I managed to sweep the cockroach off the bed and onto the floor. To his misfortune, he landed on his back, legs clawing at the air. Before he had time to turn onto his front, my sandal came down, right on target. He didn't even have time to be cute.

THWACK! THWACK! THWACK!

Mr. Cockroach could not compete with the brutality of my multiple attacks. His days of international cavorting were over. I held him up to the afternoon light by one of his mangled legs.

Victory.

It was only then that I noticed I was not alone in the dorm room. Two girls were resting on a couple of top bunks. They must have been napping, only to be awoken by my whack-dance. And now, with horror in their eyes, the pair stared at me as I stood with a mashed cockroach in my hand.

"Don't worry, ladies," I said to them with a reassuring grin on my face. "I think he's dead."

Their looks of revulsion did not fade.

With the slaughter scene concluded and my attempts at chivalry clearly not winning any points, I excused myself to take a shower. ○

OVER THE PAST few years, many regions of Southeast Asia have become hotbeds for *voluntourism*, which is the term for the multi-million-dollar industry that arranges "bite-size" volunteer vacations. For example, if my November dream had been to bathe baby elephants at an animal rehabilitation centre, it would have been entirely possible. In fact, a long list of third-party organizations was ready to make that happen for me. But there was one hitch: I would need to fork over some serious cash in exchange for the experience (and to cover the administrative costs). From my understanding, the reality of international volunteerism is that a helper probably won't be able to contribute much unless he or she has a specific expertise to offer, such as veterinary or electrical skills. Thus, money is infinitely more valuable than inexperienced hands.

If anything, voluntourism has become a rich form of irony. The "developing" world has learned that the citizens of the "developed" world — with me waving the flag for this crew — are starting to crave more meaningful experiences in their travels. In a beautiful twist of exploitation, volunteer organizations have discovered that they can charge value-starved foreigners to do menial tasks, often under the beautiful pretext of saving the world. Is this not capitalism in its most satirical state? In fact, somewhere there is a room full of Thai businessmen laughing and patting themselves on the back as they exclaim, "Can you believe they're paying *us* to shovel elephant shit? We should charge more! And after they're finished with the elephants, have those fools teach our children English!"

A fateful conversation in Israel determined where November would lead me. After departing from the goat farm, I learned that my application for an Indian visa would take a few days longer than expected. To pass the time, I decided to visit the city of Nazareth. With an increasingly voluminous beard, I thought it would be fun to wrap myself in a white bed sheet, throw on a crown of thorns and freak the hell out of the Jesus tourists. Ultimately that never happened. However, I did take a walking tour of the Old City, where I met a well-travelled woman from Dublin and told her about my wanderings up to that point.

"So, where will you be going in Asia?" she asked.

"I'm off to India next month. But to be honest, I'm not entirely sure yet where November will take me." I mentioned that Southeast Asia was a likely choice, considering the great food and inexpensive amenities.

"Laos is really great. Totally chill. You'd love it."

"Oh, yeah?"

"Have you heard of Luang Prabang?"

"What's that — like a spicy soup?"

"No. It's this charming little city in the north of Laos. When I was there, I volunteered at a drop-in English centre. I can't remember the exact name of it ... something like 'Mousy Big Brother,' I think."

By this point I was all ears. If I had learned anything that year, it was that recommendations from friends or acquaintances were pure traveller's gold. For instance, my months spent with Common Ground Relief and Goats With the Wind had been two rewarding experiences, and both had been personally suggested.

That evening in Nazareth, I did a quick online search for more information about Luang Prabang. I came across photographs of crumbling Buddha statues, stunning waterfalls cascading into jade green swimming holes, monks in carrot-coloured robes collecting morning alms, and dramatic mountains standing like chess figurines overlooking chessboard fields. The city and its surrounding region looked downright heavenly — apart from the peculiar food culture that I learned about when I came across an unappetizing photo of a roasted rodent.

Sure enough, the town was home to a not-for-profit organization called Big Brother Mouse, which invited volunteers to assist with two-hour tutoring sessions. The Laotian-run initiative was among very few projects in Southeast Asia that did not require a fee to volunteer — and this immediately appealed to me. Each morning, local youth and young adults came to the language centre to practise English communication skills. Volunteers merely needed to show up and help out. The only downside was that the organization did not offer any formal volunteer accommodation. Nonetheless, given the affordability of Laos, I figured that finding a cheap room wouldn't be a problem.

Big Brother Mouse came with a personal reference, was located in picturesque Luang Prabang and was *not* a costly pre-packaged voluntourism arrangement.

And so it was decided. ☼

OUTSIDE THE HOSTEL, evening had fallen. The main street, Sisa-vangvong Road, was closed to vehicle traffic to make way for the nightly sidewalk bazaar. Under a sea of blue and red tent awnings, local women sat with their legs folded. Their retail paraphernalia was spread out on blankets in front of them: vibrant sarongs, T-shirts with the logo of Beerlao (the emblematic lager of Laos), crisp cotton linens, baby clothes and thousands of other things. Extension cords ran like tree roots over the pavement and con-nected to a long series of dangling light bulbs. Back at the Edin-burgh Festival Fringe, I had been yelled at for permitting a sin-gle extension cord to cross a pedestrian path. The Scottish Site Manager would have grasped his chest and collapsed in horror if he ever saw the mess of lines threatening the safety of people strolling through the bustling street market. I, on the other hand, felt a wicked sense of vindication.

With its bright lights and colourful knick-knacks, the night market was pure stimulation for the eyes. Yet, as much as I wished to stop and examine all the different products, I urgent-ly needed to eat. I noticed other foreigners entering and leaving through a passageway that ran perpendicular to the souvenir market. Curious, I followed the crowds down the cobblestone alley. Bingo — dinner stalls! Despite the thrill of finding food, I proceeded cautiously, not knowing what to expect. My brain was still slightly marred by that photo of roasted rodent. I was afraid of what other culinary offerings might await, such as bar-becued dog or grilled pony privates. Fortunately, my worries were unwarranted.

If the people of Luang Prabang had not invented the art of the smorgasbord, they had certainly perfected it. Along a full street block, table after table featured plates piled a foot high with lo-cal fare: steamed broccoli, fried tofu, sticky rice and raw vege-table salads. Other concoctions that resembled rice pilafs, chow meins and noodle stir-frys added to the medley of succulent op-tions. Adjacent to each buffet, river fish and chunks of chicken were held together by bamboo splints and seared over the glow-ing embers of a grill. After the meats were sufficiently cooked, they were served on wide banana leaves, which made perfect disposable plates. Finally, a selection of beer and sodas was piled into Styrofoam coolers and drowned in ice. My concern moved from "Will I find anything to eat?" to "Which vendor offers the tastiest food?"

My strategy was simple: find the stall with the chubbiest hostess. I lined up at a busy table behind some towering Germans. Eventually a rotund Laotian woman took my money in exchange for an oval plate. I stocked up on a selection of veggies and noodles, before grabbing a clammy bottle of Beerlao to wash everything down. Then I took a place at one of the rickety wooden dining tables. Around me, the other diners exchanged the typical chit-chat that one might imagine in such a communal setting: *Where are you from? Where are you going? Have you visited the temples yet? What about the waterfalls?* It was pleasant enough, but I kept my head down and opted not to bother anyone. Oftentimes beer makes decent enough company.

The food was sufficient but not as spectacularly flavourful as I had imagined. My wallet, however, found the experience utterly delectable. The cost of the heaping plate of food was a mere 10,000 kip. That might sound like a lot of money, but it converted to approximately $1.25. At that rate, I wouldn't even need a host organization to feed me.

Once my oval plate was clean, I thanked the food vendor and headed back toward the street market. Weaving my way among the merchants, I stopped occasionally to run my hand over the bumpy fabric of a colourfully woven handbag or to examine a dead snake suspended in a jar of formaldehyde. There were no fresh fruits or mops or other domestic products that might be found at a regular market. No, the night market clearly catered to outsiders. Local entrepreneurs had learned that if they stitched an elephant onto a baby bib, tourists would swoon and sales would soar. The situation was formulaic, but it appealed to me nonetheless purely because it provided the opportunity for exchanges between residents and foreigners (and also because I'm not excluded from the elephant-loving demographic).

337

I wanted to buy stuff. But not just because I have a soft spot for fun souvenirs or because I enjoy purchasing gifts for loved ones. A new paper lampshade might look great in my future home, and I was certain that my nephew would be amused by a carved wooden tiger from the other side of the world. My wish to buy things stemmed from something different. I felt a distinct sense of economic obligation, a desire to uphold an unspoken "tourist treaty" of sorts.

For travellers, spending money is a way of honouring the unofficial economic tourism agreement. The contract reads something like this:

> "I, _____ [insert tourist name], have come to your country along with these other strangers with expensive cameras and sweaty faces. I recognize that our collective influx changes your city. You put up with our general obnoxiousness. So I'll buy stuff and make it worth your while."

This implicit agreement is customary in the *souks* and shops of most countries, and its intensity correlates directly to the presence of tourism. In other words, the more that tourism affects a region, the more the visitor is expected to spend. In Trujillo's local markets, for example, it was rare to see a foreigner; therefore, there were few expectations to buy stuff. On the other hand, I felt pressured to make purchases while wandering through tourist-dense markets in Marrakesh and Goa. Over the course of the year, I found it difficult to maintain my end of the contract. No matter how unique or finely crafted the products were, my budget remained meagre. And it was impractical — if not impossible — to load my backpack with trinkets. As a result, I often felt that I was disappointing the local people I met and that I was a bad tourist.

As I paused to examine a spread of silk scarves, a foursome of carefree British twentysomethings strolled by. I could overhear their intimate anecdote of how they got high on opium and floated down the river on inner tubes when visiting the city of Vang Vieng (a backpacker's haven). Part of me was envious — not of their intoxicated adventures or overall breeziness but of their camaraderie.

In front of me, a middle-aged European couple paused at a tent, unravelling their interlocked arms to coo over a set of bamboo placemats. I lingered to listen to the interaction. The woman, whose accent was undeniably French, inquired about the price. The Laotian salesgirl quoted her an amount similar to what the placemats would cost at a boutique in Paris. The Frenchwoman shook her head and immediately offered a quarter of the suggested price. After a few counter-offers, the French couple started to walk away. The Laotian girl hesitated, biting her lower lip and taking a moment to scan the market for other customers. She called the couple back and accepted the offered price.

During my travels, I tried to be respectful, to be helpful, to be non-invasive. At many of my destinations, such as Buenos Aires and Cape Town, I had infused money into regional economies by paying for accommodation, food and local transportation. But as I walked from tent to tent in the night market, all these good intentions were not apparent to the vendors. What was visible was my expensive-looking camera, my tallness, my whiteness. Was I a fool to believe that I was really any different from the other foreigners who wandered through the market? Even if the local merchants understood that I was in the city to volunteer as an English tutor, would that be enough to exempt me from the tourist purchasing treaty? From their point of view, the concept of a "poor traveller" must have been completely laughable.

For the first time in many weeks, I felt truly lonely — regardless of the fact that there were people around me. Sure, the night market was teeming with vendors and dotted with foreigners who were all moving and interacting with each other. But in that setting, my existence felt irrelevant if I wasn't going to buy anything. So I crouched down and purchased a bib with an embroidered elephant at the next tent. Despite what the guidebooks advise, I didn't negotiate a lower price. The vendor smiled and nodded in appreciation as she took my money. And then she immediately began to chat with the person behind me. ⬮

ALTHOUGH MANY OF the countries I visited throughout the year were significantly different on a cultural level from my Canadian homeland, most of them were tried-and-true travel destinations. For example, Peru tends to be a classic choice among travellers to South America. In the past, Egypt had traditionally been the most visited African country (primarily due to the pyramids), but in recent years South Africa and Morocco have begun to joust for the top spot. Until November, I would argue that the 10 nations I had visited were somewhat obvious choices. I had not voyaged to lesser recognizable countries, such as Suriname, Benin, Lithuania or any place ending with "—stan." None of my destinations required careful consultation with a world atlas or a freakishly profound knowledge of political geography. Because it was my first time on most of these continents, I chose to begin my explorations with some of the mainstays.

But Laos was different. It occupied a less prominent position on the world stage. For me, Laos was one of those places — up there with Zanzibar and Finland — that I knew existed in theory but that I knew basically nothing about. But, as they say, there's nothing like visiting a country to get schooled. (Okay, I don't know if anyone says that *yet*. But they should.)

As a landlocked country, Laos sits quietly in the shadows of more brazen neighbours. To the north, big brother China is ostentatious in comparison. To the south, Thailand and Vietnam are more exotic and more developed. At a hypothetical beauty pageant that pitted the reputation of Southeast Asian nations against each other, Laos might be described as the toothy girl with small breasts. Apart from Myanmar — who would probably boycott the aforementioned beauty pageant altogether — Laos is the most understated and under-visited corner of the region's popular backpacker circuit. With fewer than seven million people, it's also the least densely populated area of Southeast Asia.

Perhaps Laos is less showy because it's still recovering from a tumultuous past. According to many war historians, Laos is the most heavily bombed country, per capita, in the world. Of course, this distinction is difficult to measure, considering that countless

340

undocumented bombs explode across the world each day. But to even be in the running for this title indicates a difficult history. The most turbulent years of the past century occurred during the Vietnam War, when parts of Laos were invaded and occupied by North Vietnam. In response to the occupation, the United States retaliated with a bombing campaign. They dropped more aircraft ordnance (bombs, missiles, rockets, et cetera) on the country than was dropped during the entire Second World War. Of the 260 million bombs that rained down on Laos, some 80 million still remain unexploded. That's roughly 10 unexploded bombs per person.

During my month in Laos, I learned that the country was moving away from its war-torn past. While Laos has not changed as rapidly as some of its neighbours, certain locations have started to become westernized — especially tourist-heavy Luang Prabang. The city's main street offered a number of restaurants and bars, including a pizzeria and a swanky wine saloon. The hostels and guest houses had Wi-Fi. The monks had mobile phones. And the wealthier residents of the city had one foot in the Buddhist temple and the other in the espresso bar. ○

A FOUR-FOOT FIGURINE of a happy cartoon mouse with a gigantic pencil in his hand tipped me off that I was in the right place. The morning sun was shining outside the Big Brother Mouse office, where I stood beside a well-organized row of bicycles and mopeds. It was my second day in Luang Prabang — and my first visit to the organization where I would be lending a hand for November.

From my vantage point on the street, I could see into the open-space classroom. A group of youngsters with American accents crowded around a table, talking loudly to Laotian students. The volume of their squeaky voices made me cringe. It's odd how we often think that talking louder helps comprehension. Thanks to my experiences in Peru and Morocco, I had learned that speaking slowly and enunciating clearly were the best tactics to promote understanding. If anything, yelling made the student feel shouted at — or worse, stupid. But it wasn't just the loud voices that made me momentarily hold back. It was also the matching volunteer T-shirts. Even from outside of the building, I could read the name of a voluntourism agency branded in bold letters across one guy's chest.

But I wasn't going to pull the plug on my plans just because a group of do-gooders spoke a few decibels above sensible. I finally entered through the large garage doors and slipped off my shoes. At the reception desk, a young Laotian woman greeted me with a smile.

"*Sa-bai-dee,*" she began and then welcomed me to Big Brother Mouse.

"How are you?" I responded over the noise of the matching-shirt crew.

"I am good, *khawp-jai!*" she said, thanking me. "Are you here to help?"

"Yeah ... well, if I can."

Just then, the receptionist's attention shifted behind me to the doorway where two young orange-clad monks had entered, reaching a few inches shorter than my shoulders. She spoke to the monks in Laotian, and they responded by nodding their heads.

"Perfect, you can sit together," said the receptionist. There was no space left at the tables, but she gestured to a few plastic patio chairs stacked against the back wall. Without receiving any instruction or guidance on what to say or do, I soon found myself seated in a small circle with the two monks.

"So, shall we speak some English?"

The two devotees nodded their shaved heads in approval.

"Good. My name is Daniel."

They nodded again. I waited for them to introduce themselves, but the pair remained silent.

"I am from Canada." I pointed to a world map pinned to the wall.

More head nods.

"So ... Laos is quite beautiful, no?"

They agreed politely by raising their eyebrows.

"Do you understand what I'm saying?"

This time they nodded more energetically. Despite my teaching experiences, it still took a few failed interactions for me to realize that "yes or no" questions are not effective for jump-starting a conversation.

"What are your names?"

"My name is Sing."

"My name is Charlie."

"Nice to meet you, Sing and Charlie. What do you do?"

Sing spoke. "We are novice monks. We go to school."

"Cool. What are your favourite subjects?"

"My favourite subject is English," said Sing.

"My favourite subject is English," said Charlie.

We were on a roll!

From there, we progressed slowly. The interaction was less of a conversation and more of an interview, with me posing a variety of preliminary questions: *What town are you from? What do your parents do? What's your favourite thing to do in Luang Prabang? What do you like to eat for dinner?* Their answers were simple, but the boys understood whatever I asked them for the most part. Often Charlie would repeat whatever Sing had said word for word, indicating that he was perhaps less confident in his English abilities. I kept an encouraging smile on my face, partly because I wanted to ensure that the boys felt comfortable and partly because grinning is a great antidote against the urge to yawn.

Eventually, Sing showed some initiative and asked me a question.

"Do you like to play the Internet?"

"Yes, I do like to play the Internet," I responded, grinning authentically now. "Do *you* like to play the Internet?"

"Oh, yes. I like the Facebook."

Cha-ching! From that point the conversation became more animated. We were just some guys, hanging around and bonding over the World Wide Web. Two of them just happened to be wearing saffron robes.

After approximately an hour of chatting, the novice monks indicated that they had to depart for their other classes. Before leaving, they asked me if I would be returning tomorrow. I promised them that I would be back. They bowed their heads, slid their feet into sandals and shuffled out of the building.

The room was still buzzing with the sound of the brash American volunteers. I loitered for a few minutes, waiting for any other students who might want assistance. To pass the time, I perused a shelf near the reception area, which was stocked with children's stories that Big Brother Mouse had published and made available to purchase. The proceeds of the sales were used to further their core mission: promoting literacy among Laotian children. Most of the books were colourfully illustrated and written in Laotian script with smaller English subtitles. Books were apparently rare in the country's rural areas, and Big Brother Mouse made it their mandate to help remedy this situation.

After thumbing through the literature for a few minutes, I decided to call it a day. My session with the two novice monks had been a good introduction to my November role as a conversationalist. I figured I might as well ease into the job slowly. Besides, there were still some important details I needed to address, such as finding more appealing accommodations for the month. My present digs had too many transient backpackers passing through, which made me unsure about the security of my possessions. Plus I wanted a bit of space to unpack my bag and feel relaxed for the next few weeks. So I bid farewell to the young woman at the reception desk and was soon standing back on the road under the intense late-morning sun. ○

"How much?"

"It's 400,000 kip per week."

The young hotel worker noticed the blank look on my face. I had yet to master the conversion rate — especially when it

344

reached six digits — so his number meant nothing to me.

"You want American price?"

"Yeah, that'd be easier for me."

Several days had passed since my arrival. After leaving Big Brother Mouse that morning, I had been heading over to the national museum (the former Laotian royal palace) when I came across a guest house that had a "Room Available" sign in the window. Like many of the buildings in Luang Prabang, this was a two-storey *pagoda* with white walls and wooden trim. Less flashy than some of the more stately houses I'd seen, this house appealed to my budget. (I was content with visiting palaces. I didn't need to stay in them.) So I inquired about the room. An eager employee escorted me up to the second floor, where I did a brief inspection. The room was small, but it featured a double bed, a ceiling fan and a private bathroom with a shower. After 10 months of shared dormitory rooms, tents and various forms of hut-based shabbiness, having my own quarters seemed very luxurious. Best of all, there was a set of double doors that opened to a balcony where I could see the Mekong River if I stretched my neck.

The worker guided me back downstairs to the reception desk and proceeded to punch numbers into an antiquated calculator. He flashed the screen toward my face. It read "50.3489." After a quick division in my head, I determined it was approximately $7 a day — a great rate for a private suite with river views. Other rooms that I had seen were upwards of $20 nightly. This was too good to be true!

I confirmed that I would be back later with my gear. Outside the guest house, a young woman with bleached blond hair and Thai fisherman pants sat at a picnic table smoking a cigarette.

"How is this place?" I asked her in a low voice, hoping to get the inside scoop.

"Sometimes there's a chemically smell," she replied with a Scandinavian accent. "But other than that, it's fine."

To be honest, I didn't really know what her response meant. But it didn't seem overly negative. Besides, I could deal with chemical smells. Cleaning products have always been among my favourite odours.

Later that afternoon, I hauled my things from one end of the city to the other, pulling my backpack on its little plastic wheels for 15 minutes across bumpy cobblestones and uneven pavement. The same eager young man was there upon my arrival, so I paid him $50 for the week and headed up to my room to settle in. I immediately took an extra long shower and paraded around the room in nothing by a towel. With evening approaching, I decided to grab some food at the stalls in the night market. While I was out, I figured I might as well enjoy a glass of Argentine Malbec at the city's modern wine bar. My new low-cost accommodation warranted a small celebration, and a glass of vino did the trick rather nicely.

That evening, I sauntered back to my new abode, crawled between the sheets and turned the lights out.

But sleep did not come.

After 20 minutes of attempting to drift into slumber, my body began to feel fiery, like I was having an allergic reaction. Then I began to itch and feel queasy. As I continued to squirm, a stream of hypochondriac questions raced through my mind: *When is flu season in Laos? Did I get salmonella poisoning from the food stalls? WAIT … IS THIS WHAT MALARIA FEELS LIKE?* I finally pulled myself out of bed to flip on the overhead light. With my shirt stripped off, I inspected my body in the mirror and discovered a series of swollen red welts running down my right shoulder blade.

No. No. No. This cannot be happening to me again!

At the side of the bed, I ripped the sheets back. Lo and behold, there were bugs crawling across the mattress. This time, there were two varieties: little red ones the size of fleas and larger black ones that looked like mini ladybugs. I squished a big black bug between my thumb and index finger, and it exploded in a crimson mess that was most certainly blood — and hopefully my blood.

For a minute, I just stood there wondering what to do. Although bed bugs had been an annoyance in Buenos Aires, at

346

least I had been in the company of a friend whose disposition had taken the sting out of the situation, so to speak. In fact, bed bugs had been the catalyst for adventure. We had managed to have a good laugh about our bad luck as we wandered through the streets at midnight. This time, however, I was not amused. Another nighttime departure was not realistic. Firstly, Luang Prabang was *not* a 24-hour city like Buenos Aires. By this early hour, the doors of the other guest houses would be locked up. And secondly, I was *not* in the mood for another midnight escapade. Perhaps if this had occurred months earlier, I might have tackled a late-night photo essay of the city's French colonial architecture or attempted to sleep on an unoccupied riverboat. But at this point, I was weary and I couldn't think past my need for sleep.

I pulled the sheets and blankets back over the mattress, put down a sarong and stretched out on top, hoping that the thick layer of bedding would provide enough of a barrier. I figured that I would deal with the situation in the morning — and get my damn 50 bucks back.

Despite my efforts, all attempts at sleep were futile as the ravenous creatures managed to bite through the fabric of the sarong. After an hour of attempting to configure a solution with the bed, I surrendered. I grabbed a book and went out to sit on the concrete floor of the balcony, accepting the inevitability of a long night. I read for an hour, but by four o'clock in the morning, my eyelids became impossibly heavy and I went back inside.

From a few feet away, the bed looked so soft, so inviting, like a fresh baked cinnamon bun that smelled delicious but you knew was laced with arsenic.

What to do? I scanned the room for any non-infested cushioning. That's when I spotted the manhole-sized mat in the bathroom. I pulled it out and positioned it near the balcony doors, far away from the bed. Wrapped in my warmest sweater and a woolly pair of socks, I lay down and tried to make myself as comfortable as possible. Curled up on a bath mat on the floor of scuzzy Laotian hotel room marked a new low point in my trip. If I hadn't been so beat, I might have started crying. Despite the smell of feet wafting from the rug, I did manage to sleep for nearly two hours.

Finally, the sun rose and the time came to leave. I dreaded checking out. It was the kind of situation where nobody would come out a winner — myself for obvious reasons, and the guest house owner because he was going to lose money. *Oh God. Was there going to be an argument?* After the long, frustrating night, I was feeling a little volatile — which I would use to my advantage, if necessary. With my bags, I left the room and went downstairs to the reception area.

The eager young man who had initially shown me the room was not there. Instead, a teenaged girl sat at the desk. Curbing any hostility or unnecessary drama, I calmly let her know that I couldn't stay any longer and asked for my money back. Before I could explain about the bed bugs, she rooted through a drawer and handed over 400,000 kip. There was no argument, no inquiry, no shock. They must have been through the same scenario in the past.

At this point, it was seven o'clock in the morning. I was out in the streets with all of my possessions and no plan. Guest houses would be suspicious of a tall, dishevelled man with red eyes arriving at such an hour, looking for a room. So I slunk into a café and hoped that an espresso would alleviate my frustrations. Or at least distract me from my sense of disenchantment.

Understandably, I was disappointed that the worker had offered me a room that he undoubtedly knew had bed bugs. It made me wonder about the words of warning I had received from the Scandinavian woman in the Thai fisherman pants. Was "chemically smell" some sort of traveller's code for "DO NOT PROCEED"? How had I missed that tutorial?

I was also annoyed with myself. How could I have fallen victim to bed bugs again? I should have read the warning signs: the speckled sheets, the barrier of blankets stacked over the mattress, the amazingly low price. Yet I had been so easily lured by the affordability of the room and by the romantic views of the river.

Note to self: If it looks too good to be true, it is, you damn fool. ○

"Have you been to Pussy Hill?" Sing asked innocently. He was the same earnest young monk from my first morning at Big Brother Mouse.

"Excuse me?" I responded, smiling cautiously.

"Pussy Hill. Have you visited?"

It was well into the second week of November. I had developed a ritual of spending my mornings tutoring at the language centre. Each day, I tried to be more creative with my tutoring activities, always searching for fresh ways to keep the students engaged. Most sessions began with basic conversational questions: *How are you? What did you eat for dinner? What are you studying in school?* But depending on the students' level, our "chats" could only last for so long before they became cross-examinations. So I turned to other options. If the students were more advanced, a popular activity was to slowly read them a short story and have them transcribe the text, which they would then review together. Letting them correct each other, I learned, was an effective way to win their trust and maintain enthusiasm. In other instances, some pupils brought their English homework to the centre, and I was happy to assist them with it. Sometimes I would ask a student to select a book from the shelf, and we would work on pronunciation by reading aloud.

That particular morning, I was working with Sing, Charlie and two other novice monks. They were a timid crew, in the same way that *all* Laotian students were timid. Yet they were eager to learn. Sing was the bravest and most enthusiastic, but I was stuck by his vulgar question.

"Pussy Hill?" I repeated.

"Yes! Pussy Hill," Sing confirmed, suddenly looking self-conscious, as if I were the one making fun of him.

In my mind, I raced through the possibilities of what he could be asking. In Peru, the students had proven to have surprisingly smutty vocabulary. I wasn't sure if I was the victim of another teenage prank or simply a language miscommunication.

"Can you write that down?" I requested.

Sing pulled out his notebook. In slow, wobbly script, he

etched out the words "Phu Si Hill."

"Oh, yes," I chuckled, feeling foolish about distrusting his intentions. Mount Phu Si was the hill located in the heart of the city. It was adorned with a temple on the top and offered a superb 360-degree vista over the surrounding countryside. "I climbed Phu Si Hill on my second day here."

With the misunderstanding resolved, we proceed to talk about the other attractions in Luang Prabang. A solid understanding of the must-do activities in the city would inevitably help the guys communicate with other foreigners in the future. Heck, maybe they'd even want to take advantage of my tourist status to practise their tour-guide skills. I was a willing guinea pig.

I tutored patiently in hopes that one day I'd receive an invitation for a meal or a tour. Just like my time in Morocco, I wondered if any of the students would take me under their wing. The days ticked by. And I waited. And I waited. And I waited. ○

THE DEAD RAT looked entirely unappetizing as it sat there, lifeless on my chopping board.

Indeed, among the fresh shallots, multi-coloured hot peppers and fragrant stalks of lemon grass, the common rodent waited to be hacked into bite-sized pieces. The poor guy had been skinned and had his intestines ripped out. And then he had been splayed open like a book to dry. My challenge was to turn the dehydrated rat into Laotian stew.

After a few weeks in Laos, there were still some sights and activities that I hadn't yet experienced. A fellow traveller recommended a local cooking school that offered foreigners the opportunity to experiment with Laotian cuisine. After scouting their office, I signed myself up for a one-day class. The following morning, I was standing on the curb outside that same office with a handful of middle-aged westerners keen on learning about local grub. We were corralled into the back of a *tuk-tuk* and then whisked off to Ban Pho Sy, the largest food market in Luang Prabang. The young instructor, a playful bald man appropriately named Joy, guided us through the stalls. He pointed out a variety of foods, especially the animal products: buckets of slimy silver catfish, pink-dyed eggs, gnarly-looking chicken feet, a variety of plum-size eyeballs. With a strong command of English, Joy shared tidbits of information that we would never have accessed without a guide.

"Because Laos is landlocked," Joy said, "our cuisine was not quick to be internationalized, unlike neighbouring Thailand and China."

He paused and gestured toward a four-foot mountain of purple rice, which was almost as tall as Joy himself.

"Many Thai dishes are oily or liquidy. But in the Laotian countryside, most people eat with their fingers. Sticky rice and thicker stews are much more common."

On the tour, he also pointed proudly to a bucket of dried rats, informing us that the rodent was a traditional ingredient in local recipes. I had, of course, seen the photos on the Internet. However, there was something much more palpable about witnessing a bucket of dead rats in person.

After the official tour was complete, Joy gave us 10 minutes to wander around and gawk, to take photographs and to do all the uncouth things that tourists love to do in foreign markets. But before he unleashed us, he posed a question that would subsequently seal the fate of my afternoon menu — and my entire gastronomic history.

"You are free to roam, but first I need to ask a question." Joy was facing the group with a mischievous grin on his face. "This afternoon we will make a special Laotian stew called *orlarm*. For the stew, there will be different meats to choose from, such as pork and water buffalo. But is there anyone who wants to cook with rat?"

Snickering ensued from the class of friendly but conservative Europeans.

"Oh, I don't think so," said one grey-haired man as he patted his large belly and winced with the vigour of a thousand thespians.

"God, no! I'm a vegetarian!" added another woman, turning

her nose up as she made her food politics abundantly clear.

Joy looked unsurprised, probably laughing internally at our pitiful *falang* uptight attitudes. I wasn't certain if the offer was real or if he was merely playing the role of the "provocative tour guide" — you know, hamming it up for a bunch of paying tourists who expected a certain amount of entertainment. The group continued to look around at each other to see if anyone would gamble with his proposition.

"I'll do it. I'll cook with rat," I blurted.

Instantly, all eyes turned to me, scanning to see if I was serious. To tell the truth, I wasn't entirely sure myself. Gnawing on rodents not been on my list of life goals. However, when else in life would I ever have the opportunity to cook rat in a socially acceptable setting? When life presents an opportunity, one must seize it. Besides, paying for a cooking class only to be surrounded by a swarm of foreigners was far from a genuine Laotian experience. Wouldn't eating rat up the authenticity quotient? Furthermore, I didn't want Joy to think that all westerners were a bunch of precious food wimps. No, I definitely had to take one for the team. (Hey, western world, you're welcome!) So a couple of hours later, I found myself facing an eight-inch dead rat and the consequences of my supposed gallantry.

"Hey, Joy!" I called over to the instructor. He came sauntering to my cooking station. "Do you have any tips on how to chop this thing?" The dried beast had the texture of beef jerky and was proving nearly impossible to sever into smaller pieces.

"You have to push really hard," he replied. "Maybe use your hands."

Guided by his advice, I took the withered animal in my fingers and attempted to rip the brown, leathery carcass apart. The process was slow, since it involved twisting bones and aggressively chopping through muscle tissue. Who knew rat ligaments were so strong?

Up to that point, the cooking class had been rather delightful. Located a few kilometres outside of the city, the class was held in an open-air pavilion that overlooked a pond of pink lily pads.

We had tinkered with a variety of recipes at the heart of Laotian cuisine: a spicy grilled aubergine dipping sauce called *jeow*, herbed fish steamed inside a folded banana leaf, lemon grass craftily stuffed with chicken, and perfectly cooked sticky rice. The dishes were inspiring, but the ingredients were very "niche market" (pun intended). I've yet to find salted water buffalo skin in a typical Canadian grocery store. Regardless, I enjoyed the opportunity to learn more about Laotian cuisine and to prepare myself a meal. All of the other students in the class had to work in partners. But because nobody else wanted to cook with rat, I was able to do everything on my own. A small rat-related bonus.

Finally, after an intense wrestling session with the rodent, I had successfully partitioned him into edible pieces and piled the dried flesh into a neat little rat pack. The rest of my stew was bubbling politely over the propane element, so I slid the chunks of meat into the pot and gave it a good stirring. All that was left to do was wait.

Joy emerged with the perfect remedy for the stress that comes with having to hack up a rodent: a few bottles of wine. With glasses filled, the class toasted to our newly acquired skills and to the meal we would soon be eating. For the next short while, we wandered among the herb gardens and lotus ponds, soaking up the tranquil setting. Eventually, we headed back to the kitchen to inspect our stewing dishes.

Standing in front of the stove, I lifted the lid off the rat orlarm to examine the chunky mixture of broad beans, spring onions, pea eggplants and bits of meat, all marinating in a translucent brownish bouillon. Inhaling deeply, I expected to be greeted by sweet notes of basil, spicy scents of chili and the pungency of mushroom. Well, I was in for a big surprise.

The aroma of the rat stew was anything but appetizing.

It reeked.

I recoiled.

When I was a boy, my mother once stewed wild moose meat in a pressure cooker. When she removed the lid, the nauseating smell rushed through the house and into my bedroom, where I was quietly playing with my Lego. The moose odour crept into my nostrils. I gagged and then sped to the bathroom, where I proceeded to spew a mixture of vomit and tears into the sink. I share this anecdote because the smell of cooked moose is the only reference I have to the stench of the stewing rat: gamy, pungent, aggressive, callous. Food experts will tell you that the ambiguous "gamy flavour" comes from a mixed diet of shrubs, bark, roots and other forest delights that wild animals consume. I could only imagine what my rat had eaten to foster that type of penetrating smell. Perhaps a balanced regimen of compost and cigarette butts?

"Joy!" I called for assistance. "Is it supposed to … uh … smell that way?"

"Oh yes. Rat is very strong meat. Not for the weak."

"Well, good. I guess I nailed it then." I put the lid back on the stew and brought it over to the dining area.

Seated around the table, we had all the dishes spread before us. Steam poured from vibrant green banana leaves, snow-coloured sticky rice, purple-grey eggplant dip. Despite all the appetizing options, I felt obligated to sample the rat dish first. The stew was still extremely hot, so I used a fork to delicately extract a morsel of meat — possibly a piece of thigh? — and blew on it. While the other group members watched cautiously, I brought the rat to my lips.

I rolled the meaty chunk around in my mouth, waiting for some type of aftertaste to smack my tongue. The flesh had the consistency of chicken. But due to the fact it had been previously dried, it was slightly chewier and featured more aggressive undertones. "It's actually not *that* bad," I informed the curious onlookers. "The smell is worse than the taste."

To the credit of my dinner companions, a few of them even tried the dish for themselves. And I can confirm that not one of them raised a wrist to a forehead and fainted. Nobody served themselves ambitious portions, but together we managed to finish off most of the stew. Although rat might not be included on the menu at my next dinner party, I'm glad I tried it. If I ever happen to be stranded in some godforsaken situation with only rats to eat, at the very minimum I know that now I am psychologically prepared to chow down. Not that I want that to happen. In fact, I'm definitely *not* asking for that.

Whether you're talking about a Laotian cooking class or life in general, you have to be careful what you ask for. ○

AT BIG BROTHER Mouse, I worked with Sing and Charlie a couple more times throughout the course of the month, yet our interactions never went further than basic conversation. In general, I had different students each day, as tutors and pupils were informally matched when they arrived on site. The majority of students were college-aged men who believed that a strong foundation in English would give them a competitive edge as they pursued careers in banking, engineering or tourism, the most popular career choice.

I enjoyed my role as a language coach. Unlike my teaching experience in Peru, there was no great need for me to be entertaining. Not once did I have to act as a disciplinary figure, nor was I subjected to interpersonal friction. I simply presented myself and did my best to communicate clearly.

When the tutoring sessions had ended for the day, I spent my afternoons exploring the sights and charms of the city. In the evenings, I retired to a private room. Following the bed bug debacle, I settled on a very clean guest room for $12 per night from a woman who also ran a laundry service I had used shortly after arriving. (In hindsight, it made perfect sense to trust the house of a lady who had made my tattered clothes look fresh again.) Following nearly a year of often-dubious accommodation, I was all too happy to stretch out on a double bed in a house where the tile floors were mopped daily.

Luang Prabang wasn't just picturesque and friendly, but it was also an exceedingly *easy* place to travel. Over the previous years, the city had exploded into a tourist magnet. Local entrepreneurs have learned that foreigners — as adventurous as they might think they are — not only have a robust adoration for anything elephant-related, but they also have an addiction for the luxuries of the western world. By the end of the month, the folks at the local wine bar had learned my name. Over the weeks, I had occasionally forgone the cheap local cuisine at the night market for a gooey pizza at the Italian-inspired eatery. Grabbing a latte at the modern café became a daily ritual. Every tourist-related establishment had a wireless network and someone on staff willing to relieve tension with a low-cost massage. The inconspicuous Asian city was an epicentre of decadence.

But decadent travel experiences aren't always the most profound travel experiences.

In retrospect, I was lonely in Laos. I state this without melodrama. That's merely how the cards fell. When it comes to short-term travel, being alone can be great, even liberating. But after 11 months on the road, the absence of a confidant or a familiar friend can take its toll. That month, I found it tiresome to strike up a conversation with a new person each day — whether local or foreigner. Going through the typical "nice to meet you" social rigmarole was exhausting, *especially* after the hours of friendly but mundane chit-chat with English students. So, in the morning, I drank my latte in the company of the news headlines. In the afternoon, I gave myself a self-guided tour through a temple. In the evening, I sat at the bar and watched newly arrived couples thumbing their guidebooks. The lonesomeness wasn't debilitating. It just seemed to hover around me like a smell I couldn't quite wash out.

(Incidentally, one of the most memorable evenings of the month was when I bumped into my seventh grade teacher in the night market. To celebrate the happenstance, we went out for dinner. Over grilled fish and Beerlao, we chatted about my hometown of Prince George. If you were to tell the 12-year-old version of me that my teacher would become my social angel and drinking buddy for one night in Laos, I would have laughed. Or cried.)

I was partly responsible for the loneliness. It was my decision to get a private room. Perhaps I had set myself up for isolation. The people of Laos are certainly more shy and standoffish than those in other nations, such as India or Morocco. By late November, I began to wonder if perhaps my month would be a minor failure. Sure, I had successfully checked off most of the must-do activities around Luang Prabang. Sure, I was a competent volunteer.

But there was something missing.

That month, I had successfully secured a project but not a host. Big Brother Mouse was (and still is) an excellent initiative. Yet without a centralized volunteer program, it wasn't able to offer me a centralized community. And outside of the organization, I hadn't found a local person to bond with: no Estella to guide me through the food market, no Moses to explain local culture, no Nico to introduce me to the neighbours. (Not even a Baba G, who — love him or not — provided a glimpse into the way things were done in Goa.) As the end of November approached, I struggled with a difficult question regarding my time in Laos: *Had I achieved the immersion that I sought in my travels?* ☼

ONE PARTICULAR AFTERNOON, I found myself struggling with a case of the doldrums. The morning, as usual, had been spent with the students at Big Brother Mouse. But I wasn't quite sure what to do with the rest of my day. The museums had been visited. Each alleyway of the city had been explored. At the risk of sounding sacrilegious, the thought of another temple was tiresome. So after humming and hawing, I decided that renting a set of wheels might be a fun way to switch up the tempo of my wanderings. With a backpack containing my camera, some snacks and a couple bottles of Beerlao, I departed the guest house to rent a bicycle. It is, after all, impossible to feel drab when in the possession of an orange cruiser with a wicker basket and a cheerful bell.

Strolling parallel to the great Mekong River, I walked east toward the city centre on a bicycle hunt. The riverbank was dotted with restaurants that catered to tourists wishing to watch the daily sunset. Down the embankment at the water's edge, elongated houseboats in a selection of unruly colours waited for their next river adventure. Along the roadway, locals raced by on scooters. This path had become my preferred method to get to the heart of the town. Halfway along the route, one of the many boatmen approached me with an offer.

"You want to cross the river?" asked the short barefoot man in a baseball cap and grease-stained shirt.

I paused and considered the proposition for a brief second. Normally I was quick to reject the unsolicited offers from tuk-tuk drivers and other men who tried to sell me things, including substances of a narcotic nature. But I had heard about a cave littered with Buddha statues on the other side of the Mekong. We were standing a few metres above the official location where one could catch a boat across the river, so it was clear that this man didn't have any swindling motives. My plans for bike riding quickly dissolved with the prospect of Buddha caves and boat trips.

"Yeah, all right." The impulsive decision produced a rush of excitement: the perfect cure for the doldrums.

After waiting a few minutes at the ferry landing, I boarded a boat not much bigger than a canoe to cross the country's most important body of water. The Mekong River measures more than 4,000 kilometres, connecting Laos to China and Cambodia and acting as a political border with Thailand. The stewardship of the river is a contentious environmental issue, with multiple stakeholders affected by its welfare. The effects of hydroelectric damming and the implications of oil shipping on the river subsequently affect China, Myanmar, Thailand, Cambodia, Vietnam and, of course, Laos. As far as rivers go, it was sort of a big deal. But that afternoon, the politics of the river seemed worlds away.

The engine droned as the boat cut across the river current. The sun was nearly overhead. In the city, the heat off the pavement would soon give rise to hazy mirages. On the river, however, there was a light breeze and the familiar yet enigmatic smell of fresh water. Aboard the boat, I was joined by a couple of young mothers with babies tied snugly to their chests, an older man in a three-piece suit, three novice monks and a handful of chickens in bamboo cages. Five minutes later, we arrived at the other side. I disembarked and made my way up the steep bank into the small village of Ban Xieng Maen.

The village was strikingly different from Luang Prabang. The roadway was narrow, and a distinct aroma of manure wafted through the air. Mangy chickens darted underfoot. Intersecting the main lane, a sad-looking stream attempted to find its way to the Mekong River. Nailed to a tree was a wooden sign with a public service announcement written in both Laotian and English: "Good People, do not throw garbage away." Judging by the plastic bags lining the stream, not everyone in the town was aspiring to be good. As I moved forward, a muscular man passed me as he led a couple of water buffaloes by long ropes attached to hoops through their bovine snouts.

After walking a couple hundred metres through the quaint village, I became slightly uncomfortable. Despite being engrossed in my new surroundings, I was growing suspicious that I was being watched.

The three young monks from the river crossing were trailing me.

On the boat, I had noticed them observing me with curiosity. Who could blame them? I must have looked very exotic to them with my red beard, long white legs and western clothing. The eerie sensation of being tracked now trumped the reassuring symbolism of shaved heads and orange robes of monks. If I had learned anything from my experiences this year, notably those in Trujillo and Cape Town, it was that a group of young lads can range from innocently mischievous to downright dangerous. Just because someone is dressed up in rags of spiritual devotion doesn't mean he won't rob you blind. So I decided to stop at a food stall to order a big bowl of brothy noodle soup and temporarily delay my adventure.

Like shadows, the young monks paused on the other side of

the road — enough evidence to confirm that they had indeed been tailing me. The best approach to the situation, I figured, was to acknowledge their presence.

"Hi," I said, pivoting directly toward them and making eye contact. "How are you guys doing?"

The boys covered their mouths and giggled. One whispered to the other. Then two of the guys pushed forward the third member of their party, a short fellow with rectangular eyeglasses who was probably in his mid-teens.

"We are good, *khawp-jai*," the elected leader of the group responded timidly. Then, to my surprise, he looked directly into my eyes and asked, "Where are you going?"

I hesitated. What was the safest strategic response?

"I'm going to the temple." It was a half-truth. From the other side of the river, I had seen a temple on the edge of the village that looked intriguing.

"Where are *you* going?" I asked suspiciously.

"We are going to the cave."

My ears perked up.

The guys murmured among themselves in their own language, occasionally looking in my direction, blatantly plotting something. Were they formulating a strategy to steal my camera? I took a spoonful of hot soup and kept my eyes on them, sizing them up from the other side of the alley. The tallest was probably only a few inches over five feet, and their sinewy bodies weren't exactly intimidating. However, the right amount of piranhas can bring down the mightiest of creatures. And any insinuation that I am a mighty creature is *awfully* generous.

After they finished their planning, the leader of the group turned to me. He ironed his robe with his hands and then said in the most innocent tone, "My friends and I would like to practise our English. Can we travel with you?"

The inquiry struck a chord, especially during a month when I was so weary, when I had wrestled with a consistent sense of loneliness. At no point in my year had anyone asked to "travel with me."

"Sure," I smiled, unable to deny such a request. "We can travel together. I'll finish my soup."

Within minutes, we were walking east in the direction of the temple. The leader of the group, Somchit, did most of the talking. Like my tutoring sessions at Big Brother Mouse, the "conversation" was more of a basic interview — but this time the questions were all directed at me. *What is your work? Are you married? How many people are in your family? What do you do in your free time? What is your favourite sport? Do you like Laos? Where are you staying?* Whenever I could, I slipped in a question of my own.

Somchit revealed that he was 16 years old and that he and his friends were novice monks, studying in the city. For Laotian parents with the financial means, it was common to send their sons to a novice monk college, regardless of whether or not they'd actually become full-fledged monks. It was like the western equivalent of boarding school. In fact, you might see these orange-robed boys sending text messages from mobile phones hidden in their satchels — young men studying ancient traditions in a modern world.

We arrived to the base of a long set of stairs, which led to a whitewashed temple overlooking the valley. We climbed the 123 steps slowly and turned to look at the vista: below was the copper-coloured Mekong river, the tree-covered bump of Mount Phu Si and the pagoda rooftops of Luang Prabang. If I had been summoned to build a sanctuary for spiritual disciples to get closer to the divine, this location would have served perfectly. While I buzzed around snapping photographs of the dragon illustrations on the ceiling of the temple, Somchit and his friends sat patiently on the steps, perhaps underwhelmed by the commonplace of another Buddhist setting.

"You come to cave with us now?" Somchit asked eagerly when I emerged from the temple. "We think you will like it."

The young monks had proven to be respectful and friendly.

"Yes. Let's go."

After descending the same 123 stairs, we followed a path that ran parallel to the river, away from the village and deeper into a

361

remote forested backdrop. We passed over a footbridge above a clean creek, and then arrived at a seminary that featured a cluster of mildewy stone buildings and another understated temple. In front of the temple, a maintenance man sat with his ankles crossed atop a desk and his hands folded behind his head. He gave Somchit a key and a flashlight then asked me to pay 5,000 kip for admission to the cave. Somchit informed me that he and his friends were permitted free access to the cave because they were novice monks. For me, it came to less than a dollar.

Equipped with the key and flashlight, we marched further along the footpath, eventually cutting a sharp left turn and heading away from the river. One more set of stairs and we had arrived. A stone archway stood before us. Although it looked like a secret passage into a castle, this vine-covered entryway led directly to the bowels of the mountain. Somchit unlocked the mossy steel gates, opened the double wooden doors and motioned for me to stay with him.

The cave air cuffed me across the face. It felt warm and moist, like a natural sauna. I paused for a few seconds to acclimatize to the new environment. My eyes adjusted to the darkness and my lungs to the swampy air. After a few deep breaths, I proceeded forward, trailing closely behind my three guides, who whispered vivaciously amongst themselves.

"Use the rail," instructed Somchit, pausing from his conversation with his colleagues to shine the beam from his flashlight toward a chain-link guide rail that had been drilled into the wall of the cave.

"Yes, cap'n," I responded. I was appreciative to have a few local guides. Even if I had found the cave on my own, I'm not sure I would have had the tenacity to enter alone.

Deeper and deeper we proceeded. The dark cave featured unique stalagmites, dripstone formations that rose like mini-cities. And while I couldn't see any bats, I did see clear evidence of human activity. The steps of the staircase were bowl-shaped, suggesting that thousands of people had made their way through this cave. The Buddhas adorning the walls spoke to a specific human history. Throughout the centuries, caves across Laos were used as Buddhist pilgrimage sites, as shelters from religious persecution and as safe places to hide from the implications of French colonialism. Caves were also used as bomb shelters. As I moved deeper in the cavern, I wondered whether this mountain hollow had once been a refuge from the tempest of American explosives.

Although the sheer awesomeness of the situation was not lost on me — I was caving with monks! — it wasn't long before the stairs, the muddy path and the hot air took their toll on me. Oxygen abruptly felt in short supply. I crouched down, feeling dizzy, and took a few minutes to stabilize my breathing. For a moment, I wondered if this was when the novice monks (who suddenly looked resilient and robust) would knock me over the head with a Buddha statue, steal my wallet and camera, and then head for the hills. It would make for a perfect heist: placate the naïve traveller with gentle orange robes, entice him with an Indiana Jones cave adventure, weaken him with oxygen-depleted air, and then rob him blind. But while I was huddled over trying to catch my breath, the three novice monks waited patiently —not fussing over me but not abandoning me either.

Following a brief rest, I rose back to my feet. We had been in the cave for at least 15 minutes and had seen more or less all there was to see. Accordingly, we began to retrace our steps and eventually surfaced through the stone archway. The exterior air raced into my lungs.

Damn, oxygen is enjoyable!

I would have preferred to relax and savour the fresher air, but Somchit indicated that he wanted to return the key and the flashlights to the seminary. Soon I was trailing after the three Laotian musketeers once again as they marched back toward the small village and the boat launch.

After the gear was given back to the man with his feet on the table, I asked a favour.

"Guys," I called as I wiped my gleaming face with the inside of my elbow. "Is it okay if we take a break? Maybe have some water?"

"Okay. Yes," replied Somchit. "I know a place."

He led us to a rocky outcropping that overlooked the river and across to Luang Prabang. I collapsed to the ground, happy to give my legs some rest. My tongue was like sandpaper. I peeled off my sweaty backpack, eager to trade my camera for my bottle of water. But as I was unzipping the bag, a telltale clinking sound attracted the attention of my young tour guides.

Somchit's eyes widened. "Can we have some?"

"Some what?" I asked, trying to play stupid.

"You have beer. Can you share it with us?" Somchit specified.

Now *this* was an unanticipated dilemma. Ignorant of Laotian laws concerning alcohol, I had no idea if there was a minimum drinking age. To make matters more complicated, these were supposedly spiritual students. I'm not terribly familiar with Buddhist philosophy, but I'm certain that it doesn't encourage teenagers to drink beer. Yet the boys had guided me to a hidden cave and offered some much-appreciated afternoon company. And on top of everything, they had not even robbed me.

When a group of 16-year-old novice monks request to drink your beer, what is the most honourable course of action?

After a few seconds of deliberation, I came up with a moral loophole.

"I am going to put the beer right here," I explained to them as I placed the two bottles of beer behind me. "If they disappear, I won't ask questions."

I rotated toward the river, unsure of what would happen next. But whether they understood or even cared about my attempt to evade responsibility was irrelevant because the next sound I heard was the hiss of beer bottles opening. That was followed by the special sort of giggling that comes from boys doing something they probably shouldn't be doing.

Before us, the Mekong surged endlessly onward, forcing the riverboats to navigate the currents with care. It was one part wrestling match and one part dance. A successful passage required both assertiveness and surrender. The true art of the journey was knowing which approach to take at the right moment. ○

EACH DAY AFTER my morning tutoring session at Big Brother Mouse, I made a point of saying goodbye to the friendly young woman at the reception desk. We developed a rapport of sorts. The average visitor dropped by for a single session, maybe two if they were travelling at a slower pace. But it was rather unorthodox for a foreigner to return again and again over the course of four weeks. Perhaps the receptionist thought I was lost and just kept showing up because I had no other place to go — a quirky traveller trapped in his own voluntary time loop. Whatever the case may be, she was friendly with me. And even though it was always brief, I enjoyed our daily ritual.

"You come back tomorrow?" she would say as I slipped on my shoes.

"Yes." I would wink and nod my head. "I'll see you tomorrow."

"Oh!" Her mouth would form a perfect O, as though she were blowing out a candle. "Again! That's good."

And sure enough, the next day, I'd greet her with a wave, saying *"Sa-bai-deeee."*

Eventually, however, my last day of volunteering arrived. After a final tutoring session I gathered my possessions and stood in the reception area by the bookstands, flipping through the titles. Unlike the sense of obligation that came with buying things in the night market, I *actually* wanted a book. This was a genuine purchase. I selected a fun-looking title, *The Mouse that Sat on an Egg*, and placed the book on the desk. The smiley receptionist calculated my total.

"You come back tomorrow?" she asked in a suspicious tone as she took my money. This was my first time buying books, and the change in our routine tipped her off that something was awry.

"Actually, no," I replied apologetically. "Tomorrow I'm taking the bus to Vientiane. And then I'm off to Australia."

"Oh ..." She tilted her head to one side, pressed her lips together and paused to process my response. And then she furrowed her brow and offered a departing sentiment. "Well, you come back again sometime. You stay involved!"

It wasn't a question. It was a command.

"Yes. I would like that very much." ☺

DECEMBER

Outback, Australia

"*Daniel, can I* ask you a favour?"

Edda and I were zooming down a side road in a glossy blue Chevrolet El Camino. An hour earlier, I had arrived at a small airport on the east coast. The Aussie kink-goddess had picked me up, and we had begun a short drive south toward her hometown of Lismore.

"Sure, what's up?" I responded while looking at the green gum trees that framed the road.

"It's for a performance piece." Edda said as she ran a hand through her asymmetrical haircut and then shifted into a lower gear to compensate for slower traffic. The truck's little engine growled before relaxing again.

"Um ... okay." I knew to expect the unexpected from Edda.

"It's sort of ... how do I put this?" Edda paused. "Well, it's intimate."

Now she had my full attention. I looked at her apprehensively from across the cab of the truck. For a brief second, she glimpsed at me through her Jackie Onassis sunglasses, trying to read my eyes. She looked back to the road and then finally stated the essence of her request.

"Can you film me while I get my labia pierced?"

The question hung in the air for a brief second, requiring a moment for processing. And then Edda released her trademark laugh, her cheeks turning a delicate shade of crimson. Despite her bold personality, Edda was not immune to blushing.

"Well, I can't say that I have much experience in the documentation of labia piercing," I stated matter-of-factly. "But if you're willing to accept an amateur, I'm happy to help."

"Amazing. Let's do it today."

And with that, my afternoon agenda was confirmed.

For many people, the request might have been awkward. Truth be told, I was not without my reservations. But the year was devoted to seeking adventure and finding ways to be helpful. This meant tiling floors and teaching English but also tackling smaller, more unusual requests. Overall I felt flattered to be bestowed with such an intimate invitation — isn't the request to film a pal's labia piercing a surefire indication of true friendship?

As we merged onto the freeway, the traffic picked up speed. The truck's engine revved again. We pushed forward, and soon Edda was back in high gear. ☼

THE DESCENT INTO the Gold Coast airport had been exceptionally turbulent. As the plane lurched through the choppy air, I wrapped my hand over a small pewter pendant (an orca) that dangled on a chain around my neck. It had been a gift from my father many years prior, and I wore it on all my flights — a talisman of sorts to ensure safe transfer. Thus far, it had served its purpose flawlessly. Now I wasn't just hoping for safety as we bounced through the air. I also felt like I could use some guidance.

Eventually, the plane rattled onto the tarmac without incident, and I was soon standing in a slow-moving line at Australian customs. An hour later, I handed my passport to the chipper sun-kissed woman at the desk. She called me by an abbreviated form of my first name, like we had been friends forever.

"Hiya, Dan," she said as she flipped through the pages. "Well,

I see you've gone full circle! Are you here, Dan, for business or pleasure?"

"To see a friend," I replied. To be honest, I didn't fully know what my month in Australia would entail, though seeing Edda was at the top of my list.

"All right, mate. Have a good one!" The familiar sound of the customs stamp came slamming down onto my passport. I moved on to the baggage claim.

It took me another hour to gather my backpack and proceed through an unceremonious X-ray baggage inspection system. As luck would have it, I was flagged and forced to unpack my entire bag on a table in front of my fellow bleary-eyed travellers. Perhaps coming direct from Southeast Asia while sporting an unruly five-month beard aligned me with the profile of someone who is doing something he shouldn't be doing. The security agents mentioned that my bendable camera tripod looked suspicious, like illegal Thai wooden beads. After realizing that I wasn't a cocaine baron or professional Buddhist necklace smuggler, they released me.

Edda was not scheduled to arrive at the airport for another hour. I wandered the long corridors, eventually stopping to withdraw currency. With one of the colourful plastic Australian bills, I bought food: $5 for a latte, $10 for a sandwich. December, it seemed, would not be my cheapest month. *Welcome back to the developed world, buddy.*

My legs became tired, so I sat on a bench and watched people bustling throughout the terminal: folks rushing to catch planes, families joyfully reuniting, a discreet custodian pushing a broom. While it was pleasant to return to a culture that was similar to my own, it was still only an avatar of my Canadian reality — familiar, but not quite the same thing. In a state of fatigue, the thought of getting on the next plane to Canada wasn't unappealing.

I was feeling lost.

You see, my arrival in Australia marked a departure. Apart from seeing Edda, I had landed in the country with no specific plans and had no prospects for a work-exchange project. This

369

lack of strategy suddenly made me uneasy. December was the grand finale. And because it would be the end, I wanted it to be meaningful.

Self-doubt jabbed me in the gut. Had I made the right choice to not plan anything? Or would this month end up being something of a cop-out? I dwelled on the most important question of all: *What was the most poignant way to end the biggest year of, you know, my entire life?* Before I had the opportunity to sprint to the ticket counter and solve my concerns with a direct flight to Canada, I saw a familiar body strutting in my direction.

"Daniel!" Edda exclaimed as she pulled me close, crushing my bony frame against the softness of her breasts. "It's good to see you."

"You too."

"Let's get outta here."

With that, she grabbed my backpack and escorted me to the parking lot where the blue El Camino was waiting. I hopped into the passenger side. There I saw three yellow Post-it notes stuck onto the glove compartment:

I never knew Post-it notes could be so profound. Seeing the words seemed to instantly recalibrate my purpose with a reminder of what I was doing. Edda had that effect on people. She knew how to make a person feel welcome. Simply being in her presence made self-doubt dissolve. The last time she gave me guidance was in late January, when she waved me forward at the New Orleans airport. At the time, I had no idea what the following months would bring. Now we were at an airport once again, but on a different continent with my journey nearly over.

Maybe coming full circle was exactly what I needed. ☺

IN THE BLINK of an eye, December had arrived. How had I made it so far?

Well, logistically speaking, I knew how I had arrived to where I was. I had booked airplane tickets and showed up to each gate on time. But on a more synchronistic level, how had I made it so far?

Before setting out on the year-long adventure, I had recognized that the quest could possibly end prematurely due to a myriad of scenarios. I might get sick from one of the many water sources I'd be drinking. A close family member could be diagnosed with a grave illness. Perhaps a mugging would leave me severely injured. Or maybe I would simply reach a saturation point, leaving me unable to handle any more travel, adventure or stimulation. Yet somehow I had made it to December. I was weary and dumbfounded but still in one piece.

Had I been coasting on a gigantic lucky streak? If so, I hoped that whatever luck I had been blessed with would last a few more weeks — just long enough for me to survive the ferocious dingoes and overpriced lattes of Australia.

Luck, however, had nothing to do with how I chose my final destination. Throughout the journey, I had carefully curated my list of countries. I selected some western and some eastern, some more developed and some less developed, some where English was common and some where I'd be challenged linguistically. When it came to my final month, there were a couple of obvious choices. With only one (inhabited) continent left to visit, I figured that I would conclude in Australia or New Zealand. Both of these destinations would provide a gentle stepping stone back to Canadian culture. The allure of seeing Edda again, in addition to the more affordable ticket prices from Southeast Asia, made one nation the clear winner. My final leg would be in the land of kangaroos and boomerangs.

Originally, I hadn't planned on having no plan. As with all my other destinations, I had prepared for my stay by researching work-exchange projects. I had made considerable efforts to arrange and confirm a host. But it was the wrong time of year for the prolific Aussie vineyard harvests. The pearl farm on the north coast politely declined my application, stating that they already had a full roster of helpers. The kangaroo rehabilitation centre did not even respond to my inquiries. I found myself bumping into wall after wall, and I began to interpret this as an indication that maybe I needed to try something different. My response was to abandon the formula that I had applied to each of my previous months. The time had come to throw the metaphorical map to the wind.

And hope that luck would not abandon me yet. ○

AS AGREED UPON, I used my camera to film Edda's labia piercing later that first day. It would be gratuitous to share all the explicit details, but I can confirm that the procedure was a success. Having never had any part of my body pierced or any surface of my skin tattooed, I caught a glimpse into a foreign world, had front row seats to a unique cultural ceremony — the kind where one doesn't know where exactly to put his eyes.

Once Edda had her panties back on, we headed out to celebrate in the only appropriate way that one should commemorate a new genital jewel: dinner at a collectively run vegan restaurant. A group of Edda's friends joined us for food, wine and conversation that lasted for hours and hours. It was well after midnight by the time we stumbled back to Edda's temporary home, a comfortable bungalow she was house-sitting (for a disabled lesbian with a voracious herb garden). With a bedroom all to myself, and the opportunity for free laundry, the housing arrangement was downright lavish. That first night, the combination of jetlag and wine helped me fall sleep very quickly. An hour later, however, I awoke to a *shocking* surprise.

Something warm and furry was literally crawling between my legs. This might sound like a good time for some people, but for me it was a moment of sheer horror. I leaped from the bed and ran to the light switch.

From the bed, a rat — yes, a RAT — stood up on her hind legs.

She sniffed the air, looking rather disappointed that I didn't want to spoon with her.

I rubbed my eyes.

In my mid-REM grogginess, it took me a minute to piece together what had happened.

This furry thing was also known as Ginko, the rodent pet of the lesbian homeowner. The little creature must have escaped from her cage on the other side of the house in search of company. The bedroom door had been shut, but the rat had crawled under it and selected me as the lucky recipient of her affections.

After letting my heart rate settle, I picked up the rat, put her back in the hallway and wedged a towel under the door to prevent her from any further attempts to get between my legs. Falling back asleep was not easy due to the sound of little paws clawing on the wooden door.

Although it felt like an eternity ago, I had a made a stew out of rat just a few weeks previously. Now there had been one trying to snuggle with me, in my bed. It had to be some sort of cosmic revenge. ☼

A WEEK PASSED quickly.

After spending a rather lonely month in Laos, I genuinely appreciated the company of a friend. Edda and I went to the beach, strolled around Lismore and shared some memorable meals. Perhaps the best times were when we sat on the tattered couch on the veranda, waxing poetically about life and travel and sex and spirituality and other subjects that defy oversimplification.

Despite the good company, I struggled with that same big question: *What is the best way to complete this journey?* Understandably, I was worn out. But this wasn't justification to excuse myself from the ideals I had set. The problem wasn't my lethargy — it was my own amateurishness, my own sheer ineptitude. I didn't know what an "ending" was supposed to look like or where it was supposed to take me. This was all new to me. Closure doesn't come with a compass.

The week with Edda served a very important purpose. Between the Post-it notes and the veranda conversations, I drummed up enough oomph to face the final stretch. The best approach, I decided, was to go leave Lismore. I needed to get back on the road and travel to other corners of Australia. The final month had arrived, and I would go on a search for an ending — my ending. ○

ON THE EVE of my departure from Lismore, Edda and I retreated again to the veranda. A navy nocturnal blanket had begun to descend over the city. The weaving silhouettes of bats on the hunt for insects etched a hypnotic pattern across the sky.

With a blanket over her shoulders, Edda sat cross-legged on the couch with a pillow on her lap. On the pillow, she had a specific set of items: a punctured inner tube from a bicycle tire, a pair of scissors and a roll of black electrical tape. Her plan was to transform the rubber into a flogger, which is a kinky tool that can be used as a whip — or as a caressing apparatus. I sat beside her with a glass of whisky in my hand and my bare feet sprawled on the floor.

"So, Mr. Baylis," Edda said as she pulled on the tube to test its strength. "Are you on a good path?"

The question came out of nowhere. Knowing Edda, it was not intended to provoke or critique, simply to encourage reflection. She was intentionally giving me space to talk.

"Um … I don't know," I said, shrugging. The idea of a "good path" seemed inextricably linked to notions of destiny or fate, subjects on which I am a notorious fence-sitter. "How do we ever really know?"

By that point, Edda had reached for the scissors and was now cutting the tubing into long, narrow strips that fell into a tangled snakepit beside her.

"For me, I suppose everything just feels right," she stated simply. She grabbed a strip and whipped it against her exposed forearm. "Relationships are in order, life is flowing, doors are open. I know that I'm on a good path when I feel good about myself and about others and about the world."

I marvelled at Edda's clear spiritual compass. And her DIY resourcefulness.

"Something tells me that when I look back on my path this year, I'm going to be baffled at how seamless it was." I paused and took swig of whisky. "Don't get me wrong. There have certainly been some difficult parts, but I'm sort of baffled at how far I've come ... so I guess you could say that I'm on a good path."

Eventually Edda had a dozen strips. She lined them up and then folded the bundle in half.

"It's like this: I dreamed of seeing the world, so I got a job, made some money and then bought some tickets." Edda had given me the space, so I figured I might as well talk. "This year, I kept showing up and rolling with the punches. But the thing is, I couldn't have done this without assistance. It might sound flaky, but it's as if the universe somehow enabled this journey to happen — like it gave me the green light to proceed. The problem is that now I'm dumbfounded on what my appropriate response should be. Or if a response is even necessary."

"I've always thought," Edda interjected, "that the appropriate response to generosity is simply to be the best people we can be."

I raised my glass to Edda and took another hit of whisky. She winked and then began to form a handle by wrapping electrical tape around the folded end of her strips.

"I guess I thought that by this point in my trip, I'd be wiser — you know, have some sort of grand clarity, some sort of deeper understanding. Isn't that what's supposed to happen to travellers? But with only a few weeks left, I mostly just feel confused."

Again, Edda whipped her forearm, giving the flogger a trial run. With a look a satisfaction, she pushed the materials to the side. Then she took my empty hand between her palms. They were warm and soft.

She looked me in the eyes.

"You know what they say about stirred ponds being murky,"

she said gently. "Water can't be calm when you're moving around so much. A period of stillness after all this movement will let the sediment settle."

I nodded in silent agreement and then let my head fall onto the pillow on her lap.

Above the rooftops, the bats had completed their feeding frenzy, leaving the night sky quiet and clear. ○

FOR THE NEXT 10 days, I wandered and became a tourist in the truest sense. During the train ride from Lismore to Sydney, I watched kangaroos jump through the forest and the verdant hills of New South Wales flash past. Sydney was peppy and bustling. I took a ferry boat through the harbour, stopping to visit urban graffiti art installations on Cockatoo Island. From Sydney, I went to the Tahbilk Winery for a reunion with Matt, my fellow volunteer at the Costa Rican raw vegan farm. I don't know what I appreciated the most: the opportunity to see Matt again, the chance to see wild wallabies bouncing through wetland trails of the vineyard or the personal access to the estate's cellar.

While in Melbourne, I arranged to reunite with a Dutch fellow named Bart. I had met him on the camel tour in Morocco and subsequently bumped into him one evening at the Luang Prabang night market. This marked the third continent on which our paths had crossed that year.

The city of Adelaide proved to be a hidden gem. A Canadian couple from Ottawa generously invited me to stay at the gorgeous beachfront home they were renting. On an afternoon drive through the eastern hills of Adelaide, we looked up and saw little grey furry bundles hanging leisurely in eucalyptus trees. Nothing says "Crikey, I'm in Australia!" like wild koalas.

As I drifted across the southeast corner of Australia, I was consistently greeted with utmost kindness and treated to the best-of-the-best at no cost. Consequently, the Australian dollar became less of a burden than I had originally anticipated. To a certain degree, the bounty of hospitality struck me with irony.

Throughout the entire year, I had strived to find arrangements that provided accommodation in exchange for labour, and this ambition hadn't always led to the most "deluxe" of experiences. And yet in my final month, when all I offered was my company and a handful of stories from my journey, I was being treated like royalty. Complimentary room, board and unexpected adventures? Yes, please! Now *this* was the way to travel!

Truth be told, however pleasant it was to wander, I still couldn't let myself off the hook. I couldn't escape a sense of obligation. Despite the scenic train rides and the cutting-edge museums and the *really* heavenly bottles of vino, I feared that my expedition across the world would somehow feel incomplete if I didn't challenge myself to go beyond itinerant frolicking in the final days. I sought a more purposeful resolution or, as Edda had suggested, some stillness to consolidate my thoughts.

By the time I reached Adelaide, I had made a decision. I realized that *creating* a meaningful journey and *concluding* a meaningful journey were two different phases, two separate challenges. Therefore, at this stage of the trip, I no longer needed to focus on the foundations of engagement, helping, and connection. Instead of roaming or trying to form new relationships, I would seek out the ideal space for introspection. ○

By mid-December, I was a man on a hunt for a contemplative ending. I certainly wasn't without ideas on how to conclude the year-long project. It was simply that many of my notions were laced with romanticism and impossibility. If pipe dreaming is a crime, lock me up for life.

If I could have a poignant experience to conclude to the journey, what would that look like? It would need depth. It would need meaning. It would need to provide me with wisdom — if not from within myself then from an external source. When seeking such wisdom, where does one turn? I had an aspiration to meet someone with genuine life experience, with a connection to the natural order of things — a person with deep wrinkles and eyes that spoke of the universe. Someone who could speak to histories that most people can only read about in books. When considering the context of Australia, I naturally thought of the various Aboriginal peoples. For a wide-eyed wanderer from the West, this is both understandable and embarrassingly cliché.

In Adelaide, after a home-cooked meal and a couple glasses of Pinotage, I divulged my desires to my Canadian hosts. Unfortunately, they didn't know of any mystical elders who were waiting for a world-weary Canadian to show up on their doorstep. But they had recently driven through the outback and visited traditionally sacred areas.

One of their favourite regions was the West MacDonnell ranges, or simply the "West Macs." (Australians have an adorable tendency to condense words, such as "barbie" for barbecue and "mozzie" for mosquito.) According to the traditional legends of the Arrarnta people — indigenous tribes of the central Australian region — the West Macs were sculpted at the Dreamtime, a sacred era when ancestral spirit beings created the world. The abbreviated story is that giant caterpillars, known as the mighty *yipirinya*, emerged from out of the ground at Urlatherrke (Mount Zeil), which is the highest peak in Australia west of the Great Dividing Range. The creatures travelled east, creating the West Macs and a series of permanent waterholes. They came to rest at what is now the town of Alice Springs and then they disappeared back into the ground.

For millennia, these waterholes have been highly revered, as they were often the only source of water available in times of drought. This life-giving quality — in addition to the stillness of the outback — appealed to me. How could I *not* find something meaningful in this area?

With a bit of research into the region, I discovered a walking trail that connected these waterholes. The Larapinta Trail is a 223-kilometre footpath through the outback and is considered one of Australia's most spectacular hiking experiences. This would be *perfect*. Two weeks in isolation would provide a formidable space to think — a good long walk to clear my mind. My own white-boy walkabout.

Then I did even more research and began to second-guess myself. My first concern was that I would need to fork out a considerable amount of cash to purchase adequate hiking gear. Furthermore, there was the heat to contend with. During the summer months — December, January and February — temperatures along the trail could exceed 45°C, leading to dehydration or heatstroke or a minor medical condition called "death." After a couple days of seriously pondering the option, I accepted that walking 223 kilometres through the outback in the summer heat with absolutely zero bush training might be a foolish idea. Just maybe.

In hindsight, of course my pipe dreams of connecting with Aboriginal elders and going "walkabout" across the outback seem rather silly. But I was simply a person looking for an ending. I was a mixed-up traveller grappling with the reality that meaningful relationships simply could not be scheduled. I was a dreamer coping with the inability to plan epiphanies. I was a fool waltzing with a beast called closure.

Yet, for some reason, I couldn't get the outback out of my head.

It was the stillest place I could think of. ○

THE AUSTRALIAN OUTBACK is one of the world's most unique landscapes, a setting where survival takes a certain amount of wherewithal. For thousands of years, Aboriginal groups struggled, adapted and flourished in the region, each generation passing traditional knowledge and skills down to the next. For non-Aboriginal folks, however, the outback has proven treacherous. Even the most skilled of western explorers have met their premature demise there.

The wildlife living in Australia's red centre is infamous for being exceptionally hazardous, ranking among the world's more poisonous creatures. The common death adder, for example, is a tremendously venomous snake that delivers one of the fastest strikes in the animal kingdom. (This begs an important question: does the "common" refer to the prevalence of the snake or the frequency of death resulting from its bite?) A single sting from the redback spider can trigger severe swelling and tremors. The bite of an *ethmostigmus rubripes*, better known as the giant centipede, can induce anaphylactic shock.

But the most unforgiving thing in the outback is not a creepy crawler — it's the extreme temperatures. On an average summer day, the mercury rises well beyond what you'd find inside your local sauna. There is little natural shade across the vast landscape, and water sources are few and far between. Thus, the outback — with the combination of heat, inhospitable terrain and impossible distances — has claimed its ample share of unprepared victims. It is said that dozens of people die in the region every year. While the majority of these deaths are from road accidents, there is the occasional case of an ambitious tourist who goes for a long walk and simply doesn't return. ○

ON THE 20TH of December, I landed in the heart of the Australian outback in a small town called Alice Springs. The midday sun had baked the tarmac. As I stepped off the airplane, a wall of heat slammed me with the same intensity as opening an oven.

Without delay, I transferred to an air-conditioned coach and headed toward the centre of town. Edda had connected me with her veterinarian friend, Megan, who had invited me to stay at her home. Following the instructions I had received via email, I got off the bus in front of the Swagman's Rest motel, walked through a suburb for two blocks and found myself standing in front of a one-level concrete house with shutters covering all the windows. Megan was still at work, so I let myself into the shady back porch, as instructed. Then I collapsed onto the threadbare couch in the corner.

A short while later, I heard the screen door creak open.

"Hiya, Dan!"

A woman with dark, chin-length hair and black cut-off denim

shorts stood in the doorway. Around her knee was a bulky medical brace, the consequence of a messy roller derby wipeout that had left her requiring major surgery. I stood up as she hobbled over to give me fast but firm hug.

"Welcome. You want a beer?"

"I won't say no to that."

Megan disappeared inside and came back seconds later with two sweaty bottles of Victoria Bitter. We clinked the necks of the VBs and then crumpled back down onto the couch.

"One of my roomies is out of town, so you can take his room. No need to be bashful. Make yourself at home."

Over the next 24 hours in Alice Springs, I moved at a slow pace. In the morning, I used one of the extra bikes in the backyard to explore some of the city, which proved to be an Australian version of a Wild West frontier town. The only thing missing was a tumbleweed blowing down the quiet main street. In the afternoon, I stayed horizontal, acclimatizing. The temperature was reminiscent of the severe arid heat in Marrakech, the kind that quickly dried the eyeballs. Only it was even more intense. As I lounged in the shade, I flipped through Megan's outback guidebooks and discovered that the waterholes of the West Macs were connected by a sealed highway. The region had become a popular tourist destination, a place where visitors could learn about indigenous culture, as well as about the local flora and fauna. Many of the sites even offered camping services, such as sleeping platforms and toilets.

On my second evening in "Alice" (as the city was tagged by the locals), I mentioned my curiosity about the outback to Megan and told her that I was thinking about going exploring.

"I've been through the West Macs tons," she said enthusiastically. "There's some really great swimming. And I've got everything you need." She proceeded to run through a list of camping supplies she could lend me: a cooking stove, a sleeping bag and a portable canvas bedroll, commonly known as a "swag."

I thanked her and said that I'd be grateful to use her gear. But she wasn't finished.

"How are you going to get out there?"

"Oh, I figure I'll rent a car."

"No, no. You should take my car."

"What? … No."

"Seriously, I want to start biking more. It's actually the best exercise for my knee."

"Um, I'm pretty sure I cannot steal a car from a crippled woman."

She angled her head and raised an eyebrow, looking like an alpha kangaroo ready to start a boxing match. "Take my car."

I paused and briefly scanned her face for any sense of hesitation.

To make an adventure in the outback possible, I needed camping gear and a car. Megan offered me her camping gear and her car. The arrangement seemed so easy that my first reaction was to be suspicious. Three months from now, was I going to be solicited for one of my kidneys?

Yet, from a rational (or even mathematical) perspective, the equation was beautiful in its simplicity:

$$desire + offer = solution$$

So rather than continuing to play a faux "no I couldn't possibly" card or worrying if the universe might eventually ding me for accepting so much charity, I humbly accepted.

"I would love to use your car." ☼

I PULLED OUT of Alice Springs and pointed Megan's white compact sedan due west toward the West Macs. I progressed gradually along a two-lane paved highway called Namatjira Drive, staying below the speed limit. Outside the car window, the landscape was surprisingly colourful. It wasn't lush, but it certainly wasn't the monochromatic beige landscape that I had imagined. The topsoil was a rusty red, the shrubs and trees that bordered the highway were pale green, and the low mountain range in the distance was a faded shade of purple.

The trunk of the vehicle was packed with more than enough food. A week's worth of water filled the backseat. I had left Megan with a tentative agenda of where I'd be sleeping each night. All the necessary precautions that one should take when preparing for a camping trip had been taken. At no point in the coming days would I ever be more than 10 kilometres from the main highway that ran directly back to Alice Springs. Help would be available if I needed it.

Yet, I still felt nervous.

Was I being foolish? Going alone into the wilderness involves a certain amount of risk, and the danger is greater when the region is unfamiliar. That said, some of the most memorable moments of my trip had involved risk: travelling with Moses to Khayelitsha, waiting on the side of an Israeli highway in the dark, speeding down Indian side roads on a motorbike. I hadn't renounced my job and my apartment in Canada to sit on an air-conditioned bus or to spend a year hiding in a hotel room. This outback adventure was one final opportunity for me to take a chance, to summon braveness.

Approximately 80 kilometres west of Alice Springs, I turned north off the highway and onto an unpaved side road that led toward a ravine, a meeting place of two red rocky cliffs. The car crept cautiously forward, coming to a stop at an empty picnic area. This was my first destination: Udepata, also known as Ellery Creek Big Hole.

I stepped into the penetrating mid-afternoon sun, noting that nobody else was around. Hesitantly, I shut the car door and proceeded down the walking track toward the water and its sandy beach. The brochure from the Alice Springs tourist information centre stated that many of the waterholes of the West Macs were perfect for lounging, especially on hot days. As I stood at the edge of the Ellery Creek Big Hole, I could see why they were deemed ideal. A crowd of tall, stately gum trees with gnarly white branches and sparse foliage framed the greenish natural pool. Behind the trees were the stunning terracotta cliffs, each at least five storeys high. The fact that this oasis exists in the middle of one of the world's driest environments is extraordinary.

The brochure also explained (from an academic perspective) how the site was formed: "thousands of years of hydrological disturbances ... *blah blah blah* ... the waterhole was a geological by-product ... *blah blah blah* ... residual spring water is still found in various places across the outback ... *blah blah blah*." These practical explanations did *nothing* to change the fact that, in my mind, the site was a complete miracle, a fluke of nature.

The waterhole itself was divided into two sections: a large pool where I was standing (on the beach) and a second pool on the other side of the gorge. The farther pool was more or less hidden from sight. The only way to access it was to swim across the first large pool and through a narrow passageway flanked by the two cliffs. This provided a tempting challenge. I returned to the car to change clothes, grab snacks and blow up an air mattress, which Megan had also insisted I take.

Armed with the inflated mattress, I returned to the shoreline, ready to jump in.

Despite the inviting setting — the soft sand, the picturesque cliffs and the gentle swaying of the trees — I was blocked. The water became deep *very* quickly and turned into a murky abyss. As daring as I'd like to think I am, I have this weird thing with unfamiliar waters. It's called "I don't particularly like them." Deep pools lead to profound fears. Were there hungry weeds waiting to wrap around my ankles and pull me under? What unfriendly territorial reptiles would inform me (with their fangs) that I was on their turf?

An inner debate began to take place about whether or not I should actually go in.

"Listen, cupcake," said the pro-adventure side of me. "This is why you are here — to experience the natural beauty of the West Macs. You cannot *not* go swimming in this waterhole."

"Hey, who are you calling a cupcake?" I retorted back to myself, knowing full well that I could grab a book, sit under a tree and be quite content absorbing all the "natural beauty" in the comfort of the shade.

Ultimately, the pro-adventure side won. What eventually pushed me forward was the same rationale as going into the outback in the first place. I didn't haul myself to the centre of Australia, obtain a car and buy a week's worth of camping food to sit on the shoreline with a Costco-sized bottle of hand sanitizer in my purse.

With a grimace, I took a deep breath, threw the air mattress on the water, mounted it chest-down and pushed off the sandy bottom. As I paddled forward, the water splashed over the low plastic sides of the mattress, jolting me with its chill. My skin immediately broke into goosebumps, begging me to reconsider my decision. But there would be no turning back. Instead, I thrashed into the centre of the waterhole and toward the opening in the cliffs.

I was in the middle of the gorge when I noticed the mattress was leaving a trail of tiny bubbles. Air was slowly leaking out of my flotation device, and water began to cross over my lower back. With a deflated mattress, I was nothing more than a sunscreen-flavoured sushi roll for whatever creatures lurked below. Filled with panic, I paddled even faster.

A few minutes later, I successfully beached myself on the other side of the swimming hole with a mattress half-empty of air and veins half-full of adrenalin — there's nothing like a generous dosage of terror to get the heart racing. I tossed the mattress onto the bank, slid on my flip-flops and wandered to a small patch of trees. It looked like a perfect place to get down to business and to do what I had come to the outback to do: ruminate.

When visiting a sacred location, its wisdom can be absorbed by osmosis, no? Is it not possible to simply go into nature and allow the timeless spirituality found in the ancient rocks, the resilient trees and the millions of grains of sand to permeate the heart?

With this in mind, I sat and attempted to be still.

A minute passed.

I adjusted my legs to be more comfortable.

Another minute passed.

385

I figured that if I was going to sit for a while, I should have some water.

Another minute passed.

Uh-oh. The sun was beginning to hit my toes. I moved further up the bank to a shadier location.

Another minute passed.

Instead of attaining a supreme unity with the natural splendour, a barrage of questions began creeping forward. *What type of bird is making that clicking sound? Should I eat the tinned spaghetti for dinner? Or should I maybe attempt to cook up the dehydrated chili? Is the way that I see the colour green the same way that everyone else sees the colour green? How much beard is too much beard? Will I ever live on a sailboat?*

It quickly became evident that I lacked the skills and experience required to meditate effectively.

And then I inhaled a goddamn fly.

It's true. As I was sitting cross-legged, attempting to attain "stillness," a lentil-sized blackfly started zipping around my head. I shooed him away. He returned to walk across my cracked lips. Again, I swatted at him and attempted to return to my supreme objective of meditation in a sacred location. I decided it would be appropriate to focus on my breathing. I closed my eyes. I relaxed my shoulders. I exhaled gently and then inhaled deeply. The fly must have been resting on my moustache because that guy got sucked into my nostril.

Instantly, my eyes popped open and I started to snort.

The next few minutes were *not* graceful. Nor still. Nor sacred. I first tried to eject the bugger by pinching one nostril closed and blowing hard through the other — an unrefined method better known as "the farmer's blow." But all attempts to shoot him out failed. So I deliberately snorted the pest deeper through my nasal passages and then began a session of intense phlegmy throat clearing.

Finally, the mucous-drenched blackfly fell out of my mouth and onto my palm.

He wiggled for a moment. And then he went still.

Spiritual connection just wasn't in the cards for me that day. By the time I recomposed myself after being penetrated by a fly, a group of college-aged guys had arrived. Without the necessity of air mattresses, the gang dove into the pond, swam to the narrow chasm, climbed up the rocky sides and commenced a boisterous session of cliff jumping. Instead of attaining meditative stillness at a sacred oasis, I became an unwilling bystander at a rambunctious frat party.

So I gave up. ☼

I UNROLLED MY swag onto a knee-high wooden platform. To prevent nocturnal animal visitors, these flat-surfaced sleeping stages were designed with a single base and no sides (imagine a square beer coaster centred over a golf tee). This was ideal because the only thing worse than sleeping with a rat is sleeping with a snake.

I hopped onto the platform, crawled onto the foam mattress inside the swag and pulled the covering over me, relishing the thought of some open-air camping. In my year of adventure, there hadn't been a single night when I had actually slept under the stars. I was hoping it would be worth the wait. Out there in the desert landscape, the night sky wouldn't be muted by light pollution. Nope, it was going to be just me and the vastness of infinity.

The heavy canvas cover soon proved to be far too warm, so I pushed the shell off. I tucked my hands behind my head, waiting for darkness and the stars to appear. As I lay there, a single howl cut through the evening soundscape — the sound of a dingo moaning. A moment later, the lone caller was joined by a band of haunting wails that bounced off the canyon walls and filled the sky with echoes. This dingo chorus was unlike anything I had ever heard, somehow alarming and enchanting at the same time — like hearing what forlornness feels like.

The dingoes, however, were not my only company at Ellery Creek Big Hole. When I opened my swag, I had exposed my skin — and therefore my scent — to the night air. This attracted mosquitoes that began to nip at my legs and neck. At first I tried to ignore them. But after a few minutes, the constant stings became intolerable. I had a choice: brave the heat or brave the bugs. I chose to sweat it out. I covered my head with a mosquito net and wrapped myself in a cotton sheet. Sleeping under the stars wasn't quite the same with a cover pulled up to my nose and the protective veil of insect netting over my eyes. Fortunately, it wasn't too long before I fell asleep.

Halfway through the night, however, I awoke shivering.

Who knew the outback could get so cold? Not me. I had figured Megan's sleeping bag would be unnecessary, so I left it in the trunk of the car. I was wrong. It suddenly felt like I had entered a walk-in refrigerator. I sat up and flipped a flashlight on. The beam of light happened to fall onto the surrounding bushes, where it illuminated a pair of eyes. *Something was watching me.*

You'd think that a set of glowing eyes in the blackness of night might have triggered a fight or flight response, that my first reaction might have been to dive-roll for the nearest frying pan in preparation for zombie combat. Don't get me wrong — those eyes were *definitely* unnerving. However, in my tired and cold state, I didn't have enough energy to get overly creative about what might be stalking me or how I might fight it off.

"What are you looking at?" I yelled, startling the animal. The creature turned sideways and took off in the other direction. I could see that it was just a scrawny yellow dog. Another emaciated mongrel darted out from the bush and followed the first one. The duo had probably been circling my sleeping stage and lingering near the car, which contained what must have been very enticing smells to the canine nose.

With the dingoes gone, I hauled myself up, slipped my hiking boots half-on and shuffled awkwardly to the car to get the sleeping bag from the trunk. Back on the platform, cocooned in the swag with another layer of warmth, I frantically rubbed my skin, trying to return to sleep. ○

THE NEXT MORNING, I felt like an oxidized tin man. I rose stiffly, cold and spotted with mosquito bites. The slowly rising sun eventually took the edge off the morning chill. The gradual increase in temperature helped to lubricate my stiff muscles and to warm my crusty mood.

By mid-morning, it was scorching hot once again. I bid goodbye to Ellery Creek and sought refuge in the air-conditioned car. I headed back to the main highway and pushed further west toward the next waterhole on the map.

At Serpentine Gorge, I pulled into another gravelly parking lot, deserted except for a safari truck from a local rental agency. I positioned the vehicle tight against a tree, so it would at least be half-covered from the sun. With my backpack and bottle of water, I followed a wide rocky path through a forest of gum trees toward the heart of the gorge. Halfway along the trail, I came across a family of five. We grinned in acknowledgement as we approached each other. The littlest family member, a boy no older than six years old, was crying. "How much further do I have to go?" I overheard him say. To a certain extent, the same question was running through my mind.

Soon the trail led out of the wooded area and into the gorge. Like Ellery Creek Big Hole, the ravine had a set of steep rust-coloured canyon walls, which dropped into a waterhole — or what once was a waterhole. What remained of the natural pool was now a foot-deep brown puddle of sludgy liquid no larger than a badminton court. Insects buzzed over the slime-covered rocks at the edge of the shallow water.

It appeared that my West Mac waterhole adventure excursion had just been downgraded.

Instead of hanging around the pond, I decided to follow an official park sign indicating that visitors could hike up one side of the canyon. After a sweaty 10-minute ascent up a steep footpath, I reached the top of an overhang. The cliff was at least three times as tall as the tallest trees below. From that vantage point, I could see for miles across the craterous landscape. The West Macs formed a bumpy geological vein across the flat skin of the

389

outback. Some of the hills were patterned with sedimentation lines. In certain places, the earth had shifted, causing the lines to tilt vertically. From that perspective, the hills really did look like caterpillars.

Breathless — from both the hike and the view — I stripped off my backpack. Between the mountain breeze and the hot sun, the sweat along the spine of my shirt immediately began to evaporate.

That outback lookout would have made the *perfect* place to set up camp for the night. Unfortunately camping was prohibited at Serpentine Gorge. Even if I were audacious enough to bend the park rules, I wasn't up for the multiple hikes up and down the mountain to bring up my swag, food and other gear. Besides, I had another destination in mind. The next spot on the map was an abandoned chalet, and I figured it would be a serene place to spend a night. Wasn't "abandoned" more or less synonymous with "still"?

So I settled for an hour at the top of the cliff, enjoying the wind and stretching out my limbs. Then I slowly descended the side of the hill, walked back along the trail to the parking lot and got in the car.

Ten kilometres further down Namatjira Drive, I turned onto yet another gravel road. I guided the car as far as I could over the uneven track. I became worried about high-centring the car, so I pulled it off to the side and began walking. A short while later, I reached a cluster of scantily leafed trees and a wooden sign that read "Serpentine Chalet."

The Serpentine Chalet, or so I had read, was a posh tourist destination developed in the mid-20th century to lure travellers to remote central Australia. It was promoted as an isolated bush camp that featured all the amenities of an urban hotel. However, the chalet only managed to remain open for a few years, since it was plagued by a deficiency that seems rather obvious in hindsight: a lack of water.

I looked beyond the sign, feeling as though I had missed something. Were the heat and the lack of sleep messing with my mind? Where exactly was the chalet?

I trudged forward.

Past the signpost, a parched riverbed was filled with rocks the size of basketballs. Further down, a concrete dam contained a lagoon of mucky, stagnant water. The trees were far too sparse and spindly to hide an abandoned building. In fact, there were no shady places at all. I had a hard time picturing how this setting was once part of a luxury resort.

Sweat trickled down my face and back.

I felt dizzy, so I dropped down to one knee and steadied myself on a rock. I closed my eyes.

When I opened them again, I saw exactly what I had been looking for.

A few metres in front of me was a cracked rectangular slab of cement. It was covered in sand, barely distinguishable from the red dirt surrounding it. This was Serpentine Chalet. There was nothing left of the old resort other than a dusty foundation, a horizontal headstone marking a site of misplaced tourism intentions.

You've got to be frickin' kidding me. This is all there is?

With no shade, no water and no wind, the Serpentine Chalet site was not a viable place to spend the night — and especially not the place to celebrate Christmas Eve.

That's right. Outside the parched valley, throughout Australia and across the rest of the world, the 24th of December had arrived. A shade-less graveyard was not what I had envisioned.

In the screenplay of my outback adventure, the night before Christmas was supposed to look something like this:

[setting: abandoned building wedged between two rock cliffs]

A tall, bearded man contentedly cooks himself dinner-for-one over a propane stove. He looks sun-kissed, but half the "tan" is a layer of dirt accumulated from a day of joyfully tramping around the outback.

*Cue the kangaroo. It bounces by, pausing to wink at the man.
As a response, the man extends his arm and gives the marsup-
ial a thumbs-up.*

[camera pans out, revealing a small but sparkling waterhole]

*The man is next seen taking a sunset dip in the lagoon. His
attitude is playful as he splashes through the water, then takes
a moment to float on his back. When he exits the pool, he
forgoes towelling off and instead lets the moisture evaporate
off his freshly cleaned skin. He stretches out his arms, expressing freedom and renewal.*

Night falls.

*The man reaches into a knapsack and extracts a bottle of
whisky. He twists off the cap and salutes the full moon, which
is rising over the horizon.*

[camera pans to the night sky; a shooting star is seen]

Reality was *way* different.

I was uncomfortably hot. I was isolated. I was standing on
someone's broken hopes. And to top it all off — despite the fact
that I've never been overly sentimental about the holidays — the
knowledge that my family would be gathering for a neighbourhood tour of Christmas lights followed by a traditional meal
elicited a sharp pang of remorse.

What the hell was I doing?

In another circumstance, I might have kicked a rock or let out
a healthy yell to express my frustration. But the swampy air was
too hot for acts of melodrama.

I let my head fall into my hands. One day into my outback
"closure" adventure and I was already feeling defeated. I knew it
wasn't going to be comfortable, but I had no idea it would be so
harsh.

What was I supposed to do with myself when the thermom-eter surpassed scorching? Humans in the hottest areas of the planet allocate the hottest hours of the day for doing something specific: absolutely zilch. And that's exactly what I had hoped for. But to achieve "zilch," I needed, a relatively comfortable place, somewhere without intense sunlight.

Eventually, I stood up and slowly walked back to the car. With a map of the West Macs spread across the roof, I reviewed my op-tions. The current scenario was uncomfortably hot and unneces-sarily isolated, containing all the elements required for an emo-tional breakdown. From the very beginning of my travels, my intent was to be practical. Yet at that moment, the situation felt entirely absurd, entirely impractical. What I needed was some-thing — *anything* — that would buffer the elements and make it feasible for me to stay in the outback. I didn't need anything perfect or magical. Just something that would make me feel like I was not failing. ☼

IN DESPERATION, I went for the last resort — quite literally. The Glen Helen Resort was the last service stop before hundreds of kilometres of outback. Although it wasn't luxurious, it featured motel rooms, a backpacker bunkhouse, a pool, a bar and (most importantly) copious amounts of shade. At $30 per night, the "Stockmans Quarters" (a bunk bed dormitory) was beyond my budget. But I did happen to have the room to myself. This was an ideal balance of being in the vicinity of other people yet having my own space. And the fan rotating over my bunk was the *perfect* Christmas present.

After rinsing off the day's sweat and dust with a quick shower, I made myself a fairly anticlimactic dinner of instant noodles and then strolled into the resort's tavern. I sat on a stool and nursed a bottle of beer. At the other end of the bar, two guys in park ranger outfits were chatting together. A pool table sat un-touched. The tightly ponytailed bartender was deeply involved in her task of polishing pint glasses. I turned my attention to the large television, which blared a peppy Australian holiday variety show. In the middle of the outback, the popular Christmas stories —such as the whole "Santa Claus and his reindeer" shtick— seemed incongruous, even ludicrous. I drained my beer and retired to my bunk.

Without mosquitoes or dingoes stalking me, I slept soundly. I rested so well that the reception desk was my first point of call when I finally emerged out of the dormitory room shortly before noon. I needed to inform them that I planned on staying another night. I was in no rush to return to the graveyards and blackflies of the outback.

Later that afternoon, I walked to the Glen Helen waterhole, located a few hundred metres behind the resort at the meeting of two ridges. After surviving my experience at Ellery Creek, my entry into the natural pool (with my leaky mattress) was less of a personal struggle. Except for a myriad of fish and birds that called it home, I had the waterhole to myself. On the far side, I found a place on a sandy bank in the shade of a tree. This time, instead of trying to fulfill some sort of meditation mandate, I just sat.

The wind moved through the tall grasses on the edge of the water. The birds floated on the surface, occasionally diving under to feed on weeds. Flies circled my head. A goanna came strolling out of the long grasses, a few metres away from my sandy nook. The three-foot lizard had a dark leathery hide with yellow spotted stripes and a whip-like tail. Despite his long claws and powerful hind legs and the slithery way he moved, I didn't feel threatened.

He watched me.

I watched him.

And for a brief moment, a thought crossed my mind: *Maybe this lizard will deliver me some type of message.*

His tongue explored the air.

I held my breath.

After a few moments of our stare-down, he turned and went back into the long grass.

Back at the resort, I sat with an iced coffee on the veranda beside a dilapidated piano adorned with weather-beaten hiking boots. The dining room spilled with sounds of families and couples dining on a traditional Christmas feast. Among the clinking silverware and people laughing, the melody of a carol came drifting out the screen door. I recognized the familiar Elvis croon.

You'll be doin' all right, with your Christmas of white.
But I'll have a blue, blue Christmas.

As I was finishing my coffee, thinking about which of my dehydrated meals I would prepare for dinner, one of the groundskeepers walked by.

"Well, I think we've officially hit 40 degrees!" he said, pausing to pull off his wide-brimmed hat and fan his tanned face.

I smiled and nodded.

"So where's home to you?" he inquired.

"Canada," I replied. I wasn't feeling very chatty, but I appreciated the fact that he had attempted to make conversation. Like that first day in New Orleans with the bass player in the French Quarter, it still felt good to have my presence acknowledged.

"Oh, is that right? I just got off the phone with my son who's a ski instructor in Banff. We visited British Columbia and Alberta a couple of months ago."

He lingered and then looked me in the eyes.

"Canada, what a beautiful country."

"Yeah ... it sure is."

He tipped his hat and headed into the dining room.

Blinking rapidly, I bit the inside of my lip and looked the other way. ☼

THE NEXT MORNING, shortly after checkout time, I left the Glen Helen Resort. After two nights of good sleep, my resolve to commune with the natural splendours of the outback was replenished — or at least somewhat replenished. Once again, I drove west down Namatjira Drive, this time toward Redbank Gorge, the furthest waterhole of the West Macs. The highway was smooth. Occasionally the pavement dipped and ran directly across an empty riverbed. Bridges had not been constructed because the rivers rarely had water. When it rained, either you risked the crossing or you waited. I had no fear of a flash flood.

My foot was gentle on the gas pedal, feeling no need to rush the short drive, savouring the short parentheses of air conditioning. Sooner than I would have hoped, I reached the turnoff. I headed down another gravel lane and tucked the car in the speckled shade of a tall bush.

I loitered in the car, savouring the cool air. With the engine turned off, however, the fans stopped turning and the temperature began to rise like the inside of a crematorium. So I got out, smeared a layer of sunscreen over my exposed skin and draped a beach towel over my head like a veil, holding it in place with my trucker's hat. Then, in my flip-flops, I began to jump rock to rock along a dried creek to the waterhole. I tried to stay under the cover of tree shade as much as possible. When the sun's rays did hit my calves, it felt like I was standing with my back turned toward a bonfire. After diligently watching out for snakes along the creek bed, I finally reached a sandy bank that led to a reservoir of brownish water. This, it appeared, was Redbank Gorge.

Although I couldn't tell its depth, the pool of water was hardly wide enough to drown a picnic table. The supposed main attraction of the site was the narrow channel that ran through the rugged red cliffs. Unlike the corridor that I passed through on my mattress at Ellery Creek Big Hole, Redbank Gorge was a labyrinth that did not open up to another pool. It looked more like a swimmable hallway. If they were brave, visitors could paddle into the crevasse, explore the red walls and play with the echoes of an enclosed space.

Nobody else was there. The upside of my seclusion was the obvious lack of frat boys or crying children. The downside was that there would be no one to save me if I jumped into the water, slipped on some algae, cracked my skull on a rock and concluded my trip (and my life) with a slow, bloody death in a remote pool. That wasn't the type of stillness that I sought, so I didn't dare plunge in. Besides, I hadn't even bothered to attempt to re-inflate the leaky air mattress.

Instead, I knelt beside the hole and splashed the dark water through my hair, providing a moment of coolness. Then I sprawled in the shade of a rocky outcrop, occasionally swatting at blackflies as I read a book.

As the sun moved higher in the sky, the shade in my little alcove began to disappear. I realized that soon there would be no discernible coverage to protect me. The goanna lizard from the day before was designed to survive in the outback. But without adequate precautions of shade, clothing and water, I would surely be dead within 24 hours. Staying at Redbank Gorge would be insanity.

I was tempted to turn back to Alice Springs, where a double bed in an air-conditioned room was waiting for me. With only 150 kilometres of highway to cover, the drive would take only a couple short hours.

But I hated the thought of giving up.

I wanted to give my outback adventure one last chance.

So I came up with another plan, a compromise. I would backtrack to a waterhole that I had skipped in order to go directly to the resort. Ormiston Gorge was the only waterhole of the West Macs that I had not yet visited. There I would spend one last night of camping, one last night of adventure. Then I would return.

I dipped my towel in the murky water, wrapped it over my head again, slipped on my flip-flops and tottered out along the riverbed — a man and a landscape that were never destined to truly understand each other. ○

THE SUN HAD just disappeared when I decided to walk the trail back to the waterhole at Ormiston Gorge. The permanent pool was lined with a sandy shore and a canopy of gum trees. Out of all the locations I had visited over the previous days, Ormiston Gorge was the most beautiful with the clearest water, the softest sand and the most dramatic cliffs.

I had arrived at the site mid-afternoon and spent the remaining hours of daylight exploring a network of marked footpaths. To my delight, there had been a light breeze. The trees and tin-roofed camping platforms provided plenty of options for shade. Now, with the onset of evening, the heat had tapered.

Despite spotting camper vans and other vehicles in the camping area, I reached the water's edge to discover that nobody was around. I sat on the warm earth wondering how long it would take before the hungry insects found me. For some reason unbeknownst to me, none came. So I rolled onto on my back and looked into the dark cobalt atmosphere.

An unexpected calm.

Above, a single star appeared. One by one, like performers arriving at an orchestral stage, other stars emerged. Each particle of light was a different instrument, fine-tuning its pitch until it achieved harmony with a greater song. Without need for a conductor, the music gradually took a shapeless yet illuminated form. An opus of stars in the night sky.

I closed my eyes.

The past few days had been far more challenging than I had anticipated. The heat was draining. The bugs were aggravating. My own enthusiasm had flatlined yet again. But as I sat beside the waterhole under the starry sky, I felt a release from my difficulties — both those from the natural world and those that were self-imposed. The next day I would be heading back to the comforts of a city, and in less than a week I'd be back in my homeland.

I folded my hands across my chest and breathed deeply.

This was my final evening in the outback, my last chance to be truly "away." With that in mind, an acknowledgment materialized: I had reached the end. I had set out to travel around the world, and it had happened. The year hadn't always been easy. It had been a varied terrain of highs and lows, of unexpected delights punctuated with periods of loneliness and fatigue. At times, I had felt embraced by places. At other times, there had been an inescapable sense of isolation. But I had made it.

At that moment, something small but vital occurred.

I surprised myself by speaking the following words out loud: "I'm ready to go home."

Over the course of December, the sentiment had been brewing inside of me. In the severe outback heat, while I swatted at flies and shouted at dingoes, it had grown more intense. Nevertheless, it was surprising to have the statement leap out of my mouth, shoved forward by some subconscious force that wanted me to hear it. Something about verbalizing the words had made them suddenly very real, very true. With the explicit declaration came a mix of euphoria and heartache.

The journey was finishing, and that was okay.

There was nothing to do but let it end.

My eyes detonated. I emitted tears that dripped down the sides of my cheeks and fell into the parched sand. There, on the bank of Ormiston Gorge, I wept. Not the gentle drip of tears, like when I bid farewell to Edda back in New Orleans. Not the simple wetting of my eyes like when I said goodbye to Moses in South Africa. These were thick, heavy drops — tears laced with the expectations and realities and confusions and wonderments that came with an entire year of travelling.

I had been hungry to find a meaningful ending, largely because I was afraid of letting go of an experience that had defined me for a year as a seeker, a traveller. But now the expedition was ending, and this identity was inevitably about to shift. A part of *me* was about to disappear. Sitting under the stars, I felt a grief that I had been unready to feel. I acknowledged the sorrow that comes with endings.

"It's over," I repeated. Again and again and again.

What happened next was nothing. There were no congratulatory fireworks. The universe did not offer a shooting star. A dingo did not respond with a howl in celebration of my personal moment. I just sat there. Alone. Confused. Honoured. Exhausted. The stars kept shining. And I cried until I felt lighter.

I took a shaky but deep breath.

With this purging of tears, a space was created for a new emotion — an upwelling of appreciation broke the surface. Even though I had travelled on my own, the journey had not happened alone. It had occurred with the help of many luminous characters. The faces of the people from the past year came flashing before me: Edda, Estella, Moses, Nico, Slava and more. Back home, family members and friends had cheered me forward. A net of generous people had hosted me on the road, often giving more than I had been able to offer in return. This dream had been enabled by a cast of individuals who opened their doors and their hearts to me.

I sat up. With a dusty hand, I wiped my face. And then I whispered to the cosmos the only sentiment that made sense:

Thank you.

A couple feet away, the waterhole was tranquil, the glassy surface reflecting the twinkling night sky. The bank dropped steeply into unknown depths. A sudden desire came forth: to clean the sweat and the burden, to wash away the salt and the self-imposed struggle.

I rose to my feet, took off my clothes and stood naked at the water's edge.

I paused.

Before me was something frightening yet intriguing, uncharted yet inviting. I tiptoed forward into the black pool, the sensation instantly raising the hairs on my arms.

I paused again.

Then I filled my lungs with as much air as possible and dove forward. The cool water rushed over my skin. In the middle of the pool, I surfaced. I rolled onto my back and floated, staring upward into the sky. Exhaling slowly, I tried to remain as motionless as possible. ☼

EPILOGUE

The final night of my year-long adventure was spent sleeping in the backseat of a rental car in an airport parking lot. You'd think I might have sprung for a hotel or maybe some champagne. But I had an 8 a.m. flight to catch. And no dingo in Australia was going to prevent me from being on that plane. I wanted home.

After my night at the Ormiston Gorge waterhole, I had returned to Alice Springs and thanked Megan profusely for letting me use her car. We had beers on the couch. I had never been happier to have air conditioning. On the 30th of December, I flew to Brisbane, where I rented a car and drove two hours to Lismore to pick up some gear I had left behind. But more importantly, to have 24 hours with Edda.

On the last morning of the year, Edda and I went out for breakfast. I ordered bacon and eggs with a latte. Edda ordered gluten-free pancakes with roasted dandelion root tea. While we waited for our food to arrive, Edda didn't miss her opportunity to check in and inquire about my time in the outback.

"Darling, did you find the stillness that you were looking for?"

"Actually, not really."

"Oh?"

"But it's okay. I found out that I was ready to go home."

Edda tilted her head to the side, listening. And then she smiled in her accepting way.

"And it turns out that's all I needed." ○

EACH YEAR, LISMORE hosts a massive New Year's Eve dance party. Edda invited me to go, but I didn't feel up for a large crowd. Besides, I had that early-morning flight to catch. At sundown, we hugged. This time our farewell was not characterized by any salty storms on my cheeks — I had shed all the tears that I needed to shed.

Heading directly east, I drove until I came to the Pacific coast. As midnight approached, I found a beach and curled up in the sand, alone but content. Somebody had thrown a Glow Stick in the water, which created an incandescent gleam that danced down the shoreline like a star in the waves.

I made a few resolutions for the upcoming year: spend time with family, be a more present friend, do more yoga, play the piano again. The clock struck midnight. Further down the beach, fireworks exploded. I could hear the whoops and laughter of drunken partiers celebrating the arrival of the New Year. To me, however, the celebration was premature. I still had hours to kill and an ocean to cross.

I got back into the car and drove north. At one point, I crossed the state line into Queensland and entered into a different time zone. The car radio provided another New Year's countdown. More fireworks exploded in the distance.

Finally, after arriving at the Brisbane airport parking lot, I crawled into the backseat. As you can imagine, I didn't have the best of sleeps. The hours dripped by. Just after sunrise, I boarded a plane and flew to Seoul, where I got on a different plane that headed to Canada. My mom surprised me at the Vancouver airport. That will always be one of my most memorable reunions. Joy. Laughter. Relief. And finally, celebration.

It was the first day of January.

In the most literal sense, I had spent one year in the world. ○

IF I LEARNED anything during my 12 months of travelling, it was that naps are really great. When arriving at a destination, as I did in Peru or Laos, the first thing I liked to do was get horizontal. A nap is whisky for the soul. (Nah, just kidding. Whisky is whisky for the soul.)

My learning, however, did reach greater heights. For example, there was the slew of practical skills I acquired as I moved across the world: how to lay tile, how to make a stellar ceviche, how to milk a goat, how to ride a motorbike (and not hit cows), how to dismember a dried rat. Oh yes, and how to liaise — like a boss.

Then there were the more subtle life lessons — things that I essentially knew before I left on the trip but that were solidified by my international experiences. For starters, I confirmed that I usually like people but that I prefer not to share a room with anybody (or with other members of the animal kingdom, for that matter). I appreciate being useful but, even more so, I appreciate being *appreciated*. Stability and routine lead to a certain amount of comfort. People are generally benevolent.

And then there were the more travel-specific lessons. When backpacking, only bring underwear that you feel comfortable revealing to the entire world because you will expose your skivvies. Keep extra taxi fare with you at all times. Don't listen to your iPod while walking dark streets in South Africa — or dark streets anywhere, really. The cheapest ticket is not always the best option. Wear sunscreen. ☺

FOR THE FIRST few months following my return, I lived in my mom's spare bedroom. I spent time with family (a niece had been conceived and born in my absence). I started writing this book. Eventually I headed back to Montreal and got a new job.

I tried to find my moments of stillness. But life marched forward.

As I returned to my day-to-day existence, I bumped into old friends. The most popular question that people asked me was "What was your favourite country?"

I equally love and loathe this question. I love it because the root of it exposes a human trait that makes me happy — a yearning for goodness. We want to know where the joy was found, whether or not we want to visit that place for ourselves. I loathe it because it's impossible to answer quickly — or to answer at all.

Yes, I had a favourite goat.

No, I did not have a favourite country.

In fact, I couldn't make a sweeping assessment of any of the nations I visited because I only experienced one nook, one microcosm. Some projects were more joyful or simply easier than others. By this point in the book, I'll bet you can take an informed guess at which ones I am talking about.

The set of criteria that I had established for a "successful month" in the early legs of the journey — New Orleans, Costa Rica, Peru — did not waver much throughout the year. *Did I have a chance to be helpful? Was there something compelling or intriguing about the physical setting? Did I sample authentic local cuisine? Did I acquire a new skill? Did I have an opportunity to connect with either a local or fellow traveller?*

Those questions were important to keep in mind. But as it turned out, every single experience had value. Each place offered a slice of life in a different corner of the planet. Each month was successful. Just like the "biker beta test" in India, the months offered up their own little nuggets of insight, even when things didn't go as I had anticipated. Sometimes a broken plan is a better plan. ☼

Now that I've written a book about work-exchange and volunteer travel, I suppose some folks might ask me for advice on the subject. Here are a few quick tips: If there's a specific type of volunteer experience you want to have, be willing to pay for it. Good reviews are helpful, but personal recommendations are best. Be prepared to work hard, but respect your limits. Also: bring cookies. Everybody likes cookies.

When I was dreaming of the trip, there were experiences that I thought I would like to have, such as visiting an ashram or volunteering at an orphanage. But as I travelled, I began to understand the littleness of a month. I also realized that many of my dreams were romanticized ideas that served me far more than anyone else. So keep in mind the motives behind your choices.

For those who haven't yet figured out the top-secret algorithm to my travels, I'm going to break it down right now. (Just promise me you won't tell anyone else — copyright pending!) The entire methodology of my journey can be summarized in three important steps:

1 *Find host (this step can be skipped if you want).*

2 *Book ticket.*

3 *Go.*

For those who are truly hoping to set forth on an adventure, probably the main thing to do is focus on that third point: be brave and go. Or at least fake braveness and go.

That's pretty much what I did. ☼

I NEVER EXPECTED my year-long trip around the world to be perfect. I don't even know what perfect adventures look like. Maybe it's what we see in travel advertisements — the happy white couple with their backpacks, standing at the edge of a mountain with arms triumphantly stretched over their head as the sun sinks over the African plains. As far as I understand, the truest form of travel is not meant to be perfect. I had cooking classes and bed bugs. I had baby goats and loneliness. I had African sunsets and an African mugging. The journey was imperfect and impeccable at the same time.

Now if you'll excuse me, I'd like to end here.

I've got work to do.

On being still.

Daniel Baylis
Montreal, Canada
☼

ASSOCIATE TRAVELLERS

WHEN I RETURNED from my travels, I went for lunch with a friend. I told her about a book I envisioned writing and asked her if she would be my editor. She jumped on board with little more than a handshake. Monique James — you are a lighthouse, a mother, a dictionary and a comedian all wrapped into a single lovely human being. Thank you for keeping the editing process fun and for forcing me to stay on track with such amazing one-liners:

– *"As it stands, the ending of the vignette focuses on the negative aspects of your stay, which ultimately makes you sound like a whiner."*

– *"Zzz. Could you say something more positive or more negative? Or funny? Or sarcastic? Or something more interesting than 'was OK'?"*

– *"This vignette is not a vignette. Nothing happens."*

– *"This makes you sound like a cheap bastard. I won't let you do it!"*

– *"Sorry, too many donkey mentions already."*

Monique, this project would not have happened without you. Thank you for believing in me. ☺

Thanks to the people and organizations that hosted me during my year: Common Ground Relief, The Farmer, Horizon Peru, Con Tacto Hotelero, Seventies-80s, YACD, the delightful Frenchman named Nico, Pleasance Theatre, Goats With the Wind, YogaGypsys, Big Brother Mouse and the divine Edda.

The flights from my year-long journey were made carbon-neutral thanks to the readers my blog (*danielbaylis.ca*) and the participation of *Offsetters.ca* — that was the best birthday present! ○

Thanks to a stellar indie publishing team: Jennifer McFee, Michel Vrana and Emrys Miller. For trudging through early drafts and for the honesty, thanks Maggie Panko.

To my friends in Montreal (and Toronto!) who let me roam yet still welcome me home: I love you guys. Mille fois merci.

And finally, thank you to my family for the assurance that I will never be without a bed or a meal. ○

The printing of this book was made possible by over 250 generous dreamers: Matt Joycey, Meaghan Wyatt, Marc-Antoine Saumier, Alicia Savage, Matt Borgatti, Jeffrey Cufaude, Vanessa Groshong, Jonathan Burgoine, Ethan Wright, Alice Kos, Katerine-Lune Rollet, Richard Rhyme, Andrew Down, Hector Rodriguez, Stephane Courchesne, Vicki Muise, Cathy Baylis, Elise Legault, Samuel Sauvageau, Glynis Rumsey, Francois Lachapelle, Chas Holzworth, Naomi Scheyen, Daniel John, Trisha Hortsing, John Baylis, Kathryn Maytham, Sandra Grant, Virginia Barratt, Raymond W. Walsh, Jeffrey Spivock, Anne Randall, Fleur Hardy, Kelsey Mori, Ken Monteith, Krispahlyn Daria, Meghan Walford, Trudi Johnson, Ashley Diener, Christopher DiRaddo, Monica Park, Kathy Baker, James Alexander Dunphy, Gracie Wegwitz, Benjamin Wegwitz, Ryan Wegwitz, Lisa Baylis, Brad Lucas, Joss Drolet, Jacynthe Smith, Kathy Lalonde, Jeffrey A. Ward, Denise Ondaro, Sarah Hamilton, Erin Bandola, Roseanne Harvey, Hilary McGregor, Veronique Beaulieu, Kelly Fremmerlid, Andrea Padgett, Nicolas Revel, **Konstantinos Katsiapis**, Daniel Van de Mark, Ilana Segall, Tessa Wilkie, Jaron Eilkie, Marie Mutl, Régine Buès, Lynn Habel, Annalise Ferro, Jon Barrett, Eddie Coleman, Lucy Kitchen, Amanda French, Alain Lessard, Stella Artuso, Candice Walsh, Samatar Abdillahi, Dominic Tremblay, Jen Gonzales, Pierre Campeau, Jenny Phan, Marielle Albert, Matt Cordell, Julie

Butterworth, **Bao Phac Do,** Kathleen Doyle, Mylène St-Pierre, Yvette Beaudry, Peter Taraba, Aurelia Roman, **Racheal Martens,** Lauren Jane Heller, Christopher Desrosiers, Doug O'Neill, Sergio Alvarado, Holland Gidney, Guillaume Langlois, Audrey-Eve Beauchamp, Rhonda Buckland, Lara Farcasan, Naomi Petkau, Lee Sullivan, Chantal Smith, Laurie March, Sean Keener, Teri Foureyes-Awasis, Mary and Norman Gidney, Richard Phillips-Kerr, Leslie Plant, Thomas Caley, Quoc Dung Le, Alborz Arzpeyma, Christopher Spear, Michelle James, Travis Robertson, Robyn Fadden, Patrick Dao, John R Ahchong, Kathy Iselmoe, Emily King, Maizie Monroe Bernard, Boris Fournier, Jamie Taylor, Annika Baltzer, Thomas Collombat, Barbara Reimer, Francis Paquet, Rosanne March, Courtney and Scott Campbell, John and Dale Howe, Genevieve Vallerand, Mary Ann Thomas, Xavier Blais, Laura Fairbourn, Joseph Messina, Judy McGregor, Rob Rollins, Anny Chien, Randall Shirley, Jacqueline Celemencki, Pete Holliday, Cyrille-G Francoeur, Hjalte Betak, Hugh Bartlett, **Kirsten McKenzie,** Shelly Finch, Myriam Dali, Jeff Wood, Lee Wood, Curtis Bathurst, Simon Pow, Eric Bolduc, Joe Doul, C. Charles, Thach H. Nguyen, Marnie and JP Martin, Conni Biesalski, Allison Russell, Nathalie Rivard, Anne Pascale Quinty, Nancy B Pilon, Lindsay Bell, Erik Calhoun, Guy Deom, Noema Perez, Reg Baylis, David Abramovich, Elizabeth Wells, Susan Kenney, Richard Webster, Kayla West, Daniel Hunley, **Shadia Garrison,** Toula Drimonis, Jeanne Gan, Natalie Karneef, Kathy Gelinas, James Calvin Slusser, Evelyn Sloboda, Vanessa Schnepf, Holly Haimerl, Catherine Lily Richardson, Heather Braiden, Faith Lloyd, Melanie Klien, Linda Truglia, Gregg Rowe, Agata Golab, Amber Mathews, Shelley Fitzpatrick, Alicia Montplaisir, J&K Pierotti, Kathy Bobyn, Alfonso Stefanelli, Todd Mundt, Ahmar Husain, McKenna Erin Raney, Patrick Louche-Pelissier, Annemarie Dooling, Wil Mowrey, Jeneah Lightfoot, Jessica Place, Jen Wagner, Laurent Bui, Maddy Wright, Funmilola Adigun, Michael Catlin, Betty Esperanza, Lori Giampa, Nick May, Mark Symonds, Alan Chaffe, Dana Shawish, **Eric Pineault,** Igal Avrahami, Alan Conter, Robyn Naylor, Kerri (& Keith) Warkentin, Marc-André Monette, Cheryl Christie, Dora Yu, Helene Marcoux, Cheryl Sparks, Alain Mankarios, Melanie Reis, Jorge Enrique Prieto, Alessia Guthrie, Levi Hasting, Rick Moreira, Maxime Lefrancois, Carleen Kyle, Signy Arnason, Rebecca Jeffery, Eimear Ryan, Helen Heenan, Nora Newell, Jocelyn Scammell, Daniel Allen Cox, Joseph Mesiano. And last, but not least, the incomparable Laura Delany.

PROJECT PATRON

www.NAisGood.com

ABOUT THE WRITER

DANIEL BAYLIS WAS born in British Columbia, educated in Edmonton and refined in Montréal. He holds a degree in Human Relations from Concordia University, has planted more than 250,000 trees and has run a grand total of one marathon. His professional credentials include articles for *Fast Company, Huffington Post* and *The Guardian,* as well as content collaborations with Tourisme Montréal, *enRoute Magazine* and N/A Marketing. In his spare time, he enjoys yoga and drinking Malbec.

Find him at *www.danielbaylis.ca.*